REBELS TO REELS

A biography of Combat Cameraman Daniel A. McGovern USAF

JOSEPH MCCABE

GALLOWGLASS

DISCLAIMER

Every effort has been made by the author to ensure that the material contained within this work is correct and that sourced information, accompanying photographs and other images have been properly attributed. Every effort has also been made to correctly identify the subject matter of photographs and movie stills reproduced herein and also where and when they were taken. In some cases all contemporary records of such images have been lost or are unobtainable. In such cases the author has cited the subject matter and locations based on independent research or simply as *anonymous*. Should more factual information become available, every effort will be made to make revisions in future editions.

Note: Photographs and movie footage or stills taken from the latter made by Dan McGovern or any other US military cameraman/photographer in the course of his/her duties, even if not turned in during service and subsequently retained in private collections, remain subject to US *Copyright Law Section 105(a)*. The US government has not asserted a claim to these photographs/movies/movie stills. Therefore, they are in the public domain. For further information see *Compendium of US Copyright Practices, Section 313.6(c)*. It was not USAAF photographic practice to officially credit individual photographs to individual service photographers. Apart from his known movie footage Dan McGovern also took many photographs during his military service and would undoubtedly on occasion have accessed, retained and shared photographs taken by other military cameramen/photographers and visa versa. Dan also freely shared many USAAF/USAF images following his military service.

Published by Gallowglass Publishing, 8 Parnell Street, Carrickmacross, Co. Monaghan, Ireland.

Cover imagery: *Main photo courtesy of the McGovern family; Nagasaki ruins photo, US National Archives; IRA Riflemen photo, Waterford County Museum and crashed B-17 Hell-Cat photo, The Ken Synder Collection courtesy of Eric Barko. Colourizations by Rick Foss. Flying cameraman cartoon motif featured was the logo of the First Motion Picture Unit/USAAF.*

For my mother, Verney.

Also dedicated to
Combat Cameramen and Combat Camerawomen
past, present and future.

CONTENTS

INTRODUCTION

As one of the very first Americans into Japan within days of the Japanese surrender at the end of World War 2, Dan McGovern filmed the immediate aftermath of the atomic bombs in the devastated cities of Hiroshima and Nagasaki. This biography in part, is the story of how McGovern and his cameramen filmed throughout Japan in defeat and of how their harrowing atomic footage was suppressed by the US government for decades.

We also learn how earlier, in the wake of Pearl Harbor, McGovern became a designated photographer/cameraman to President Franklin Delano Roosevelt before training the very first cadre of World War 2 combat cameramen for the United States Army Air Forces. McGovern himself eventually deployed to England with the 8th Air Force. This is also the story of how *Big Mack* trained those cameramen and of his own six hazardous combat missions over Nazi occupied Europe as he shot combat footage for the celebrated documentary *The Memphis Belle – A Story of a Flying Fortress*. The narrative then turns to McGovern's post-war years including his involvement in filming early experiments with former Nazi rocket scientist, Wernher Von Braun and later atomic test detonations on Bikini and Enewetak atolls.

We learn also of Dan's involvement in the *Roswell Incident*, *Project Bluebook* and subsequent UFO investigations and also of his interactions with some of the most notable figures of his day. These included actors Clark Gable and future US President, Ronald Reagan; top directors including William Wyler; Generals MacArthur and Eisenhower and even Japanese Premier, Hideki Tojo. The story then focuses on McGovern's remarkable civilian career at the height of the Cold War and during which time his long suppressed atomic bomb aftermath films were finally declassified – new information about which is revealed here for the very first time.

However, Dan McGovern's remarkable story begins not in America, but in his native Ireland and in the years prior to and during the turmoil of the conflict that was the Irish War of Independence. This biography contains Dan's eyewitness accounts and also the background to that conflict. The son of a policeman of the Royal Irish Constabulary, he experienced first-hand how the Irish Republican Army waged its guerrilla war against British rule in Ireland. As a boy, he even had close associations with the nemesis of the IRA – the infamous Black and Tans.

Author, Joseph McCabe, is from the same hometown in Ireland as Dan McGovern and met and interviewed him there. In the pages which follow, McGovern's first-hand historical accounts and unique insights have been compiled with the author's extensive additional in-depth research to finally chronicle what was a truly remarkable life story.

———

*To enhance your reading experience of **Rebels to Reels** a selection of film footage shot by or under the direction of Dan McGovern, as referred to later in this biography, as well as additional relevant material, can be viewed on the **Rebels to Reels** companion website* **rebelstoreels.com.**

PART 1

Formative Years in Ireland

A BARRACKS HOME

Carrickmacross

Lt. Daniel A. McGovern of the United States Army Air Forces boarded the Douglas C-54[1] transport aircraft at Atsugi naval airfield some thirty miles from Tokyo, Japan. He was bound for the United States. His route home would take him to Harmon Airfield on Guam in the Marianas Islands, to Kwajalein Atoll in the Marshall Islands, then to Hickam Field in Hawaii and on to San Francisco from where he would eventually fly to Washington DC. It was June 28th 1946. Once in Washington, McGovern would once again meet with General Orvil A. Anderson at the Pentagon, or the *squirrel cage* as the lieutenant called it. It was Anderson who had made the difference. Anderson had immediately seen the potential of what McGovern had proposed and crucially, at a time when he needed support most among the higher echelons of the United States Army Air Forces, it was Anderson who had provided it.

Big Mack McGovern, by which he was more commonly known, was now finally on his way home after almost five years service during and immediately after World War 2. His contribution had not been to shoot a rifle or a machine gun in war-ravaged Europe or in the Pacific Theatre of Operations, although he had now served in both. His job had involved shooting of an entirely different sort. McGovern was by now a highly experienced military combat cameraman, photographer, producer, director, film editor and Army Air Forces combat veteran. His shooting, with a few exceptions, had been done with a camera.

The six-feet-five inch tall USAAF lieutenant was exhausted, but he was nevertheless content that he had finally completed two filming projects which had become a personal quest of dogged determination and perseverance almost ten months before. On the plane with McGovern were seven sturdy US Army issue footlockers. They contained the master negative reels, a positive print and other associated materials of a completed black and white movie documentary which he knew had accurately recorded, with powerful imagery and hard-hitting facts, the aftermath of two of the most important but infamous events in world history – the dropping of the atomic bombs on Hiroshima and Nagasaki.

In the days before the surrender, a team of Japanese cameramen had started to film the material devastation and the human cost of the atomic bombs in what was left of both cities. They had continued their documentation work even after hostilities had ended only for their production to be shut down by advance elements of the American occupation forces. McGovern, however, had interceded. The Japanese filmmakers had then, under his supervision, finished their location filming and carefully edited their footage into a completed black and white documentary film entitled *Effects of the Atomic Bomb on Hiroshima and Nagasaki*. McGovern was now taking the completed film back to the United States but, even already, the fact that such a film existed at all, sat uncomfortably with many in the halls of power in Washington.

In addition to overseeing the completion of the black and white documentary he had also simultaneously led a second team of American cinematographers and support crew. It was with this team that McGovern had himself travelled thousands of miles across Japan filming at over thirty major locations in addition to Hiroshima and Nagasaki. Under his leadership this team had filmed over 100,000 feet of footage of Japan and its people as it emerged from the protraction of war, but exclusively in vivid colour. From this footage the lieutenant now intended to produce a second documentary which he had provisionally entitled *Japan in Defeat*. It was the United States Army Air Forces which had provided the financial and human resources needed to complete both filming projects.

For all but the first three weeks of his time in Japan, McGovern had been attached to the United States Strategic Bomb Survey, the USSBS. For this survey he had also filmed and photographed the effects of American bombing on all manner of targets throughout Japan. The imagery captured would also complement a scientific USSBS report which would be published later detailing the US Army Air Forces' overall bombing campaign. Within days of arriving in Japan and with General Anderson's support some weeks later, the film documentation of this important historical material had become the main purpose behind Dan McGovern's personal intentions in the Land of the Rising Sun. In time, the footage he either shot or directed there and particularly that of the destruction of Hiroshima and Nagasaki, would represent the most unique historical visual record of those events for future generations around the world.

A TERRIBLE RESOLVE

Amid the destruction and the uncertainty surrounding its total Allied occupation, Japan and its people were by now coming to terms with losing the Pacific War into which they had plunged the United States back on December 7th 1941. This had been, of course, with their surprise attack on Pearl Harbor. Indeed, Japanese Admiral Isoroku Yamamoto had been right in his belief immediately after Pearl Harbor that his country's attack on the United States had *only managed to awaken a sleeping giant and to fill that giant with a terrible resolve*. With its resulting dead, wounded and displaced and with its great cities and industrial centres now in ruins, Japan now lay defeated and conquered.

Big Mack had been amongst the very first Americans ordered into Japan after it had capitulated. He had been sent there initially only to make newsreel films for the United States 20th Air Force news pool and to supply that film material to a group of visiting high profile American and Allied news correspondents. Only later had he been transferred to the USSBS. It had been a long war for McGovern but then again long periods of conflict and strife were nothing at all new to him or to the family in which he had grown up. This was because indirectly, it was another war, decades before on the other side of the world, which had set in motion the long chain of events which had brought him to Japan in the first place. He had witnessed that war unfold too and also to its conclusion, but that was back in the land of his birth – in Ireland.

Daniel Alphonsus McGovern was born in the Royal Irish Constabulary police station in Monaghan Town in north County Monaghan, Ireland on December 6th 1909. He was the second child to Daniel Senior and Margaret McGovern. County Monaghan is located in the south of Ireland's ancient but long troubled province of Ulster. One perk of the job for an RIC man was that living quarters for married couples were often available in the larger RIC barracks.[2] Such was the case in the Monaghan station where the first three of the McGovern children, Margaret, Daniel and Isabella, had been born. The couple would go on to produce a family of five boys and five girls. Constable McGovern had acquitted himself well so far in the course of his mainstream policing duties. He was popular with everyone and his superiors took note of his leadership qualities. In April 1912[3] when Dan was still only three years of age, his father was given the temporary rank of Acting Sergeant and the McGoverns transferred over twenty miles to the south-east to the remote police station at Corrinshigagh in south County Monaghan.

Daniel McGovern, aged 5. It was common practice in Ireland at that time to dress very young boys in petticoats. This was a throwback to the ancient superstition that the fairies would take only boy children and that any child wearing petticoats would be left alone. **Photo courtesy of the McGovern family.**

Corrinshigagh was only a stone's throw across the River Fane from County Armagh and the family remained there until they transferred once again after Daniel McGovern Senior, collar number 57787, passed his sergeant's exam on 1st November 1913. They moved only five miles away though, to the police station in the village of Inniskeen.[4] Dan Senior now permanently wore 3 large chevron sergeant's stripes and with the exception of only a few brief temporary postings elsewhere, was in charge of a unit of several subordinate constables there.

By mid 1915, Dan's father had transferred again – this time to his District Headquarters seven miles from Inniskeen – the RIC station in Carrickmacross, a large market town which boasts one of the widest main streets in Ireland. It would be here that the sergeant would serve out the remainder of his days in the Royal Irish Constabulary. It was also here over the ensuing years that his young son and namesake would witness his first significant historical events. As it would turn out, they would certainly not be his last. Already by now, events had started to unfold which would eventually transform Ireland and the lives of the McGovern family forever. For Daniel, his early years growing up in Carrickmacross would be fraught with uneasy tensions and frequent violence.

Carrickmacross, or simply *Carrick* to which its inhabitants usually refer to it, back then, as today, was world famous for its beautiful and intricately stitched *Carrickmacross Lace* veils and ornamental lace showpieces. As an Ulster town it predominantly looked more towards its provincial capital of Belfast, rather than to Dublin for the majority of its trade.

On the eastern side of the Main Street and right in the centre of town, was the McGovern family's new home. It was an impressive and imposing three-storey cut limestone building which was decorative but purposeful. The station stood some 60 feet high at its brick built chimney level making it one of the tallest buildings on the street. The Carrickmacross Royal Irish Constabulary District, also referred to as the South Monaghan District, was administered within the RIC command structure from its Belfast Ulster headquarters which, in turn, took its orders from headquarters in Dublin.

What was more commonly called Carrickmacross RIC *barracks* had four Georgian style windows on its first and second storeys and was fronted at ground level by decorative wrought iron railings which converged on an offset entrance porch with a flat roof. The porch protruded some six feet from the main building and was flanked by the station's three ground floor windows. A wooden flagpole rose from the centre of the porch roof from which flew the British Union Jack. Centred over the front door of the porch and the centre top of its two side walls were large ornately painted cast iron RIC crests which could be seen from anywhere on the Main Street. The crest comprised a crown over a harp emblazoned with shamrocks underneath and also incorporated a belt and buckle Order of Saint Patrick motif. This was a device which had its origins in the prestigious British Order of the Garter.

Sergeant McGovern was now one of anything up to eight RIC officers[5] who manned Carrickmacross RIC station but this did vary from time to time. The McGoverns were allocated family quarters in the barracks basement which was a family apartment or flat. These quarters were accessible, not just from within, but also via an external door directly under the building's entrance porch. Exterior cut stone steps serviced the basement flat from the Main Street above with access to these steps being via a side gate in the building's wrought iron protective railings.

The east side of the Main Street of Carrickmacross showing the Royal Irish Constabulary barracks circa early 1900s. A gateway opening in the side railings of the barracks at street level is visible. This was the access point down to the McGoverns' RIC family quarters in the basement of the building. **Photo: ©National Library of Ireland.**

Right and left of the basement front door, two additional large windows provided adequate natural light at least for the kitchen-cum-living room area of the McGovern's new home. A cleaners' room and storage area to the rear adjoined the flat and it was here that the overall basement area could be accessed from the rear of the RIC station from the ground floor corridor above via a wooden staircase. By now Danny, as he was known during his boyhood years, had three brothers – Malachy, born 1912; Eugene, born 1913 and John born in 1915, bringing the

McGovern brood to six. Danny's father, the sergeant, was a man of a generally quiet disposition but this sometimes belied his strong authoritative demeanour. He stood over six feet tall and was well built with a kindly face underneath the nose of which sat a full moustache which was common to menfolk of the period. A strict disciplinarian, he raised his strong and confident voice only when necessary. Occasionally though he could be short-tempered.

Dan Senior's main hobby outside his work was breeding pedigree greyhound dogs for racing purposes which he now kept in a homemade pen not far from the barracks and close to the town centre. The dogs were raced at the greyhound track just outside the neighbouring town of Dundalk several times a year. A fast dog would occasionally mean race prize money and additional income for Danny's father and possibly even more earnings in stud fees now and then. To ensure that they were in peak fitness, one of Danny's regular chores was to exercise his father's greyhounds which usually meant long walks throughout Carrick keeping a tight hold of as many as six taut greyhound leads at a time. Dan's father smoked a pipe and only drank occasionally. He particularly enjoyed *a wee sup of the crator*[6] at Christmastime.

Margaret was a seamstress who was always well dressed. She was also a dedicated homemaker. A native of Ballymena north of Belfast, she was a pretty brunette of average height. Her tone of voice was soft with a slight lilt common to her native County Antrim. A great cook, she had a great love of music and she was extremely religious. "I can remember her often singing or humming hymns and she was always very concerned about family health," Dan remembered. Daniel Senior, in the course of everyday conversation, frequently called his wife Maggie. In point of fact, this was a name Margaret absolutely hated and she regularly chastised her husband for using the term.

The children of RIC men who resided in barracks were referred to by other RIC personnel and indeed by some members of the public outside as *Barrack Brats*. Back then in Ireland it was common for youngsters not to start primary school until the age of seven.[7] As a result Danny and his siblings initially availed of pre-school tutoring in the barracks itself for several years from the age of three from local tutors who came in on a daily basis. The McGovern Barrack Brats were no different to other school-children in that they were given homework to do before the tutors left for the day. This was usually done with chalk and slate sitting around the kitchen table in the station basement quarters and closely scrutinised by their father.

Daniel McGovern Senior pictured as a constable in his RIC uniform. **Photo courtesy of the McGovern family.**

Then, as now, the station itself was accessed via its public porch-way. This led to a hallway with a private sergeant's office on the left. Directly opposite was a six feet wide, narrow but sturdy, well-worn wooden counter that opened out to the station's busy public enquiry office – the Day Room. It was here, across the counter, that the public conducted its business with either the duty sergeant or an assisting constable. This was where the main day-to-day business of the RIC in Carrickmacross was conducted. It was the hub of operations.

The Day Room was accessed by a doorway just to the right of the public counter. Always sitting on one side on the counter was a large hardback daybook 2 feet long, 1.5 feet wide and four inches thick, into which was entered every enquiry and occurrence of the day with the date, time and nature of what had occurred. New pages were allocated to record each day's busy policing activities and a new daybook was provided for every year. Beyond the counter on its opposite wall the Day Room contained a large 8 feet X 5 feet map of the policing district which was located over the fireplace. This map clearly displayed local and outlying areas and also all the RIC sub-stations and huts which were located in villages and rural areas within the district. A small annex room off the Day Room contained a wall mounted telephone which connected the station with the outside world including its eight smaller sub-stations. The telephone number was clearly marked on the body of the telephone – Carrickmacross 24.[8]

In addition to its telephone, this room also contained a police telegraph system which was used to send and receive encrypted operational reports with RIC main headquarters in Dublin Castle as well as with provincial headquarters in Belfast.[9] Behind the Day Room leading to the rear of the building was the corridor which, near its end, serviced the basement area's internal rear stairwell and the McGovern's flat. From the Day Room this corridor first led to holding cells on the left and opposite those were Head Constable and Sergeants' offices – including that of

Danny's father and a Break Room where policemen congregated during their breaks in the course of their shift. The station's guardroom or armoury, where its considerable array of firearms were securely stored, was also located close by.

THE FORM YARD

Near the rear entry gates of the form yard of Carrickmacross Royal Irish Constabulary barracks. This photograph was taken in early 1921 and following a successful poitín raid in which the still and other distilling paraphernalia have been seized. Pictured LTR are Constable Johnston, Sergeant Daniel McGovern Senior. Head Constable Palmer, Head Constable Patrick Brannigan (Plain Clothes), Constable Thomas Conboy, Constable Lynch and Sgt. Peter McGoldrick. The illicit distilling of what was known as the 'Mountain Dew' was rampant throughout Ireland at the time. **Photo: ©Glór Na Gael Collection, Monaghan County Museum.**

Ground floor operational areas in the RIC barracks and some first floor offices had electric lighting[10] with the remainder of the building still reliant on gas or paraffin oil lamps for nocturnal illumination. The first floor of the police station comprised the offices of District Inspector John Maunsell and his direct subor-

dinate senior Head Constable Patrick Brannigan[11] as well as
offices for supporting administrative personnel. The top floor
contained barrack billets for the younger single officers. The
ground floor corridor also led to a back door beyond which lay
the back yard of the station.

Mack McGovern recalled: "This was always called *The Form*.
The idea being that it was here, within the confines of the station
property and protected all around by high walls, that policemen
could form up in ranks either for inspection purposes or prior to
leaving for routine or special patrols." Also situated to one side of
the rear eastern wall of the form was a 25 yard practice shooting
range with three targets behind which was an eight feet high
bullet backstop of neatly built jute sandbags. This was mainly
used for pistol practice. The ground directly in front for several
feet was coated by now with damp and hardened sand which had
gradually been released from the sandbags over many years due
to innumerable bullet strikes. The form also contained several
open sheds. The first contained about a half dozen or so sturdy
black bicycles.

Most RIC mobile patrols consisting of one or more
policemen were, at this stage, still conducted on bicycles and it
was not uncommon for RIC bicycle convoys of various sizes to
be observed out and about on the highways and byways of the
Carrickmacross RIC District. Even then, strict discipline would
be observed with the policemen cycling along in columns of twos
often accompanied by a senior officer. The second shed
contained the barrack's fuel with adequate stocks of coal, slack
and firewood. This shed also housed a large oil tank which
contained paraffin oil to fuel the station's many oil lamps as well
as the portable *Bullseye* police lanterns the officers used when
patrolling at night time. Pedestrian and vehicular access to the
form yard was through a pair of strong wooden gates which hung
under a cut stone archway serviced by an alley to the Main
Street. The McGoverns soon settled into the routine of family
life, such as it was, as it revolved around the working practices of

the head of the family in the busy police station that was Carrick RIC barracks. Margaret had soon made their basement accommodation there as comfortable and as homely as she could for her growing family.

---

1. Large numbers of these long-range Douglas Aircraft Company manufactured four engine transport aircraft were used in the early days of the occupation of Japan as they were throughout the later occupation years. General MacArthur himself arrived in Japan having been flown to Atsugi in a C-54. According to Joe's Snyder's book, *Para(graph) Trooper for MacArthur,* the occupation troops of the 11th Airborne Division were flown into Japan on a fleet of C-54s.
2. These were normally reserved for the Sergeant-in-Charge who had responsibility for the overall smooth running of the station itself. The one exception to this arrangement was if a sergeant happened to have teenage daughters. This was deemed too much of a distraction for young constables as they went about their work – PSNI Museum, Belfast. As Dan McGovern Sr. was only an ordinary sergeant, it can be deduced that the quarters were free at the time and thus allocated to him.
3. This was the same month that *R.M.S. Titanic* sank en route to New York.
4. As Sergeant McGovern went about his policing duties in Inniskeen, a young boy was growing up there who would go on to become one of the most celebrated poets and writers Ireland has ever produced – Patrick Kavanagh.
5. Deduced from IRA observations, RIC photographs of the time and Peter McGoldrick of the RIC Online Forum. A minimum of six and possibly as many as eight regular RIC policemen were stationed in Carrickmacross before the Black and Tans arrived.
6. Irish term for whiskey.
7. This is according to the written account of Dan's brother Malachy.
8. This was the actual telephone number of Carrickmacross RIC station at that time. – PSNI Museum, Belfast. Telephones came into regular police use towards the end of the 1800s with the first police models being introduced in Glasgow.
9. Encrypted telegraphs had been in Crown police use as early as 1850. Kieve, p245.
10. Electricity was supplied to the station by the Carrickmacross Lighting Company.
11. There were different grades of both RIC District Inspector and Head Constable rank.

2

THE IRISH WAR OF INDEPENDENCE

Rebellion in Britain's First Colony

IRELAND and the Irish had existed under the constant domination of Great Britain for 700 years. It had been the very first colony of the British Empire. Over the preceding centuries, the British had successfully brought their ways – their language, their infrastructure and engineering expertise, as well as their education, legal, judiciary and monetary systems, but to a mainly subservient Ireland. The general Irish population, for the large part, had settled into something of a grudging acceptance of the British presence in Ireland but this imposed juxtaposition had been opposed by sporadic acts of rebellion against British rule. Insurrection was always just under the surface in Ireland and down through the centuries it had frequently boiled over. Young Danny McGovern was in the midst of many elderly people in Carrickmacross who could still recount the horrors of the Irish Potato Famine of the 1840s, *The Great Hunger*.

He could remember Ireland's Easter Rising in 1916 when the Irish Volunteers and other smaller militant groups staged a rebellion against British rule mainly in Dublin. Over eighty years later, Lt. Colonel McGovern, reflecting on the Easter Rising recalled: "I was only a very young boy at the time but the Easter

Rising changed our very way of life. It had a big effect on our family. When they shot the leaders of the Rising, those executed became martyrs for the cause of Irish freedom." Fourteen leaders were shot including the seven signatories of the *Proclamation of the Irish Republic* which had been read aloud by one of them, Padraig Pearse, outside Dublin's General Post Office. All had been court-martialed in secret without proper legal representation and shot before a British Army firing squad in Kilmainham Gaol in Dublin.

In fact, two of the rebels executed in the wake of the Rising had spent time in Carrickmacross in the years prior to it taking place and had attracted huge attendances eager to hear their message of Irish Independence. These speakers had been none other than Pearse himself and Roger Casement.[1] The executions caused widespread public revulsion and served only to galvanise the resolve of the majority of Irish people firmly against the British establishment. The result was that politically all strands of Irish nationalism now assembled under the banner of an Irish political party whose name in English translates to *We Ourselves.* This party favoured severing ties with Britain altogether and its name was Sinn Féin. Later, during 1917, the Irish Volunteers began to reorganise.

By the time young Danny McGovern turned ten years old in December 1919, he had settled in well to his new home. He was now attending the local primary school which, in Ireland even today, is referred to as a *National* School. The Patrician Brothers Boys' National School sat not far from the barracks on O'Neill Street in the shadow of the neo-gothic Saint Joseph's Catholic Church with its elegant and soaring limestone spire. By and large Danny was enjoying a happy childhood and had made many friends his own age in and around the town where his father had been stationed now for seven years.

Every day, during his school breaks and after his school day had finished, he enjoyed the freedom of walking and running the corridors of the barracks and the form yard to the rear outside.

As a *Barracks Brat* he was largely ignored by the policemen as they went about their work, but during quiet periods at the station most would acknowledge him with a smile and a bit of a friendly chat. In the course of any given year new RIC men of various ages would arrive to their new posting at the Carrick-macross barracks. Some stayed on and Danny got to know them quite well, but others soon moved on again as more attractive postings to other areas nearer home became available. For the large part, morale amongst the officers and men of Carrick RIC station was good, but Danny's father was also well aware of the growing political tensions in Ireland and throughout the community in which he served.

OBSERVING THE POLICEMEN

The uniform of the Royal Irish Constabulary was very dark green. Since 1911, the tunic had a high collar and black crown embossed buttons augmented by collar and arm insignia and with an epaulette on each shoulder. Every officer also wore a brightly polished chain and whistle on his tunic. The whistle was kept in the left breast pocket and was traditionally used to raise the alarm and to summon other police officers within earshot in the event of assistance being required in an emergency. The whistle chain was anchored to the inside of a tunic button hole to avoid loss and was always visible as a decorative addition to the uniform.

As was the case with Sergeant McGovern, rank markings were sewn onto the tunic just a few inches above each sleeve cuff. This was to ensure that they could be clearly seen even if such a more senior officer was donning his waterproof cape at night or during periods of inclement weather. A black leather belt with an S buckle, usually incorporating an optional black revolver holster, leather truncheon pouch and rectangular ammunition pouch, was worn around the waist of the tunic. The uniform trousers always matched the tunic – at least for now. RIC service footwear was a pair of black highly polished leather hobnail boots. Head attire was usually the typical bobby helmet of the time, or a visor cap depending largely on rank and personal preference. The RIC badge or helmet plate comprised the RIC motif.[2] Even aged 89, Mack could remember: "Usually, my father wore a police visor cap but there were occasions when he would wear the RIC police helmet which had a spike on top of it."

It was as a very young boy that Danny became aware of the comings and goings of the policemen as they went about their daily and nightly duties either in the barracks itself or out on the beat throughout the town. He also observed shift changes, his father and other policemen dealing with the public at the Day Room counter and also the tedious paperwork being undertaken by officers hidden away behind desks piled high with statements, summonses, charge sheets and other documents in the administration offices upstairs. He became used to observing individuals being taken into custody at the barracks where they were processed and interviewed by RIC officers for many different crimes and misdemeanours. He observed statements being carefully taken by officers with pencil and paper to be typed up later from prisoners, witnesses and complainants alike and he saw how charges for various offences were preferred. During the day he frequently accompanied his father and other police officers on foot patrol throughout the town.

When observing the policemen, most importantly of all perhaps, Danny began to understand how the chain of command between the different ranks played out in his barracks home. To that end he also observed the constables as they frequently formed ranks for inspection. This was undertaken in the form yard to the barracks' rear either by his father or by other senior officers. The policemen also fell in to conduct regular arms drills. In the immediate years ahead Danny would come to fully understand how the more senior officers like his father instilled discipline and heightened the sense of duty in their subordinates. This was a grounding that would stand to Danny well in future years.

The First World War finally ended in November 1918 but even before the guns fell silent, another enemy was manifesting itself, not just in Dan McGovern's home town, but all across the world – the Spanish Flu. Carrickmacross had instances of the flu throughout the first half 1918 but no deaths. However, that all changed when, in July, the flu started to become particularly virulent. Before the end of 1918 as many as three funerals of flu victims a day were being observed in the town and schools, including Danny's, were closed for long periods.[3]

The British then called a General Election in December 1918. Whilst election rallies undoubtedly helped to spread the deadly flu, the electoral result in Ireland was a landslide victory for Sinn Féin contesting its very first General Election. The party won a resounding and historic victory taking 73 out of a possible 105 Irish seats. Then, on January 21st 1919, twenty-seven Sinn Féin MPs, instead of attending Britain's Westminster parliament in London, assembled as pledged at the first sitting of a new but illegal parliament of the Irish Republic – Dáil Eireann – at the Mansion House in Dublin. The Dáil elected representatives present were not called MPs but Teachta Dála, or TDs. The absent forty six were incarcerated by the British. Despite the fact that under British law the Dáil was illegal and seditious, its members had a clear mandate from the Irish people following Sinn Féin's sweeping election success. The Easter Rising of 1916 had had no such mandate.

———

On the very same day that the first Irish Dáil convened in Dublin, two RIC men were shot and killed by Irish Volunteers operating independently in Soloheadbeg, County Tipperary in southern Ireland. The officers had been guarding a cartload of gelignite explosives which was being delivered to local mines.

The shots which killed the two RIC men were the very first of the Irish War of Independence, a guerrilla campaign which would rage for two and a half years until July 1921 and which young Danny McGovern would witness first hand. An offensive strategy was soon however, adopted by the Irish Volunteers[4] dispensing with independent operations like that of Soloheadbeg in favour of a proper command structure. This was with the Volunteers' resourceful and resilient Director of Organisation and Intelligence, Michael Collins and its Chief of Staff, Richard Mulcahy, issuing orders from GHQ in Dublin.

Just like the Fenian movement before it, the leadership of the Irish Volunteers still clearly viewed the RIC as Britain's eyes and ears in Ireland and the main threat to aspirations of an Irish Republic. It now set out an effective strategy to destroy it as a force including its informants and to seize its weapons. In order to do this, ruthless war would initially be made on smaller more vulnerable RIC stations. With this strategy, Collins envisaged that the RIC would be compelled to withdraw to the larger urban-based stations effectively leaving large swathes of Ireland un-policeable. However, for the large part, it would be 1920 before the strategy would be put into widespread practice with any great effect.

THE RIC BOYCOTT

Meanwhile, in parallel with the military campaign, the Dáil decreed a new strategy against the British in Ireland in order to make an Irish Republic a reality. It would destroy the fabric of British civil governance in the country by ignoring it and running its own counter state in parallel instead. Dáil Eireann would take over the civil administration duties both at national and local level from the existing British-run authorities. In keeping with this strategy and in addition to it, in County Monaghan the Irish Volunteers established what were referred to locally in Carrickmacross as Peace Patrols or Volunteer Patrols.

However, they were also referred to as The Irish Police and represented a direct alternative to the RIC.[5] Now, to further alienate the RIC in its local communities, Dáil Eireann also adopted a policy of social ostracisation, a boycott campaign, against RIC policemen and their families.[6] Interaction with the local community in which it served had always been one of the key cornerstones for the efficient functioning of the Crown's police force in Ireland. As a result a large proportion of the Irish public now disengaged from the RIC man in both his official and personal capacities in the community in which he served.

In Carrickmacross, a number of policemen were soon assaulted and their families threatened. Threatening letters were received and windows broken in known RIC family homes at several locations throughout the town. One young woman was threatened with death if she went through with her marriage to an RIC constable and another had her hair shaved off after she was seen talking to a policeman contrary to the boycott order.[7]

Gradually, the Dáil boycott of the RIC began to be even more rigidly enforced by the Irish Volunteers in Carrickmacross. The rebels decreed that anybody found interacting with the RIC in the area were also to be boycotted by the general public and a list of these people made. Up to this point the RIC had still largely managed to maintain at least some access and interaction with the local community. Now, however, as across most of Ireland, the boycott began to be forcibly imposed raising the effectiveness of the tactic with more or less immediate effect.

To augment the activities of its Peace Patrols, which were now increasingly undertaking police duties, Sinn Féin parish based tribunals and arbitration courts were also set up in South Monaghan[8] to deal with criminal and civil cases respectively which had resulted from the activities of the Peace Patrols. These Parish Courts ran parallel to the British Petty Sessions courts which had existed in the country under the Crown for centuries and directly challenged their authority. The local population began to refuse to attend the British Petty Sessions and gradually the Parish Courts began to increase the cases heard before them at the expense of their British counterparts.

Later, the Parish Courts were superseded by the better organised Dáil Courts.[9] Soon, Carrickmacross RIC station had virtually no callers at all and the Petty Sessions Courts had virtually no cases to hear either. Despite the boycott, Sergeant McGovern was not subjected to it to the same degree as many of his colleagues. There may have been several reasons for this but in this regard Mack McGovern said of his father: "My father knew all the locals. I have always felt that he knew a lot more about what was going on than he let on and I think that is what saved him. I wouldn't call him an informer but he was Irish to the core and I think that he felt that the domineering attitude of the British was just too much." With increasing frequency young Danny and his siblings were beginning to feel that they too were being set apart from their peers in the local community in which they lived.

As was the case with all RIC children, they were beginning to experience some problems at school and elsewhere emanating from the Dáil boycott order. In Danny's case this was something which would come to a head later. The Irish Volunteers came under the control of Daíl Eireann later on in 1919 effectively becoming the army of the new state. At this point the Irish Volunteers adopted a new name – the *Irish Republican Army*, but it would be more commonly referred to by its abbreviated form – the *IRA*.[10] In this capacity it continued to wage its military campaign against the British in conjunction with the Dail's own administration activities and its campaign of civil disobedience.

By the end of 1919 and as young Danny McGovern turned ten years old, eleven RIC men and three Dublin Metropolitan policemen had been killed at the hands of the IRA.[11] By now no RIC man travelled anywhere unless he was armed. The McGovern family had been in Carrickmacross now for almost ten years and Danny's father, 47 years old, had just been given a temporary promotion to Acting Head Constable.[12] Dan explained: "Head Constable Brannigan had been sick and as a result my father took over many of his duties."[13]

In 1920, IRA attacks on RIC facilities started to escalate in County Monaghan as throughout Ireland. In the early hours of Sunday February 14th 1920, the first major IRA operation took place in South Monaghan on the direct orders of Michael Collins himself. Four IRA companies attacked the remote outlying Ballytrain RIC station on a four crossroads only eight miles north-west of Carrickmacross. It was this attack which marked the start of offensive operations in earnest by the IRA in South Monaghan during the War of Independence. A gun battle ensued as an IRA detachment placed a large explosive mine against a gable wall and gave several warnings to the garrison to surrender. It refused and the mine was detonated destroying much of the building. Miraculously, none of the six RIC men inside were killed with some only receiving relatively minor injuries.

However, the rebels then assaulted the building and captured it and its occupants. The surrendered policemen were subsequently released unharmed but the attackers made off with all the arms and ammunition they could find. It was a major coup for the IRA as it was the first surrender and capture of an RIC station in Ulster. Danny McGovern's father, now with additional policing responsibilities, attended the scene. As a result of this attack, RIC personnel were withdrawn from Ballytrain and the other outlying sub police stations and police protection huts back to Carrickmacross District Headquarters where RIC strength and activities were now consolidated. Most of the now vacated outlying stations were soon put to the torch by the IRA.

The stations of Inniskeen and Corrinshigagh, where the McGovern's had lived when they first arrived in South Monaghan, were burned to the ground. All across Ireland outlying police stations were subjected to a similar fate. By early March 1920 nearly 500 outlying police barracks and police protection huts across the country had been evacuated of which 400 would eventually be destroyed by the IRA by the end of

June.[14] Soon in the South Monaghan RIC District, only the Carrickmacross and Castleblayney RIC police stations were occupied and operational and had not been burned to the ground by the IRA.[15] Whilst in 1914 there had been 21 RIC stations throughout County Monaghan that figure would soon stand at a mere 9.[16] As the IRA military campaign continued, the boycott had by now become extremely effective against the operation of the RIC in other ways. Eventually, many shopkeepers refused to even serve members of the force. Then, one by one, those in Carrickmacross who had been making a regular income from the police station for years reluctantly informed Sergeant McGovern and other policemen that they were no longer in a position to supply goods or services essential for the running of the station.

Soon the supplies of food, coal, paraffin oil, firewood, everyday groceries and other essential items dried up. Even the charwomen, the cleaning ladies at the station who had always been an inadvertent source of local intelligence through their everyday gossip, soon resigned. Elsewhere, dockers at Dublin and other ports refused to handle British military or police matériel destined to be distributed to military and police barracks across the country. Railway workers, lorry and bus drivers, either out of patriotism or in fear of reprisal from the IRA, also refused to haul not just British Crown supplies but also British soldiers and Royal Irish Constabulary policemen.

By the end of May 1920, 66 policemen and 5 soldiers had been killed with 79 policemen and 2 soldiers wounded. In addition 351 evacuated barracks had been destroyed and 105 damaged. Occupied RIC barracks had also been attacked with 15 destroyed and 25 damaged. In an attempt to obtain explosives and signalling equipment, 19 Coastguard stations and lighthouses were also raided by the IRA.[17] For the RIC man danger and possible death now potentially lurked around any corner, behind any window or behind any hedgerow. This ever present threat began to take its toll. The RIC in Carrickmacross soon drastically scaled back what had been its few remaining routine patrols and investigations throughout the local community. This was a scenario now being played out at those remaining RIC police stations all across Ireland which were still manned. As a result morale in the RIC ranks plummeted. Many officers, under pressure from distraught wives or family members, resigned in favour of less dangerous occupations or retired altogether. Out of a force of 9,500 over the summer months of 1920, over 500 policemen had resigned.[18] Recruitment could not keep up with the resignations.

Across Ireland the RIC became a demoralised and depleted force – a shadow of the force it had been. As the months of ever-present danger and dejection rolled on, the policemen in Carrickmacross had somehow still managed to come off relatively unscathed. During the first few months of 1920, custom-made armour plate shutters and armoured double front doors had been fitted to Carrickmacross RIC barracks.[19] Both shutters and doors incorporated loop holes to shoot firearms through and to allow observation. This was a defensive measure from which by now most major RIC barracks benefitted in anticipation of IRA attacks. These shutters and doors could be slammed closed in seconds and used as firing points in the event of an attack. However, there had been no attack against Carrick RIC station – at least not yet.

Mack McGovern remembered: "The killings, ambushes, bombings and the boycott of the policemen had a serious effect on the RIC. Manpower and morale were at a very low ebb." The machinery of British administration in Ireland had by now all but seized and across the country chaos reigned. The Irish Republic in the eyes of many people throughout Ireland was already a reality. The fledgling state, although still under the thumb of Britain, was grappling free. It now had its own parliament, its own local authorities, it was collecting its own taxes, it had its own army, its own judicial system and its own police force enforcing its own laws.[20]

A NEW HOME

Margaret McGovern had growing concerns for her husband's safety and for that of her growing family. By now Danny had two new baby sisters, Genevieve and Anna, bringing the children in the family to eight. Eventually, due to the increasing violence and threat level against RIC members in the South Monaghan RIC District, the McGovern family were moved out of their barracks basement flat. Mack explained: "We were moved out of the police barracks because of the trouble. It became increasingly dangerous not just for an RIC man like my father, but for mother and my brothers and sisters and me to live within the confines of the barracks compound."

The McGoverns' new home was a cottage rented by the RIC,[21] which stood on the property owned by the nuns of The Sisters of Saint Louis. It stood several hundred yards downhill from the town on a laneway called Distillery Lane and nestled beneath a copse of trees and adjacent to a large old and long defunct distillery building which gave the lane its name. Distillery Lane wound on past the cottage and the old distillery to become the Convent Avenue, a popular local walkway which ran west to east about a mile and a half through convent farm-land flanked by leafy mature trees and well kept fencing on both sides. The cottage had originally been built for the manager of the distillery but had subsequently been occupied by a succession of gardeners instead who tended to the many gardens of the convent complex.[22] In more recent years, however, the cottage had been vacant. It had been rented by the nuns to the Royal Irish Constabulary for Acting Head Constable McGovern and his family who soon moved in.

The cottage was built of thick stone walls. It sat between Distillery Lane and the periphery of the convent's vast sports field which curled around into a kidney shape at one of its corners and ran right up to the boundary fence within several feet of the McGovern's northern gable. Downstairs the dwelling had several windows front and back and solid wooden half doors front and rear. The living room comprised a large family sized kitchen with a small alcove dining area on one side and a big cut stone fireplace with a cast iron stove installed on the other. The stove was nearly always continuously lit and on its hot plates on top the contents of a saucepan usually bubbled around a well-worn wooden spoon. In the oven, soda bread was frequently on the rise and emanated a pleasant aroma throughout the cottage. There was also a cupboard with display shelves which now held Margaret's willow pattern fine china plates and beneath that, on the sideboard, stood her precious silver tea service. Much to Margaret's delight against the remaining kitchen wall, the cottage had an upright piano. The McGovern's also had a violin which all the McGovern children were encouraged to learn.

Overall, the kitchen-cum-living room was cosy, clean and impeccably tidy. Access to the two bedrooms upstairs was via a stairwell near the kitchen's front door and the only natural light which pierced the bedrooms did so through two narrow skylights set in the Bangor Blue slated roof above each room. Right outside the front door of the cottage was a wooden rain barrel into which rainwater was directed from the spouting on the roof. Given the Irish climate, the barrel was usually full to the brim. In the dryer summer months water could also be obtained in buckets from a hand pump further up Distillery Lane near the main convent building.[23] The cottage had good circulation of air which was important given that the deadly Spanish Flu had arrived in Ireland only a few short years before. By mid 1920, however, its contagion had largely dissipated. Tuberculosis or consumption known locally as *The Con,* was still, however, very common in Ireland at the time.[24]

The cottage was not serviced by electricity, so the McGoverns used mainly paraffin kerosine lamps to light their new home at night-time. There were no sanitary facilities either, so chamber pots, more commonly called *guzunders,*[25] were to be found under every bed upstairs whilst outside, in one corner of the vegetable and flower garden to the rear, was a wooden privy which was used mainly during the daylight hours to answer the call of nature. Chickens, ducks and a rooster patrolled the cottage property in their daily quest to locate and pick food morsels wherever they were to be found. The additional space also meant that a pen could now be built in the garden to house the sergeant's greyhounds and Danny now walked the lean racing dogs regularly along the long and leafy Convent Avenue.

Meanwhile, Irish Republican Army attacks on the RIC and Dáil Eireann's counter state activities and its campaign of civil disobedience against the British continued to increase. The British felt compelled to take extreme measures to restore law and order. They had by now started to introduce a new foil to take on and quell the IRA, Dáil Eireann and any *Sinn Féiner*[26] who dared to challenge Britain's authority in Ireland.

---

1. *Farney in the Fight for Freedom* – P.V. Hoey.
2. Garda Síochána Museum.
3. From *Dundalk Democrat* archive, 2nd November 1918/ Louth County Council archive. The Spanish Flu pandemic was the deadliest pandemic in recorded history. It killed more people in a single year than the bubonic plague killed in its four years in the 14th century. Estimates state that as many as 60 million people may have died from it worldwide and in Ireland it claimed 10,600 lives. World War 1 is sometimes blamed for the spread of the flu. It is believed that American soldiers initially brought the highly infectious but moderate flu strain to France in April 1918. It was called *Spanish Flu*, not because it originated there, but due to the fact that Spain was neutral during World War 1. All major belligerents in the war did not want enemy spies reporting the true effect the flu was having on their population which was useful intelligence. Details of the pandemic in these countries therefore, were greatly suppressed. On the other hand, the uncensored information about the flu was published in the Spanish press and then related to other countries hence *Spanish flu*.
4. This was at a meeting in Dublin between Collins and one of his ace spies – Detective Sergeant Eamon *Ned* Broy of the Dublin Metropolitan Police. A clerk in Brunswick Street police station, now Pearse Street Garda Station in Dublin, he had access to virtually all British police intelligence documents. Broy had always been sympathetic to Irish nationalism and decided to become a double agent. Collins and Broy met in the first week of April

1919 and the strategy to best undermine and attack the RIC was formulated based on Broy's advice. It was Broy who arranged Collins' and Séan Nunan's infamous night inside Brunswick DMP station on April 7th 1919 where they spent hours reading the RIC and DMP *G Division* intelligence files gleaning valuable intelligence for the IRA.

5. *Dundalk Democrat* archive, via Fr. Peadar Livingstone Collection, Monaghan County Council *War of Independence Files*.

6. *Farney in the Fight for Freedom*, P.V. Hoey.

7. iBid.

8. *Irish War of Independence 1919 - 1921* Timeline, University College Cork.

9. *Monaghan's War of Independence 1919 - 1921*, Terence Dooley.

10. In his Witness Statement to Fr. Peadar Livingstone in Monaghan County Council's *War of Independence Files,* Volunteer Patrick Corrigan of South Monaghan states that the term Irish Republican Army/IRA had first been used unofficially in 1914 after the Irish Volunteers split. This had been as a result of John Redmond's attempt to entice them to serve in the British Army in The Great War as a means to an end of achieving Home Rule for Ireland.

11. *Timeline of the Irish War of Independence.*

12. As this was only a temporary promotion Danny's father was still technically a sergeant and he will be referred to as such in the narrative hereafter.

13. Brannigan, who held a senior Head Constable rank, later returned to duty. Sgt.McGovern, however, appears to have retained his Acting Head Constable role. This was most likely due to the fact that later, Brannigan was absent having been posted to take charge of the RIC in the neighbouring town of Castleblayney in an attempt to control the reckless behaviour of the Auxiliaries.

14. UK Government sources.

15. Witness Statement, Patrick Corrigan, Fr. P. Livingstone archive, War of Independence Files, Monaghan County Council.

16. PSNI Museum, Belfast.

17. *The Black and Tans* (London) 1959, p47, Richard Bennett.

18. An Garda Síochána Museum.

19. The armour plate shutters and front doors can be seen on the building to this day.

20. Partially sourced from Hopkinson *The Irish War of Independence.*

21. Any dwelling into which an RIC man and his family intended to move had to have the approval of a senior RIC officer. The author believes that the transfer of the McGovern family out of Carrickmacross RIC barracks was on the instruction of District Inspector John Maunsell who resided in *Iona House* in Bath Street (Now Farney Street) which had been rented from the nuns with whom Maunsell and his family would have had daily contact. The District Inspector's house and the convent's main building and school yards were only separated by the narrow Distillery Lane which was in regular use. The McGovern's cottage was only several hundred yards down the same lane from Maunsell's rented house.

22. The convent building still dominates the southern approach to Carrick-macross town. It was built on the original site of Essex Castle (built circa

1630) and occupied by the 3rd Earl of Essex, Robert Devereaux. A few miles east of Carrickmacross at a place now called Essexford, his father Robert, the 2nd Earl of Essex, had met with his Irish Chieftain adversary Hugh O'Neill, the Earl of Tyrone in 1599 to discuss peace terms during the Nine Years War. The 2nd Earl of Essex was executed for treason in 1601.

23. Cottage description from the written account of Dan's brother, Malachy.

24. A 1912 report found that TB related deaths in Ireland were 50% higher than in England or Scotland with the vast majority occurring amongst the poorer classes.

25. In present tense Irish terminology of the time as a chamber pot in a bedroom *guzunder* the bed.

26. As the British authorities collectively called anyone suspected of doing the bidding of Dáil Eireann or the IRA.

3

THE BLACK AND TANS 1920

A Rough and Dangerous Task

THE BRITISH HAD COME up with a plan of action. They were going to fight fire with fire. By January 1920 the British government had advertised in British cities for men who were prepared to *face a rough and dangerous task* to augment the ranks of the RIC in support of British policing in Ireland. The formation of this force was instigated by the then British Secretary of State for War –Winston Spencer Churchill, who proposed a Special Emergency Gendarmerie[1] which would become a branch of the Royal Irish Constabulary. However, the idea of such a force utilising ex-servicemen had first been suggested the year before by both Unionist leader, Walter Long and the British Army's Commander in Chief in Ireland, Sir Fredrick Shaw.[2]

This force had now been raised to re-enforce the ranks of the RIC and to physically strengthen the defences of all police facilities in Ireland. It would also take the fight to the IRA by mounting a determined counter-insurgency campaign against it and to do everything in its power to eradicate the activities of the newly elected and established but illegal Irish Government - Dáil Eireann. Amongst other duties, members were to act as escorts for agents of the British Crown, to provide crowd control and also to act as guards and sentries when the need arose. It was hoped that this new special force would do much to restore British order in Ireland. The pay was well above average for the time too – 10 shillings a day with free board and lodgings. By comparison, basic pay for a British Army infantryman was a tenth of that – 1 shilling and 6d per day. Two years after millions of men had returned from the trenches of France, Flanders and elsewhere and with many finding themselves unemployed, there had been no shortage of recruits for the new RIC police augmentation service and its ranks were filled mainly by former British soldiers between the ages of 20 and 27. This force would soon become infamous as the Black and Tans and a reign of terror in Ireland was to follow. Dan McGovern said of the introduction of the new British force: "In point of fact, England was bringing in its military forces disguised as policemen and that was the whole crux of it."

Such was the urgency of the British government to take control of the deteriorating situation in Ireland that some recruits found themselves on the evening boat to Dublin having successfully sat their interview for the new force only earlier that day.[3] The proscribed regular basic training for a *regular* RIC man was six months. By comparison, the Black and Tans had in the region of three weeks rushed training and sometimes even as little as three days policing instruction[4] at the RIC depot in the Phoenix Park and other sub-training depots including that at Gormanstown in County Meath. 9,500 of these new Black and Tan recruits were deployed as special constables from these depots to police stations throughout most of Ireland to augment the dwindling ranks of the RIC.[5]

In the same month that Cork City's Republican Lord Mayor, Tómas McCurtain, had been assassinated in front of his family, the Black and Tans first deployed throughout Ireland on March 25th 1920. Platoon sized units of Black and Tans, usually comprising in the region of 27 special constables, were deployed to augment the regular RIC in their urban stronghold garrisons throughout Ireland. However, this unit number varied. Little if any were ever deployed to the mainly unionist counties of north-eastern Ulster.

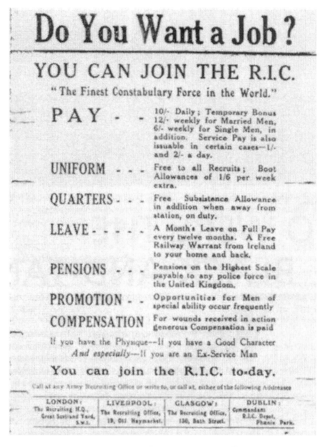

A Royal Irish Constabulary recruitment advertisement which appeared in many British newspapers. Successful applicants would become the notorious Black and Tans.
Image: Anonymous source.

The Black and Tans got their nickname because of a shortage of police uniforms which saw them kitted out in a mixture of dark, almost black, police rifle green uniforms as well as the much brighter army khaki uniforms. Mack could remember: "Their uniforms were a mixed bag of black tunics and tan pants but some of them had khaki tunics and black pants." These hodge-podge uniforms differentiated them from both the British Army and the regular RIC.[6] By mid-summer 1920 the Black and Tans were flooding into Ireland to help quell the now raging countrywide IRA guerrilla war and Dáil counter-state activities against the British establishment. Despite their nickname being applied by the Irish soon after their deployment in Ireland, the moniker *Black and Tans* was not at all despised by its members. The Tans frequently referred to themselves verbally or in printed matter as the *Black and Tans* or the *Black and Tan RIC.*

Whilst the Black and Tans were formed to augment the RIC, the regular British Army, when required, now found itself augmenting the Black and Tans. For the large part the British Army, when interacting with the general population had exercised restraint. The Black and Tans, however, showed no restraint whatsoever. It was soon apparent to the Irish population including the mainstream RIC, that the Black and Tans were an ill-disciplined rabble more intent on terrorising the population in Ireland than on augmenting the efforts of the police. Mack McGovern said of them: "They were a reckless, hard-drinking bunch of bastards."

On August 9th 1920, the British introduced the *Restoration of Order in Ireland Act.* This banned the Dáil Courts, driving them underground and was intended to clamp down on IRA and Sinn Féin activity by introducing courts martial rather than jury trials and providing for powers of internment. On 31st August 1920 and to procure additional weapons and ammunition, the IRA conducted what became known as the General Raid for Arms. This was on unionist homes across County Monaghan and neighbouring counties. In many cases the houses were often identified to the IRA by sympathetic local postmen. However, the occupants of some houses in County Monaghan chose to defend themselves and fired on the IRA raiders. These ensuing gun battles resulted in the fatal shooting of four IRA men and the wounding of several more. Two of the dead rebels had been shot during gunfire exchanges at unionist houses in Sergeant McGovern's Carrickmacross RIC District.

TANS ARRIVE IN CARRICKMACROSS

Towards the end of September[7] a convoy of distinctive military lorries packed with Black and Tans and bristling with weaponry entered Carrickmacross. Apart from the increasing danger associated with remaining in their family flat, there had been another reason why the McGoverns had been moved out of Carrick police station – to make billet room available for the Black and Tans. As elsewhere throughout Ireland, the Black and Tans had been sent to Carrickmacross to quell the growing subversive activities of Sinn Féin and the IRA. By then the Tans and what would soon be referred to as the *Old* RIC faced the IRA's 5th South Monaghan Battalion which now consisted of 330 men split into 11 companies roughly drawn along parish lines. Each company varied in strength from between 20 to 60 men. Towards the end of 1920 one thousand men were in the ranks of the IRA's County Monaghan Brigade.

The Tans immediately set about familiarising themselves with the localities to which they had been posted. Mack McGovern's first sight of them in Carrickmacross was when two Tans walked past the cottage in Distillery Lane and on to the old distillery. They tried to gain entry to the disused building only to end up blasting the padlock off the front door with two shots from a Webley pistol. The Tans conducted a search and then left. In addition to the fitting of its armour plate front doors and shutters, the regular RIC had taken some additional steps to fortify Carrick police station. Sandbags, for example, had been placed on all front facing window sills as an additional measure of protection. However, it was the Black and Tans who now really bolstered defences at the building.

They first set to work filling more jute sandbags from which a 6 feet high frontal defensive wall was built at street level and along the outside edge of the entire footpath in front of the building. This defensive wall then turned in at right angles on both its flanks and butted to both ends of the station's wrought iron railings which contained the access gates to the McGovern's former basement home. This measure now necessitated pedestrians having the imposition of walking around the exterior of the sandbag wall on the Main Street itself to continue past the RIC station. This new exterior defensive wall contained a single, constantly monitored, open access point through which the station's front porch and entryway could be reached from the outside and the Main Street from the inside. Strands of barbed wire were festooned across the front of the sandbag wall except at its access point.

Now, as an additional measure to fortify the building's façade, large wooden frameworks supporting mass chicken wire were erected at sloping angles along the entire width of the building's façade from the top of the new sandbag wall to a height just beneath the first floor window sills. A further chicken wire frame ran at a more obtuse angle from the sandbag wall to the roof of the station's entry porch at first floor level. Around the edges of the porch roof an additional five-feet high sandbag wall was built which backed onto the main front wall of the building. Access to this elevated strongpoint could only be obtained from Head Constable Brannigan's office window directly behind. With the sandbags obscuring the bottom of Brannigan's window this access point was not visible from ground level.

From the centre of this defence point rose the wooden flagpole on which now flew, not the Union Jack, but a different flag – the flag of the Black and Tans with a black and tan background on which was emblazoned the RIC crown over harp crest. This was a clear warning to local inhabitants and particularly to the IRA and other Sinn Féiners, that the Black and Tans were now in residence. The Tans had in fact, built themselves a typical British Army Sangar – in this case a temporary front perimeter defensive structure. With the addition of the sangar the lower extremities of the front of Carrickmacross RIC station at least, were now largely protected from any future attempt by the IRA to attack it at ground level with small arms, grenades and other projectiles.[8] Dan remembered that the Tans soon became the dominating factor. "Our RIC former barracks home became a regular military compound." Some fortification was also provided to the rear of the building but to a lesser degree than to the front given that the existing form yard already provided considerable protection. However, strands of barbed wire were also employed here to re-enforce the form's perimeter walls.

FOOT PATROLS AND CROSSLEY TENDERS

With the fortification measures at the barracks complete, the Black and Tans commenced day and night foot patrols throughout the town area. Several times a day and several times during the night they would carefully emerge, one by one, with rifles in hand from the fortress that was now Carrick RIC barracks via one of the twin armoured front doors and undertake foot patrols throughout the town. Patrolling in groups of twos and threes, sometimes the Tans were accompanied by a regular RIC man. They always undertook sweeps of the Main Street and along its entire length from the town's imposing courthouse at the very bottom of the northern end of the Main Street as far as the bottom of Castle Street. This was as far as Callan's of the Bridge pub at a road junction on the southern approach to the Main Street and only a quarter mile as the crow flies from the McGoverns' cottage. The Tans would usually then just return to the safety of the RIC station at the centre of Main Street before patrolling again later. IRA intelligence watched and noted the movements and habits of the Black and Tans very carefully.

Young Danny eventually met his first Black and Tan who was driving one of the very distinctive lorries on which they had first arrived in Carrickmacross some weeks before. These were the

Crossley Tenders. They were a 25/30 horse power medium-sized high speed reconnaissance vehicle. The Crossleys were utilized by the British Army and the RIC in Ireland from 1919 until British withdrawal in 1922. They would become synonymous with the Black and Tans. It was not long before Danny was invited to travel on RIC and Tan Crossley Tender patrols outside the barracks and throughout the district. It would become a regular occurrence. As a result, Danny got to see first hand the behaviour and tactics of the Tans. "I went along for the excitement. I was out with them many times. As a matter of fact a photograph of a group of Black and Tans on their Crossley Tender was even taken right in front of our cottage in Distillery Lane at one point," he recalled. "The Black and Tans would roam the countryside hell bent on putting down anti-British insurrection. They were ruthless in their approach. They would think nothing, for instance, of running down a farmer's chickens or whatever else happened to be in the way. I saw that."

Initially, Sergeant McGovern often accompanied the Tans on their Crossley patrols but, after a while, when their notorious heavy-handed methods of enforcing British rule became more apparent to him, he preferred to see them off instead. He would simply watch them clamber onto their Crossley Tenders bristling with weaponry in the form yard and drive out under the barracks yard archway to the Main Street and away as they attempted to re-assert British authority in the South Monaghan RIC District.

The Black and Tans on their Crossleys soon became a common sight on the roadways of South Monaghan either on patrolling duties, or on operations to raid houses for known IRA gunmen, weaponry or intelligence leads. In fact, any Sinn Féiner throughout the South Monaghan police district could now expect to be monitored, lifted, questioned and even interned with brutal efficiency. The Black and Tans became greatly feared by the public at large who soon actively avoided travelling on the roads if at all possible, in fear of meeting them. Raids were soon commonplace and particularly at night when suspects were likely to be sleeping and literally could be caught napping. The IRA, however, soon employed effective counter measures to deal with the Crossleys as Dan remembered: "They would dig trenches in the road always just around a bend and camouflage them with tree branches. The Crossleys would drive right into the trenches. The IRA would also cut down a tree and drop it across the road. This would always be on the blind side of the road."

The rebels had identified that Crossleys had very weak rear axles which, when driven into a trench, would fail – disabling the vehicle and leaving its occupants more vulnerable to attack.[9] Often two trenches would be dug with enough room between them to permit other regular traffic such as horses and carts and cyclists to continue on their journey having negotiated an S type manoeuvre through the trench obstacles. This trench tactic would often precede ambushes with the IRA having taken up attack positions behind adjoining hedgerows. As a result Crossley tender patrols took to carrying steel planks with them which were used to bridge ambush trenches.[10] The Black and Tans also sometimes bypassed such IRA obstacles by driving through gates onto adjoining farmland and exiting at the nearest gate beyond the obstacle. Where more than one tender was used on convoy duty and to counter ambushes, the Tans adopted the practice of spacing each vehicle approximately 150 yards apart.

Crossley Tenders also had a very distinctive engine sound which frequently gave warning to IRA men and civilians alike that a raiding party of Black and Tans and RIC were on approach. Due to this the Tans soon learned to dismount their Crossleys some distance from the location they intended to raid and far enough away so that the engine noise would not carry to alert those upon which they were about to swoop. Instead they would approach on foot and surprise their quarry. Arrests and convictions against Republican rebels soon started to increase significantly. Mack recalled: "It was the leadership, the older ones of the IRA that they were mainly out to capture." Soon dozens of IRA men of all ranks and ages were either interned or on the run. The large numbers of rebels on the run and unable to work soon led their leadership to take advantage of their availability. In essence, these men now became full-time revolutionaries. The IRA amended its guerrilla tactics to incorporate these fugitives into much larger but highly mobile and effective IRA units which worked alongside existing IRA battalions and companies. The IRA *Flying Column* was born.

Flying Columns continuously travelled around the various IRA companies in any given county on training or operational duties. Two operated in County Monaghan and throughout the other County Monaghan RIC districts of Monaghan and Clones, the number of both regular RIC men and Black and Tans killed or wounded as a result of IRA ambushes continued to rise. In South Monaghan and particularly since the arrival of the Tans, the local IRA had gradually started to attack the RIC with increasing frequency. This, however, had initially been with only limited success and so far, no policeman, regular or Tan, had as yet been killed or seriously wounded at the hands of the rebels of South Monaghan.

The IRA's lack of success in its attacks was in part due to the fact that arms and ammunition were always in short supply. To augment what they had, rudimentary hand grenades and buck-shot for shotguns were manufactured on kitchen tables or outside in sheds and away from prying eyes. The limited supplies of commercial gelignite, detonators and safety fuse wire, such as that used in Ballytrain, were replenished either by being smuggled into the country or simply skimmed and spirited away from local quarries where the material was used commercially for blasting rock faces.

On 11th February 1921, a Tan foot patrol was ambushed on the edge of Carrickmacross town centre leaving two of the special policemen wounded in the legs before they managed to scramble back into the sanctuary of their barracks compound. Another attack in the town on a wet night on 15th April 1921 clearly demonstrated the shortage of quality ammunition in the ranks of the IRA and the inadequacy of its home-made supply. The IRA ambushed the Black and Tan nightly street patrol at Castle Street as it approached the town centre. The rebels took cover in an elevated position within the convent grounds using the castellated wall there for cover.

Black and Tans pictured soon after their arrival in Carrickmacross outside the McGoverns' cottage in Distillery Lane. Daniel McGovern Jr. was present when this photograph was taken and as a boy often travelled with the Black and Tans on patrol on this and other Crossley Tenders. The McGovern household was largely a 'dry house' where alcohol was rarely consumed but the Tans are clearly seen here drinking in the course of their duties. **Photo: ©The Glór na nGael Collection, Monaghan County Museum.**

As the Tans walked beneath the IRA guns, the rebels let fly at their quarry with a shotgun fusillade. With careful aim having been taken on their unsuspecting adversaries at no more than 30 yards range the shotguns suddenly boomed. The homemade buckshot could clearly be heard as it repeatedly struck the wet rubber capes of the Black and Tans. However, instead of having the desired effect at such short range, the lead behaved no better than grains of rice on impact and simply tickled the policemen who quickly levelled and fired their .303 Lee Enfield rifles and Webley pistols towards the rebel positions. Not a single Black and Tan was even wounded as the IRA withdrew cursing its poor quality ammunition.[11]

SPIES AND PERSONAL SCORES

The RIC boycott and the IRA warnings to enforce it had been very effective but not completely so. Frequently, in the South Monaghan RIC District, carefully laid IRA ambushes to counter Black and Tan convoys, raiding parties and foot patrols came to nothing. This was due to a mixture of bad luck, bad ammunition and still surprisingly good RIC intelligence. Sometimes the Tans simply deviated off their normal routine but, more concerningly for the IRA, it was frequently due to the fact that information was still being supplied to the RIC from spies in the community which resulted in the Black and Tans being re-routed or with-drawn to barracks altogether. Many of the IRA men in the South Monaghan IRA battalion, as well as others throughout the county brigade, suspected that what they referred to as a *Mutual Husbands Protection Club* existed in Carrickmacross.[12] This, it was thought, was between the wife of the top policeman in the district, RIC District Inspector Maunsell and that of one of the leading IRA officers in South Monaghan.

The IRA ruthlessly executed spies and in South Monaghan it shot numerous people as such. This included several spies known to have been planted in the community by the Black and Tans. In one case Dan McGovern's father and his police colleagues were called to a scene where an informer was found buried upside down on remote farmland with his boots clearly protruding from the ground as a stark and gruesome message to other would be RIC *plants* and informers.

Also in South Monaghan, as doubtless was the case elsewhere in Ireland, many unscrupulous members of the local community were not averse to using the services of the hated Black and Tans to their own advantage to settle personal scores. A person with a grievance towards another would often settle it by contacting the Black and Tans by letter or by approaching them in confidence with concocted information about a rival's supposed involvement with the IRA. Given the Tans' reputation for swift reprisal, their response would be predictable. The rival's home would be raided and ransacked and the individual arrested, jailed and sometimes even shot dead on the spot resulting in that person being conveniently out of the way.

Meanwhile, the ongoing ostracisation of the RIC did not leave the McGovern family entirely untouched. As the son of a policeman in the service of the Crown during the boycott it meant that, now with increasing frequency, Danny was being bullied and picked upon by some of the other boys both during and after school hours. "It was becoming difficult for me to get along with the other young fellows," he recalled. "Fights which arose due to my father being a policeman were common. They would beat me, kick me and gang up on me. Soon, as a result, I had to leave class a full half hour before the rest of the boys to avoid being beaten up."

SPARRING WITH THE TANS

One day Danny was set upon by a number of boys not far from his new home. Their leader was the son of a local Sinn Féiner. Dan was stripped of his clothes and thrown into the river which meandered through the convent grounds.[13] Shivering with the cold, Danny gathered what items of his sodden clothes he could from the river before slowly climbing out. Soaking wet and miserable, he was noticed by a passing Black and Tan Crossley patrol, picked up and taken not home, but back to the RIC station where Sergeant McGoldrick cleaned him up, gave him some oddments of dry clothing and then took him home.

Danny's father was away elsewhere on temporary duty. Margaret was shocked when Sergeant McGoldrick explained what had happened to her son. Dan recalled: "When mother saw the state of me she was in tears. She said one Hail Mary after the other." Later, the Black and Tans sent word to the cottage that they wanted to see Danny at the barracks the following day. They were going to teach him how to defend himself in the event that he was ever set upon again. The next day at the barracks, Sergeant McGoldrick and several Tans took Danny aside and taught him numerous personal defensive techniques which would complement his already considerable height advantage. He learned fast. It was not long before he had to put his newly acquired defensive skills to good use.

Some weeks later Danny was walking across a narrow wooden plank which spanned a mucky section of Carrick's Main Street between two sections of stone footpath when Pete Sinnott, the local Blacksmith's son, approached from the opposite direction. The boys confronted each other and stopped in the centre of the plank – standoff! "It was a Sunday and I was on my way to Mass and I had my nice little suit on," Mack remembered. "Pete insulted me and insisted that I step aside into the gutter to let him pass and then, to get his way, he pushed me. Then he pushed me again. I just took one step back and landed a haymaker punch on his nose which effectively landed Pete in the gutter himself! I then just walked on delighted with myself that my new found skills had stood to me."

Due to the ongoing Troubles, work demands on Sergeant McGovern's time was increasing and he was beginning to be notably absent from the family home. Perhaps due in part to this development, Danny started to visit his old home in the centre of town usually along with his brother Malachy and especially after school. The boys would often do their homework there with the help of the regular police constables and the Black and Tans.

Despite the brutal and ruthless methods they employed in their efforts to quell rebellion in Ireland, it soon became apparent across the country that the Tans did not work well in the role for which they were recruited – to augment the RIC. Their presence throughout Ireland only served to swell the ranks of the IRA whose guerrilla tactics the Tans were hopelessly ill-trained to effectively fight against.

On July 27th 1920 and in an attempt to address this, Sir Henry Hugh Tudor had personally raised a second but smaller augmentation force to further bolster the RIC in its efforts to crush the activities of the IRA and Sinn Féin. This was the Auxiliary Division, Royal Irish Constabulary, known as the *Auxiliaries* or *Auxies* , but ultimately its members were also referred to by the native Irish population as Black and Tans. The members of this new force often referred to themselves as *Tudor's Toughs*. The Auxiliaries were made up exclusively of ex-army officers referred to as Temporary Cadets who were to serve only a one year tour of duty in Ireland. They also operated more independently of the RIC. As it transpired, the Auxiliaries were to earn an even fiercer reputation for brutality throughout Ireland than their Black and Tan RIC counterparts.

REPRISAL KILLINGS

A sequence of events soon unfolded which would prove to be amongst the bloodiest of the entire conflict that was the Irish War of Independence. These tit-for-tat events would bring the conflict to an entirely new level of viciousness and serve only to further polarise the British from their Irish subjects and the RIC from the local communities in which it served. What transpired would also ultimately bring what was also known as the Anglo Irish War to a head.

On 20th September 1920 a young medical student was captured by British soldiers when the IRA party to which he was attached ambushed a British Army lorry collecting bread from a bakery in Dublin. A 15-year-old boy soldier was shot dead. Two more soldiers were seriously wounded and later died of wounds. The 18-year-old IRA man arrested was a medical student. His name was Kevin Barry. The following day, Monday 21st

September 1920, a Royal Irish Constabulary District Inspector, Peter Burke, was shot dead by the IRA as he drank in a pub in Balbriggan in North County Dublin. In revenge the Black and Tans burned down or damaged 49 houses and several pubs in the town and beat two local men to death. This became known as the Sack of Balbriggan.

Then, on 25th October 1920, after 73 days on hunger strike, the Cork TD and the Lord Mayor of Cork City, Terence McSwiney, died in Brixton Prison in England. McSwiney had succeeded his slain friend, Tómas McCurtain, as mayor. The circumstances of McSwiney's death caused widespread revulsion not just throughout Ireland but also worldwide.[14] Less than a week after that, on 1st November 1920, having been tried and convicted despite hopes for clemency given his age, Kevin Barry was hanged in Mountjoy Prison in Dublin.[15] He was the first Irish rebel to be executed since 1916 and his death fuelled even further anti-British sentiment throughout most of Ireland.

Across the country the War of Independence and the resulting chaos and tit-for-tat reprisals continued unabated. On the morning of Sunday 21st November 1920 Michael Collins sent out his assassination squad to addresses around Dublin City where British agents were known to reside. Twelve were shot dead or fatally wounded. That afternoon Crown Forces including I Company, a detachment of RIC Auxiliaries along with regular RIC, arrived at Croke Park in Dublin where a Gaelic football match between Dublin and Tipperary was under way.

They opened fire indiscriminately on the crowd and the players, killing 14 and wounding over eighty. One of the dead was a Tipperary player named Mick Hogan (24) from Grangemockler in that county. Later that day two IRA prisoners, Peadar Clancy and Dick McKee, along with a civilian named Conor Clune, were shot dead whilst in British custody at Dublin Castle. Due to the killing which occurred over the course of that day it became known as Bloody Sunday. In a reprisal on 28th

November 1920 the IRA ambushed a convoy of the hated Auxiliaries at Kilmichael in County Cork killing seventeen.

As the reprisals continued Crown Forces then burned down
the centre of Cork City on 11th December causing an estimated
£20 million in damage. As the city burned, fire tenders deployed
to douse the blazes, had their water hoses bayoneted by the Tans.
In a deliberate affront to taunt the local public for some time
afterwards, the Auxiliaries appeared in public wearing burned
bottle cork on their caps. The burning of Cork had been in retal-
iation for an IRA ambush of a patrol of Auxiliaries earlier that
day that had left one dead and another twelve wounded.

TENSION AND TERROR

On 18th December 1920 a company of Auxiliaries on Crossley
Tenders entered Carrickmacross for duty in the South Monaghan
Police District. They had been sent from Dublin to augment
both the regular RIC and the Black and Tans. Whilst they would
regularly patrol in the Carrickmacross area they were based in the
neighbouring town of Castleblayney. This was none other than
the notorious I Company which had been involved in the Croke
Park massacre. They soon had the local populations of both
Carrickmacross and Castleblayney in a state of *tension and terror*.

As a result of this behaviour, Sergeant McGovern's boss,
District Inspector Maunsell, was constantly in Castleblayney. He
also now put Head Constable Brannigan in charge of the RIC
barracks there. These officers and others of the regular RIC were
abhorred with the conduct of the Auxiliaries.[16] Brannigan also
lived with his family externally from the barracks in Carrick but
now, like all RIC men, was required to spend considerably more
nights on duty in the Carrick station.[17] Similarly, Sergeant
McGovern too was by now spending almost all his days and
nights at the barracks. Dan remembered that his father was only
managing to get home to see his family at the cottage for short
periods of time and that the strain was beginning to show.

Then, on December 22nd 1920, British Prime Minister David Lloyd George introduced the *Better Government for Ireland Bill* to the British House of Commons which proposed the partitioning of Ireland. By now half the 1,500 Royal Irish Constabulary barracks across the country had been abandoned with most having been subsequently burned to the ground by the IRA. When not out on patrol, the policemen and particularly the *old* RIC men, had become virtual prisoners in their own police stations. However, in Carrickmacross and despite their already desperate reputation, several Black and Tans had still managed to get out and about to meet local girls.

Temporary Constable Walter Perkins from the Isle of Wight, for example, was considerably more mannerly and courteous than was customary of his Tan colleagues. He was very popular with his fellow Black and Tans and regular RIC men alike. Surprisingly, despite the ongoing RIC boycott, Perkins, in his more mannerly way of dealing with the local population, was considered by many of the locals to be *not a bad fellow*. Perkins was a WW1 veteran of Gallipoli, Palestine and Egypt. He had suffered considerably from shellshock as a result of his experiences during the First World War and had subsequently found it hard to hold down work as a result on returning from the trenches.[18] Soon after his arrival in Carrickmacross he had met a local girl and was now engaged to be married. Given the boycott Perkins' intended was running the risk of ostracisation and banishment from the local community. In any case the IRA attacks continued as did the Black and Tan patrols and round ups, but with only a varying degree of success on both sides.

---

1. Some claim that the Black and Tans were a *special reserve* of the RIC. However, others refute this. For the purposes of this narrative they will sometimes be referred to as *special constables/policemen* to differentiate them from the regular RIC.
2. Townshend, Charles, *The British Campaign in Ireland, 1919-1921* (1975).
3. Black and Tan Special Constable Douglas Duff, Recollections, IWM.
4. *Sword for Hire*, Douglas Duff, p59.

5. *Black and Tans, British Police and Auxiliaries in the War of Independence,* D.M. Leeson, pages 193-196.

6. A precedent for this had been set at the beginning of World War 1 in Britain when mass enlistment into the British Army had also resulted in a shortage of uniforms. Police tunics and trousers had been used then to augment what army khaki uniforms were available. These mismatched uniforms were worn during recruit training until more khaki garments became available. Later, fitting issues also arose with Black and Tan uniforms due to the fact that the average height of an RIC man was 5'9" and a British soldier 5'7".

7. The Dáil Court sat openly in Carrickmacross Courthouse in September 1921. The Black and Tans would never have permitted this to happen and with the British crackdown, the Dáil Courts soon relocated to secret venues including its rural makeshift jail and even to cow byers. The author concludes therefore that the Black and Tans only arrived sometime shortly after the Dáil Court sat in the town's courthouse in September.

8. An elderly relative of the author related to him details of the extensive fortifications placed on Carrickmacross RIC barracks when the Black and Tans were in residence. These details are largely consistent with the photograph which appears later in this narrative but which shows an Irish tri-colour on the flagpole. The author believes this photo was taken shortly after the Irish Free State forces took possession of the barracks. From further research it appears that, at some point after the handover, some or all of these fortifications were removed when the truce was signed only to be re-instated during the Irish Civil War which followed.

9. Gerald Stone, British Officer, Devonshire Regiment. Recollections, IWM.

10. These may have been an early form of lightweight pierced steel planking (PSP).

11. Witness Statement, Vol. Brian McMahon. *Irish War of Independence Files,* Monaghan County Council.

12. iBid.

13. The Proules river.

14. UCD archives.

15. Barry was hanged by John Ellis, the same hangman who had hanged Roger Casement in 1916.

16. *Dundalk Democrat* archive/Louth County Council.

17. It is highly likely that Brannigan also had to spend some nights at Castleblayney RIC station having been placed in charge there.

18. Info gleaned from local Carrickmacross historian Larry McDermott, Royal Irish Constabulary Forum/Peter McGoldrick and P.V. Hoey's *Farney in the Fight for Freedom.*

4

THE BARRACKS ATTACK

Gelignite and Fusillades

IN A HOUSE in the parish of Corduff outside Carrickmacross on the night of Friday 29th April 1921, a group of IRA men collected jute sacks containing dozens of sticks of blasting gelignite. Each of the explosive sticks was eight inches long and approximately an inch thick and most were strapped together in bundles of five. There was also an assortment of other explosive material including large bags of industrial blasting powder and other explosive oddments. The IRA had decided that its 5th South Monaghan Battalion, as part of a much larger brigade force, would audaciously attack the RIC and the Black and Tans in their heavily fortified Carrickmacross District Headquarters.

The plan, just like at Ballytrain weeks before, was to blow a massive hole in the barracks to force the RIC garrison to surrender and to capture its arms and ammunition. The station would then be set on fire and destroyed using petrol and tar. Buoyed up by the success of Ballytrain, eighty handpicked IRA brigade volunteers from all over County Monaghan,[1] including flying column active service members, started to converge on Carrickmacross town centre. By now garrisoned there, including Sergeant McGovern, were up to 35 RIC men of which at least twenty five were Black and Tans.[2] Like that of the Ballytrain attack, this was a virtually moonless night. Four rebel detachments crept into the town centre from the west at around 10.30pm. Three detachments accessed the rear of three adjoining three-storey buildings and took up positions at first floor level overlooking central Main Street and directly opposite the town's now heavily fortified and formidable police station.[3]

Carrickmacross police station pictured shortly after Crown Forces had vacated it in 1922. Note the Irish tricolour which now hangs from the flagpole. The heavy fortifications installed by the Black and Tans are clearly still in place. Daly Bros. Hardware and Ironmongery store is immediately to the right of the barracks. **Photo: ©Monaghan County Museum.**

At ground floor level these Main Street buildings contained O'Hagan's pub, Shannon's drapery and shoe shop and the adjoining Hand's pub which also housed a drapery shop. The fourth rebel detachment took up positions above another business premises further down the street. The elevated positions of these IRA detachments meant that they could bring fire to bear on the barracks' ground floor windows and on its front door over the new sangar's sandbag wall and through its chicken mesh wire. This negated what protection the new defensive measure afforded the RIC from small arms fire.

The job of these IRA men, when the time came, was to engage the RIC in the barracks and any policemen who might attempt to exit onto the Main Street from either the front door or via the alleyway which serviced the barracks' form yard. A young man was locked in a room in Shannon's and in O'Hagan's, Mrs. O'Hagan and her sister were locked in a rear room for their own safety. The Hand family, were led downstairs and locked in their cellar where they settled down unsure of what was to happen next.

Upstairs in these buildings the IRA gunmen quietly took up firing positions at the first floor windows. It would be hours yet before they would go into action. As they settled down and waited, the IRA volunteers peered through the windows and across the street at their heavily fortified target, the features of which could clearly be made out by a dim electric light suspended half way across the Main Street between the rebels and their main objective. Meanwhile, elsewhere in the town and via an alleyway from O'Neill Street, an assault party entered Smith's yard located directly behind the barracks.

In addition to their weapons some of these men were heavily laden with the bulging jute sacks containing their gelignite and other oddments of industrial explosive material plus a bucket of hand grenades. Others carried tins of petrol and buckets of well diluted flammable tar. Further down the alleyway fifteen men stood to in anticipation with their weapons loosely pointed over a low boundary wall towards the barracks rear now only some 60 yards away. The job of these men was to prevent any of the RIC garrison from escaping from the rear of the building and to fight their way into the police station via Daly Brothers once the explosives had blown and the adjoining barracks wall had been breached. However, that would be several hours away yet.

THE EXPLOSIVES DETACHMENT

The remainder of the town centre assault party comprised a specialist six man explosive mine detachment led by the IRA's commander who was a Tipperary man who worked for the Great Northern Railway in north County Monaghan. Dan Hogan was the brother of Mick Hogan, the Tipperary footballer who had been killed at Croke Park on Bloody Sunday. Hogan and his band of rebels now stood directly behind their objective – the rear of Daly Brothers Hardware and Ironmongery store which, from his perspective, adjoined the RIC station and which stood immediately to the left of it. It was another key objective to the success of the whole operation.

Now carrying the sacks of explosives, the tins of petrol and the buckets of tar, they made their way up several steps to Daly's back door and broke in. About ten minutes elapsed before movement was again detected at Daly's rear door. A comical line of both men and women in various stages of undress and with some clutching articles of clothing and others still pulling some on, then emerged being urged on by the IRA men. With some still protesting and cursing the intrusion, the occupants were quickly ushered out the rear doorway, through the yard outside and towards the waiting IRA detachment in the alleyway. These individuals were the live-in staff of Daly's who had just been roused from their beds upstairs by the armed rebels and ordered out of the building for their own safety.

Just about the same time as Hogan's explosives team set to work in Daly's, Sergeant McGovern rose from his armchair in the cottage, re-buttoned his tunic, buckled his police belt and grabbed his visor cap. He had been home for a much needed meal break with his family but now it was time to return to the barracks where he would spend yet another long night on duty. Mack McGovern recounted his recollection of what happened next. "It was about 11.00pm and my father decided to go back up to the barracks. As he finished a mug of tea he asked us boys which of us was going to walk him up to the first light on Main Street." Usually one of his sons gladly escorted their father on the fifteen minute walk before going to bed.

The public electric light to which the sergeant referred was the first of only three electric lanterns evenly spaced along the length of the street and which hung no more than 20 feet or so above it. The second hung over the Main Street near the RIC barracks and a third illuminated the bottom of the town's main thoroughfare. All three lanterns were suspended from long wire cables which ran between opposite facing building façades each illuminating the darkness of the April night.

The first Main Street lantern, the nearest to the McGovern's cottage, hung at a street junction on the southern end of the town centre. This was just before Main Street began to slope downhill to become Castle Street. The sergeant's walk from the cottage would take him up Distillery Lane through part of the convent's school grounds and past the gable of another house where his boss, District Inspector Maunsell, lived with his wife and family.[4]

To reach the first light the sergeant would then enter Bath Street, turn left and continue past the wrought iron railings of Saint Finbarr's Church of Ireland and its spire which dominated the southern end of Main Street. Danny said he would go. Half way up Distillery Lane, his father suddenly stopped abruptly and grabbed Danny's hand. He said to his son: "Daniel, look straight ahead. Keep talking but don't make any sudden moves or anything like that." He then asked his son: "When was the last time you were at Confession to confess your sins to God?" Dan replied somewhat puzzled: "Oh, I'm alright, father." He then asked the reason for such an unusual question. The sergeant replied: "Well, both of us may very well soon meet Him, Danny!"

Mack recounted the moment: "By the way my father had suddenly gripped my hand intensively, I knew that something must be wrong, but I did not know what he was talking about. I knew later that my father meant that we might well be meeting our maker that night. He had caught sight of something I could not see." Sergeant McGovern had, in fact, spotted an IRA detachment just up ahead armed with rifles, shotguns and bandoleers. These men had entered the main convent yard opposite Inspector Maunsell's house at the top of the laneway. His attention had first been attracted by a slight glint of metal. The sergeant had spotted one of another two elements of Hogan's attack force which were on their way to take up additional ambush positions a short distance away.

The first position was the other side of the main convent building and once again behind its high battlement walls which overlooked the roadway half way up Castle Street and close to St. Finbarr's Church and the town centre. The second ambush position was just below this and beyond where the battlements ended to become a low wall with iron railings on top which incorporated a gateway into the convent grounds. This firing position was in the Sisters of Saint Louis cemetery which was set back one hundred yards and slightly beneath the surface level of the roadway on which the nightly tan patrol would first appear as it approached the town centre near the conclusion of its patrol. With its walls and railings, the little cemetery offered the rebels good cover and a good field of fire onto Castle Street.

A HELLUVA LONG WAY ROUND

Danny and his father continued cautiously on their way to the top of Distillery Lane, turned left and stopped once again in front of St. Finbarr's Church but just outside the reach of the illumination of the first light. The sergeant looked around and then down at his young son. They were being watched by a smaller detachment of concealed rebels who been been detailed to watch Inspector Maunsell's house closely.

When the explosion occurred at the barracks, Maunsell was to be arrested and frog marched the 300 yards or so from his house to the RIC barracks where he would be encouraged to make his garrison surrender. "Daniel," said the sergeant to his son, "go back to the cottage and tell your mother that there is going to be an IRA attack tonight. Tell her to put mattresses against the windows and when the shooting starts to get all of you to lie down flat on the floor downstairs. None of you are to venture outdoors." He added motioning with his head: "Don't go back the way you came. Go the other way down Castle Street by Martin's Hill. Do you understand me, Danny?"

"Yes, father," his son replied. He repeated what he had been told. Mack recalled years later: "Now, that was a helluva long way round." Father and son separated and Danny followed his father's instructions. He started to run down onto Castle Street. This brought him under the high convent battlement walls as he ran. He had no idea that the rebels were now taking up their firing positions on the battlements above him and also in the small convent cemetery from where Danny was also observed as he ran by. Only earlier that morning the Sisters of Saint Louis had buried one of their number there and now, in the semi-darkness, as the rebels took up firing positions there, they found that the earth on the new grave was soft underfoot.

Dan explained that he took such a roundabout way home that night out of fear of meeting IRA men, that it took him between forty to fifty minutes to eventually get back to the family cottage. "I ran like a hare and eventually made my way through streams and brambles by Martin's Hill to get back. It was not an easy job at night with no roads to follow in the darkness. I told mother exactly what father had told me to tell her and she immediately got us children to help her to place mattresses against the windows for protection." Margaret McGovern then huddled together with her children in the kitchen of the cottage and waited.

Meanwhile, under the intermittent illumination of several of the Main Street electric lights, Sergeant McGovern had made his way to the barracks without incident. He had been observed by the IRA below their positions in the buildings opposite as he walked. Once safely inside, however, he reported what he had seen. As a precaution, all armoured shutters on the windows were promptly slammed shut and the doors secured. Once inside, Danny's father was part of a garrison of which 6 RIC officers and 20 Black and Tans were now present. The remaining 7 Black and Tans were out on mobile patrol throughout the town.

The IRA explosives party inside Daly's worked by candle-light. They first went about removing the fireplace which was set into the wall beyond which, less than two feet away, was a corresponding fireplace in the RIC barracks Day Room. This was the weakest point in the wall. Both buildings, whilst having their own smoke flues, were serviced by the same chimney stack. After considerable effort and with the least noise, the fireplace was eventually prized from the wall and lifted away revealing the recessed fire hearth leading into the long winding chimney above. Four 7 lb bags of explosive blasting powder were first laid in the hearth at the base of the chimney.

On top of these was placed 3 bundles of gelignite. Other miscellaneous explosive material was also carefully placed. Around this huge explosive charge was built a double row wall, five feet high comprising bags of maize, cement and significantly, ammonium nitrate artificial fertiliser, all taken from stock on Daly's shop floor.[5] Dense packing of the same material was also placed on top of the explosive charge. The purpose of this surrounding material was to direct the ensuing blast towards the barracks. Now, into each of the three bundles of gelignite was carefully placed the end of a six foot long safety fuse. The mine was almost ready.

Other IRA men sprinkled the petrol and poured the tar based liquid they had taken with them in each of Daly's rooms. In preparation for the blast, the IRA detachments across the Main Street and upstairs in the three shops which had been waiting patiently for hours were at last given the order to prepare to fire. They now began to break out the glass of the windows in front of them with rifle and shotgun butts. This was to avoid being injured by inward flying glass when the explosion occurred and when the garrison would return fire. The falling glass smashed onto the footpath of the Main Street below breaking into smithereens. This action further alerted the RIC garrison.

Within moments, Head Constable Brannigan and Sergeant Peter McGoldrick cautiously emerged from one of the barracks' double front doors and then from the sangar entrance and onto the Main Street with each of the senior officers scanning for danger as they walked. They had been accompanied from the barracks by Brannigan's dog. They eventually turned left and made their way to Daly Brothers next door. The dog followed at their heels. The breaking glass had also alerted the Black and Tan nightly patrol which had by now started to make its way back up Castle Street towards the town centre and just when and where the IRA had predicted it would. In the semi-darkness each Tan was now frozen on the spot having raised his rifle towards the town centre after hearing the breaking glass up ahead.

To the direct right flank of the Black and Tan patrol, the IRA men now had the silhouettes of the Tans in the sights of their shotguns, pistols and what few rifles they had. Each volunteer now controlled his breathing to only slow faint breaths and started to squeeze their trigger fingers. Any second now. Head Constable Brannigan and Sergeant McGoldrick meanwhile, had attempted to peer in through the front windows of Daly's premises. Now highly suspicious, they moved on further and started to bang repeatedly on the door shouting out and demanding admittance. The IRA explosives detail had been rumbled. At that point a single shot rang out from across the Main Street which was instantly followed by a deafening torrent of shotgun, rifle and pistol fire directed from the three IRA firing points opposite the barracks.[6]

"GET UP! THE BLOODY PLOUGHMEN ARE IN TONIGHT!"

Amid the IRA firing there was a loud yelp. The dog was hit and dropped dead at the feet of Brannigan and McGoldrick. Mortal danger now sent the two senior RIC officers scurrying back along the front of the sangar's sandbag wall within seconds, juking and ducking as they withdrew until they were safely behind it. In their immediate wake, bullets and buckshot repeatedly struck the ground and the sandbags to their right as they ran. With the IRA guns continuing to fire on them, the policemen eventually managed to scramble back inside the station itself.

At Daly's fireplace the IRA mine detachment had suddenly ducked for cover as a single rifle round struck the footpath, ricocheted and came flying through the front window, cracking the glass, before whizzing on and lodging in the ceiling above them. They instinctively ducked their heads deep into their shoulders.[7] Now they also began to hear a muted excited commotion from directly beyond the other side of the wall. They heard an unmistakable English accent declare: "Get up! The bloody ploughmen are in tonight!" Sergeant McGovern and the entire police barracks now leapt into action, grabbing their weapons and taking up pre-designated positions at all front and rear windows.

The rebels at Castle Street now immediately opened fire on the Tan patrol which returned fire towards their attackers on the convent walls. The Tans fought their way out from under the IRA guns towards the town. A Tan, however, lay mortally wounded on the street, his Glengarry cap and rifle either side of him. In the cottage Margaret and her children quickly lay down flat on the kitchen floor.

Mack recalled that moment almost eighty years later: "Sometime after midnight all hell just broke loose. The gunfire was really close. We could hear spent bullets striking our slate roof and that kept our heads down. We were scared. Nobody wanted to go outside." The family in their cottage, only 500 yards away, had clearly heard the IRA in the convent grounds open fire on the returning Black and Tans.

The special policemen had been caught in the open. They now made their way frantically towards their base with the wounded being aided and urged on by their comrades. They eventually reached the relative safety of the outside sangar and then the double front doors of the barracks. Once inside the building, they slammed the doors shut behind them. Several relieved but exhausted Tans now lay back against the doors to catch their breath. To their shock several rifle rounds from across the street struck the doors but instead of bouncing off the armour, penetrated it narrowly missing them. Sergeant McGoldrick now realised that the electric lantern suspended in the centre of the Main Street outside the barracks was working to the detriment of the RIC garrison.

He grabbed his newly issued Lee Enfield SMLE .303 inch service rifle, cocked it and pushed the muzzle through a loophole in one of the armoured window shutters. He took careful aim through the weapon's V sights and squeezed the trigger. *Bang!* The single round travelled through the chicken wire mesh and struck the electric lantern, shattering it and plunging the centre of the street into darkness.[8] As at Ballytrain, an attempt was made by the policemen to raise the alarm that they were under fire in Carrickmacross by using both the telephone and priority RIC telegraph to contact Dublin Castle and Belfast. All lines were dead. The IRA had cut the wires. Standard attack procedure.

Many other RIC men had also pushed their new .303 rifles through the rifle loops of the armoured window shutters. However, RIC men were now conspicuously absent from manning the loops in the front doors. With firing positions limited, the Black and Tans would take turns returning fire through the window shutters. Everybody else inside the garrison would help to ensure a readily supply of ammunition and take cover as best they could.

Vigorous fire was returned by the police garrison and directed at the IRA positions opposite, smashing the remaining glass and pock marking the facades of the buildings. Before long the IRA detail to the rear of the barracks was surprised when it too came under rifle fire. RIC bullets whizzed overhead and ricocheted off the wall behind them. They did not return fire. They were under strict orders only to shoot when the regular police and Tans ran towards them outside or when they engaged the police in the barracks itself. These rebels were, however, surprised, given the darkness, at the apparent accuracy of their opponent's shooting.

It was later ascertained that the garrison had anticipated a possible attack from the rear. They had applied a line of white paint to much of the top of a wall, immediately behind the IRA gunmen's position. This white line could easily be seen from the barracks and provided an effective aiming point. Inside the barracks a Lewis machine gun was made ready for action and taken by several Black and Tans to Head Constable Brannigan's first floor office where they clambered out with the machine gun past the wooden buttressed base of the flagpole. Now, despite sporadic fire directed their way, the Black and Tan machine gun crew managed to place their weapon across the top of the sandbags. One of the Tans aimed it at the smashed windows opposite and opened fire. Bursts of "Rat-a-tat-tat"… "Rat-a-tat-tat"…now repeatedly overtook the already loud cracks and booms of gunfire which echoed throughout the wide Main Street amplified by the tall buildings on both sides.

As the machine gunner aimed his weapon at the muzzle flashes in the windows opposite, the Tan beside him crouched low behind the sandbags as he prepared several more of the drum ammunition magazines for the Lewis gun to ensure a constant stream of fire. Once done, he picked up his specially adapted rifle, removed the safety and commenced firing rifle grenades towards his attackers positions across the street. Most exploded harmlessly on the ground. Whilst the deployment of the Lewis gun certainly managed to keep IRA heads down, it did not deter them and shots were exchanged across the street for a full ten minutes before there was any momentary lull in the fighting.

Suddenly outside, the darkness of the night disappeared as a brilliant light now filled the night sky bathing both sides of the entire Main Street with a bright flickering illumination. In the expanse now visible between both sides of the street hung a pall of grey smoke and the smell of cordite permeated the air. This sudden light took the IRA men somewhat by surprise and the shooting suddenly stopped altogether on both sides for a moment until the withering fusillades of rifle and machine gun fire resumed, this time initially from the barracks garrison. The bullets tore into the IRA positions opposite which were now more clearly defined. The sudden light was a flare.

The RIC and the Black and Tans used flare guns called Verey Lights which would be fired high into the sky either to illuminate an area at night or as a distress signal. The Tans had discovered that, even if under siege in their barracks, a Verey flare pistol could be safely used to best effect by firing the pistol directly up a chimney from any fireplace that was in regular use, effectively using it as a large gun barrel. The flare would exit the chimney pot at the top and continue dead straight up in the air, thus maximising its effectiveness. Furthermore, it was a much safer way to fire the flare gun without being shot at.

A DAMP SQUIB

Inside Daly's, the IRA explosives detachment was almost finished its task. However, each man was getting edgy. The end of each of the three safety fuses was split with a penknife to insure a good ignition. As the firing outside intensified, the explosives men now hastily finished packing the remaining portion of the deflection wall which they had built around the explosive charge and from which the three fuses now protruded. It was 2am and after over three hours preparation, the mine was ready at last.

One volunteer now used his candle to light all three fuses which were *splitting delightfully*[9] as they quickly withdrew. Outside now, everybody took cover and prepared for the blast. Several agonising minutes passed. Nothing could be heard only the continuing exchanges of fire from the Main Street. Five minutes passed. Still nothing. Time ticked on even further and eventually, after twenty minutes, there still had been no explosion. Something had gone wrong.

In the alleyway some of the IRA men, on realising that there was a problem with the mine, wanted to go back in and check the fuses again. Hogan, refused to let them re-enter the building. The IRA men on the Main Street and elsewhere throughout the town now realised that the crucial plan to explode the mine to gain access to the RIC station had failed.[10] Nonetheless, a ferocious gun battle continued to rage on across the Main Street for another three hours.

During further lulls in the shooting, the Black and Tans could clearly be heard singing cockney songs in unison inside the RIC stronghold at the top of their voices – goading their attackers as they attempted to keep their own spirits up. The battle continued unabated. The British garrison regularly sent up more Verey pistol flares to illuminate the street. Then, at one point, a party of Tans made their way out the front door of the barracks, through the sangar defences and partially across the Main Street, hell bent on firing grenades with another specially adapted Lee Enfield rifle as well as incendiary bombs through the smashed window positions where the IRA men were ensconced. However, sustained IRA fire checked them and drove them back into their besieged barracks. Eventually, as the dawn started to break at 5.30am, Hogan blew his whistle three times. It was the signal for the rebels to withdraw. One of their number had been wounded in the course of the night's exchanges of fire. He was assisted from the scene by several comrades.

Carrickmacross 1930s. Locals Tommy Dudgeon and James Mills stand in the doorway of what was Hand's pub and drapery, Main Street. The walls are still peppered with bullet strikes from the RIC and IRA firefight in April 1921. What appears to be residual smoke damage from the fires started by the Black and Tans is still visible on the shop façade. Disused electrical insulators just below one of the first floor windows may indicate where the early public lighting power cables were attached and crossed the street near the barracks opposite and on which the lantern was shot out by Sergeant McGoldrick. Shannon's business premises is to the left of shot. The author believes that it was Shannon's to which Dan McGovern was referring as the building he saw the morning after the attack which had collapsed in on itself. **Photo via Noel Jones ©Monaghan County Museum.**

Some time passed but once sure that all the IRA men had withdrawn, the Black and Tans crossed the street. They tossed incendiary bombs into the buildings where the IRA positions had been. The occupant families evacuated their buildings but the Hand family had remained locked in their cellar since the IRA had arrived the night before. They only saved themselves by frantically breaking a hole through a partitioned wall through which they eventually escaped. The local fire brigade was called but could only begin fighting the blazes after it was certain that the shooting had stopped. Mack remembered: "The battle had raged all night long." Everybody in the cottage was by now very concerned for the safety of the man of the house.

---

1. Some accounts say 60 men, but given the many detachments deployed 80 is more likely.
2. An exact breakdown of RIC numbers pertaining to regular and Tan constables in the barracks that night could not be ascertained by the author. P.V. Hoey, in his book, *Farney in the Fight for Freedom*, states that the overall RIC garrison at Carrickmacross was 35 strong at the time of the attack. An article following the attack in the *Dundalk Democrat* newspaper puts the garrison *in the barracks at the time* at 20 but this may be omitting those out on foot patrol.
3. The author's account of the overall attack is based on the Witness Statements of IRA Volunteers Tom Carragher, T. Ward, Jim Coyle and Brian McMahon, Fr. Livingstone archive, *War of Independence Files*, Monaghan County Council; *Farney in the Fight for Freedom* by P.V. Hoey, newspaper archive material *Dundalk Democrat* and also from the article *When I Was A Little Counter-Revolutionist,* by Malachy McGovern published in *The Chimes* college newspaper, Cathedral College of the Immaculate Conception, New York City, May 1933. Other details gleaned from local knowledge handed down to the author and from additional research.
4. This was *Iona House* rented to District Inspector Maunsell by the Sisters of St. Louis.
5. Given its explosive properties whether using the fertiliser in this manner was intentional or not is unknown.
6. The fourth IRA firing party had been told to hold fire as they were to be used in reserve. However, it is not known if this was observed. They were to provide what is called enfilade or side on fire if required and may certainly have done so when, late in the engagement, the Tans emerged and attempted to attack the IRA positions opposite the barracks.
7. This may have been the round that killed the dog. One of the explosives party in Daly's hardware store in his Witness Statement also recalls hearing gunfire breaking out elsewhere in the town. This was most likely the IRA opening fire on the returning Black and Tan patrol.
8. An account of the IRA bullets penetrating the barracks front doors and Sergeant McGoldrick shooting out the public light was related to the author by the sergeant's grandson, Peter McGoldrick, Administrator of the *Royal Irish Constabulary Forum.*
9. Vol. Tom Carragher lit all three fuses with the candle and described them as *splitting delightfully* before he withdrew.

10. Jim Coyle, in his Witness Statement, states that he had been told that one of his senior IRA officers had placed three bags of salt on the bare fuses deliberately sabotaging the mine. Another account states that, in the final hurried minutes to pack the remaining areas above the mine and given that this was done only with the aid of candlelight, the fuses were accidentally pulled out of the explosive charge.

5

THE TRUCE AND THE BARRACKS HANDOVER

The Necessity to Leave Ireland

LATER, on the morning of Saturday April 30th and given the night's events, Margaret McGovern was frantic with worry about her husband. So when it was a little brighter, young Danny McGovern and his brother Malachy anxiously got on their bicycles and cycled up from the cottage to the town centre eager for news of their father. Daybreak had brought the full impact of the attack into clear view. The façade of the RIC barracks was now peppered with bullet marks as were many buildings on the opposite side of the street which held the IRA positions. All windows in these buildings were now nothing more than a mangled, jagged and contorted jumble of wood, glass and metal – smashed to pieces by the constant unrelenting gunfire.

Behind the destroyed windows of the barracks the armoured shutters had been opened but were now peppered with bullet and shot strikes which had removed paint on impact. Opposite the barracks was a gaping hole in the top portion of Shannon's drapery and shoe shop. The roof had collapsed having burned for hours. The adjoining Hand's pub and drapery had also caught fire and had been substantially damaged. Mack remembered what he saw that morning: "The police barracks was standing, but across the way two buildings and their shops were completely gutted. Fires were still burning and the interior of one of the three storey buildings had collapsed in on itself. I remember that furniture and iron bedsteads were hanging precariously in that building and that firemens' leaky hoses were scattered around the Main Street." Hundreds of townspeople had by now gathered to survey the scene as a lorry was backed up in front of the gutted Shannon's premises. The vehicle was soon loaded up with half burned shoes and clothing.[1]

BOXES OF GELIGNITE

Dan remembered what he saw on the other side of the street: "As I cycled along I saw Black and Tans who had big linen aprons on. They were taking the boxes of gelignite[2] and black blasting powder out the door of Daly's Ironmongers store next door and into the RIC barracks. The McGovern boys hastily entered the barracks to look for their father and soon spotted him. He was alive but as Dan recalled: "He looked terribly worn out. We gave father a big hug and then he grabbed me by the shoulders and asked: 'How is your mother and the rest of the family?' Danny told him all was well.

In the course of the battle, the IRA had one casualty who had been wounded but who would survive. However, one Black and Tan had been killed in the Castle Street ambush when fire was first opened. Several more had been wounded and some badly. The Tans were seething with rage and wanted revenge. This is why they had recklessly ran out onto the Main Street shouting obscenities before being forced back inside by the IRA fire. This act had demonstrated their infamous ill-discipline and how it could backfire against them. Dan remembered that when he was in the barracks at this point, he saw the body of the Tan who had been killed on Castle Street in one of the holding cells. "A Black and Tan was killed that night. I'm certain of that but there were no regular RIC casualties." He remembered that he and Malachy also saw a wounded Tan seated by the fireplace in the station Day Room with a nasty gaping bullet wound to his jaw. The wounded special policeman asked another Tan, who was standing in the doorway of the Day Room just opposite, for a cigarette. "The Doc says you're not supposed to smoke with that wound," his comrade advised him.

"Damn the doc!," came a sharp reply as he motioned with his hand for the cigarette before receiving it and smoking it anyway.

A REPRISAL AVERTED

Danny, Malachy and their father then heard a commotion coming from the back of the barracks. The boys then followed their father from the Day Room, through the corridor, to the rear of the building where they stood in the back doorway overlooking the form yard. The fortified yard was buzzing with activity. Some other wounded Tans were being given first aid there.

In the yard close to the entry gates, a Crossley Tender lorry had been driven up. Its engine was running and close by stood Sergeant McGoldrick with a group of Tans who were getting ready to board the Crossley. McGoldrick walked over to the McGovern boys at the back door. "Your father was in the midst of a battle here last night boys," he declared. Young Danny looked past Sergeant McGoldrick. He could see that the Black and Tans were obviously incensed and wanted revenge. The boys were witnessing a reprisal patrol about to set out to round up local rebels.

"Let's get that bastard, Hogan!," one agitated Tan exclaimed. He was referring to Dan Hogan whom the RIC authorities knew was most likely the IRA commander during the attack. They were, of course, correct in their assumption. The Tans were out for blood and wanted to get their revenge on the IRA. However, at this point Danny walked out further into the yard from his father and brother. He now witnessed his father take control of the tense situation.

"Standing on the step, father told the Tans in his commanding voice that, should any one of them leave the barracks, they would do so over his dead body." 'Bear witness as my son stands near you!' father warned." As the senior officer, he then ordered Sergeant McGoldrick to dismiss the patrol immediately. McGoldrick did as he was instructed but there was hesitation on the part of the Tans to comply. However, they eventually dismissed, albeit reluctantly and the form gates were closed.

"My father, the strict disciplinarian, wielded considerable sway." said Mack recalling the moment. He added that, given that the Black and Tans had already burned the buildings opposite, his father was convinced that if they had been permitted to leave the barracks yard that morning, considerable needless bloodshed would have resulted as the Black and Tans were bloodthirsty for revenge. However, due police process was observed instead. There would be no reprisals that day.

Later on that morning Sergeant McGovern told Danny Junior to get his bicycle as they were going for a ride. Dan Senior was going about his investigations into the previous night's events. The boy did as he was told. Father and son cycled together up Main Street and then half way down Castle Street where the sergeant first briefly viewed the roadway where the Tans had been ambushed. They then entered the convent complex and left their bicycles to one side.

Danny and his father soon found themselves at the Saint Louis Convent cemetery which had been one of the IRA ambush positions. "We went to that area and looked around," Mack recalled. "My father spotted a coat[3] hanging over an iron spiked fence which surrounded the nuns' graveyard and also the imprints of boots on the grave of the nun who had just been buried the morning before. There were also numerous spent rifle cartridges lying on the grave," Mack remembered. Several decorative spikes on top of the cast iron railings which surrounded the small square shaped cemetery were now bent and distorted having been struck by Black and Tan bullets.[4]

Part of the castellated wall from which the IRA ambushed the Black and Tan patrol in April 1921. One Tan was killed on the roadway below. Further to the right of shot the road becomes the Main Street of Carrickmacross. **Photo: ©Joseph McCabe.**

The Sisters of Saint Louis cemetery as it appears today. It was on the railings here that Sergeant McGovern with Dan Jr. found the torn coat containing the notebook. In 1921 this position offered a clear view of the roadway in front. **Inset:** *A spike in the cemetery's iron railing bent from the strike of a Black and Tan bullet can be seen to this day.* **Photo: ©Joseph McCabe.**

The IRA position where Danny and his father now stood was almost directly between their family cottage and the roadway. The Tans had continuously fired on their attackers at this position the night before. Many wayward Tan bullets had overshot, only coming to ground at the cottage and in a wide area around it. This was why Danny and his mother and siblings had heard the numerous bullet strikes on their roof earlier in the night. The sergeant examined the jacket and searched the pockets. "He took something out and I believe it was a book or a notepad or something. As he looked through it he said to me: 'Do you know, Dan me lad, both of us could have been killed last night. The good Lord protected us Thank God.' He then told his son to go on home to the cottage. "All I know is that he spent the rest of the day making enquiries throughout the area finding out the whereabouts and movements of certain individuals. I think my father knew who was involved to a certain degree but nobody was ever charged. Nothing more ever resulted from those particular enquiries." Mack recalled.

A FATAL ERROR

That Saturday in the immediate wake of the barracks attack, shops in the town were forced to close for the day by the Black and Tans. With the damage and destruction caused to businesses in the town centre, the Black and Tans also thought that they might capitalise on possible strong public feeling against the rebels. Throughout the town Black and Tan notices appeared warning the public to co-operate with the police against both the IRA and Sinn Féin. For a time a curfew was also imposed from 10.30pm at night.

Danny McGovern's father might have been successful in stopping Black and Tan reprisals on the morning after the barracks attack, but the Tans were still hell bent on revenge. They soon received intelligence from a spy regarding the location of an IRA flying column which had taken part in the attack. The intelligence was accurate. The IRA men were bivouacked in a very remote disused dwelling house known as John Frank's[5] five miles west of Carrickmacross in the townland of Corrybracken in the parish of Magheracloone.

The Tans drove on their Crossley Tender to within a mile of the IRA camp and dismounted to then employ their now standard stealthy tactic of approaching their target on foot. Using a map provided by their spy as a guide, they attempted to navigate the maze of local rural boreens only to soon become hopelessly lost. Along a by-road and adjacent to a complex of mid 19th Century buildings known as Barton's Mill, the Black and Tan raiding party stopped for a moment in an attempt to establish its bearings. The Tans gathered around one of their number with a candle to scrutinise the map. However, they were seen from the mill by an IRA sympathiser who immediately took off across the fields to warn the flying column of the police presence in the area. At some point later, the Tans, still unsure of where they were, eventually but unknowingly approached the location of their quarry.

The forewarned IRA men, however, had by now taken up ambush positions, had loaded, cocked and levelled their weapons towards the roadway and now lay in wait in the pitch darkness. They listened intently for any sign of the approaching Tans. Nothing could be seen or heard but unknowingly, the Tan patrol was walking right into the IRA ambush. Just then a Black and Tan, in a quiet but careless action, reached into his pocket and pulled out a packet of cigarettes. He took one from its box and placed it between his lips still scanning the darkness around him.

Having hastily slung his rifle over his shoulder, he next slid his matchbox open as he walked, took a match from it and stopping only just momentarily on the roadside, struck the match to light his cigarette. Just then the crack of an IRA rifle rang out from an adjacent hedgerow. The Tan was dead before he hit the ground, the first pull on his cigarette being his very last. A brief firefight broke out and a commotion ensued as muzzle flashes intermittently pierced the darkness. However, fire could only be exchanged merely towards the general direction of each side. The Tans quickly realised that it was more prudent to withdraw rather than to try and fight it out with the unseen IRA men in an area they knew well. They slipped away leaving the body of their dead comrade on the roadside behind them.

In the weeks after both the Carrick barracks attack and the ensuing Corrybracken debacle, public notice warnings from the Black and Tans started to appear throughout the town and in the outlying rural areas. These notices referred to letters supposedly received at Carrick RIC station from the IRA which had threatened further RIC lives and the lives of their families. The RIC notices offered a showdown between the Black and Tans and their IRA adversaries and warned that swift retribution against known individuals with Republican sympathies would follow any such further attempted attacks on the RIC in South Monaghan. However, at the time the IRA believed that the letters purportedly received by the policemen, had been contrived by the Tans themselves simply displaying their frustration at being unable to quell Republican activities in the area. In any case the IRA was preparing an answer.

THE KYBER PASS AMBUSH

A month later on Tuesday 30th May 1921, an IRA flying column took up ambush positions along a 400 yard stretch of roadway at Tullyvaragh on the Castleblayney Road, approximately three miles outside Carrickmacross. This had been the scene of previous ambushes and for that reason the stretch of road had earned the ominous nickname of the Kyber Pass, to which it was now referred by both sides. This was after the infamous Afghan mountainous pass where the British and other invaders had been ambushed time and time again by local tribesmen. Its Irish version was well named. Several IRA planned attacks had recently been aborted there. This time, however, IRA intelligence expected a convoy of two Crossley tenders to pass through the Kyber Pass at approximately 3.00pm. These vehicles would contain large detachments of the hated I Company auxiliaries who were billeted in Castleblayney. The Auxiliaries would be travelling southwards towards Carrick where they would be augmenting the RIC and the Black and Tans there and undertaking patrols. Suddenly an outlying scout shouted out: "Look down on the Carrick side!" Suddenly a large column of RIC comprising mainly Black and Tans were visible on the road. They were not coming from Castleblayney but from Carrickmacross.

Instead of mounted on Crossley Tenders, they were travelling in columns of two – on bicycles. This unexpected RIC cycling patrol had left Carrickmacross RIC station only 30 minutes before for Castleblayney. They were lead by D.I. Maunsell and he and his fifteen subordinates were all wearing their rubber rain capes and cycling two abreast. Maunsell was known never to leave his barracks on bicycles without at least half his garrison.[6] The IRA opened fire and in the ensuing half hour gun battle one of the Tans was killed and many more seriously wounded. The dead Black and Tan was Walter Perkins.

Perkins' death deeply affected the entire Royal Irish Constabulary garrison at Carrickmacross. For two days following his death on Wednesday 31st May and Thursday 1st June, businesses in the town were again forced to close by the Black and Tans who also ordered people entering the town to turn around and go home. As arrangements were being made to return the dead special policeman's body to his family, Sergeant McGovern, as Acting Head Constable, was given a special assignment by D.I. Maunsell. Along with two subordinate constables he would accompany Perkins' body on its final journey and attend the funeral in Sandown on the Isle of Wight.

Whilst Danny's father was away, IRA intelligence observed that five new replacement Black and Tans arrived in the town[7] as violence and civil unrest all over Ireland continued with no end in sight. One direct result of the Tullyvaragh ambush was The

Big Sweep which took place across County Monaghan as well as Cavan and Leitrim. Three regiments of the British Army, including cavalry units and a Royal Air Force aeroplane supported by RIC Black and Tans and Auxiliaries – 6000 men in all, started a systematic sweep through County Monaghan.[8] As the McGovern brothers were leaving their school in Carrick one afternoon, an RAF two-seater biplane flew low over them and dropped leaflets to the local population asking it to support the RIC and warning that any assistance given to the IRA would have repercussions. Some of the leaflets fell into the school grounds, onto the street-way in front of the school as well as onto the grounds of the adjoining St Joseph's Church. When Dan and his brother Malachy and the other excited children started to gather the leaflets, their teacher, Brother Paul, roared at them: "Don't pick those up. Leave them where they lie!" Of course, after Brother Paul had returned inside the boys picked up the propaganda leaflets anyway.

On another occasion Malachy witnessed an RAF biplane land on level farmland not far from the McGovern's cottage. The pilot got out and walked around the aircraft, got back into it and took off again.[9] In all 900 people were arrested across County Monaghan during The Big Sweep. Approximately 60 of those rounded up were taken initially into RIC custody in Castleblayney for questioning. Twenty five of that number were from the South County Monaghan area and were imprisoned in jails in Britain or in Ballykinlar internment camp in County Down.

Resulting directly from The Big Sweep, fourteen wanted men from the area remained on the run from the RIC. This necessitated them to be armed at all times and to move from safe house to safe house.[10] The sporadic fighting and civil chaos dragged on in the South County Monaghan RIC District as it did elsewhere throughout Ireland. The days of ordinary community policing for the RIC were long over. Now, simply walking or cycling the quarter mile or so between the barracks and the cottage to see his family, continued to be fraught with risk for Danny's father. Yet, he had never been directly confronted or threatened by the IRA in any way and for that, he was thankful. Margaret lived in daily fear for her husband's life as Mack remembered. "The short time he would spend at home was usually just for his meals." By now, however, an end to the Irish War of Independence was in sight.

THE POINT OF STALEMATE

Both sides now found themselves at the point of stalemate. The British government envisaged that the IRA's effective guerrilla campaign, which had already cost so many lives and which was costing the Crown an inordinate amount of men and money to counter, would continue indefinitely. The deployment of the Black and Tans and the Auxiliaries had only been counter-productive and severe criticism was now being levelled at the British establishment for the brutal actions of both.

With Dublin Castle, the British seat of power in Ireland at crisis point, the British by now realised that their coercion approach would never work in Ireland and that furthermore, they could never now hope to win over the hearts and minds of the Irish people. On that point Dan said of his father: "I think that my father also thought that the British government putting in the Black and Tans to take care of policing activities was just a step too far." In any case, Britain had also lost the worldwide public relations battle with regard to its nearest neighbour and first ever colony. Even King George V had made known his displeasure at British actions in Ireland. Now, British Prime Minister David Lloyd George, decided to make peace overtures to the Irish through Sinn Féin's Arthur Griffith.

The British Government held the view that in offering to negotiate it would strengthen its own hand in the event that the Irish refused to enter talks. In addition to the RIC, British troop numbers in Ireland had now grown to 50,000.[11] The IRA, with its continuous acute lack of effective arms and ammunition, generally felt that the armed struggle could not continue indefinitely. Finally, weeks later on 8th July, peace talks commenced between both sides. A truce was signed on the 9th July which came into effect on 11th July 1921 which ended the Irish War of Independence. After two and a half years of war a total of 513 RIC men had been killed and another 682 wounded nationwide.[12] British Forces were subsequently confined to barracks until further notice and the IRA officially stood down its campaign although there were a number of IRA attacks reported on British Forces even after the truce had come into effect. Despite the death and destruction, the attacks, the daily threats, the boycotts and the obvious hostility from the local community against the RIC, Sergeant Daniel McGovern had emerged unscathed. His wife and family understandably, were extremely relieved. By 1921 the family had increased to nine children with the birth of their final girl, Elizabeth.

Following lengthy negotiations in London the Anglo-Irish Treaty was eventually signed on 6th December 1921 providing for the establishment a year later, on 6th December 1922,[13] of the self-governing Irish Free State. The new state would initially be a dominion within the British Commonwealth of Nations under the Government of Ireland Act 1920. The first time that the *Commonwealth of Nations* was referred to rather than the *British Empire* was on the official Treaty document ending the Anglo Irish War.[14] The treaty also provided a clause whereby Northern Ireland, consisting of the pro-British and strongly Protestant populated counties of Antrim, Armagh, Derry, Down, Fermanagh and Tyrone, could opt out of the new state and form its own parliament but loyal to Britain which it exercised resulting in the partition of Ireland. The new southern Irish parliament, Dáil Eireann, only narrowly passed the treaty. It would later result in the bitter Irish Civil War and the deaths of countless Irishmen on both sides including Michael Collins himself.

In January 1922 British and Irish delegations sat down together and it was agreed to disband the Royal Irish Constabulary. The process began on a phased basis within weeks. The Black and Tans and Auxiliaries were withdrawn by the British to six designated withdrawal centres in the south of Ireland. The Tans in Carrickmacross and the Auxiliaries in Castleblayney withdrew to their nearest sub-depot at Gormanstown Army Camp in County Meath just south of Drogheda. The Irish-born regular RIC men would soon know what options might be open to them. The following month Sergeant Daniel McGovern was part of the RIC delegation which officially handed over Carrickmacross RIC station to the Irish Free State Forces on February 4th 1922. His sons Danny, by then 13 years old and his younger son Malachy (11), were both present with their father for the handover proceedings. In his eighties, Mack McGovern still had a vivid memory of what transpired in the barracks that day. "I remember that on that particular day we were accompanied by a group of Sinn Féiners who were now dressed in light green well-tailored khaki uniforms with Sam Browne belts and swagger sticks."

A RAGING BONFIRE

An inventory was made of everything including the barracks, the grounds, furniture, weapons, motor vehicles and bicycles. "I walked along with my father as that inventory was taken," Dan recalled. The delegations of RIC men and Free State Civic Guards determined what was to be retained at the station, what was to be returned to the British authorities and what was to be burned in a large bonfire out in the form yard. Constantly fuelled by reams of documents and billowing thick black smoke, the bonfire would rage for days.

Danny and Malachy watched as the signature of Acting Head Constable Daniel McGovern was placed on the inventory of Crown property and the official Document of Handover of Carrickmacross RIC station. It was one of multiple signatures on the document which, once signed by representatives of both parties, effectively ended at a stroke the existence of the Royal Irish Constabulary in Carrickmacross. The sergeant and his sons then left the barracks and returned to the family cottage. It would be another sixty years before Daniel Junior would visit Carrick police barracks again.

With the treaty signed, Danny's father, now reverting back to his sergeants rank, at 51 years of age and with a wife and nine children, was at a crossroads in his life. Many RIC officers would retire. Some would join the new replacement Civic Guard of the Irish Free State which, within a year would be renamed An Garda Síochána. "I don't know why my father decided not to go with the new Irish police force. Perhaps he had a premonition or something," Dan said years later.[15] Many like him would opt to join the newly formed Royal Ulster Constabulary which was the new police force for the six northern counties of the newly formed Northern Ireland. Others would emigrate to Britain and many more would opt to join other police forces in other parts of the British Commonwealth. A great many chose to emigrate to Canada. Many more to Australia and New Zealand or to Palestine and a new gendarmerie there for which recruiting was ongoing in Britain at the time.

Daniel McGovern Sr. knew that there were options, but it would not be a decision he alone could make. That night the McGovern family sat down to discuss their future. The sergeant explained to Danny and his siblings that he was now, in essence, Persona Non Grata as far as the Irish Free State was concerned. He told them also that the family had six months to leave Ireland. "My father pointed out that the British Crown would give us free passage and land in Canada or Australia."

Margaret McGovern then strongly stated in her soft Antrim accent: "No. We're not going to any English territories. We're going to America." She added that she would write to her brother, John McCauley in New York, requesting him to sponsor the family so that, when the time came, they could emigrate to the United States. Danny's father made the point that if the family went to America there would be no assisted passage. They would have to foot the entire cost themselves. Margaret, however, was adamant and with that the decision was made. The following morning Daniel saw his father in plain clothes rather than in his customary uniform. Very soon now he would be Daniel McGovern, civilian.

THE AUCTION

*The McGovern family passport photograph taken on the convent playing field and beside their cottage before they left for America. **Back Row** LTR: Margaret Jr, Daniel McGovern Sr and Daniel Jr. **Front Row** LTR: Isabella, Elizabeth (on lap), Eugene, John, Malachy, Genevieve and Mrs. Margaret McGovern with infant Anne on her lap. The main building of the Convent of St. Louis can be seen in the background through the trees. Beyond and to the left of this building was the roadway on which the Black and Tan was killed in the IRA ambush on the night of the barracks attack.* **Photo: ©Glór na nGael Collection, Monaghan County Museum.**

On April 2nd 1922 the Royal Irish Constabulary officially ceased to exist but the full disbandment process would not be completed until August of that year.[16] Two days later on 4th April 1922, Daniel McGovern Senior was pensioned off but only at the rank of sergeant. With the Irish War of Independence now over and with a political settlement, Danny soon found that even at school attitudes towards him as the son of an ex RIC man had already changed for the better. He was no longer being harassed. No longer either did he have to leave school half an hour earlier than everybody else. He was now just one of the boys.

Sponsorship from Margaret's brother John to enter the United States was arranged and permission granted by the US authorities for the McGoverns to emigrate there. With no Crown emigration assistance, steps had to be taken by Danny's parents to supplement their savings to fund their journey. Dan remembered what had to be done. "The result was that we had to sell off everything we had to make as much money as possible to get us all to America."

The family held an auction one Saturday in mid September 1922 on the large school playing field attached to the Convent of Saint Louis and not far from their rented gardeners' cottage. The auction was advertised a week in advance with a classified small advert in the local newspaper as well as on posters around Carrick. Many dozens of people attended and the auctioneer on the day was Mr. Lonergan. Several prized pieces of family furniture were sold along with cutlery, delph and china, paintings, tools, clothes, bicycles, childrens' toys, books, jewellery and so much more – in fact everything that Daniel and Margaret McGovern deemed unnecessary for their trip to America. The sergeant's pedigree greyhounds were sold and as she watched her furniture being carted away Margaret McGovern's lip quivered. Dan also recalled: "Mother squeezed my hand when her prized silver tea service came up for auction and finally she broke down crying when it was sold off too." Shortly afterwards a photograph of the McGovern family was taken on the convent playing field. It would be the last of them taken in Ireland.

On September 22nd 1922, the McGoverns left Carrickmacross for the last time to board a ship for America the following day. The date they left the town was noted in the diary of Main Street publican, William Daly, who also recorded that it was *a dull day*. All eleven members of the McGovern family travelled by train to the port of Derry on the north-west Irish coast. "I recall that somebody there, seeing our large family, asked my father: 'Are all those yours? You're going to America with all *them?*' before we boarded the Anchor Line vessel the *RSS Cameronia.*"[17] This was a brand new 16,000 ton, single stack trans-Atlantic ocean liner.

The McGoverns were Third Class passengers for their crossing to America but, once aboard, they were assigned two staterooms given that they were eleven in number. For Dan it was an adventure. "We explored that ship from one end to the other," he remembered.

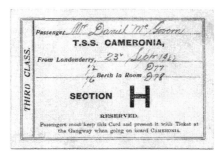

A treasured family heirloom. The Anchor Line Third Class ticket issued to Daniel McGovern Senior for his family's passage to America on the liner 'RSS Cameronia'. Having left Carrickmacross the family of eleven sailed from the port of Derry on Ireland's north west coast on 23rd September 1922.
Photo courtesy of the McGovern family.

However, it wasn't all plain sailing as they crossed the Atlantic Ocean. The McGoverns also endured storms and terrible seasickness for days on end during their voyage to America. Finally, after ten days at sea, they sailed up the Hudson River and into New York Harbor. Margaret, 39, held her one-year-old daughter, Elizabeth in her arms as her husband lifted three-year-old Anna onto his shoulders. The remaining children, Margaret,14; Daniel Jr.,12; Isabella, 11; Malachy, 10; Eugene, 9;

John, 7 and Genevieve 5, all leaned over the side rails of the *RSS Cameronia* as the family sailed past the Statue of Liberty and the towering skyscrapers of Lower Manhattan. Tug boats soon came alongside to nudge the big passenger liner into Pier 54. It was October 2nd 1922. A new chapter in the lives of the McGoverns had begun.

---

1. According to the article *When I Was A Little Counter-Revolutionist* by Malachy McGovern published in *The Chimes* college newspaper, Cathedral College, New York City, May 1933.
2. Dan's father told him later that it was gelignite which was being removed.
3. One of the IRA men who had been shooting from the cemetery somehow got hung up by his coat on the railing spikes as he tried to escape. In desperation he tore the coat asunder to free himself leaving it behind. This is according to the article *When I Was A Little Counter-Revolutionist* by Malachy McGovern as #1 above. The account was more than likely related directly to Malachy from his father, the former RIC sergeant.
4. The railings have been partially repaired over the years but a single deformed spike can still be seen on the cemetery railings today.
5. Even today many different Marron families reside in the Corrybracken area. Then, as now, they were given additional monikers or even nicknames to differentiate between them. The owner of the disused house had been John Marron – a member of the Marron family known as the *Franks* after his grandfather, Frank Marron. Local folklore has it that for years after the Black and Tan was shot dead on the roadside in Corrybracken the unexplained spectre of a cigarette being lit was often observed in the darkness of night on the exact spot. The phenomenon ceased after the local priest said Mass at the location. The account of this incident between the Black and Tans and the IRA has been passed down through the author's family and was related to him by his uncle, Brian McCabe.
6. Witness Statement, Brian McMahon, Fr. Peadar Livingstone archive, *The War of Independence Files*, Monaghan County Council.
7. It was the opinion of several IRA men that a second Tan, McWhirter, had also been killed in the attack and that this fact was suppressed by the RIC. One IRA account states : ...*there were reports of two bodies being shipped out.*
8. According to plans seen by South Monaghan Volunteer Brian McMahon in the former British Army HQ in Parkgate Street in Dublin after the British had left. These plans made provision for the 6000 strong security force to move into County Monaghan in a four-pronged pincer movement. – *A Fist to the Black Blooded*, Hugh MacMahon.
9. Based on a written account by Daniel's brother Malachy in later years.
10. *Farney in the Fight for Freedom* – P.V. Hoey.
11. Cottrell, Peter *The Anglo-Irish War The Troubles of 1913-1922*, p20.
12. Pakenham, Frank (1972).

13. The Republic of Ireland did not come into existence until 1949 following the adoption of a constitution earlier in 1937.

14. Cottrell, Peter *The Anglo-Irish War The Troubles of 1913-1922*, p20.

15. The fact that young Danny's father did not opt to join An Garda Síochána and was subsequently given six months to leave Ireland may have been due to the fact that he had assumed the duties of *Acting* Head Constable – a senior rank in the RIC.

16. Chris Ryder, *The RUC 1922–1997*.

17. In later years and during *WW2*, the *Cameronia* was the largest troopship to take part in the D-day Landings on 6th June 1944 – *Cameronia/Empire Clyde - The Ships List*.

PART 2

America and the Military

6

THE EARLY YEARS IN AMERICA

The Bronx, New York

THE *RSS CAMERONIA* firstly disgorged its First and Second Class passengers who would go through a simple entry process and be on their way. For the McGoverns, however, as steerage immigrant passengers, their entry into the United States would take a little longer. The family disembarked from the ship and boarded a ferry which took them across the bay to New York's immigration processing centre – Ellis Island. The McGoverns entered the Great Hall of the immigrant inspection station where they had to wait for several hours in the lines of immigrants ahead of them before eventually being called for medical and legal inspections.

The family was split into two separate processing lines. Danny and the older boys went through with their father in one line whilst Margaret and the girls went through in a second line. Mack recalled: "I can still smell the aroma of the disinfectant, the carbolic soap and the *Lysol* going through that area. The concrete floor of that building was dark grey and wet. I stood there in front of the doctor in my shorts. My brother Malachy's leg must have looked crooked in some way because the doctor asked: "Is that leg lame?" Dan's father replied "no" that it was just the way the boy was standing and told Malachy to straighten himself up at once. One by one the family passed through the inspection process until finally, with their approval paperwork in their hands, they were successfully through and free to start their new lives in America. "We all got through fine," Mack remembered. Outside they were met with great excitement by Margaret's brother John, a bricklaying contractor and his wife and family who had sponsored the new immigrants for their migration to America. After the appropriate hugs, kisses and handshakes the McGoverns soon arrived at Uncle John's two storey brick home on 127th Street.

NEW KID ON THE BLOCK

The McGoverns stayed with the McCauleys for several months before eventually finding a home of their own on 589th East 139th Street in The Bronx in a predominantly Irish neighbourhood. Danny's first winter in America brought with it the reality of a bitterly cold New York. The freezing conditions and often heavy snowfall did, however, have its advantages. Danny, Malachy and their pals from East 139th Street often took to their sleds and sped down the hill at Saint Anne's Avenue or a little further away in Saint Mary's Park. In the often sweltering heat of summer by contrast, they cooled off by spending many fun filled hours at a favourite swimming spot in the East River.

The McGoverns eventually moved several times as more suitable homes became available. "Finally we wound up in an apartment at 1966 University Avenue. That was up near Columbia University," Dan recalled. The family settled in well to their new life in America and soon the everyday perils of being the family of a policeman back in Ireland under constant threat of death or wounding from the IRA was but a memory – a great relief to Margaret in particular. Daniel McGovern Sr., the former RIC sergeant with his good background, education and policing experience, soon got a job as a railroad patrolman at the New York, New Haven and Hartford Railroad Station.

The apartment block at 1966 University Avenue, The Bronx, New York where the McGovern family resided.
Image: Google Earth.

Before long Dan Sr. was promoted to Head Police Officer and instead of wearing a uniform he now wore civilian clothes and carried a concealed pistol. He would remain in that job for 21 years. Margaret made a comfortable home for her husband and nine children and soon produced a tenth child, another son, Terence, the last of the McGovern children and the only one to be born in the United States. Margaret made sure Daniel and the rest of the children were always well turned out, well mannered and kept busy attending to whatever chores needed to be done around the house. Margaret, religious as ever, saw to it that the Rosary was said every evening and that Mass was attended every Sunday morning as a family.

Apart from the smaller ones, all the McGovern children were now happily attending school in their new neighbourhood. Margaret always made sure also that they were attentive to their studies. Dan remembered: "Throughout that entire period of growing up all of us got our education and the peculiar thing for me was that because of my schooling in Ireland, which must have been pretty good, I had practically finished my second year in High School early and when I was still only 13 years old."

An important part of the education for the McGovern children, Dan remembered, was obtained at home. In the evenings Margaret and her husband and the eldest children would help the youngest with their homework just as they had back in Ireland. "The education of our whole family was a wonderful togetherness I remember. It was nothing for us to sit down and talk about any subject. We had to recite and we had to read. If there was a volume on Shakespeare or History or something we had to read whatever it was and each one of us had to compete with the other. That was part of our education."

Dan got a job as a delivery and errand boy at a local store. He and Malachy also got newspaper delivery routes. "I delivered *The Bronx Union* newspaper. We used to buy our newspapers in those days for a penny and a half and then, when you sold them, you made two cents on each of them." In the family tradition over those first years in America, Danny's father continued to instruct his sons on how a young man should always carry himself. "Father taught us boys how to be manly, how to speak and walk straight. It was part of a tradition that was instilled in you.[1] In parallel Margaret looked after the feminine requirements of the girls.

THE FIRST CAMERA

It was in his spare time during his early teens that Dan started to get greatly interested in two things that would eventually lead him to his chosen career. The first was photography. Dan bought his first camera in 1927 and this ignited in the young man a passion that would stay with him for the remainder of his life. "I studied photography and did everything I could to learn how to take good photographs."

He soon amassed considerable technical and perspective skills behind the lens and made the decision that he wanted to pursue a career in professional photography. He began to get work as a news and industrial freelance photographer in New York City. Then, in 1928, he moved his focus of attention so to speak to moving pictures. It was to be a significant move. "I got myself a hand-cranked, 16mm^2 movie camera and started to learn the basics of using that and soon I was making my own movies." He was eighteen.

The second interest which would shape Dan's future was his first experience of the military. It was around this time that he was selected to attend the Citizens' Military Training Camp, the CMTC. This was run by the US Army. These were military camps held for a month every summer which offered an opportunity for young men to obtain military training without the obligation of call-up or active service.

Dan immediately liked the military life and he would continue to attend the Citizens Military Training Camp for another four straight summers. "We were paid $21 per month plus subsistence. I think this was one of the finest things that ever happened to me because, apart from the military training, it gave me an insight into working with other boys my own age and also how to be competitive in sports and things of that sort." Danny had other interests too. He took an interest in Ham radio.[3] "I knew some of the guys my own age who had ham radios and it was interesting to listen to foreign radio stations or police broadcasts that were happening somewhere."

However, a year earlier in 1927 personal tragedy had befallen the McGovern family and tempered what had been their successful transition to life as an immigrant family living in the United States. The McGovern's youngest child, Terence, the only one who had been born in America, contracted diphtheria and died at the age of four. "This hit my mother particularly hard," Dan remembered. Then, almost two years after this family tragedy, came the 1929[4] Wall Street Crash which was subsequently followed by The Great Depression. "One of the things about a large family such as ours in that particular type of environment was that it was hard for an awful lot of people because everybody was out of work. In our house though, all us boys and girls stuck together to help make ends meet." Any money made in individual part-time jobs was pooled into a common fund so that nobody wanted for anything. "It was all about family togetherness and teamwork." All through these difficult early years in America ex-Sergeant McGovern's RIC pension came as regular as clockwork every month. This was in addition to his railroad police salary. This sustained the family through tough times and beyond The Great Depression for many years.

THE NEWSREELS

With his skills behind the camera improving all the time, Dan was picking up more and more work in New York as a freelance photographer, but by now he was also becoming very adept as a cine-cameraman too. Whilst he continued to provide excellent photographs to print publications he was now also increasingly providing freelance quality movie footage shot all over New York and its environs to the audiovisual news productions of the day. These were shown in cinemas all across America before main feature movies – the Newsreels.

Back in the days before electronic devices and news apps and with television only in its infancy the masses around the world obtained news mainly from only three sources – newspapers, radio bulletins and from the newsreels which were popular short filmed documentary style news reports with sound narration. Some of the more prominent newsreel companies of the time in the United States were *Movietone News*, *The March of Time*,

Columbia Pictures News and *Universal Newsreel.* There were many more. These American parent newsreel companies also operated newsreel subsidiaries which distributed their newsreels in cinemas in other countries around the world.

For a month every summer though, Dan continued to acquit himself well during his annual camps with the CMTC. "I became what was known as a Blue Candidate or a leader. I passed all my courses and took up gunnery and leadership and everything under the sun including map reading and things of that sort." Between his photographic work and his summer military camps Dan had by now obtained and excellent foundation in both the proficient use of the stills and moving pictures camera and the military way of life.

He was subsequently asked to take an aptitude test for the US Army. He passed and was then offered some army correspondence courses too which he subsequently accepted and completed. The United States Army now offered Daniel a commission as a second lieutenant in the Infantry. "I refused it because I wanted to get into photography not the infantry." Daniel also displayed an early interest in aviation related photography and had ideally wanted to join the New York based Air National Guard's 102nd Observation Squadron where he could put his photography skills to best use. He applied but was unsuccessful. However, his chance would come again.

Sadly, in 1931 tragedy struck the McGovern family again when Dan's younger brother John was badly hurt in a fall when he was sixteen. "John fell on some steps and badly injured his head and his arm and after that he just wasn't capable of taking care of himself." John needed special care for the rest of his life. By way of some consolation, Margaret in particular was delighted when two of her other sons, Malachy and later Eugene, with only a year between them, both decided to become Catholic priests and subsequently went off to a seminary to study for the priesthood. Despite the economic depression, Dan's older sister Margaret Mary had by now become an executive secretary for a large insurance company. His sister Isabella became a seamstress. Her mother had trained her well in the artful use of the needle, thimble and thread. "Isabella was the funniest of the whole bunch. She was a clown," Dan fondly remembered.

By now Dan and all but the two seminarians were still living in the McGovern household. The youngest remaining children were at this stage only approaching adulthood – Genevieve, Anna and Elizabeth, who by 1933 were 16,14 and 12 years old respectively. By then the family had moved several more times eventually settling into a bigger seven room rented apartment on New York's 301 East 193rd Street.

A LUCKY BREAK

Towards the end of 1933 America's economy had started to emerge from The Great Depression and it was around this time that twenty-five-year-old Dan got a lucky break. He heard through the grapevine that the 244th Coast Artillery of the New York National Guard was looking for a full-time photographer. "I applied for the job and I got it so I joined the National Guard as an enlisted man."

Soon he was sent on his first assignment on a two week Bomb Scoring course to Oswego in Central New York State. "A tug pulled artillery targets on a barge behind it on Lake Ontario and the gunners fired their 155mm guns from the shore. The idea was to land a shell just close to the target. That was designated as a hit. An actual hit would have destroyed the target. I photographed this with a special type of photo instrumentation 5 inch by 7 inch box camera."

Dan photographed each gun crew as they fired at the barge and the resulting photographs were used to interpret the fall of shot for each gun for correction and competition purposes. He recalled one interesting aspect of the gun crews of the 244th Coast Artillery that he photographed on that assignment. "One of the battalions was made up entirely of White Russians and former Cossacks.[5] They were a fantastic group of gunners who would always win competitions."

By early March 1934 Dan was running a photographic laboratory. He gained valuable photographic experience with the 244th. Over a period of almost three and a half years with the unit he continued to hone and perfect his skill with the stills and movie camera. Then, at the end of April 1937, he finally got another chance of the posting he really wanted. "I finished up with the 244th and finally got into the 102nd Observation Squadron and I was promoted to corporal." It was the first of many promotions.

Meanwhile, Dan's brother Malachy, who had been attending the Catholic seminary for over four years, was on the verge of becoming a priest. It would never happen. There were already too many existing seminarians and also an unprecedented number of new incoming vocations. As a result of these factors, the decision was taken by the seminary's hierarchy not to advance Malachy and several more of his classmates any further in their studies for the priesthood. In any case, Malachy was beginning to have doubts about his vocation anyway. Dan: "So, in his fifth year, he left and eventually went into the insurance business."

In fact none of the McGovern brothers would become priests as tragedy was to sadly strike the family once more. "My brother Eugene was the brilliant one of the family. He had a fantastic mind but he died in the seminary from an obstruction of the bowel." The obstruction had arisen due to stomach cancer. In less than ten years Dan had lost two younger brothers in tragic circumstances and had another seriously injured. One brighter development at the end of this period was that Dan had been assigned to take social photographs at a National Guard night out at Pine Camp in upstate New York to which a number of girls from the local hospitals had been invited. Despite being busy at his craft that night, he managed to meet one of the ladies in attendance. Virginia Scott was a native of Buffalo, New York and was a pharmacist at a local hospital. She and Dan soon began dating.

---

1. Even as an elderly man Dan McGovern still stood with the same bearing and often as not, with his hands smartly tucked behind his back.
2. 16mm film was a small format black and white film developed for amateur home movie use. However, so vivid was its later colour variant that it would be pressed into service for US military use. In later life McGovern would use 16mm colour film to capture striking images of both conventional and nuclear war which resonates to this day.
3. Amateur non-commercial radio communication.
4. In 1929 another individual well known at least to former RIC sergeant Daniel McGovern Sr. arrived in New York having emigrated there from Ireland. That was non other than former IRA commander and now former Irish Army General, Dan Hogan – the man who had been instrumental during the IRA attack on Ballytrain barracks back in 1920 and who had later led the attack on Carrickmacross RIC station in 1921 on the night when Sergeant McGovern had been on duty there. Hogan had served with the Free State Irish Army in the Irish Civil War and became its Chief of Staff in 1927. However, following a falling out with the new Irish Minister for Defence, Desmond Fitzgerald, Hogan resigned and decided to emigrate to America. He was seen off on the ship to America by his former IRA commander General Eoin O'Duffy who, having resigned from the Army too, was now the commissioner and most senior officer of the new police force in Southern Ireland which had replaced the Royal Irish Constabulary – An Garda Síochána.
5. Cossacks were fierce highly experienced, sword wielding cavalry soldiers. They formed the core of the Russian *White* Army which was loyal to the Tsar during the Russian Revolution. The Tsar, however, was deposed and executed by the communist revolutionary, or *Red* Russians. Cossacks originated from what is today The Ukraine.

7

BATTLESHIPS IN THE DESERT

Ground Mapping and the Presidential Appointment

OF THE 29 observation squadrons in the Air National Guard the 102nd was the oldest and most prestigious having been established in 1908, a year before Dan McGovern was born. It was based at Miller Field, Staten Island, New York and was a mapping squadron for the National Guard 27th Infantry Division also undertaking air transportation and repair duties.

Even greater emphasis had, by this time, begun to be placed on the importance of aerial mapping for military purposes and each division was assigned its own mapping group which photographed designated areas of ground from the air. These photographs were then used to make accurate military maps but they were also useful for general reconnaissance purposes. Some of the fliers of that particular group had, in past years, been part of the famous American *La Fayette Escadrille* contingent which flew very successfully in the French Air Force during WW1 and before America entered that war in 1917.

The 102nd Observation Squadron specialised in aerial photo reconnaissance and mapping and when McGovern joined it flew a variety of aircraft including the Northrop BT-1 monoplane, the Douglas O-43 monoplane, the North American O-47 monoplane as well as some older Consolidated PT-3 Husky and Douglas O-38 biplanes.[1]

The author believes that the aerial mapping photographer in this 102nd Observation Squadron promotional photograph is Dan McGovern. This photograph was taken by American stock photography pioneer H. Armstrong Roberts in California in 1942 when Mack was undertaking ground mapping work with the squadron there. **Photo: Alamy Stock Photo.**

As a result of its lineage the 102nd attracted the rich and famous to its Air National Guard ranks. Amongst the officers and pilots with whom Dan was working was a young Captain Thomas J. Watson Jr. whose father had founded the IBM Electronics company. In later years Captain Watson would go on to transform the company into the corporation we know today. Another was First Lieutenant Fred W. Castle who would go on to win a Medal of Honor posthumously in WW2 for his heroics in a burning B-17 bomber over Belgium and after whom the former Castle Air Force Base in California was named.

At his new base at Miller Field, New York, Dan was first trained and tested in the latest up to date US military standard photography and movie making techniques. Because he became so proficient in the use of both still and motion picture cameras he was always in demand and he initially criss-crossed the United States on various photographic assignments with his unit. His first assignment with the 102nd was on a 21-day trip from Miller Field which included photographing the visits of the 102nd pilots and aircraft to other air bases across the country. Dan flew in the passenger seat of open cockpit aircraft. "That was hop, skipping and jumping all the old air bases – Offutt, Barksdale, Wright Field and others and it was very interesting to work with these people. Some days we'd fly 300 or 400 miles."

As he went about his assignments and given that the officers in his unit were mainly from wealthy families, he was frequently rubbing shoulders with the well-to-do. In 1939 he was flown out west to photograph the big San Francisco International Exposition at Treasure Island in San Francisco Bay. The exposition, among other things, celebrated the recent opening of the new Oakland Bay Bridge and the Golden Gate Bridge the latter having been completed only two years before. "I covered all that," Dan recalled. "I had never mixed with people who had money before and these people knew their etiquette and social graces, but I was no daw either so I was well accepted." Dan was always told in advance to which sort of event they were flying. "They would tell me what type of clothes to bring. If I was going somewhere formal for instance I was told to bring a dress uniform or to take civilian clothes instead." However, as accurate maps were essential for military purposes and particularly in wartime, Mack McGovern was soon trained in the finer techniques of aerial mapping. In the days before satellite imaging accurate detailed and cost-effective topography of large areas of ground was obtained by taking multiple photographs at high altitude which were then matched together into photograph mosaics to create a broader and very accurate master image from which maps were then developed and printed.

Dan was taught the necessary photographic skills for what was generally referred to as ground mapping in great detail at Miller Field and he soon found himself assigned to aerial ground mapping with increasing frequency. He was trained in the latest ground mapping methods of the time by Master Sergeant John W. *Toby* Tabasco,[2] the senior 102nd non- commissioned officer in charge of photographic training and organisation.

Mack remembered: "He ran the show and I had a great incentive to learn. Toby also taught me a lot about the leadership role of the Non Commissioned Officer. The officers flew the planes but the noncoms like Tabasco were there to train people like me so that we knew exactly what we were required to do as part of the photo observation team. Tobasco was the type of guy you couldn't pull anything over. It you tried it you'd know. He had no favouritism."

The master sergeant, Dan noted, had the peculiar habit of holding a cigarette between his lips which was always unlit. Mack also remembered what would transpire if he had a gripe with somebody else in his outfit. "It was fists out the back and many times I got my butt kicked just for being a big mouth but that's just the way it was. You had to do your studies, take your tests and do the work assigned to you. I was a stills photographer, I was a motion picture cameraman, I was an aerial photographer. I was taught how to photograph enemy positions from the air and things of that sort. I was considered a bit of an all-rounder." He was soon promoted to sergeant. By now the officers and men of the 102nd rarely if ever referred to Dan by his Christian name or rank with the exception of formal occasions. To almost everybody in the unit the big

Irishman was by now simply *Mack* McGovern or given his 6ft five stature, *Big Mack* McGovern – the photographer. Mack remembered: "We didn't have much in the sense of weaponry and things of that sort but we had first rate pilots and cameramen with a lot of spirit. We were a first class photographic organisation."

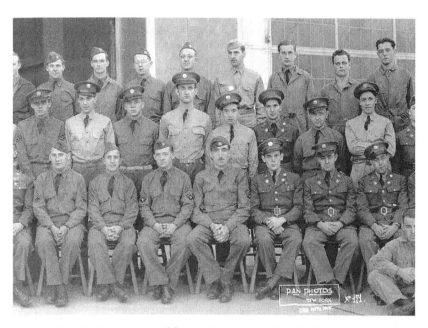

Dan McGovern, pictured front and centre with the 102nd Observation Squadron, Miller Field, Staten Island, New York. This photograph was taken on 17th October 1940 shortly after Mack was promoted to sergeant and only two days after the squadron was called up to full-time service prior to World War 2. McGovern did not know it then but he was two days into a full-time Air Force career that would last 21 years. **Photo courtesy of New York State Military Museum.**

Later that year on October 15th 1940 all the members of the 102nd were taken off reserve status and called to full-time service for a 12 month period as part of the then United States Army Air Corps. Mack: "I didn't know it at the time but, as it turned out, from then on I would be in for the duration of the war and in the service continuously until I retired in 1961." In a revamp in

June 1941 the United States Army Air *Corps* became the United States Army Air *Forces*.

A TIME OF SORROW

One pleasant Tuesday afternoon Dan was showing movies outdoors in a forest for some Air National Guardsmen when a telegram arrived. It was sad news. Dan's mother Margaret, had passed away.

With the youngest surviving McGovern child, Elizabeth, by now eighteen, Margaret had raised her family and stood by her husband and made a great job of both. She had been the guiding light and a pillar of strength to the McGoverns through thick and thin, not just through the difficult years back in Ireland but also through the better years of their new life in America. Despite her great attention to family health she was diagnosed with cancer some time before. Margaret subsequently died on August 25th 1941 aged 59, leaving her husband Dan

Margaret McGovern pictured in her latter years in New York.
Photo courtesy of the McGovern family.

Senior, the former sergeant and their two remaining sons and 5 daughters distraught at her loss and with a great void in their lives. Dan never forgot the way the military handled that sad situation on that occasion. "The military really took care of me. The Red Cross and the USO were both great too. Those people were just dedicated and the women particularly so. They had everything arranged. The guys had taken up a collection and I was on my way home to New York for the funeral. That's what I call teamwork and consideration for a military man."

One day Sergeant Mack McGovern was on photographic assignment at Fort McClellan in Anniston, Alabama where he was undertaking year-long aerial photography and mapping duties. This was with the 102nd in support of the 27th Infantry Division. Just the day before Mack had celebrated his thirty-second birthday. He was hailed from some distance away by a 102nd colleague named Billy Menefee. "Billy's father was in the newsreel business in New York. I was on my way to the latrine when Billy shouted to me: "Hey Mack, the Japs have just bombed Pearl Harbor…!" It was December 7th 1941. "I couldn't figure out were that was and I replied: 'Where the hell is Pearl Harbor?" The next day President Franklin Delano Roosevelt went to Congress and declared war on Japan. Three days after that, on 11th December 1941, Adolph Hitler declared war on the United States. With his adopted country embroiled in a world war, Big Mack's life was about to change drastically yet again.

In January 1942 the 102nd Observation Squadron transferred to Morrow Field two miles east of San Bernardino, California. There they joined another squadron – the 115th Observation Squadron, which had been based in California. Both squadrons would be working closely with the US Army Corps of Engineers.

"We put up our tents at Morrow Field and it was freezing, colder than heck," Dan remembered. The squadron would be using mainly two seater North American O-47 monoplanes that had been specially designed for ground mapping. Dan's position, as usual, was in the back seat. At the same time other elements of the 102nd were assigned to anti-submarine patrols off the Los Angeles coast. In March 1942 the 102nd Observation Squadron became a component of the 69th Observation Group. Mack said of his outfit of that time: "We were all highly qualified all round cameramen, mappers and aerial photographers."

On 1st April 1942 Sergeant Daniel A. McGovern sent a wire to Buffalo, New York for the attention of Ms. Virginia Scott. Despite Mack being posted on various photographic assignments around the country, the couple had continued to correspond and had got on so well that the wire read: "Why don't you come out here and marry a fool?" It wasn't an April Fool's Day joke either. Virginia accepted and the couple were married in a military ceremony at Morrow Field on 20th June 1942. Now happily married and living locally to his base, Dan continued his aerial ground mapping assignments throughout California as the United States ramped up its construction of new wartime military bases and other facilities.

One of the new facilities which Dan mapped was the former Virginia Dare Winery which was going to be a new base for P-38 Lightning fighters. Today the former base is better known as California's Ontario International Airport. "All the grapevines were dug out and the runways were quickly built." He recalled that one of the problems with mapping for such facilities was avoiding excessive natural rainwater run-off from nearby higher ground. "There was no time to worry about that. They were putting a fighter base there and it had to be built in record time."

For many years afterwards heavy rains in Ontario resulted in part of the runway being flooded. "This was because it is located on the base of the Cucamonga Wash which comes down from the mountains," Dan explained. Later on Dan and his fellow photographers also mapped the dry lake of Muroc, California which is located in the Mojave Desert.

In future years this area was to become one of the most substantial air bases in America and McGovern would play a part in that. For now, however, he concentrated on his aerial training and on honing his photography skills in the air which were improving all the time. "Now, that was really something. It really helped me as it was the best training ever was. Apart from photographers we became what they call Geodetic Surveyors." Dan now found himself not just taking aerial photographs but also working in the laboratory back on the ground where he was taught how to develop his photographs and to then combine them into the high quality composite mosaics from which the ground maps were made.

Dan McGovern, second from left, pictured with his 102nd Observation Squadron colleagues in California in early 1942. **Photo: AFHRA.**

Dan pictured in temporary camera stores at Morrow Field, San Bernardino California in 1942. **Photo: AFHRA/McGovern family.**

Apart from high quality single exposure cameras being used over an area of ground being surveyed, specialist nine lens cameras became available capable of taking high altitude wide-angle photographs in one single exposure. "I also had to write an analysis of the area of ground that I was after photographing and that was also part of the training." In addition, he shot useful movie camera footage of the survey areas that was also analysed to give an additional dimension to the aerial mapping survey. He was soon promoted again, this time to the rank of Staff Sergeant.

Meanwhile, his brother Malachy had also joined the services. He received a direct commission as an Ensign in the United States Navy and would serve in Naval Intelligence for the duration of the war. Ensign McGovern was posted to England and worked in the US Navy code room below the then US Embassy in London's Grosvenor Square. This facility handled secure high priority trans-atlantic communications including those between President Roosevelt at the White House in Washington and Winston Churchill at 10 Downing Street in London.

Back in California, as it happened, the United States Navy had built a full scale concrete and wire re-enforced three dimensional replica of a Japanese battlecruiser warship at Muroc on an area of ground called Rogers Dry Lake. They called their creation the *Muroc Maru*[3] and it was used to train bomber pilots and bombardiers on the proper techniques for low level attack approaches towards enemy shipping. As he was regularly in the air in the vicinity Dan took several photographs of this battleship in the desert and turned them in on his return to base once they had been developed. Some days later he landed back at Morrow Field only to be summoned to the office of his boss Master Sergeant *Toby* Tobasco.

In his office Toby was standing there with a scowl on his face and with Dan's *Muroc Maru* photograph prints in his hand to which he pointed: "Now look here McGovern, Goddamn it, you're always full of these tricks. What the hell's a battleship doing in the desert?"

Staff Sergeant Dan McGovern, USAAF and Ensign Malachy McGovern, US Navy pictured together in Washington DC in late 1942. Back in Ireland both brothers had been present at the handover of their father's RIC barracks to Irish Free State forces in 1922. **Photo courtesy of the McGovern family.**

The 'Muroc Maru' as it appeared from the air at Muroc Dry Lake, California as a B-25 Mitchell bomber flies past. It was used by aircraft crews to practice and perfect attack techniques against enemy shipping. **Photo courtesy of the US Air Force Test Centre History Office.**

Dan smiled and swiftly explained that he hadn't produced a trick photograph. "It's there, Toby, it's actually there." The corporal gave the master sergeant the co-ordinates. "Well, I'm going to fly up there tomorrow," replied Tobasco, "…and if it's not there I'll have your ass…!" The following day Tobasco was flown to the concrete battleship and when he returned to Morrow Field, Dan was waiting for him. The master sergeant climbed out of the aircraft with his customary unlit cigarette hanging from the side of his lip. He jumped to the ground and walked towards McGovern.

"Well?" enquired Dan.

"It's a big son-of-a-bitch, isn't it!" replied the laughing Master Sergeant Tobasco.

A SPECIAL APPOINTMENT

With his ground mapping duties in California completed in the latter half of 1942, the 102nd Observation Squadron was redeployed. Part of it was sent to Australia on further photo mapping duties. McGovern would not be going to Australia. He had been handpicked to join the Press Section of what was called the 16th Photographic Squadron (Special)[4] based at Bolling Field in Washington DC. This was an elite special group which specialised in the photography of VIPs. These included White House and Pentagon VIPs such as ambassadors, the military Chiefs of Staff, State Department officials and …..the President of the United States of America. McGovern had been detailed to be a designated photographer and movie cameraman to President Franklin Delano Roosevelt.

"When I got to the White House I had to wear civilian clothes. Dress was always formal but these clothes were provided with the job." However, given his height and unusual frame everything had to be tailor made. "I'm six feet five inches, I've big hands, big feet and I wear a 38 inch sleeve. As a photographer I went along with the Presidential party and on Presidential trains and the like. I became very adept and specialised at this type of photography." However, as President Roosevelt was disabled due to polio, Mack also had to be very careful to avoid capturing this fact in his photographs and film footage. In addition, to do his job right, he also had to learn how to keep a low profile. "Big as I was I was able to do it and you could never find me in things. If there was a tree I'd hide behind the lee of the tree. With my civilian clothes I'd mingle with the crowd."

In any situation Dan would pick his moment and get the best possible photo or film scene and then melt into the background once again. Once he was satisfied that he had enough photos, for example, he'd slip out of the room and get to his darkroom where he'd immediately process the negatives. "I would then bring the picture proofs up to the President's aide in the White House who would hand them to the President who would then pick out whichever ones he liked." However, Dan's time as a designated photographer/cameraman to President Roosevelt ended due to something which occurred at Bolling Field in December 1942.

THE PRESIDENTIAL FAUX PAS

Normally, in keeping with official Presidential protocol, 45 degrees right and 45 degrees left directly in front of the President is kept clear and nobody ever walks in the space in between. "The reason for that is so that the Secret Service can have a clear view. You never cross the President's path. You never go around the back of him either. I still see it today with the Secret Service."

Dan though, made a mistake. On the afternoon of 8th December 1942, Secretary of State Cordell Hull[5] and President Fulgencio Batista of Cuba were arriving together at Bolling Field and the plane had taxied up. "Hull and Batista walked from the plane towards Roosevelt and just as I was about to take a photograph of them as they approached the President, somebody got in my way and I stepped out of line to get a better position."

Dan had inadvertently strayed into the no-go area. He had literally stepped out of line. A colonel who was behind Dan saw his
mistake and grabbed him to pull him back. However, Roosevelt
had noticed this and said: "Let the sergeant get his picture." Dan
got his picture and many more over the course of that day and
also later that night at the official dinner at the White House to
mark Batista's visit.

*President Batista of Cuba is welcomed to Washington by President Franklin
Delano Roosevelt. Moments before this photo was taken and as Batista
approached the President, McGovern had inadvertently broken protocol and
the 45 degree rule.* **Photo: Associated Press.**

The following morning however, he was summoned to the
War Department at the Pentagon which was still under construction at that time. "I called into an office and soon stood before a
major who told me that what had happened at Bolling Field had
been a breach of Presidential protocol and that I was no longer to
be in the 16th Photographic Squadron." Despite President

Roosevelt's intercession, Dan knew in his heart that he had been wrong in breaking the 45 degree angle rule. However, despite his Presidential faux pas McGovern's career was about to take yet another remarkable turn. The Pentagon major then softened his tone. He concluded by informing Dan that, regardless of the breach of protocol, he was to be transferred elsewhere anyway as he had been chosen by the top brass for another very important assignment. The major explained: "McGovern, you've been hand-picked to go back to California as the NCO In Charge of Army Air Force combat cameramen training. You're going to Hollywood!"

---

1. Rosenfeld, Susan and Gross, Charles J. (2007), *Air National Guard at 60 – A History*.
2. 169 NCOs from the 102nd Observation Squadron became officers and Staff Sergeant Tabasco was one of those. He eventually retired a colonel.
3. McGovern stated that the *Muroc Maru* was blown up and removed in or around 1956.
4. The 16th Photographic Squadron was another ground mapping and photo processing squadron. As it was based in Washington DC, McGovern's *special* detail was attached to it for the purposes as outlined. There may have been several photographer/cameramen on Presidential duty.
5. Almost exactly a year before on 7th December 1941 it was to Secretary of State Hull that the Japanese ambassador had handed the infamous 14 Part Message which was essentially a declaration of war. The document had, however, been delivered in or around an hour *after* the Pearl Harbor attack had already commenced.

8

TRAINEE CAMERAMEN AND THE HOLLYWOOD SET

The First Motion Picture Unit

IN MARCH 1942 and as the United States Army Air Forces rapidly expanded, Commanding Officer, General Henry *Hap* Arnold, commissioned the establishment of a motion picture unit for his Air Forces. This would be completely independent of the army. Up to this point, film making

within the US Army was solely the responsibility of the US Army Signal Corps. The personnel to fill the ranks of the Air Forces' motion picture unit, however, would comprise professional film makers, actors and technical personnel who would be recruited mainly from the civilian population.

This was at a time when General Arnold and many of his Army Air Force contemporaries strongly felt that the Air Force should be re-constituted as a branch of service completely independent of the army rather than as a branch of it. It was held therefore that professionally produced Army Air Force films would greatly help to make the case for Air Force autonomy when the time came for any future shake up in the structure of the United States armed forces. General Arnold appointed the head of Warner Brothers studios, Jack L. Warner, producer Hal Wallis and scriptwriter, Owen Crump to establish the new film unit. Dan: "The navy had John Ford, the army had Frank Capra and the Army Air Forces had Jack Warner." The result was the First Motion Picture Unit, the FMPU, which was located where the bulk of the talent required to fill its ranks were already located – Hollywood, California and production of wartime documentary movies ensued. All its members were already highly experienced in the many wide and varying skills required for the professional production of motion pictures.

With its personnel now working solely in the service of the United States Army Air Forces the new independent professional unit would eventually produce more than 400 documentary style propaganda, information, training and morale films. These films would be used to demonstrate the work of the Army Air Forces deployed across the world to the American and worldwide public. Nine months later, in November 1942,[1] General Arnold further directed that FMPU would also take on the responsibility of training a cadre of combat cameramen cinematographers who could be sent across the world to record actual combat film footage and other aspects of the USAAF's involvement in all theatres of war in which it would operate.

Arnold stated: "*The Commanding General, Army Air Forces, has advanced personal interest in the work of the AAF Combat Camera Units and has defined their mission as follows: 'Cover thoroughly with both still and motion pictures the activity of the Army Air Force to which they are attached particularly [and] whenever possible, combat operations both on the ground and in the air.'*[2] Part of the job of the Army Air Forces combat cameraman would be to photograph the accuracy of bomb strikes on given targets as well as other port, dock and industrial facilities. The enemy's war machines were also to be filmed so that the USAAF could learn their secrets, their modes of operation and the tactics adopted.[3]

All such footage could then be used to best effect in the production of new films which would be then distributed either within the Air Forces themselves or released to the public newsreel companies around the world. Even before November was out small and incomplete detachments of already experienced cameramen were hastily sent to United States Army Air Forces overseas to commence film documentation.[4]

CAMERAMEN SELECTION CRITERA

The Army Air Forces now set about recruiting its trainee combat cameramen who, on successfully passing the course, would be given the specialist designation Gunner/Photographer. Before being selected applicants had to comply with five initial criteria. They had to meet the necessary physical requirements, be between 20 and 45 years old, show outstanding initiative and an alert mind, a high sense of responsibility and demonstrate a steadfast performance under high pressure. They had to have some motion picture camera experience and be able to prove an interest in cinematography.[5] To train its cadre of new combat cameramen the Army Air Forces now also had to find the best and most qualified cinematography instructors.

As he was already a serving highly experienced aerial cameraman in the Air Force, Dan McGovern had been quickly chosen, promoted yet again to Technical Sergeant or Tech Sergeant as it was more commonly called and seconded to the FMPU to train combat cameramen. Of the five experienced cameramen chosen as instructors, Mack was the most senior. In mid December 1942 McGovern packed his bags and took the train across the United States and arrived in Hollywood. The new FMPU, or *Fum-Poo* unit as it would soon become known to its members, had been based at several other Hollywood facilities since its formation but these had proven to be unsuitable for the needs of the First Motion Picture Unit. In October 1942 it had relocated to the Hal Roach Studio complex at 8822 West Washington Boulevard, Culver City[6] which, McGovern remembered, was an excellent base of operations. Because of the nature of the specialist work that was to be carried out there and the professionals involved, military discipline was relaxed. Saluting was more or less optional and the various ranks usually addressed each other on a first name basis.

The extensive Hal Roach Studios which were designated Fort Roach during World War 2. **Photo courtesy of The Culver City Historical Society.**

Hal Roach himself was a reservist in the Signal Corps and aged 50, had been called up to full-time service with the Army Air Forces in June 1942. He later commanded his own experimental Combat Camera Unit. The Hal Roach Studios had produced films starring many household names in the movie business including Laurel and Hardy and Harold Lloyd and the studios were often referred to as *The Laugh Factory of the World.* Now though, for their wartime duration, the studios were referred to as Fort Roach and comprised a total of 55 buildings on a 14 acre site. These included six very large sound stages, film editing suites, make up suites, costume, animation, sound and music and special effects departments. There was a carpentry shop in which movie sets were built and where wooden props were produced as well as a sculpture shop. Fort Roach also had a backlot with numerous exterior film sets, equipment storage facilities, a motor pool, catering and administration buildings and four Army Air Forces aircraft at its disposal close by.[7]

On the night when Dan eventually got there, tired after his long train journey, everything was in a state of confusion. "People were running here and people were running there. This was in the early days when we were preparing to go to war. Even though there were a lot of Hollywood types running around in their tight fitting uniforms, I couldn't even find out who the hell was in charge!" Eventually Mack spoke to another sergeant who directed him to Sound Stage Number 5 where he was instructed to find himself an army canvas cot in which to sleep. Mack found that there were over two hundred men and their cots on Sound Stage Number 5.

These were the trainee combat cameramen who had met the criteria and who had been handpicked from all across the United States because they already had the adequate basic knowledge required of motion picture camerawork. These were the men McGovern would train. The next morning a whistle blew and the trainee cameramen arose from their cots. They were called to order and told to form ranks for a roll call outside in the assembly area. This was directly in front of the First Motion Picture Unit headquarters building. "Corporal Davenport, aided by a PFC Mandelaro,[8] started to call out the names which were followed with 'Here!' or 'Present!' in a haphazard unmilitary way." Dan didn't like it and his military leadership training was about to kick in. Trainee combat cameramen or not, these men were now soldiers of the United States Army. The corporal eventually called out: "McGovern"....and again… "McGovern…is McGovern here?" In front of the whole assembly 6 feet five Dan, who could be clearly seen by all, replied: "Are you addressing Sergeant McGovern, Corporal?"

"Are you McGovern?" came the reply. Dan walked out in front of the ranks of men, stuck out his big hand towards the corporal and said: "Corporal, you give me that list and take that PFC with you and get the hell back in over there. I'll show you how to organise a morning call." Dan assumed command of the ranks of men before him and then addressed the entire assembly which now including the red-faced corporal and the PFC. "The fact that I had been sent out there to train the cameramen gave me the confidence to do that," Mack explained.

"How many of you men have had military training?," he asked. "Come on now. Put up your hands." About a dozen men put up their hands. Dan now broke up the large group of over 200 trainees into 12 separate platoons each with a man with military training in charge. The next order he gave was to instruct the new groups to move to a nearby car park where he instructed them to undertake some physical on-the-spot training before breakfast as was common in the army.

As the trainees would find out, physical exercise, in various forms, would be an important part of their overall combat cameraman training over the course of the coming months. On their way to breakfast the entire group passed between two massive sound stages singing army cadence songs at the top of their voices. "I got them singing together to build a spirit in them. Anyhow, that's how I got the whole damn thing going and their training started," Mack remembered. A little later Big Mack was standing outside when a Major Teitelbaum, complete with beige coloured riding britches, tan riding boots and with a swagger stick walked up to him accompanied by the obviously aggrieved Corporal Davenport. The major started to angrily make a point, poking Dan with his swagger stick as he did so. "McGovern, I'm going to prefer charges against you for insubordination," the major declared. Dan interjected: "Major, don't poke me with that stick."

"What's your problem, sergeant?" replied the major.

"Don't poke me with that stick," Dan repeated.

"You've insulted my sergeant major."

"What?" said Sergeant McGovern now taken aback and a little angry.

"He's a corporal!" Dan pointed out.

"You're coming with me now to see the adjutant," the major declared. Dan paused and assessed the situation.

"Okay. I'll be right with you," he answered.

THE FMPU ADJUTANT

Dan walked into the headquarters building after the major and Corporal Davenport and into an office where a young captain sat behind a desk. He was a typical reservist and Hollywood type with a tan and sure enough, a tailored uniform. Dan looked more closely at the face. The name plate on the desk read *Capt. R.W. Reagan* and the penny dropped. It was none other than Hollywood actor and future President of the United States, Ronald Reagan. He was also the Fort Roach Personnel Officer. Dan explained that he had been seconded to the FMPU as the NCO In Charge of combat photography training.

"Captain, I was assigned here directly out of Pentagon headquarters to take over the training of combat cameramen. That's what I was assigned to do. There was nobody here to tell me what to do so I assumed the leadership role." A short conversation ensued. Reagan looked Dan over and then called his secretary to his desk asking her to bring a duty roster clipboard which he promptly closely scrutinised for McGovern's name amongst the combat cameramen instructor personnel. "It's all true!," Reagan declared. "All right Sergeant McGovern, apologies for this. Carry on with your training."

"Thank you, Sir," said McGovern who then turned to the major despite his more senior rank and stated: "Don't you ever poke that swagger stick in my ribs again. Don't you even point it at me!" Dan elaborated a little bit about Ronald Reagan. "The fact was Reagan was a man that we all looked up to. He admired discipline and leadership as was the case when I made my point to him with the prima donna major. Even though he was a movie star of some importance he was never the type that would throw his weight around. He was always considerate to people and their problems and especially to the enlisted men."

FMPU Adjutant and future US President Ronald Reagan pictured at his desk in Fort Roach in Culver City. It was into this office that Dan McGovern was hauled by Major Teitelbaum when he first arrived at FMPU. **Photo courtesy of the Ronald Reagan Presidential Library.**

However, now the cameramen for General Arnold's Combat Camera Units or the CCUs, to which they would be more commonly referred, had to be fully trained. They had to be ready to go to war at the end of another three months. "So it was a crash course to get the first cameramen trained up and deployed as quickly as possible," Dan recalled. He soon discovered, however, that whilst billeted there and unlike other personnel already well established at Fort Roach, the combat cameramen personnel were actually not to be trained on the studio site at all. For its Camera School facility the First Motion Picture Unit had leased Camp Arthur Letts, a boy scout camp on ten acres, located in Runyon Canyon in South Los Angeles and approximately four and a half miles south east of Fort Roach. The camp was adjacent to a ranch owned by Hollywood actor Errol Flynn.[9]

"That was up in an area called Bynum's Heaven in Studio City," Dan remembered. He wasted no time in setting up his combat cameraman school so that the training of his new charges could commence. "Every day I marched them to and from the camp, rain or shine, through the streets until eventually temporary quarters were put up there so that they could sleep there too. That's where we trained them and from there came the nucleus of the combat camera teams for the various Air Forces." Dan's initial twelve training groups, however, soon expanded. "In a month we had organised sixteen combat camera units," he recalled. For the duration of training, each of these basic CCUs was given a letter designation, A to Q and typically comprised 23 men of which 15 would be NCO combat cameramen on combat flying status. The remainder of the unit would be mainly officers and ground technical specialists such as camera repair technicians.[10] However, as it would turn out, a CCU could later be enlarged to comprise anything up to 37 men – usually seven officers and between 20 to 30 enlisted ranks.[11]

Officially, McGovern was attached to Combat Camera Unit F but, as the senior instructor, moved throughout the other CCUs for training purposes. Regardless of size, a Combat Camera Unit on deployment was usually broken down into various smaller detachments as required for a variety of assignments with its Air Force. All men, cameramen or otherwise, would be unit specialists in some aspect of motion picture photography or support. A unit would be assigned to each of the

16 Air Forces which were the 1st to 15th Air Forces along with the 20th Air Force of the United States Army.[12] It was decreed that only combat cameramen who were non-commissioned officers were allowed to fly missions and never officer cameramen. However, as it would turn out, this was a rule which would not always be strictly adhered to.

———

TRAINING THE CAMERAMEN

The trainee combat cameraman course was 17 weeks in duration. Each of the groups was given training on rotation between the instructors with one group often combining with another and all under the watchful eye of Mack McGovern.

For the first eleven weeks[13] the trainees received practical and theory classroom instruction. Big Mack initially taught each trainee a few important ground rules. They now had to think like a documentary and newsreel cameraman.  They always had to be ready for the unexpected and to film interesting footage whenever the opportunity arose.

Dan taught his trainees how best to position themselves to film in a variety of environments in order to maximise their coverage but to minimise their risk of wounding or death. He taught them to always keep fresh filming perspectives in mind and the benefits of also shooting their subject matter from reverse angles whenever possible.

He stressed to them at all costs to avoid becoming a participant in the action themselves as, to do that, meant that they were losing the action that they were there to capture. It was also drummed into the combat cameraman trainee what not to film in order to avoid inadvertently capturing security sensitive footage resulting in censorship issues.

THE EYEMO 35MM MOVIE CAMERA

Mack thoroughly instructed each trainee in every aspect of the movie cameras they would use to film the activities of the United States Army Air Forces on deployment all over the world. Supported by numerous training instruction pamphlets and manuals, trainees were taught the technical aspects of the rugged handheld Bell & Howell Eyemo model 35mm movie camera and its variants. Built in Chicago and weighing almost ten pounds, this was the functional well-made silent camera that was to be mainly used by the combat cameraman either in the air or on the ground to film the war as it unfolded around him.

The Eyemo 'Hard Front' 35mm movie camera. **Photo: ©Richard Bennett, cinemagear.com.**

At this early stage of the war the Eyemo was finished in a matt black crinkle paint but some were already beginning to arrive with a factory coat of flat olive drab green instead reflecting their military status. In the event that American camera manufacturers could not keep up with Army Air Forces demand, the First Motion Picture Unit was directed to buy or lease suitable cameras wherever and whenever required.[14] Regardless of colour a small black and white plastic label riveted to the top of the camera body declared: *Property US Army Air Forces*. The trainee cameramen all received advanced training on all aspects of the Eyemo's operation and maintenance and also on the camera's spare parts inventory. Mack explained all about the camera's simple settings and other features and about its lenses and filters.

Just like the infantryman with his weapon, all Mack's trainees were trained to strip and reassemble the Eyemo and when they had mastered that they where then taught how to do it again –

blindfolded. For this task Mack lined up his trainees in a queue before a single table so that each took his turn to strip and assemble the Eyemo and to then load and unload it with film but with the blindfold on as the others watched and learned. Mack sat down at the table first, put on the blindfold and stripped and assembled the Eyemo very quickly before returning to the end of the queue as the next man sat at the table. The training group was being watched by a group of officers. "I remember there was a Captain Ray Flinsky there who remarked: 'This guy can't be that good?' Mack replied to the Captain with a big smile: "Do you want me to do it again, Captain?" Eventually, even blind-folded, all the trainees could strip and assemble the Eyemo movie camera as quickly as Mack himself.

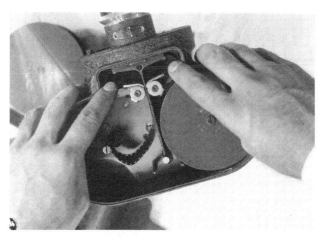

Loading the Eyemo 35mm movie camera. **Photo courtesy of Leatherby Libraries, Chapman University, Calif.**

The trainees were taught how to use light meters and all they needed to know about the characteristics of the various types of film available for both movie and still cameras. Such film, in most cases unexposed and unprocessed, was collectively known in the trade as the *raw stock*. However, they also learned that the term *raw* was also applied by cameramen to unedited film footage. The trainees learned how to properly load a fresh film spool from the raw stock into the Eyemo's film chamber and then they learned how to properly unload it. The good practice of loading and unloading in subdued light or even total darkness whenever possible was emphasised. To that end they also learned how to load and unload the camera blindfolded.

HEADS AND TAILS

The Eyemo was usually loaded with what were called Daylight Spools of 100 feet of film which, once removed from their packaging, could be quickly loaded and unloaded without the risk of light contamination. Daylight Spools were factory spun and came with a light blocking paper strip wrapped around the outside circumference of the unexposed film on its spool. A Daylight Spool also had four or five feet of a blank *leader* at the start or *head* of the spool and also at its end, known as the spool's *tail* or *foot*. These leaders had a special coating on one side which blocked light contaminating the film during loading and unloading thus eliminating the requirement for total darkness.

Once loaded with film and with the camera's side door back in place, it was drilled into the trainees to always reset the Eyemo's footage dial to *zero* with each reload. This small dial turned as the cameraman filmed so that, at a glance, he always knew how much unexposed film remained. The camera could then be wound up.

With its cranking key inserted on the camera's right side, Mack now taught the trainees the correct camera cranking technique. This was to repeatedly half turn the considerable weight and bulk of the camera itself with one hand whilst the inserted key was held and flicked with the wrist of the other hand in the opposite direction. It was easier that way rather than attempting to wind up the action with the key like you would a clockwork toy. Ten full revolutions of the key wound the spring to its full extent. To run a single 100 feet film spool through it the Eyemo required at least two full winding operations.

When run at the standard 24 frames per second a 100 feet film spool captured one minute of footage. Mack trained his charges to get into the habit of always rewinding the camera's mechanism to its full extent after every continuous exposure or scene that they filmed. This practice only rewound the spring and not the film. This was to ensure that full mainspring power was always available for the unexpected. He also taught them to always remember to *run down* or fully release their camera's mainspring at the end of a day's shooting which prolonged the life of the spring. The combat cameramen trainees were shown how to rectify potential problems which might arise with the overall camera system from time to time. If a mainspring failed, for example, the camera could also be manually hand-cranked with its smaller crank handle accessory.

The Eyemo was already renowned for its reliability and simplicity and when maintained and used correctly in normal conditions the Eyemo gave little trouble and its finely machined clockwork mechanism exposed film very smoothly before the camera had to be unloaded, reloaded and wound up once again – in normal conditions. As Mack was to find out, in Air Force use the camera would also have its drawbacks.

The most basic Eyemo camera models were fitted with a single lens and were known by cameramen as *hard front* Eyemos. All came with a simple grip handle which screwed into the camera's threaded tripod attachment point in its base. Alternatively, a simple strap was attached which supported the back of the left hand as the camera was being held. Mack taught his trainees various new ways to properly hold their camera to minimise shake – *to keep the jiggles out of it* as they put it and also how to avoid sunlight flair in all filming situations.

He taught them extensively about the correct use of those Eyemos which incorporated triple swinging or rotating lens turrets – the models M and Q. The Q model incorporated the *Spider* lens arrangement with its three lenses set wider apart than the M model on three extended arms.

THE SPIDER EYEMO

The ubiquitous 'Spider Eyemo' with its rotating lens turret. This camera is often referred to as the camera that filmed WW2 *so regularly was it photographed with combat cameramen in all theatres of war.* **Photo: ©Richard Bennett, cinemagear.com.**

Probably more than an other this became the ubiquitous Eyemo image of World War 2 when pictured with the combat cameraman. An Eyemo with a swinging lens turret gave the combat cameraman the option of instant lens selection with a simple partial revolution of the turret dispensing with the time consuming need to remove and replace single lenses for various filming tasks. Unlike today's *view through the lens* or reflex cameras, the basic Eyemo used only a simple fixed cylindrical offset viewfinder. This was incorporated into the centre of the camera's removable door on its left side and it framed what was intended to be shot. However, some Eyemo variants also came with a *correction* viewfinder which revolved on an adjustable offset axis. Such viewfinders could be adjusted using either an external dial or a small revolving turret incorporated into the front of the viewfinder into which was set a single viewfinder lens or up to three such lenses. The Eyemo Q model also had an improved *focusing* viewfinder. The trainee combat cameramen also received instruction on the hard front Eyemo Type 71 variant which was a customised Bomb-Spotting camera. This was used during bombing raids for filming the results of ongoing bomb strikes on the ground. However, if the opportunity arose standard Eyemos could also be used for the same purpose.

Dan also instructed his trainees on the correct use of the Eyemo when used in conjunction with its tripod and on advanced camera panning techniques when using this stable filming platform. When using the tripod the camera could be wound up with its longer cranking handle instead of its cranking key. The tripod configuration, however, was cumbersome and was restricted to use in safe environments. As access to resources was always going to be limited in the combat environment Dan stressed to his trainee combat cameramen the importance of improvisation as they went about obtaining their footage either on the ground or in the air. The trainees learned, for example, how to improvise when no tripod was available as would certainly be the case in the actual combat environment.

The Eyemo Q model camera could also be used in conjunction with a 400 feet external magazine allowing four minutes of footage to be obtained. If available, a small battery powered electric motor and drive spring could also be attached. When using external magazines with the Eyemo, given their larger spools, loading and unloading the magazine was a more complicated process compared to simply using daylight spools inside the camera itself. The larger spools of the magazine were usually prewound in advance of a shoot by the cameraman from bulk film stocks. There was no light blocking tape or special coating with this film and unloading and reloading the magazine was achieved by placing it as well as a film canister, inside a specialist accessory called a Changing Bag which, in essence, was a portable darkroom. Internally, the bag blocked out all external light ensuring that the photosensitive film was not contaminated when the side access covers of the magazine were removed inside the bag.

When using the changing bag the cameraman, by feel alone, first *un-canned* a replacement fresh spool of film from its canister. He then removed the magazine's side covers, unloaded the exposed spool from the magazine, *re-canned* it in the same canister from which he had removed the fresh spool and loaded the new unexposed spool into the magazine. The magazine's side covers were then reinstalled before the entire reloaded magazine was removed from the changing bag and fitted onto the rear of the Eyemo. This process resulted in only a minimal waste of film due to unavoidable exposure. The changing bag could also be used by the combat cameraman in any situation where the transfer of film between canisters was required. For the trainees using the changing bag soon also became second nature. Many training hours were also devoted to the smaller format 16mm Bell & Howell Filmo movie camera with which high quality colour footage could be shot. Dan explained: "Colour film was very sought after but it was expensive so we only used that for special assignments." The slightly smaller Filmo 16mm camera had the same basic design and characteristics as the Eyemo and was a camera which Mack himself would have considerable use for in the immediate years ahead. It had a film spool and magazine length similar to the Eyemo.

The Eyemo military movie camera in its classic tripod configuration and fitted with its magazine and electric motor. **Photo: Alamy Stock Photo.**

Training was also given on other 16mm contemporaries of the Filmo such as the 16mm Victor or Auricon movie cameras. 16mm colour footage, it was also explained, could be blown up into the larger 35mm format if required for black and white newsreel use. The trainees where also taught everything they needed to know regarding the use of the 35mm Mitchell Government or GC larger format high speed movie camera. This version of the Mitchell had been introduced in 1940.[15] However, when running, the GCs were noisy and for this reason McGovern also gave his charges some additional instruction on the operation of the similar but more advanced Mitchell NC and BNC models. This was so that he could also train them on the operation of compatible sound recording systems for these cameras in the event that the Army Air Forces ever called upon them to film using sound.

The trainee combat cameramen were given instruction on the operation and maintenance of the electrically powered 16mm Gun Sight Aiming Point or GSAP movie camera. This was a black robust film cartridge fed compact camera about six inches long by 4 inches wide and 2.5 inches thick which was usually fitted with a 35mm lens. The cartridge contained 50 feet of film or 700 individual frames. The GSAP was normally placed flat in the wing or fuselage of a fighter aircraft and synched electrically to the *fire* button on the pilot's control yoke to shoot when the guns were fired capturing the action as the pilot saw it.

Such footage was useful for training purposes and for confirming enemy aircraft kills claimed by a pilot. As McGovern was to discover, such cameras and the dramatic footage they could capture would have other useful applications later. Each trainee was also issued and trained on the 2X3 inch Graflex made Baby Speedgraphic stills camera as part of their work would also involve some still camera duty on deployment. At the time this was the smaller version of the most popular 4 X 5 inch large format press camera in America but training was also given on the larger Speedgraphic too. In this capacity Dan also passed on

The 35mm Mitchell GC Government Camera. This is a chronograph model GC used for filming high speed action. McGovern would also put such specialist GC cameras to very good use in his post-war years. **Photo: ©Richard Bennett, cinemagear.com.**

his considerable stills camera experience and techniques to the trainees. He gave instruction on some of the standard 16mm cassette cameras in use at the time such as the Bell & Howell Filmo Autoload movie camera.

Given that they were going to war the trainees were also taught the various ways in which all cameras could be destroyed rather than to allow them and their film footage to be captured by the enemy. They were shown how to roughly frame and test the potential of subject matter using a simple alignment technique before they even raised their cameras. This was to hold both arms outstretched at eye level with the hands held vertically and with the thumbs outstretched horizontally at roughly at 90 degrees to the index fingers. Roughly, the edges of the index fingers represented the two sides of a potential viewfinder frame and the thumbs the bottom edge.

When sighting a potential scene in this manner and particularly with one eye closed, the distance between both hands could be varied thus giving the cameraman an initial idea of either the best distance from which to shoot his subject matter or the most suitable lens to employ. McGovern also passed on accurate methods he had mastered for judging both distance as well as natural light intensities simply by eye. These were two basic but important skills that the combat cameraman in particular was going to need to get the best results from his camera.

Every attempt to film a scene constituted a single *take*. Mack's charges learned how to deal with footage takes with which they were unhappy – the *No Goods* or *NG takes*. In order to let the film editor know later that takes were *No Good,* McGovern taught his rookie cameramen to film a close up of the inside of an outstretched hand at the end of the unwanted take several feet from the camera lens – a clear message to the experienced film editor – *Do Not Use.* They learned how to properly store and label exposed film canisters and how to properly mark caption sheets and production slates. Unlike the more elaborate clapper boards used in big budget commercial motion pictures, the simple production slate sufficed to serve the same purpose for the combat cameraman's needs. It was drilled into McGovern's trainees to remember to *always put a slate on it* before attempting to shoot a scene.[16]

The Gun Sight Aiming Point or 'GSAP' camera which captured combat footage from the pilot's perspective. McGovern would put it to other uses later. **Photo: ©Richard Bennett, cinemagear.com.**

After every new spool of raw film was loaded into his camera the cameraman filled in the production slate with the details of the footage about to be filmed. This was usually just with a piece of chalk. The trainees were taught how filming a few frames of the production slate prior to a take ensured correct film editing continuity. Ideally, a production slate was permanently sub divided into painted white pre-categorised rectangles on a black background into which was written, the location, the camera-man's name, the date, the reel number, scene or take number and where relevant, the director's name. As it would frequently turn out, the production slate would often be hastily improvised in some fashion or other.

In addition to the production slate *Caption Sheets* in partic-ular were also important. These contained much more detailed information. Each exposed canister of uncut negative shot – the undeveloped and unedited film, had to be accompanied by a regulation Army Air Force/First Motion Picture Unit printed paper caption sheet. This had to be filled in by the camera-man/cinematographer and placed inside the film canister with the exposed uncut negative film. It was stressed to the trainees how this detailed information was also crucial for editing and continuity purposes later on during the film production process.

Dan McGovern (back left) and a group of his combat cameramen trainees pictured at Camp Letts in the Hollywood Hills in early 1943. Until tents were later provided on site at the camp Technical Sergeant McGovern marched his trainees over four miles each way every day from Fort Roach.
Photo: AFHRA/First Motion Picture Unit Historical Group.

The caption sheet contained crucial information – the film's title, the cameraman, the combat camera unit, the date, the type of camera, film and lenses used, where possible a synopsis of the contents scene by scene, take numbers, where it was shot, the length of film, observations on filming conditions at the time, the type of light etc. and whether the content film was silent or accompanied by sound. Finally, each canister of uncut film also had to have a content label placed on the outside. This simply contained the film title, where it was shot, the type of film, the cameraman, the CCU and the canister number.

The processing of exposed movie negative film was not normally the job of the combat cameraman. However, Mack taught his trainees how to develop exposed black and white film on deployment just in case the need should ever arise. It was also explained how a rough version of a film production called a *workprint* was prepared from exposed film and how film prints could also be duplicated for various purposes known in the film trade as the *dupes*. The trainees learned all about editing and about film splicing techniques so that their footage would always be shot with continuity of the finished product in mind.

In keeping with what was their basic *Army* designation the trainees were also taught how to field strip and fire the 1911 Colt Automatic Pistol and the M1 Carbine and put through a modified form of commando and warfare instruction. This helped to ensure that they were in peak physical shape for the job ahead.[17] Barracks and personal kit were regularly inspected and any breaches of army regulations reprimanded. McGovern's charges were often inspected in full battle kit outside the main office of the First Motion Picture Unit at Fort Roach by their senior officers. Simulated combat, even on the ground, also afforded an opportunity for the trainees to safely perfect camera skills and to practice filming techniques.

As there were no Air Force bombardment units and associated training facilities located close enough to Hollywood, for the final seven weeks of the course Dan and his charges relocated to Las Vegas Army Airfield, Nevada. Here they were given additional training as Gunner/Photographers.[18] Given that they were going into harm's way aboard fully operational aircraft in warzones around the world the combat cameramen also had to be ready in an instant to stow their cameras and to act as spare crew members when the need arose. Of that part of the combat cameraman's job Mack explained: "As a Gunner /Photographer the combat cameraman often had to drop his camera and take up a machine gunner's position. For us there was no such thing as a free ride."

The trainees were given 5 weeks[19] practical gunnery instruction. They were trained how to field strip, reassemble, load, fire and clear the Browning AN.M2 Light Barrel .50 calibre machine gun which they would encounter on many US aircraft and then they were trained to do it all again but this time wearing the heavy leather mittens needed at the highest altitudes as protection against the extreme cold. Mack recalled: "Mostly it was learning how to load the gun and how to track a target."

The trainees were also given practical instruction in First Aid so that, if needed, they could attend wounded airmen in combat. They were also drilled again and again in aircraft profile recognition using silhouette boards of the most common Allied and enemy aircraft they might encounter until they could recognise them all to the satisfaction of their instructor. This was to avoid accidentally shooting at their own planes in the heat of battle. They were also familiarised with the Army Air Force aircraft types on which they would soon film all around the world.

The remaining weeks of the course were used to hone their newly acquired cinematography skills in the air as Dan recounted: "We were often up over my old mapping area at Muroc." This was over the Mojave Desert and beyond it to the south west and across the state line in California. Mack had honed his own aerial photography skills in this area and he was now passing on those same skills to his trainees.

At the end of their training all trainees were given practical and theory examinations. The final pass mark had to be obtained by any given trainee at which point they were given the rank of Technical Sergeant. As something of an incentive notably higher grades were also rewarded with a higher rank.[20] The trainees had earned their stripes and were now qualified Non Commissioned

Officer or NCO Combat Cameramen. Among the first of these trained by Dan McGovern were the combat cameramen assigned to the 9th Army Air Force. This CCU would now lose its unit *letter* training designation to become the 9th Combat Camera Unit.[21] This was the first CCU to deploy overseas and was soon filming action in the air and on the ground in North Africa.[22]

In addition to training his combat cameramen and their support crews Technical Sergeant Mack McGovern also worked closely with another special group back at Fort Roach. These were the specialist top tier elite groups of movie directors, actors, cameramen and technical staff who now, instead of making lavish entertainment movie epics for the big Hollywood studios, were using their movie industry cameras and the studio facilities at hand to produce the high quality training, morale and propaganda films which their country now needed.

They were the best at their craft in America and included movie directors William Wyler, John Ford, John Houston and John Sturges; actors Alan Ladd, William Holden, Clark Gable, Van Heflin, Burgess Meredith, Lee J. Cobb, George Montgomery, Arthur Kennedy and many more in addition to Ronald Reagan. These actors and directors were broken down into various groupings to produce their assigned films.

As the First Motion Picture Unit was based in Hollywood Mack pointed out that there was a certain amount of make believe involved in some of the film productions. "They had mock ups there of every weapon in the Air Force inventory. There were even mock-ups of complete planes or cutaway views of a whole aeroplane. Some scenes were faked. I could always tell because the lighting was too good or the guy behind the gun was too pretty in his brand new flying gear."

By the end of April 1943 McGovern had finally completed his task of instructing the cameramen in the training programme he had established and he had achieved this on schedule. With the 9th Combat Camera Unit already deployed his remaining units and their newly qualified cameramen were officially assigned as the Combat Camera Units of the remaining United States Army Air Forces in either the Pacific or European Theatres of War. These men were the core of the combat cameramen of the First Motion Picture Unit who would shoot World War 2 for the United States Army Air Forces.

DEPLOYMENT OVERSEAS

McGovern now also left Fort Roach in Culver City. He was needed elsewhere. Mack had left a solid foundation and others would now take over the combat training mantle at Fort Roach to provide replacement combat cameramen whenever and wherever they were needed. This would be from what was called the Cameramen Replacement Pool and that was based, for now at least, at source at the combat camera school Mack had established at Camp Letts – the boy scout Camp at Studio City.[23] The school would, however, soon relocate to the more suitable Pacific Military Academy[24] premises in Culver City and only a few miles from Fort Roach.

Many of the specialist elite cinematographers, technicians and actors such as adjutant Captain Ronald Reagan would remain at Fort Roach as the unit continued to produce its training, information, propaganda and morale boosting films for the duration of the war. Combat Camera Unit F was now deploying to England with the 8th United States Army Air Force as the 8th Combat Camera Unit. Dan McGovern was designated NCO/IC – the Non Commissioned Officer In Charge of the unit's combat cameramen. He would be leaving American shores within weeks. First, however, he would spend some time with his family in New York from where he would then embark for the war in Europe sailing en-route within sight of the land of his birth, Ireland. "We were finally heading to war, to England and to Europe as a team," he recalled.

––––––––

1. By direction in a memo from General *Hap* Arnold to the Director of Photography Army Air Forces dated 10th November 1942, *The History of the First Motion Picture Unit* 1944 – Scanlan.
2. iBid.
3. *Fighting With Film*, Hall Wall, *American Cinematographer*, September 1943. p324.
4. By direction in a memo from General Arnold to the Director of Photography Army Air Forces dated 10th November 1942, *The History of the First Motion Picture Unit* , 1944 – Scanlan.
5. *Motion Picture Photography – A History 1891 to 1960* – H. Mario Raimondo-Souto, p267.
6. *Hollywood Commandos*, Gregory Orr Productions.
7. *First Motion Picture Unit Movie*, US Army Air Forces; US National Archives and *The History of the First Motion Picture Unit* , 1944 – Scanlan.
8. Private First Class Albert J. Mandelaro would himself later train as a combat cameraman.
9. Additional details of Camp Letts gleaned from *Hollywood Heights – Los Angeles' Forgotten J.B. Lankershim Monument, The L.A. Daily Mirror* (online article) and *Briar Summit Open Space Preserve* (online article).
10. *1st Combat Camera Unit, A History*, 405th Bomb Group Memorial website. It can be deduced therefore, that in or around 240 FMPU trainee cameramen were recruited in the very first intake.
11. *USAF Combat Camera* website.
12. There were no 16th to 19th Air Forces.
13. *Historical Study of the Army Air Forces First Motion Picture Unit*, Ross H. Vincent Jr. p31.
14. *The History of the First Motion Picture Unit.*
15. The *GC* was based on the standard *Mitchell* studio model but did not have its special effects features.
16. However, production slates do not appear to have been used in aircraft during actual combat missions.
17. *First Motion Picture Unit Movie*, US Army Air Forces, US National Archives.
18. *Historical Study of the Army Air Forces First Motion Picture Unit*, Ross H. Vincent Jr. p31.
19. *The Rear Gunner*, FMPU training film (1943).
20. *Motion Picture Photography – A History 1891 to 1960* – H. Mario Raimondo-Souto p267.
21. From research it appears that the original *Letter* designated training CCUs were simply renamed to reflect the Air Force to which they were assigned. However, CCU strength and personnel were not always the same as the original training unit.
22. *Armed With Cameras,* Maslowski, pages 157-158. From the author's research a memo headed *A Brief Outline of the Photographic Activities of the Army Air Forces* dated 5th April 1943 recorded in Scanlan's *History of the First Motion Picture Unit* states that 6 CCU's of 9 officers and 23 men each had by then

already been dispatched to AAF's around the world with another 9 CCUs being organised for immediate assignment. The latter 9 CCUs which would be deployed by the end of May included McGovern's own 8th Air Force CCU. This indicates that training was somewhat expedited for these earlier deployed units further demonstrating the urgency to get the new Combat Camera Units into the field as quickly as possible.

23. *The History of the First Motion Picture Unit*, 1944 – Scanlan.
24. Not a trace remains of the Pacific Military Academy, once located at Cattaraugus Avenue, Culver City.

9

VIEWFINDERS AND BOMBSIGHTS

Chelveston, England with the 305th Bomb Group

TECHNICAL SERGEANT DAN MCGOVERN arrived on assignment at the air station of the 305th Heavy Bombardment Group, 8th Air Force at Chelveston, Northamptonshire, England two weeks later on June 1st 1943. He had docked in Liverpool only the morning before and made his way the 180 miles to the air station which was located approximately 40 miles north-west of Cambridge. The 8th Combat Camera Unit in total comprised a team of 6 officers and 21 enlisted men.[1] The CCU in turn was split up into eight[2] individual filming detachments of varying sizes depending on the assignment.

Each detachment had several combat cameramen often including a specialist such as McGovern as well as other support personnel and was assigned to individual 8th Air Force air stations throughout England.[3] The 8th Combat Camera Unit, just as it had as CCU F, remained under the command of distinguished Academy Award nominated cinematographer and later movie director, Major Teddy Tetzlaff. At Chelveston McGovern was the senior non-commissioned officer of the 8th CCU's Detachment B, a specialist colour detachment, comprising 2 officers and four NCOs.

The 305th Bombardment Group, or simply the 305th Bomb Group, was known throughout the United States Army Air Forces as the *Can Do* outfit. Whilst it was rightly proud of its *Can Do* moniker it had been hard earned over Nazi occupied Europe with the lives of American airmen since it arrived in England in September 1942. "By 1943 we were just learning how to fight with heavy bombers and how best to fly daylight missions," Dan recalled. McGovern's arrival in England coincided with a massive expansion of the 8th Air Force in terms of men and matériel. It was also a time when new aerial strategies were being devised and implemented as Brigadier General Ira Eaker sent his bombers out day after day to attack the targets of Hitler's Third Reich. Chelveston was, even by then, a massive wartime US Army Air Force base[4] from which Boeing B-17 Flying Fortress heavy bombers flew on missions against German facilities mainly on or near the French coast. Targets included U-Boat submarine pens and enemy fighter and bomber airfields.

By 1943, the 305th Bomb Group had a total complement of approximately 294 officers and 1,487 enlisted men to fly and support 48 heavy bombers.[5] The air base sprawled over 700 acres and was previously an RAF station before the arrival of the Americans. It now had the USAAF designation *Station 105* for security reasons. As enlisted men McGovern and his team were billeted in one of the many wooden prefabricated Tar and Paper huts on one of Station 105's communal areas. Bunks were aligned inside in neat barracks order but overall the interior was spartan, often cold and draughty and heated only by a single solid fuel pot belly stove. For now, at least, this was home.

In the centre of the airfield was the station's control tower and a short distance from that beyond workshops, aircraft hangars and stores was McGovern's new base of operations – a standalone building which was the base photographic laboratory. McGovern's Detachment B moving picture cameramen would now share the photo lab with its existing well established tenants, a small group of dedicated Army Air Force stills Photographers/Observers and specialist photo technicians – the 305th Bomb Group Photographic Unit. Between their already well-equipped laboratory and its darkroom or the *Black Hole* as they called it, these stills photographers were busy. Already every month they were printing off thousands of hand taken direct vertical as well as oblique photographs of enemy targets and areas of interest. They were also responsible for the remotely shot but bulky HTX still camera. This was either the Eastman Kodak K-24 or the Fairchild K-17 which was mounted in the belly of the aircraft. Both shot remotely once the bombs were released.

All photographs obtained by the USAAF Photographer/Observer were useful for intelligence, reconnaissance and bomb spotting purposes with the latter helping to determine the success or otherwise of the bombing raid on which they were photographed. These photographers also shot still photographs on the ground for historical and public relations purposes. With the presence of McGovern and his team also shooting stills, although to a lesser extent, there was a certain amount of stills overlap. However, the main task of McGovern and his team was to commence visual documentation with movie cameras and much of that would be in glorious colour.

The 8th Air Force's efforts complemented RAF Bomber Command's existing night-time area bombing campaign which the latter had been waging since 1940. Whereby the RAF concentrated on bombing raids on German targets at night, the Americans opted mainly for a precision daylight strategic bombing campaign in the interests of greater accuracy and navigation. The down side of this strategy was, of course, that it was considerably more dangerous for the American crews as bombers could be clearly seen by enemy fighters and ground anti-aircraft flak units. The American Army Air Force top brass decreed, however, that it was worth the risk. The result was an unrelenting British and American around the clock combined bomber offensive campaign against military and industrial targets all across Nazi occupied Europe.

A western view of the control tower, hangars and workshops of 'Station 105'
at Chelveston. **Photo: The Ken Snyder Collection/Eric Barko.**

The sprawling 'Station 105' at Chelveston as seen from the air during the
war. **Photo: United States Air Force Historical Research Agency.**

When Mack McGovern joined the 8th Air Force in England in June 1943 it was approaching the completion of its first year of combat operations. Even by then over 38% of its heavy bomber crews were being lost.[6] The workhorse of the 305th Bomb Group, the Boeing B-17, is probably one of the best known aircraft of World War 2. It was a high-flying, four-engine long-range heavy bomber with a wingspan of almost 104 feet. On average, the B-17 had a range of almost 2000 miles and could carry 8,000 lbs[7] or four tons of bombs and burned 225 gallons of gasoline an hour.

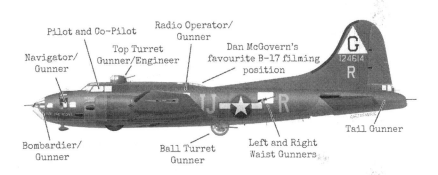

305th Bomb Group B-17F 'We The People' as she appeared in August of 1943. This bomber and her crew would feature in the footage shot by Dan McGovern when he was stationed at Chelveston, England with Detachment B of the 8th Combat Camera Unit. **Image: ©Gaetan Marie.**

The B-17 had a crew of ten with an average age of 21. It was well able to defend itself, bristling with as many as 13 Browning .50 calibre heavy machine guns prompting the name – The Flying Fortress. Each matt olive green painted B-17 with its regulation white US stars over a blue circle on its fuselage and right upper wing was maintained by a team of five mechanics, one of which was the Crew Chief. This supervising mechanic signed off on all maintenance work on his B-17. At Chelveston the crew chiefs and maintenance teams were soon replacing almost sixty engines a month on the group's 48 strong bomber fleet. As a result of ongoing maintenance and the sometimes protracted repair of battle damaged B-17s, crews rarely flew the same bomber all the time and it was common practice for individual crew members to be reassigned temporarily to other crews to make up numbers. Even before McGovern arrived in England in the summer of 1943 the B-17 had acquired an iconic status, not just because of its crews' daring exploits, but because of its mythical ability to sustain extensive battle damage and still get its crews home.

A contemporary of the B-17 also in the bomber inventory of the 8th Air Force in Britain at the time was the Consolidated B-24 Liberator. This was an aircraft which was also used in great numbers for bombing missions over Nazi occupied Europe. However, it had a lower altitude ceiling in Europe given its bomb load and was more difficult to fly in formation.[8] It would never achieve the iconic status of the B-17. One Liberator pilot in particular also had close associations with the First Motion Picture Unit throughout the war. Major James *Jimmy* Stewart, the acclaimed Hollywood actor, had starred in the very first FMPU production *Winning Your Wings* in 1942. Already a skilled pilot before the war, in 1944 he became the commander of the 703rd Bomb Squadron of the 453rd Bomb Group based at Tibenham in Norfolk 90 miles from Chelveston. Stewart would fly twenty combat missions over German occupied Europe. Also with Stewart's 453rd Bomb Group was a radioman/gunner who would also make a considerable contribution to motion pictures after the war. This was actor Walter Matthau.

McGovern's 305th Bomb Group at Chelveston comprised four squadrons each of 12 B-17s – the 364th, the 365th, the 366th and the 422nd Squadron. For identification purposes the squadron letter code was painted on both sides of the fuselage of each plane in big regulation insignia blue letters and respectfully these fuselage codes were WF, XK, KY and JJ.[9] An additional capital letter followed this squadron code to identify individual aircraft. Several weeks after McGovern's arrival at Chelveston all aircraft in the group were also assigned the tail code Triangle-G on the large vertical stabiliser and upper right wing[10] of its aircraft. This was a white equilateral triangle on which was painted the letter G also in regulation US Army insignia blue. Regardless of the firepower of the B-17 a lone bomber was always vulnerable but to the 8th Air Force the adage *safety in numbers* was taken to the extreme. Flying Fortress aerial formations were essentially built[11] from multiples of one basic core component – a simple *V of 3* B-17s called an *element.*

A formation of 305th B-17s at altitude showing the classic 'V of 3' bomber element in the foreshot. **Photo: The Ken Snyder Collection/Eric Barko.**

Depending on a number of factors a given squadron could be flown comprising two elements of six B-17s and later three elements of nine or sometimes two elements of 5 and 7 B-17s. Each bomb group such as the 305th had its complement of 48 bombers but on a mission it flew only three squadrons theoretically with a maximum of 36 B-17s with the fourth squadron's planes being maintained whilst its personnel rested or availed of additional ground training. Bombers and crew members from the resting squadron were, however, also sometimes required to make up numbers in the three flying squadrons. During 1943 due to losses, damage repair, essential maintenance, lesser target priority and the evolution of formation tactical structures, the 305th Bomb Group would usually fly with considerably less than 36 aircraft.

When it commenced operations in England in August 1942 the early formations sent out over continental Europe were group size for the large part and with only relatively simple formation structures built using multiples of these V of 3 components. Any enlarged constituent component in any formation was also frequently referred to as an element. The bomb groups flew to the target each line astern or one behind the other at varying altitudes and distances apart. However, losses had been heavy. This was particularly due to fighter pilots of the German Luftwaffe having identified that these formations were most vulnerable when B-17s of the leading groups were attacked head-on.[12] The way the American formations were then structured had exposed the glaring lack of sufficient frontal machine guns on the Flying Fortress but it was also apparent that not enough of the formation's existing defensive guns could be brought to bear against the attackers in mutual defence. As a result the 8th Air Force started to experiment with other tactical defensive formation structures to achieve a better mutual defence for its bombers.

THE STAGGERED FORMATION

Just before Dan McGovern's arrival at Chelveston it was the 305th Bomb Group which had perfected a formation structure to address this frontal attack defensive deficiency. Under the command of then Colonel Curtis E. LeMay,[13] a new and improved *staggered* formation strategy had been developed offering better mutual defensive capabilities for the groups as they flew into combat. This had evolved into an arrangement called the Compact Combat Box in which individual bomb groups normally flew 18 B-17s but in a much tighter flying formation. This was soon expanded to 21, 27 and later to the maximum 36 B-17s flying as a group as more bombers became available for maximum effort missions.

A flight deck view of a typical tightly flown symmetrical staggered squadron formation of B-17s. **Photo courtesy of United States Air Force Historical Research Agency (AFHRA).**

During McGovern's time in England, the 305th Bomb Group sent out between 12 to 28 B-17s on all its mainstream raids with the latter number being mustered only once against the oil refineries of Ludwigshaven, Germany on 30th December 1943.[14] With this new formation arrangement the vertical and lateral alignment of each bomber, the element of which it was a part and subsequently also each squadron in the group were all staggered symmetrically in flight so that no two B-17s in the same vicinity flew at the same altitude or exactly abreast of each other. The bombers now flew much closer together and often with less than thirty feet[15] between them horizontally and with 75 to 100 feet between them vertically. To put this formation structure into context any crew member on a B-17 who could see other bombers surrounding him knew he could avail of mutual protection from the formation's interlocking machine gun fire against attacking fighters. B-17s furthermost inside a compact combat box with the most bombers diagonally left and right, above and below them were generally afforded the most protection and it was in this vicinity of the formation that McGovern and his cameramen would usually fly. "I always flew in the middle or what was also called the *medium* section of the group because that was part of the tactics we had, not alone from a safety point of view, but also from a photographic composition point of view. To get the best results filming formations of bombers you needed to have aircraft both in the foreground and above you. It was a matter of getting your shooting angles correct. That was the technique that we used and it worked," he recalled.

However, any B-17 on the outside edge of the formation either at the front, back, left or right flank or at the top and bottom was more vulnerable as it did not have the same level of mutual protection as the other bombers. These B-17s were usually the first in the gunsights of attacking German fighters and the most vulnerable position of all in any formation was the trailing B-17 in the rearmost lowest position. This position was known with good reason, either as *Coffin Corner* or *Purple Heart Corner*[16] and its occupant B-17 was the *Tail End Charlie*. From the ground or above the group compact staggered box resembled an arrowhead. It was approximately 650 feet long by 1200 feet wide and in side profile the group combat box also resembled an arrowhead or wedge and had a depth of approximately 900 feet.

Each of the three squadrons of the formation flew in their combat box with the *Lead* squadron element at the front flanked by the *High* squadron element slightly behind and *above* the Lead squadron. The *Low* squadron element flew slightly behind and below the Lead squadron. In the event that the forth squadron or other additional aircraft and crews were occasionally required to fly on maximum effort missions for example, the group combat box could be enlarged by adding a fourth element in what became the lowest rearmost position of the formation.[17] This was known as the *Low Low* element similarly configured as the other squadron elements and adding 300 feet to the vertical depth of the three squadron group formation. The compact combat box defensive strategy was subsequently adopted by all other 8th Air Force bomber groups. To maximise the effectiveness of the compact combat box for the purposes for which it was intended and regardless of group or squadron size, tight formation flying was essential all the way to the target and back again.

Generally, over enemy territory every effort was made to tighten up the formation as much as possible. Once tightly flown these combat boxes were effective in achieving better mutual defence and tighter bombing patterns. Crucially, it also ensured that, when released, the bombs fell away freely and not inadvertently on the other bombers below.

As early as 17th April 1943 the 305th Bomb Group had been part of a wider 8th Air Force experiment in which three neighbouring individual bomb group compact combat boxes, usually comprising in the region of sixty B-17s, flew together with each group also stacked diagonally to become an even further enlarged single combat box.[18] These were known, for now at least, as Provisional Combat Wings or Wing Boxes.[19] The mass wing formations, however, were ungainly and on approach to the target had to temporarily break into their smaller group components in order to accurately bomb the target usually in single file.

Once bombing was completed the individual groups reformed into their mass wing boxes once again. Later these wing boxes few missions together flying one behind the other and spaced a mile and a half apart and at varying altitudes in an even larger grouping which, during McGovern's time at Chelveston, would be designated as the 1st Bomb Division.[20] The length of a B-17 mass formation depended ultimately on the number of groups flying together in their respective wing boxes and subsequently on the length of the further enlarged Bomb Division bomber stream. Dan McGovern flew and filmed from bomber streams of between 100 to 200 B-17s which were typically between ten and twenty miles long.

As the build-up of the 8th Air Force progressed throughout the latter half of 1943 the bomber streams would regularly become even longer. Chelveston was to be Detachment B's main base of operations and most of its filming assignments would take place there or having flown from there. However, Detachment B cameramen would periodically also film on or from neighbouring USAAF B-17 airfields too and with other bomb groups within the 8th Air Force which were flying the B-24 Liberator bomber. Sometimes to augment the work of other camera detachments, they would focus their camera lenses too on the important support role played by the medium bombers and on fighter groups based at airfields elsewhere which protected the heavy bombers such as those of the 305th. Now though, the 305th was about to take the fight deeper into Nazi occupied Europe on some of the most dangerous long penetration bombing raids of the war. Technical Sergeant Daniel McGovern would be with them camera in hand.

---

1. According to McGovern. *Scanlan's history of FMPU* says 7 officers and 23 men.
2. *History of the First Motion Picture Unit,* 1944, Scanlan.
3. During November 1943 the 3rd Combat Camera Unit also arrived in Britain to cover additional activities of the expanding 8th Air Force. The 4th Combat Camera Unit also arrived in Britain that month where it commenced documenting the activities of the newly deployed 9th Air Force. One 9th AF pilot who specialised in flying photo reconnaissance and bomb spotting missions with combat photographers and cameramen was Major Eugene T. O'Brien who was also originally from Dan McGovern's hometown of Carrickmacross in Ireland.
4. Almost everybody had a bicycle for personal transportation on the base. Station 105 at Chelveston used over 1.5 million US gallons of water per month. Hardly a trace of the base remains today. The site has largely been returned to farmland.

5. Bomb Group, Personnel Strengths, Wikipedia. No source available.

6. *Strategy for Defeat - The Luftwaffe 1933-1945*, Williamson Murray.

7. Maximum normal bomb load.

8. According to navigator Robert O'Boyle, 486th Bomb Group who flew in both B-24s and B-17s. – Raymond McFalone interview, You Tube.

9. Historians of the 305th Bomb Group generally agree that almost all colour footage of the Chelveston 305th BG bombers showing WF, XK, KY and JJ fuselage codes and the group's Triangle G tail marking is almost certainly all McGovern's footage.

10. The *Triangle G* motif also appeared on the underside of the left wing. The USAAF star insignia appeared on the opposite wing, top and bottom.

11. **Note:** Formations were quite complex and the author has simplified how they were constructed somewhat in the interests of clarity. Information largely sourced from the film *Target for Today* (1944) produced by the First Motion Picture Unit in which McGovern's footage appears and from John Rickard of historyofwar.org. Some additional information gleaned from *Hells Angels*, the 303rd Bomb Group website. Later formations adopted more horizontal alignments for the basic 3 bomber *V* flights.

12. The 305th Summary of Operations report following a raid on Billancourt near Paris on 4th April 1943 in which the 305th was lead group records concern about German fighters now adopting new tactics and attacking head-on in waves of 3 to 5 fighters abreast with each wave 1000 to 1500 yards apart. The report states: *Recommended: Lead group must have a larger percentage of nose guns or preferably fighter support throughout the mission. These attacks will definitely have some effect upon the morale of the leading group*.

13. LeMay had transferred out of the 305th to other 8th Air Force command duties on 15th May 1943 only two weeks before McGovern joined the group. – American Air Museum in Britain.

14. Based on American Air Museum in Britain mission archive figures and includes B-17 numbers which constituted the larger combat wings. It excludes missions were smaller numbers of B-17s were required. From researching the 305th Summaries of Operations from earlier in 1943 the group also sent out 28 bombers to Bremen on 17th April and to Kiel.

15. Estimated from existing formation footage.

16. The Purple Heart medal was awarded to US servicemen wounded in action.

17. Where oddments of B-17s were insufficient to form V of 3 elements they simply flew with existing squadron elements as designated at the mission briefing.

18. On 17th April 1943, seventeen days after the first reports of the new German head-on attack strategy, the 305th Summary of Operations, following a raid on Bremen, states that the group flew 28 of its B-17s as part of a staggered combat wing with two other groups as the 102nd Combat Wing. A second combat wing comprising three additional groups was also part of that bomber force. The 305th Summary of Operations for the Bremen raid states: *The new Staggered Combat Wing formation is very effective in warding off head-on attacks*. However, subsequent Summaries of Operations indicate that the 305th reverted back to flying with four or five other

groups line astern of each other suggesting that the initial combat wings flown were experimental. According to its later Summaries of Operations for the following missions the 305th later flew as part of combat wings to Huls 22nd June '43, to St. Nazaire 28th June '43; to Villacoublay on 29th June '43 and to Hannover 26th July '43. The 305th again flew in combat wing formation to Kassel on 28th July 1943 and also for the Schweinfurt raid of August 17th 1943 on both of which Dan McGovern filmed.

19. Given the large number of bombers which comprised combat wings accurate navigation was imperative. To this end the lead plane of the wing carried two highly experienced navigators in the nose. – William F. Pennebaker, 390th Bomb Group via Raymond McFalone interview, You Tube. Later in the war a third navigator located in the radio room specialised in radar assisted navigation.

20. Later the 1st Air Division.

WILLIAM WYLER

Project 114/25 Missions

IN AMERICA back in June of 1942, acclaimed Hollywood director William Wyler met with USAAF General Carl Spaatz. The general was about to embark for England where he would take charge of the deployment of the 8th Air Force. Wyler convinced Spaatz of the importance of the work of his new Air Force being documented on film.[1] Shortly afterwards Wyler himself joined the 8th Air Force and the First Motion Picture Unit with the immediate rank of major with orders to make a film about Spaatz's new command as it took the fight to the Germans from England. Wyler first went to Fort Roach in Culver City as he set about assembling a team and equipment for the job now at hand.

Major Wyler left the United States for England at the end of July 1942 with cameraman William H. Clothier and *RKO Studios* soundman Lt. Harold Tannenbaum, now also of the First Motion Picture Unit. Dan recalled: "These were special elite groups made up from the American Society of Cinematographers. They were specialised teams." Wyler's small advance crew soon learned, however, that all their professional cameras, sound equipment, raw film stock and other essential production equipment had been lost in the Atlantic when the vessel on which it was being carried to England was sunk by enemy action. Clothier temporarily borrowed one complete camera unit from the US Navy.[2] At least one aspect of Wyler's aerial filming up to February 1943 appears to have been an instructional film for the US Army Air Forces aimed at merely demonstrating the defensive capabilities of the B-17 bomber.

Hollywood Director Major William Wyler (Centre) pictured in England with his filming crew colleagues William Clothier (Right) and William Skall on the camera in the B-17 right waist gun position. Left is British war correspondent Cavo Chin. **Photo courtesy of AFHRA.**

This footage was not shot over the dangerous skies of occupied Europe at all but over safer skies and with American pilots flying Spitfires acting the part of enemy aircraft and making attacks on Wyler's camera ship.[3] The director was, however, also working on the outlines at least of what were other possible film productions. One was a documentary called *Rendezvous* which focused on the joint efforts of the 8th Air Force and the RAF Bomber Command against Germany. Another was *Phyllis was a*

Fortress which focused on one American B-17 on one mission. However, despite a considerable search, suitable and available sound recording equipment could not be found. As a result and rather than remain grounded, soundman Tannenbaum volunteered to quickly re-train as a combat cameraman under the instruction of his colleague William Clothier and also volunteered for aerial combat.[4]

Now, despite the Air Force rule that actual combat cinematographers were to be non-commissioned officers, Major Wyler, Captain Clothier and now Lieutenant Tannenbaum, started to fly combat missions mainly with the 91st Bomb Group of the fledgling 8th Air Force based at Bassingbourn in Cambridgeshire. Tragically, however, on a raid to bomb the Nazi submarine pens at St. Nazaire, France in April 1943 Tannenbaum (47) was lost when the B-24 Liberator on which he was filming was shot down.[5] He was the first Army Air Force motion picture cameraman to be lost during World War 2.[6] He would not be the last. By now Wyler's efforts pertaining to his film project outline ideas including *Rendezvous* and *Phyllis was a Fortress* had evolved into something else. He was now formulating his cinematography and directional efforts into what had become an Army Air Force *Project of Special Interest*.

THE MAGIC 25

In early 1943, in an effort to boost morale and crew rotation replacements, the 8th Air Force had introduced the 25 mission combat tour.[7] Each crewman had to endure a tour of 25 bombing missions over occupied Europe after which he would be stood down. These experienced crew members were usually rotated home but they were also frequently utilised for the training of replacement crews either in America or on deployment to 8th Air Force training bases such as Langford Lodge in Northern Ireland where the knowledge gained from their combat experience was used to train the replacement crews which were about to enter the fray at bomber stations in England. The twenty five mission combat tour gave the crews a personal target of their own but even then the odds of an 8th Air Force crewman surviving his twenty five mission tour stood at only one in five with most crews never making it past their fifth mission.[8]

It was the magic 25 mission target yearned for by the crews that appears to have been the inspiration for Willy Wyler. With the introduction of the 25 mission tour Wyler decided to now concentrate his efforts into one single film project. This was to now make a full colour twenty minute short documentary to tell the story of the first B-17 bomber and crew to complete 25 bombing missions over German occupied Europe. As it would turn out, however, *the first* was to have different connotations. Wyler now considered suitable bombers to be the star of his short documentary. In any case this production would give its viewers a fly on the fuselage experience of a single 8th Air Force bomber and its crew based in England as it waged war against Nazi Germany on its twenty fifth mission. The film would focus on all aspects of the bomber and its crew on the day of their twenty fifth mission – preparations on the ground, the bombing mission in the air and the eventual safe return to base.

Later, on June 1st 1943 and on the same day that Dan McGovern arrived at Chelveston, 8th Air Force overall commander Major General Ira Eaker[9] issued a memo directing that a single bomber and a specially selected crew which had completed 25 missions be chosen to be sent back to the United States on a war bond tour.[10] Eaker's directive now ran parallel to Wyler's earlier instigated and ongoing film subject matter. With this convergence the first assignment was handed to Dan McGovern and his team on arrival in England – to film suitable material for Wyler's *Project 114/ 25 Missions.*[11] However, the war bond tour would be long completed before Wyler's film documenting the exploits of *his* bomber and *its* crew on their last raid would hit the cinemas. Mack remembered: "My particular job then was to support that documentary team."

Before McGovern's arrival Wyler had earlier centred his attentions on a B-17 called *Invasion 2*. He had filmed considerable footage of her only for the bomber to be shot down on a raid to Bremen on 17th April 1943. Now, instead of *Invasion 2,* a number of other B-17s at various different bomb groups became strong contenders to be the star bomber of Wyler's new documentary. Amongst those now in contention were *Connecticut Yankee* and *Delta Rebel 2* both of the 91st Bomb Group based in nearby Bassingbourn and *Hell's Angels* and *Jersey Bounce* both assigned to the 303rd Bomb Group based at nearby Molesworth airfield eight miles away from Chelveston. A B-17 called *Murder Incorporated* of the 385th Bomb Group based at Great Ashfield airfield 70 miles to the east was also approaching twenty five missions.[12] One Chelveston B-17 bomber in contention too was *Old Bill* of the 422nd Bomb Squadron. Mack McGovern filmed on the ground with the detachment's many cameras including Eyemos and Mitchells and with one particular Mitchell GC he liked and for which he had assembled and matched a nice selection of lenses.

However, by now his favourite camera for his ground work was of a tried and tested if somewhat unusual design. This was the Akeley 35mm Pancake motion picture camera. It was referred to as the *pancake* due to its central body which was circular like a drum. It had been purposely designed for exterior documentary work and was particularly useful when utilised to capture fast action and when shooting from difficult angles. The Akeley had been used extensively during World War 1 and now, despite approaching obsolescence, it was as rugged and reliable as ever and it had always been a quiet running camera. This latter attribute was important as by now the Akeleys on the inventory of the United States Army Air Forces could facilitate sound.

Dan and his team soon learned that they could produce nice tight little stories about the bombers and their crews with only 100 feet of colour film not just on the ground but later in the air too. "We could do 20 scenes in which you establish the airplane, establish the crew, establish the bombing up of the airplane and later on go on the mission with them and tell their story in four minutes." For the first month at Chelveston Mack and his team also filmed and documented other aspects of everyday life on the base mainly for the purposes of Wyler's documentary. They filmed at a time when the 8th Air Force was preparing to probe deeper into enemy held territory fighting an aerial war of attrition thousands of miles from home.

The Akeley 35mm movie camera. This became Dan McGovern's favourite camera for filming on the ground. It had a unique design, excellent low light capabilities and also a quickly deployed tripod. **Photo: John Weinstein courtesy of Field Museum, Chicago GN92519_036Ad.**

They filmed the mission briefings and then the crews as they were taken to their respective B-17s out on the field on their concrete hard stand areas where they prepared for take-off. They filmed the B-17s as they taxied one behind the other on the outer perimeter track. They filmed the mass take-offs and the formations as they assembled over the airfield. They filmed the officers and men based at the elevated control tower as they played their important part in what was the careful choreography of aerial warfare being played out at all bases all across East

Anglia and the Midlands of England on any given mission day. They filmed also the often overlooked work of the maintenance personnel as they maintained and repaired the bombers and also the efforts of the ordnance personnel as they *bombed up* the B-17s and replenished the ammunition for the machine guns in preparation for each new mission.

As dawn breaks a B-17 takes off from Chelveston for another mission.
Photo: The Ken Snyder Collection/Eric Barko.

Mack and his small team soon learned a few tricks to get the best out of their filming efforts. "If we could we usually avoided filming the unit designation marking on the rear vertical stabiliser of a B-17 so that the footage could be used anywhere and once you're filming a plane in the air you can't tell the difference – a plane's a plane. It was easier to intercut the film that way." Dan explained that if they needed to emphasise a unit designation they filmed the unit marking up close on the tail and with careful editing, intercut that into where it was needed in the film. "That was a little secret we had but we had to do it that way otherwise there would be too much footage shot that could not be used." The 305th was already well on its way to completing a total of 480 combat missions overall by war's end.[13]

McGovern and his team also captured on film the tension and the anticipation of the seemingly endless waiting for the bombers to return. He filmed the increased activity in the control tower, the gathering of almost everybody on the base at Chelveston into groups of all sizes as everyone looked upward, listened intently and scanned the sky eagerly in all directions for the first faintest sign of the first bombers and their crews to return. When they did arrive back over the field, McGovern filmed the returning B-17s overhead often trailing smoke and firing flares indicating wounded on board or technical trouble arising from battle damage.

He filmed the ambulance and fire crews as they mobilised to be ready to render assistance; the landings and often the crash-landings and the wounded being removed from B-17s often so heavily damaged that it was a miracle that these aircraft returned at all. He filmed too the dead and the often bloodied remains which were always reverently removed. McGovern and his cameramen filmed those same bombers being expertly repaired by the maintenance crews overseen by their crew chiefs and made ready to run the gauntlet of German flak and fighters again and again and again. So many bombers were not returning at all. They filmed also the worried dejected faces and captured the terrible sense of sorrow and loss.

By comparison McGovern and his team filmed the men off - duty and relaxing in whatever ways and whenever they could. In fact, they filmed just about every aspect of life on the busy airfield that was Station 105 at Chelveston. In addition to his work for Wyler and in keeping with the mainstream purpose of his posting in England, McGovern and his team filmed the men and aeroplanes of the United States 8th Army Air Force for other reasons. In this regard Dan recounted: "There was some well-rounded coverage made and nearly all of this was shot in 35mm black & white with some special material shot in 16mm colour."

*Technical Sergeant Dan McGovern pictured with an Eyemo 35mm camera
in England in late 1943 and shortly before he was commissioned as an
officer. The three service 'hash' bars on his left forearm sleeve denote his nine
years Air National Guard and full-time enlisted service up to that point.*
Photo: The McGovern family/AFHRA.

Mack took footage that could be scrutinised by Air Force experts for tactical purposes time and time again as the bombers strove for improvement at every level. Such footage was also used in training films and to tell the story of the 8th Air Force on its deployment in England for morale as well as historical purposes. All wide and varied footage received from the Combat Camera Units was also checked for what was called *newsreel value.*

Newsreel pools had also been formed by each branch of the United States Armed Forces into which news stories, photographs and film footage was supplied or pooled to support the many American, Allied and other worldwide media organisations always hungry for war information at the time. "Most exposed film was sent back to New York," Mack remembered. This was to the First Motion Picture Unit's Combat Picture Section. This was another specialist detachment based on the sixth floor of a multi-storey office block at 1 Park Avenue, New York[14] where all footage was firstly processed after which the team there decided then how best it could be utilised for the Army Air Forces.

Footage with newsreel value was distributed from there once it conformed to wartime censorship regulations. Mack: "If the services had not created that type of arrangement for the newsreels they would have been bugged by hundreds and hundreds of news people so instead we had the news pool and the stories and images went to everybody." All footage was also stored at this FMPU New York office.

It was around this time also that the United States Army Air Forces was also preparing to launch its own new informative in house newsreel service *Army Air Force Combat Weekly Digest.* For this new production regular wide and varied content would be required from every combat camera unit operating throughout the world. It was also FMPUs Combat Film Section in New York which filtered all incoming material from the Combat Camera Units around the world for the new weekly digests. The first was screened in August 1943 and this and all subsequent digests until the end of the war focused on all aspects of the recent activities of all United States Army Air Forces.

Another bomber and its crew stationed at Chelveston that was strongly in contention to be the star of Wyler's documentary was *SNAFU* of the 422nd Bomb Squadron. *SNAFU* was one of the original bombers with which the 305th Bomb Group had been equipped when it arrived in England. However, it had acquired something of a love/hate reputation with the many crews who flew on her due mainly, to ongoing maintenance issues. *SNAFU* was well known to be contrary. Many superstitious airmen on the base at Chelveston had come to the conclusion that the bomber simply didn't like being called *SNAFU*, that it hurt her pride and that she showed it. She was sulking and abjectly refused to respond to good treatment.

Given that it was common practice in the 305th for crews to fly many different B-17s on the base, some pilots flatly refused to fly *SNAFU*. Still, despite the misgivings, *SNAFU* continued to always take her various crews home despite often significant battle damage. During the time McGovern was at Chelveston *SNAFU* was flown most often by Lt. Clifford Pyle and his crew. Dan filmed hundreds of feet of film of *SNAFU* and her crew on the ground. "In fact I filmed a six minute clip of *SNAFU*. The *f* in that stands for something naughty but we liked that plane so much that we documented the way of life of the crew – how they worked together as a team, how they had fun and prepared to go into battle together."

SNAFU'S CHANGE OF ATTITUDE

As much as Dan wanted *SNAFU* and her crew to be the stars of Wyler's documentary, it became apparent that perhaps the name *SNAFU* might not be the most appropriate name to introduce to the American public. This was given what the letters of the acronym actually stood for. In any case, there were already moves afoot to change her name from among Lt. Pyle's crew, from other flight crews as well as from her ground crew. This was because of *SNAFU's* long history of stubborn and sometimes unexplained mechanical problems – engines refusing to start, low oil pressure, starter burnouts, a leaky oxygen system, a heating system which would not work and turret trouble. A name change therefore might change the attitude of the B-17.[15]

Dan and his cameramen also played their part in persuading the crew of *SNAFU* to change the name of their bomber to something else. "I spoke to Lt. Pyle and the crew for about ten minutes one particular day in an effort to persuade them to change the name." Subsequently, the name *SNAFU* was at least painted over with matt olive drab paint. For a while she was simply referred to by the last three numbers of her tail code – *614*. Then, after considerable thought and several more raids, *SNAFU* was soon renamed *We The People* after the first three words of the American Constitution. The name was chosen possibly with a view to being the star of Wyler's documentary and the bond tour Stateside in order to better encapsulate a bomber with which everybody back home would best identify. In any case, it was remarked by many on the base, that almost immediately her oil pressures went up, the engines ran smoother and when parked all four of her propellers were always perfectly aligned. Her frequent mechanical troubles soon became a thing of the past. Dan filmed additional footage of the bomber and its crew with its new moniker now confident that it would be the B-17 chosen for the bond drive and to be the star of William Wyler's documentary.

VISITING DIGNITARIES

McGovern filmed many dignitaries and VIPs who visited Station 105 at Chelveston and many of those made their appearances there in the first week of July 1943. The first of these to arrive on McGovern's watch was World War 1 American fighter ace Eddie Rickenbacker. Actor and comedian Bob Hope, singer and actress

Frances Langford and musician Tony Romeno also arrived there as part of a USO[16] tour and put on a show in the main hangar. In addition to the mainstream everyday footage captured on the base by Mack and his cameramen such additional film content would also be screened in cinemas for the folks back home in America and even further afield.

Lt. Clifford Pyle and the crew of the newly re-named B-17 'We The People'.
Photo courtesy of United States Air Force Historical Research Agency.

That same week American war correspondent William Shirer visited the base and was photographed directly in front of *We The People* as he chatted with her crew about their exploits with the bomber. All *We The People's* propellers were perfectly aligned and everything was looking good. The B-17 and her crew were poised for greatness.

Also in July of 1943, but back in America, Wyler had realised the full potential of his subject matter. He had decided to extend his original Two Reel short documentary into something considerably longer and had, by now, also settled on the B-17 that was to be the star of his new production.[17] Despite the fact that both he and William Clothier had by now filmed on combat missions and had amassed considerable material, Wyler now needed much more additional combat footage to interlace throughout the now to be extended *Project 114/25 Missions* film project and he needed the cameramen of Detachment B to get it. The time had now come for Technical Sergeant McGovern himself to take to the air on the increasingly dangerous B-17 combat raids over enemy-occupied Europe.

By his own choice Big Mack would fly on the first one himself. "Our mission was to photograph combat flights, to get pictures of the targets and of enemy action. As I was the NCO in Charge I did the first one myself rather than send someone else to do it." Flying with the 305th was going to be a dangerous assignment and McGovern knew it. By war's end a total of 760 USAAF flight crew based at Chelveston alone would lose their lives in bombing raids over occupied Europe.[18] As it would turn out, several of Sergeant McGovern's Detachment B cameramen would be amongst them.

---

1. William Wyler – *The Life and Films of Hollywood's Most Celebrated Director*, Gabriel Miller, p222.
2. *History of the First Motion Picture Unit*, 1944, Scanlan.
3. A photograph of Wyler and his team taken as they stood at a B-17 in Bassingbourn has an accompanying caption on the rear stating this information.
4. Apart from McGovern's first hand accounts additional background information on how Wyler came to make *The Memphis Belle – A Story of a Flying Fortress* has been gleaned from *History of the First Motion Picture Unit*, 1944, Scanlan; *Five Came Back,* Mark Harris *and Armed With Cameras*, Peter Maslowski.
5. Tannenbaum was filming with the 93rd Bomb Group. According to Peter Maslowski's book *Armed With Cameras,* this was his very first combat mission.
6. *History of the First Motion Picture Unit*, 1944, Scanlan.
7. According to *Combat Crew Rotation, World War 2 and Korean War*, Historical Studies Branch USAF Historical Division (1968) new 8th Air Force

commander, Brigadier General Ira Eaker, on 31st December 1942, ordered that all combat crews *will be relieved from duty on completion of 30 sorties and 200 hours.* Major General Jimmy Doolittle subsequently adopted a rotation policy of 25 – 30 sorties and 150-200 hours. Subsequent discussions between Generals Eaker, Doolittle and Major General Carl Spaatz resulted in the latter option being adopted as *a reasonable basis for rotation.* This, of course, left some latitude to increase the mission cap to 30 which subsequently resulted in mid 1944 much to the disgruntlement of the airmen who yearned for home and loved ones. The mission tour was further increased to 35 by late 1944.

8. National Museum of the Mighty Eighth Air Force and *The Eighth Air Force V The Luftwaffe* , The National WW2 Museum, New Orleans respectively.

9. General Carl Spaatz had assumed command of the 12th Air Force in North Africa in December 1942.

10. Dr. Harry Friedman, Memphis Belle Memorial Association (MBMA) presentation, National Museum of the US Air Force, 18 April 2018.

11. *History of the First Motion Picture Unit,* 1944, Scanlan.

12. B-17 *Delta Rebel 2,* as stated of the 91st BG also possibly completed 25 missions first. However, it was shot down on a raid over Gelsenkirchen on 12th August 1943 – *Masterfortress Log,* Dave Osbourne. The 93rd BG flew liberators. In February 1943 a B-24 Liberator of the 93rd Bomb Group *Hot Stuff* became the first 8th Air Force heavy bomber to complete 25 combat missions. However, on May 3 1943, en route to the United States for its war bond tour, the bomber crashed in Iceland due to bad weather killing 13 on board including USAAF Lt. General Frank Andrews. There was one survivor. – National Museum of the United States Air Force.

13. 305th Bombardment Group Memorial webpage/Chelveston-cum-Chaldecott Parish Council.

14. Whenever possible undeveloped negative footage was shipped from Air Forces all around the world in an Air Transport Command pouch to this New York office on a daily basis. *History of the First Motion Picture Unit,* Scanlan.

15. Lt.Clifford Pyle, pilot, 305th Bomb Group Stories, Chris Coffman.

16. United Services Organisations. Many big name entertainers did their bit for the US war effort by entertaining the troops in USO concerts in far flung theatres of war.

17. In his book *Five Came Back* author Mark Harris states that during July 1943 William Wyler convinced the 8th Air Force to send the crew of the bomber chosen to Hollywood so that their voices could be recorded for his new documentary. The narrative also states that the fact that the crew had become national heroes was ample justification for a more substantial film.

18. 305th Bomb Group Historical FB Group.

THE ELEVENTH MAN

That Nuisance Bastard Cameraman

DAN MCGOVERN FLEW his first combat mission on 14th July 1943. He would hitch a ride on a B-17 of the group's 365th Bomb Squadron named *Moonbeam McSwine,* named after the unkempt but voluptuous female character in the *L'il Abner* syndicated newspaper comic strip created by cartoonist Al Capp. At 6 feet five inches tall, Mack gave an undertaking to skipper, 1st Lt. Jack Kney, that he would try his best not to get in the way as he sought out the best camera angles throughout the aircraft as he filmed. Kney was known throughout the 305th for smoking cigars through his oxygen mask when flying missions. McGovern would base himself at the radio operator's station for the duration of the mission and film mainly from in and around the middle of the aircraft.

As a combat cameraman, Dan was not technically designated as flight crew. Nonetheless, he would face the same dangers and extremes as everybody else on board on these missions. "I was the 11th man and as such at the start I was referred to as *that nuisance bastard cameraman.* On the surface of it I was always made welcome but I also got the impression that crews did not like having an eleventh man on board. I always thought that they felt that it upset their tight equilibrium as a unit and that some also felt that it compromised their luck holding out. So I had to earn my keep." However, to surmount this problem, Dan had already figured out a novel way to gain a measure of acceptance with the crew members with whom he would fly. On the morning of the mission McGovern was called in the early hours.

Breakfast in the NCO's Mess Hall of Station 105, in what were known as the Communal Areas of the base, was usually powdered egg and sausage but if the crews received fresh eggs instead of the powdered variety it was usually indicative of a very difficult mission ahead. As with all bomber crew members about to go on operations, eating and drinking, although necessary of course, was kept to an absolute minimum. The reason for this was that whilst possible, answering the call of nature at altitude in freezing temperatures wearing a cumbersome flying suit and strapped into a parachute harness would be a challenge to say the least.[1] The fact that the crews had been woken up at all was usually indicative that the mission would go ahead. The egg for breakfast that morning had been of the powdered variety.

After breakfast the General Briefing for the raid took place in Building 27. This was a large brick structure located a half mile or so from the Communal Areas across the airfield in the Operations Block and not far from the station's main entrance. All combat cameramen flying missions from Station 105 at Chelveston attended the mission briefing in Building 27. Many of the crew members availed of transport to get there but, in the peace and quiet and first light of the morning, many officers and NCOs preferred instead to walk from their respective Mess Halls. This took them through the buildings in the adjoining communal areas to a now well-worn earthen pathway and across the airfield to the Briefing Room. It was here that the latest target for the 305th Bomb Group would be revealed. Once inside, prior to the start of the briefing, Lt. Kney introduced Dan to the other members of his crew. In addition to Kney the flight crew comprised his co-pilot Lt. Jim Oakley; Navigator 2nd Lt. Edward

S. Child; Bombardier 2nd Lt. Andrew P. Demitropoulos and Flight Engineer and Top Turret Gunner T/Sgt. Charlie V. Kiefer. The remainder of the crew was designated as the combat crew.

The crew with which Dan McGovern flew his first mission to Villacoublay. Lt. John Kney is seated in the pilot's seat with LTR on Top Turret: Radio Operator T/Sgt. Doug Lane, Co-pilot Jim Oakley and Bombardier Andrew P. Demitropoulos. Standing on the B-17's wing are LTR: Ball Turret Gunner S/Sgt. Lyle E. Lyons, Right Waist Gunner S/Sgt. Kenneth Snyder, Tail Gunner S/Sgt. Lewis A. Hill and Navigator Lt. Edward S. Child. Crouching in front are Left Waist Gunner S/Sgt. Emil E. Lewison and Engineer and Top Turret Gunner Charles Kiefer. It is more than likely that the B-17 is the 'Moonbeam McSwine' which this crew considered to be 'their' aeroplane. **Photo: *The Ken Snyder Collection/Eric Barko.***

All NCOs on all bombers in the United States Army Air Forces held the minimum rank of sergeant.[2] This was the *Moonbeam McSwine's* crew and although they occasionally flew other B-17s, they considered the *Moonbeam their* aeroplane.[3] Just as he had with *SNAFU* and her crew, McGovern would get to know them well. Mack took a seat with the rest of the crew. They were now among over 200 B-17 crew members facing a large operations map which covered a gable wall of the building. The map, however, was largely obscured with a blackout blind. The flyers always waited in anticipation for the blind to be drawn to see where they were going and the target that was to be hit as some targets were feared more than others. Order was called and the briefing commenced. The moment that all crew members referred to as *The Highlight* had come.

After some brief introductory words the Briefing Officer rolled up the blind revealing the map of southern England, the English Channel and most of continental Europe. There was a noticeable collective sigh of relief throughout the room. A long red tape could now be seen on the map running from the base at Chelveston to the target and between which were a number of mission checkpoints. The first was the AP – the Assembly Point or Splicer Point which was located over the English Channel. This was the rendezvous point where twenty B-17s of the 305th would form up into their combat wing with the 92nd and 306th Bomb Groups.

The route then changed course in a dog leg where the red ribbon now ran across the French coast and on to another pin on the map. This pin was close to the end of the ribbon and slightly short of the target itself. This pin identified the IP – the Initial Point. This was where the bombers would turn for the target to commence their bomb run.[4] The Briefing Officer put the end of his pointer stick where the ribbon ended. He then declared: "Gentlemen, the target for today is Villacoublay, Paris."

McGovern's first raid would be the 8th Air Force's mission Number 73 against the DuNord Aircraft Works, one of several manufacturing facilities throughout the German Reich pressed into service by the Nazis to assemble the much feared Focke Wulf 190 fighter. Also to be targeted in Villacoublay was a large aircraft depot, aviation machinery workshops and surrounding airfields from which the German Luftwaffe flew offensive operations. Villacoublay was the primary target and one of three to be hit by the 8th Air Force in German occupied France that day.

The 8th had bombed Villacoublay before and raids on this and other German aviation related targets had been earlier devised as part of *Operation Pointblank* by the USAAF's General Carl Spaatz and the RAF's Air Marshal Arthur *Bomber* Harris in June 1943. *Operation Pointblank,* which had commenced on June 10th, was aimed at disrupting production at the factories supplying the German Luftwaffe with aircraft as well as the Luftwaffe's support infrastructure. This was particularly in advance of the overall Allied invasion of continental Europe which was being planned at the time.

MILK RUNS AND ESCAPE KITS

This target was three hours flight time from Chelveston. It was what the crews referred to as a Milk Run as it was considered an easier raid with less risk and a far better chance of survival. This meant less exposure for the B-17s and their crews to either Luftwaffe fighters or to the primary defensive ground anti-aircraft gun positions known as flak batteries. Each flak battery comprised four or six guns. German anti-aircraft defence was also the responsibility of the Luftwaffe, the German Air Force and its flak guns were the greatly feared 88mm and 105mm heavy cannon. Both were very accurate and very effective even beyond an altitude of five miles.

Flak fire was leading fire and was always aimed at an area of sky in which Allied aircraft would be by the time the flak rounds exploded. The German fire control personnel, the plotters who supported the flak batteries over which Allied aeroplanes flew, targeted their oncoming enemy aircraft therefore by anticipating their position. This was achieved using optical rangefinders but the flak guns were also radar controlled. The plotters instructed the flak crews on the course, speed and altitude of the approaching formations and the guns were aimed and fired using repeatedly revised aiming points and altitudes. German flak shells travelled 1000 feet per second and could be pre-set to explode at any height sending hundreds of white hot metal shards in all directions killing, maiming or damaging anything within one hundred feet.

This combined defence method accounted for more Allied aeroplanes than enemy fighters and 40,000 flak guns protected Reich-held territory. The heavy flak guns were also augmented by many tens of thousands of smaller calibre secondary defensive rapid fire cannon and machine gun positions. Areas where enemy flak was anticipated along a mission route were referred to by the American flyers as *Flak Alleys*. Due to the relatively short flight time on the Villacoublay raid there would be no accompanying fighter cover with the bombers on McGovern's first raid. Instead, five YB-40 gunships would fly throughout the American formation as a deterrent to German fighters. These were modified very heavily armed B-17s.

Furthermore, due to the shorter distance, petrol consumption of the four big Wright Cyclone nine cylinder radial engines on each bomber would be less of an issue for the crews. As it would transpire, however, Milk Runs would be few and far between for Dan McGovern as he flew, camera in hand, into the teeth of Hitler's Third Reich. Given the target, there was also some irony in the fact that this was also Bastille Day, France's national holiday and when its population normally celebrated its liberty. However, this was already France's third Bastille Day under the yoke of Nazi occupation.

With the help of a projector located in the middle aisle of the Briefing Room, the crews were shown large aerial reconnaissance photographs and additional maps of the target. Useful navigational landmarks were also pointed out. An intelligence officer then gave estimations of expected flak and fighter hazards enroute and over Villacoublay and a meteorologist gave details of expected weather conditions along the route and over the target at which point bombing altitudes where announced. Secondary targets were also revealed. These were to be bombed instead in the event that the primary, for any reason, could not.

Another ribbon on the map displayed the route away from the target to the Rally Point, the RP, where the groups would reform again into their various wings for the mass formation flight home. Details of flight leaders for the various B-17 wings were also revealed and the importance of maintaining tight formations to maximise the effectiveness of the protective high, centre and low combat boxes stressed. Compass headings for the run onto the target and the day's radio frequencies were made known as were details of the type of bomb loads now on board the B-17s. 1000lb GP or General Purpose bombs or Incendiary bombs could be carried but for this mission the *Moonbeam* had been loaded during the night by the ordnance personnel with 10 X 500lb GP bombs.[5] Even now, outside as the briefing continued, individual ordnance as well as maintenance ground crew specialists were still undertaking last minute checks on all the bombers which were flying to Villacoublay that morning.

Each B-17, now fully laden, was 30 tons in weight.[6] Emergency landing airfields in Southern England were also pointed out to be used by returning B-17s stricken with battle damage or by fuel shortages and unable to make Chelveston. After questions were taken from the floor the station commander then gave a pep talk to his airmen and wished them luck. Watches were then synchronised in what was called *Hack Time*[7] and the briefing concluded with the dismissal of the crews.

All crew members were also given escape kits which would be of use if they were shot down and on the run in enemy territory. Catholic, Protestant and Jewish chaplains at this point also made themselves available for a few moments of collective prayer and individual reflection. As with most raids at least some of these young American flyers would not be coming back. The crew members now left the main Briefing Room and made their way individually to a series of huts close by where more detailed information was imparted to them. Lt. Kney was handed his

Battle Folder with the very latest maps and other information pertaining to the mission about to be flown. All these additional briefings were to ensure that the group as a unit would drop the tightest pattern of bombs possible resulting in heavy damage being inflicted on the fighter factories and airfields of Villacoublay.

EXTREMES OF COLD

McGovern rejoined Kney and his crew and next went to the Personal Equipment Room. This was more commonly known as the Crew Room. It was here that crew members picked up their heavy protective leather shearling flying suits and other items of flying equipment. At altitude the B-17 bomber was un-pressurized. With its large often open dorsal hatch above and with the waist gunners just aft keeping vigil against marauding German fighters through open gun ports the radio compartment where McGovern would be located would be largely open to the elements.

At a cruising altitude as high as 29,000 feet, where the B-17's performance was at its most efficient, this meant extremes of cold throughout most of the bomber of between – 40 to – 60 degrees Fahrenheit. The pure natural wool fleece of the shearlings and the matching heavy boots and mittens provided considerable insulation from these extremes. The thick leather from which the flight jacket, pants, flight boots and mittens were made was tanned brown on the outside and retained the raw natural wool on the inside.

The white wool fleece was turned outward to form the collar, bottom seam and cuffs of the exterior of the flying jacket. These shearling jackets, trousers and flight boots were oversized to facilitate other items of uniform clothing being worn underneath. In the temperature extremes at altitude if Dan even touched the metal of his camera with his bare hands continuously for too long the skin would freeze and stick to the metal.[8] Furthermore, prolonged skin contact with the B-17's glass or even the plastic transparent plexiglass in the bomber's turrets and nose could also cause frostbite.

As another measure to help counter the extreme cold combat crews were also issued with a one-piece light blue cotton step-in electrically heated flying suit. This was the *Blue Bunny* and contained copper heating elements sewn into the material similar to a modern electric blanket. It warmed a crew member's torso and extremities. The suit was plugged into the B-17s electrical system and turned on to an adjustable temperature. The result was comfort, warmth and mental alertness at altitude resulting in greater concentration on the job at hand.

Mack and all the crew members also turned out their pockets in the Crew Room and placed every small item of personal property in numbered fabric pouches which would be redeemed on their return – most of the time. This was to avoid letting the Germans glean any small piece of intelligence from personal items in the event that a crew member was either captured or killed in action. Some crew members donned their heavy shearlings and Blue Bunny at this stage. Others preferred to do so a little later at the B-17. All picked up their parachute and its separate harness, their oxygen mask and hose, *Mae West* life preserver and their bailout oxygen bottle.[9] Dan was also issued with a soft supple leather flying *helmet* incorporating goggles and headphones and with a throat microphone for the B-17's intercom to allow him to communicate with the rest of the crew. Snyder and Lewison, the two waist gunners, meanwhile, also picked up their single .50 calibre Browning machine guns from the armourer's shop where they had been cleaned, oiled and stored after the previous raid.[10]

Dan and his host crew and all the other bomber crews were now driven in a motley selection of well used trucks and jeeps to the Dispersal Areas. A long concrete taxiway or perimeter track surrounded the entire base and its three converging runways. The frying pan shaped hardstands on which the B-17s were parked or *dispersed* were 150 feet apart and ran onto the perimeter track. These hardstands were the Dispersal Areas. They ensured easy access to the runways but this dispersal arrangement also lessened potential damage to aircraft in the event of either enemy attack or a *bombing up* accident.[11]

It was now 5.30am and much brighter but it was still just under an hour from take-off. This allowed ample time for the waist gunners to fit their Brownings to their mounts and if required, for all crew members to liaise with ground crew personnel, to undertake their own checks on the B-17 and to make any personal preparations for the mission ahead. As always at this point the aircrews became a little more quiet and subdued. Now on the concrete hardstand and under and around the *Moonbeam McSwine,* what remaining Blue Bunnies, heavy shearlings, headsets, throat mikes and other essential pieces of flight equipment that had to be worn along with the cotton flying suit or standard uniform pants and shorts were put on and either zipped or buttoned up. Then, by assisting each other, the yellow Mae Wests and the heavy duty cotton weave parachute harnesses were strapped on securely and every strap and buckle tightened snugly. Assistance was also given to the waist gunners to don their heavy armoured flak jackets which had earlier been delivered to the hardstand along with protective steel helmets for the crew.

Unlike the standard M1 helmet with which Dan and some of the other crew members had been issued, the waist gunners' helmets had been specially customised with additional steel flap panels added to the sides to afford more protection. For now everyone simply clutched their helmets which would be worn later. For Dan walking in the thick leather flying attire with his box of cameras, his parachute and grasping his helmet and other equipment was restrictive. The B-17 flight deck on the other hand, had engine heat directed there providing some warmth from the extreme cold at altitude to those in the front section of the bomber. As a result the pilots and other members of the flight crew, unlike their combat crew colleagues, usually compromised in some way or other to wear less of the protective but restrictive shearlings.

Lt. Kney now gave a final briefing underneath the nose of the *Moonbeam McSwine* after which its crew members and Mack, now along with a second passenger, dispersed and clambered aboard their B-17. In addition to McGovern the 365th Squadron Commander, Major Charles Normand, was flying on the *Moonbeam* as an observer. He was now the twelfth man.[12] Each member of the flight crew threw his parachute and flight bags into the aircraft ahead of him before using a small set of steps to then enter the flap hatch located six feet off the ground and beneath the port side of the nose. Once inside the hatch was closed behind them. Dan followed the combat crew members into the aircraft via a second hatch door located on the starboard side and near the tail of the aeroplane. Each crew member now made his way to his respective flight position and commenced his own preparations in advance of take-off.

The B-17 was already a hive of activity. Burdened with his equipment, Mack began his walk up the B-17's aluminium deck which, at a slight incline beneath him, clanked as each footstep on the bare metal deck echoed as the sound amplified within the closed aluminium fuselage. He made for the radio compartment. To get there he had to carefully negotiate his way past Lewison and Snyder, the two leather and flak jacket clad waist gunners. Both were located at rectangular windows opposite to and in very close proximity to each other towards the back of the plane. They were already busy visually checking their guns and ammunition feeds. Dan squeezed around the upper support mechanism of the belly ball turret assembly beyond which the radio compartment lay. Once there he carefully stowed his camera box on the deck of the radio room just in front of his seat which was forward on the starboard side of the compartment. Mack stowed his parachute. He had already been shown how to don it and also how and where to evacuate the bomber in a hurry in the event that it was hit and was going to go down.

Both Mack and Lane buckled themselves into their seats. Just ahead of the radio compartment McGovern could see into the B-17's bomb bay through the centre of which ran a narrow catwalk flanked by the plane's bomb racks. Each individual bomb had a fuse arming wire which was attached to the bomb rack in which it was held. With their safety pins having been manually removed, once the ten bombs were released over the target gravity armed the fuses for the remainder of their downward plunge. The narrow catwalk permitted access to and from the flight deck where lieutenants Kney and Oakley were already in their seats and had started their long sequence of pre-flight checks. Just below and beyond the flight deck was the nose section where navigator Lt. Child and Bombardier Lt. Demitropoulos were at their positions.

Everyone on board plugged the leads of their headsets and throat mics into the main intercom sockets. The intercom system was open circuit so everybody on board heard everybody else once they started to speak. They plugged their individual oxygen hoses into the regulators of the B-17's onboard oxygen system and then the electrical cables of their heated suits into the aircraft's 24 volt *Reosat* panels – all, that is, except Technical Sergeant Dan McGovern. "I couldn't get an electrically heated suit that would fit me so instead I wore a couple of pairs of long johns, two pairs of socks and a scarf which my Aunt Rose knitted for me!" Ever since he had initially enlisted back Stateside and with his oversized 6ft 5 inch frame, even regular uniforms had to be specially made for Big Mack McGovern.

For security reasons radio silence throughout the airfield was observed prior to the start of all missions. Now, towards the centre of the field, a sergeant stood twelve feet up from the ground on the exterior concrete viewing platform of the airfield's brick built olive green control tower. It was here that all twenty pilots in their B-17s on their designated hard stands were now looking. The sergeant pointed a flare gun into the air and pulled the trigger. A white flare raced skywards trailing smoke. This was the signal to *Start Engines*. First started was the port outer Number 1 engine with an initial whine of the kinetic starter motor and then a staccato of cracks as the nine cylinders fired, coughed and spluttered in sequence sending the propeller on its first revolutions before the engine caught and roared to life amid a plume of black smoke and fiery exhaust blasts. Next started was port inner engine Number 2, then the starboard inner Number 3 engine and finally the starboard outer Number 4.

Amid a drone of engine noise the B-17 now shuddered and vibrated to varying levels of intensity. With all propellers now rotating the pilot increased the throttle on the engines a little in order for them to reach the correct engine operating temperature. This was the engine *run-up*. After ten minutes or so another flare flew skywards from the control tower. This was the *Start Taxi* flare. All pilots signalled their ground crews below to remove the two wooden chocks from both undercarriage tyres which prevented the big bombers from obtaining the initial inertia needed to begin moving. Two ground crewmen, in a well synchronised movement, swiftly pulled the chocks from the front of the bomber's tyres and ran clear of the B-17 in different directions and away from its spinning propellers.

TAKE OFF

The *Moonbeam* was now ready to roll. Behind her the grass rippled intensely – forced flat by the backwash of the four big propellers. Now on the airfield the combined noise of 80 Wright Cyclone engines was deafening. Lt. Kney released the brakes. Very slowly now the wheels of the big B-17 began to move and its speed gradually increased. At a snail's pace the skipper guided the bomber from its hardstand until it slowly took its place in the procession of bombers that gradually edged its way along a section of the mass concrete taxiway and towards the end of the designated take-off runway. Amid the deafening crescendo of engine noise the twenty bombers lined up on the runway in two columns abreast of other but they would take off one by one in a well rehearsed order and each individual bomber crew now waited its turn. All but one of the B-17s was adorned with colourful names and noseart – *We The People* was there and *Big Moose, Flat Foot Floogie, Man O' War, Centaur, Lady Liberty, Sitting Bull, Windy City Challenger, Patches, Kayo, Sunrise Serenader, Rigor Mortis, Sizzle, Pappy's Hellions III, Hell-Cat* and *Me and My Gal* as well the *Lallah V* and *Vanishing Virgin*.[13] Now amongst their number was the *Moonbeam McSwine*.

305th Bomb Group B-17s lined up on the runway at Chelveston await the 'Go Order' to take off. **Photo: The Ken Snyder Collection/Eric Barko.**

Up ahead the lead aircraft waited, already lined up in its designated column at the start of the runway. Its pilot watched a signalman in a plexiglass dome atop a large chequered black and white flying control trailer out towards the centre of the field. Then, with his hand-held Aldis signal lamp pointed straight at the lead ship, the signalman flashed a continuous bright green light which was clearly seen by the pilots. This was the *Go Order* – the signal to take off.

The lead bomber started to move, quickly gathered speed, roared down the runway and soon took off. A steady stream of bombers then did the same every 20 to 30 seconds or so. In a matter of minutes the *Moonbeam* with Mack McGovern on board rolled to the start of the runway too and Lt. Kney swung the bomber into the wind. Ahead, a line of B-17s could be seen at varying heights and distances away as behind, the remaining planes in the two columns waited their turn to commence take off also.

Over the din of the engines the rest of the *Moonbeam's* crew heard Kney's crackled voice through their earphones telling them, as he released the brakes once more, that they were about to take off. The B-17 lurched forward. The *Moonbeam's* throttle control quadrant was in the Central Control Panel just in front of the instrument panel and centred between the pilot and co-pilot. With one hand each Kney and Oakley now simultaneously gripped the four throttle levers which protruded from the quadrant's top slots and eased these inboard and outboard engine controls forward in unison to achieve the necessary revs and manifold pressure required for take-off. The engines gradually roared louder and louder before becoming one continuous drone as the bomber quickly began to gather speed down the runway with every passing second.

Flight Engineer, Sergeant Kiefer, was now in his take-off position crouched between the shoulders of his skipper and co-pilot. He had set four propeller pitch control levers located on the front of the quadrant console to *full pitch* take off position and now firmly held them there. He would control all the propeller levers for the duration of the flight except when he was manning his top turret.[14] Paying close attention to the instrument panel, Kiefer had the additional responsibility of maintaining the correct RPM on each engine and he also called out the airspeed to the pilots during take-off and landing. The tail and waist gunners now temporarily joined Mack and Lane in the radio room until the B-17 was airborne. The transfer of their combined weight forward lightened the tail and in any case, the radio room was deemed to be the least dangerous place to be in the event of the bomber not making it into the air not that anywhere else would be any safer given their bomb load. McGovern now felt the sheer power of the four big radial engines in unison as he held on wherever he could to secure himself and his camera box a little better.

Through the small rectangular porthole to his right the concrete and grass could be seen rushing by. Further out were lines of vehicles and in the distance across a large expanse of grass, ground crew including crew chiefs, mechanics and other ground maintenance personnel could be seen. They watched *their own* B-17s intently just in case anything might not look right at the last minute or in case anything out of the ordinary might occur that might compromise an aircraft's performance on the mission.

Elsewhere on the airfield a fleet of red fire control emergency vehicles stood by with their crews also watching the take-off intently just in case. Beyond the grass and all along one section of the concrete perimeter track where the *Moonbeam* had been minutes before the last B-17s were now taxiing slowly and preparing to take off too. Each aircraft would go through exactly the same procedure as the *Moonbeam*. Their turn would come. There was now a distinct smell throughout the B-17 which was a fusion of petrol fumes, oil and leather. The vibration and shuddering of the aircraft was more intensive now as the big bomber trundled down the runway its speed increasing all the time. The roar of the engines of McGovern's heavily laden bomber remained constant as the aircraft approached the required 140 knots necessary for a safe take-off. Still holding on tight in the radio compartment Dan was apprehensive but then again, as always, so were all on board at this critical point. One mistake during take-off and the aircraft would crash and be blown to kingdom come.

Soon the bomber's deck was level. The tail was up and a few moments after that the ground fell away below them. The vibration suddenly lessened and the engine noise changed in pitch. The B-17 was airborne. Mack soon had his first bird's eye view of Chelveston air base as the *Moonbeam McSwine* banked and he heard the engines throttle back slightly as the gunners returned to their positions aft.

Now the aerial choreography began. Take-off had been arranged so that the 3 B-17s assigned to each V element took off one after the other. Each plane immediately formed up with its two sisters into the simple V element at approximately one thousand feet. Each element then flew westwards towards a signal omitted from a *splasher* navigational beacon located some ten miles away on the 8th Air Force maintenance depot outside the neighbouring village of Little Staughton. The airspace above and between Little Staughton and Chelveston was the group's designated Assembly Area.

Each element made a wide sweeping 180 degree turn and started to fly the first of a continuous circuit above the English countryside between both villages. On the ground as each remaining bomber took-off it too formed up into its flight of 3 and joined the aerial circuit above, each slotting into its correct element position. Two V elements merged, one flying above and slightly behind the other, into squadron formation.

As it continued to fly the circuit each designated squadron eventually formed into its correct Lead, High and Low position until finally, on or around three thousand feet, the 305th group combat box formation was complete. Hundreds of American bombers were doing exactly the same thing now at designated group assembly points having taken off from bases all over the Midlands and Southern England. The 305th formation now fell in behind a single brightly coloured Assembly or Formation B-17.[15] As this assembly ship now led the formation for one last pass over its base at Chelveston below, Mack snapped an aerial photograph of Station 105. From the *Go Order* was signalled to the lead bomber to take off to this point almost an hour had passed. The assembly ship now set course for the pre-determined Wing Assembly Point over the English Channel where the 305th would now rendezvous with the 92nd and 306th Bomb Groups to form into its combat wing mass formation in which it would fly to the target. This was the first checkpoint Mack had seen on the map back in the station Briefing Room.

As the bombers climbed at a rate of three hundred feet a minute the temperature dropped two degrees for every 1,000 feet gained. At the Air Force prescribed 10,000 feet it was time for everybody now to put on oxygen masks. 10,000 feet was precautionary but oxygen was certainly needed above 15,000 feet where the air was thinner. Failure to go on oxygen would mean passing out from anoxia after one minute and certain death after twenty. As Sgt. Lyons climbed down into his ball turret to take up his position there, McGovern checked his still and movie cameras and film stock and prepared his lenses for later. All was in order. The formation continued its climb above the clouds and was soon out over the English Channel.

---

1. In the event that crewmen did have to relieve themselves during the many hours of long missions they used a *relief tube* or *leak tube* located in the bomb bay. If they had to defecate there was a chemical toilet on board but this was disliked by the crews who instead often preferred to use cardboard boxes in which spare pre-filled ammunition boxes were supplied. In addition and in advance of each mission the ground crew for each B-17 also stowed empty standard metal .50 calibre machine gun boxes on the ship. Regardless of the method used these *Poop from the Group* containers where unceremoniously jettisoned from the bomber in flight. When this happened over Germany all too frequently it soon came to the notice of none other than Adolph Hitler himself who publicly rebuked the American bomber crews for dropping more than bombs over the Reich. Occasionally, this waste matter also struck other bombers behind much to the anger of their crew members.
2. This was so that in the event of being shot down and taken prisoner of war they would automatically be of sufficient rank to excuse them from manual

labour which lesser ranks were obliged to do in captivity under the Geneva Convention. Similar minimum rank structures existed in the RAF for the same reason.

3. Mission Diary of waist gunner Ken Snyder/Eric Barko.

4. Bomb runs were made into the prevailing wind. – William F. Pennebaker, 390th Bomb Group.

5. 303rd Bomb Group mission report. From all bomb groups researched for that mission the bomb load was the same.

6. *The Air Forces Story*, Chapter 14, *Schweinfurt and Regensburg,* (Film).

7. Every airman in the entire 8th Air Force had his watch set to exactly the same time. This, for example, was to ensure the punctual arrival of individual bomb groups at Assembly Points exactly one minute apart before they formed up into their respective combat wings. – B-17 pilot Arnold M. Singer, 390th Bomb Group via Raymond McFalone interview, YouTube.

8. McGovern and the combat cameramen may also have used fine silky Rayon undergloves which were sometimes worn under the heavy mittens in particular by USAAF navigators, radiomen and bombardiers. These may originally have been RAF issue. The soft Rayon gloves protected the hands sufficiently when the mittens had to be removed. They permitted short term tasks to be accomplished where greater dexterity was required with the heavier mittens being put on again as soon as possible. In Dan's case, however, his oversized hands may also have precluded their use.

9. The bail out oxygen bottle was either strapped to the wearer or later carried in a special pocket of the shearling pants. It permitted the crew member to breathe normally during freefall until they fell to an altitude at or lower than 10,000 feet where normal breathing was possible and after which the parachute could be deployed. Failure to use a bailout bottle during freefall could cause unconsciousness rendering the faller incapable of deploying his parachute in time. However, many crew members preferred not to carry their bailout bottle during the entire mission or even at all as, since it was under pressure, it could explode if hit by flak causing serious injury.

10. The waist guns were easily removed. The remaining guns were usually cleaned and oiled in situ on the bomber.

11. Halpenny, 1981 p11.

12. Waist gunner, Ken Snyder, identified a Major Charles *Norman* in a handwritten caption which accompanied a photograph in his collection (reproduced later in this chapter) taken of McGovern with the Kney crew and the *Moonbeam* following this mission. On closer examination of the photograph the author believes that this was in fact, Major Charles Normand and who, in all probability, piloted the B-17 at some stage of the flight.

13. Based on known B-17s serving with the 305th BG on 14th July 1943 as gleaned from *B-17 Fortress Masterlog* by Dave Osbourne. Some allowances must be made for B-17s which might have been unserviceable on this date.

14. Even today on airworthy B-17s the engineer retains responsibility for the propeller levers throughout the entire flight.

15. An Assembly or Formation aircraft was normally a war weary but flyable B-17 or B-24 that was painted in a more visible colour scheme so that it could clearly be seen by the aircraft they were to lead to the Assembly Point.

12

CAMERAS AND CONTRAILS

Filming Aerial Combat

ONCE AT THE Wing Assembly Point the brightly coloured Assembly B-17 turned around to return to base. The twenty bombers of the three squadrons of the 305th Bomb Group now formed up with 15 B-17s from the 92nd and another 24 bombers from the 306th Bomb Group to form what, at that stage, was called a *provisional* combat wing. In addition, also forming up there was a second provisional combat wing comprising 19 B-17s from the 303rd Bomb Group, 20 from the 379th and with another 18 bombers from the 384th Bomb Group[1] all configured in their own respective Lead, High and Low combat box formations. Each combat wing would fly one behind the other at the standard formation speed of 150 to 155mph.[2]

For his first mission McGovern would film from a formation of 116 B-17s which had now set course for France. Once above 10,000 feet McGovern had found that he had much to contend with before he even got around to pointing a camera at his subject matter. At this stage of the war most B-17s were still fitted with a constant flow oxygen system.[3] This system required the crewman to adjust his own oxygen regulator flow at his flight station in order to deliver sufficient oxygen to compensate for altitude. There were also extra oxygen ports to facilitate passengers. Changes in altitude were relayed to all on board and adjustments made on each individual regulator accordingly.

Once the crew went on oxygen during the mission the co-pilot or sometimes the bombardier, as the designated Oxygen Officer, called out for an oxygen check from all crew members every fifteen minutes to ensure that nobody had passed out. To allow crew members to move around the bomber above 10,000 feet, small standard *walk-around* oxygen bottles were provided at each crew station. These bottles were usually attached onto clothing or to a harness on the wearer's midriff area with a strong crocodile clip and had enough oxygen for up to twenty minutes depending on altitude and demand. The walk-around bottles could be recharged from the bomber's primary oxygen supply from a recharging valve on the regulator panel at any crew position in the bomber. Between his camera and oxygen adjustments McGovern had to concentrate hard. Now, somewhere over the Channel each gunner pointed his guns at an empty section of sky and test fired the Browning .50 calibres with a short burst of fire. The heavy guns on their cradles and mounts shook and vibrated violently with the repeated recoil as their intermittent reports broke through the drone of the bomber's engines.

Just behind Mack's position, dozens of spent brass cartridges pinged as the waist guns ejected them all over the deck. All the time the formation climbed higher and higher until it eventually levelled off at a cruising altitude of 29,000 feet. Mack again took his Baby Speedgraphic stills camera from his box. Now he would put the first phase of his *11th Man Plan* into action. He began to carefully move about the B-17 using his walk-around bottle taking photographs of every member of the crew. "I promised each of them that I'd send a picture back to their girlfriend, wife, parents or whatever in the States and that's what I did." The thought of loved ones back Stateside receiving a professionally taken picture of a crew member doing his duty in the war was appealing. He arranged it that these particular negatives were sent on to the FMPU's New York section where the photographs were printed and from there they were sent out all across the United States to the 305th crew members' loved ones with whom Dan flew. However, he would do much more than that.

Having removed the mittens, unloading and reloading the film slide holder at the back of the Speedgraphic camera was, at this point of the ascent, still relatively straightforward. However, as the *Moonbeam* gained altitude the temperature became noticeably colder to all on board and would soon start to have a bearing on the safe handling of the cameras. Apart from filming with his 16mm Filmos on this his first mission, Mack, like on all his subsequent missions, would take many still photographs that captured the crew as they flew, the other bombers around them and also aspects of the dangers to which all in the formation would soon be exposed.[4]

The skipper now ordered everyone on board to don his steel helmet as the *Moonbeam* flew closer to angrier skies. Mack welcomed the order. Already, given his 6 feet five frame, the twelve people on board and the many protrusions from the confined fuselage space, he had already managed to bang his head several times as he moved through the bomber. Dan, like everyone else, put his helmet on over his leather flying headgear and fastened the chinstrap. At this point the bombardier, Lt. Demitropoulos, entered the bomb bay from the cockpit area and just forward of Mack's position in the radio room. Standing on the narrow catwalk above the bomb bay doors he reached across to all bombs in the port and starboard racks and pulled out the ten arming pins. This was the first step in rendering the bombs live. Dan now returned the stills camera to his box.

As filming was going to be something of an unknown quantity until he ascertained what worked best for him up there, the box contained several different movie cameras. It was the colour footage needed for William Wyler that was foremost in Mack's mind. He had his 16mm Filmo but he also carried a Bell & Howell 16mm spring wound cassette camera which, given its smaller rectangular size and ease of loading and unloading might, Mack thought, prove useful. However, cassette cameras had a much smaller film capacity and captured less footage, so he retrieved his standard Filmo 16mm and wound up the action.

Up here, as it transpired, even winding the camera was a slow process. The protective leather mittens might also have inhibited the normally simple function of pushing the trigger button when shooting the Filmo. However, for his first ever mission Mack had anticipated this and had implemented a plan. "I cut a hole in my right mitten just where my index finger was. The mitten was big enough for me to stick my finger out for the few minutes when I was filming and then pull it back in again when I wasn't. That's how I filmed up there." Mack concentrated first on filming the crew of the *Moonbeam McSwine* each one at his position but working as a tightly knit team each reliant on the other. For filming with the colour 16mm cameras he would use both 15mm and 35mm lenses.

A FAVOURITE FILMING POSITION

The vast majority of his subject matter would, however, be external. From his training days in Nevada and from examining the interior of B-17s he had already identified the best filming positions from which he could easily switch around on the bomber to capture the type of exterior footage he needed. The position with the most potential he found, was shooting from the radio room through its wide hatch directly above. Here and with the plexiglass hatch cover open, he found that his 6' 5" height would work to his advantage. His head was exposed to the onrushing slipstream as it protruded considerably out this hatchway but the perspective it offered was worth it. Tightly wrapped up in his shearling leathers with Auntie Rose's scarf around his neck covering his throat and intercom mic and with his May West, leather flying helmet, steel helmet, goggles and oxygen mask, Mack carefully peered around him and prepared to film.

First, however, he took just a moment or two to take in the sight of an American bomber formation close up at altitude for the first time. As he looked around him, camera in hand, Mack was in awe at the spectacle of which he was a part – the sheer size of it, the statement that was this projection of American air power. What wonderful film material it was and he would capture it all.

This restored out-take frame from William Wyler's documentary shows an 8th Combat Camera Unit cameraman filming from the open radio room hatch of a B-17 bomber. This was McGovern's favourite filming position where his additional height was a great advantage. This cameraman films with a more compact cassette movie camera. Dan McGovern pioneered the use of these cameras for filming at high altitude in extreme cold conditions.
Restored Image: 'The Cold Blue' courtesy of director Erik Nelson.

It was a beautiful day[5] but in every direction the glare was considerable. Far below beneath the mass of bombers little cloud cover was now to be seen. Above, beyond and all around the *Moonbeam* brilliant white vapour contrails could be seen emanating from the engines of every B-17. The contrails resulted from the hot engine exhausts of the bombers as they moved through the cold moist air at altitude. The more moisture the whiter the contrail. Contrails varied from raid to raid but the downside was that often at high altitude large formations such as that in which McGovern was now flying could be seen approaching by German fighter pilots fifty miles away. Mack raised his Filmo to his goggled eye, filled the viewfinder and started to film.

B-17 vapour contrails as viewed aft beyond the vertical stabiliser of the 'Moonbeam McSwine'. This is one of the many scenes filmed by Dan McGovern from the radio room dorsal hatch during his first bombing mission which was to Villacoublay, France. A film frame from William Wyler's 'The Memphis Belle – A Story of A Flying Fortress'. **Restored Image: 'The Cold Blue' courtesy of director Erik Nelson.**

Firstly, shooting aft and upwards from the radio hatch, he captured a long wide angled scene of those contrails above and behind him including the Moonbeam's vertical stabiliser within shot. In other scenes he documented the many flying characteristics demonstrated by the other B-17s around him. He filmed close-ups of individual bombers nearby in the formation and other wider angled scenes to capture the sheer mass and depth of

B-17s in which he was flying as they headed to Villacoublay with their deadly cargo. Mack recounted: "By shooting through the radio hatch I could also look over my shoulders and see the engines and I could turn with the camera to face directly forward from there too."

McGovern would film also through the open waist gun ports, from the cockpit, through the plexiglass of the front bombardier's position and when the opportunity arose, from the top turret and tail gunner's positions. He captured the typical bobbing motion of many B-17s as they flew almost abreast of each other. He filmed too the pretty girls painted into the wonderful artwork on the side of the bombers' noses – the nose art. As the bombers flew on to their target Mack caught also the rotation of the top and ball turrets as the strong sun glinted off the plexiglass. He fondly remembered: "I think some of the most famous shots I ever got were taken on that particular mission."

Despite his extra under layers to make up for his lack of a heated suit, Dan found the intense cold extremely challenging. It was starting to bite and bite hard. "I was still colder than hell!" Up here it was regular to see a crewman remove his face mask for just long enough to clear ice from inside it before putting it back on again. An oxygen feed blocked with ice could be just as lethal as any German bullet. Mack noticed also that the extremes of cold had started to affect his Filmo. "It was so cold up there that I started to have camera problems. Several malfunctions occurred." At temperatures this cold the fine grade lubricating oil in the camera mechanisms frequently froze.[6] There was also a possibility that camera mainsprings could fail suddenly if wound to their full extremities.

In addition to these camera issues, McGovern soon discovered when he went about winding his Filmo, that the heavy sheepskin mittens were hardly conducive to the finer workings and handling of the motion picture cine-camera although it could be done. Loading and unloading film, for instance, represented a further challenge as to undertake this relatively simple but delicate task Mack had no option but to remove his mittens. He had to be very careful. At this altitude even the few minutes it took to undertake this task left the hands and fingers numbingly cold. Extended contact with the now freezing metal of the camera would undoubtedly result in frostbite.[7] The staggered formation continued on its south-easterly course and no sooner had it approached the French coast than Lt. Kney reported that the wall of flak bursts had appeared ahead of the formation.

A B-17 over its target pictured from the waist of a neighbouring bomber as it flies through a thick field of German flak. **Photo courtesy of AFHRA.**

The pilot warned everybody on board to now watch for the appearance of German fighters. Once the bombers crossed the enemy coast the 88mm and 105mm flak guns pummelled McGovern's formation filling the sky around and ahead of it with large black puffs of exploding anti-aircraft rounds. Shrapnel of all shapes and sizes started to fly in all directions and into many of the aircraft in Dan's formation, damaging many. As the formation continued along its course to Paris the flak field was particularly heavy and more accurate than expected. The waist gunners concentrated hard to spot any approaching enemy fighters in the far distance but unusually they had not appeared. The flak though now intensified and was more accurate the closer they got to the French capital. This was also largely due to the fact that, by now as instructed, the formation had commenced its decent from 29,000 feet. They would start their bomb run towards Paris, only twenty minutes away now, from the IP – the Initial Point – the third pin in the map. Still, there was no sign of the German fighters. Of the original 116 bombers which had taken off from southern England several hours earlier, fifteen had returned to base at various stages of the outward flight due mainly to mechanical trouble. 101 B-17s now arrived over the IP. In keeping with bombing procedure at this point the mass formation now broke temporarily into its smaller bomber groups to attack the targets below in a column one after the other.

THE BOMB RUN

The twenty bombers of McGovern's 305th Group, now tightened up as the *Moonbeam* and those ahead, left and right, above, below and behind approached the target. These bombers were now in perfect bombing formation as they started their bomb run to the targets at Villacoublay. Two minutes out from the target the lead 305th B-17 opened its bomb bay doors and Lt. Demitropoulos and all 305th bombardiers behind simultaneously did the same. Daylight and wind now flooded the centre portion of the B-17. With his camera reloaded, fully cranked and ready, Mack now crouched down in the radio room behind the step-through of the bulkhead which separated the radio room from the bomb bay immediately ahead. He peered down at the patchwork quilt which was the French countryside below him as it gradually became the urban suburbs of Paris. Now, at this crucial stage, each B-17 could not afford to slide out of position even to avoid the flak. This was the most crucial few minutes of the entire mission. Demitropoulos would not use his Norden bomb sight. Today he was simply a *toggler*. Having flicked its safety cover away, his hand was now on the bomb release toggle. He carefully watched the 305th's lead ship. Only the Lead Bombardier of McGovern's group formation peered down the eyepiece and crosshairs of his Norden bomb sight in the nose of the lead B-17. Making last minute allowances for wind drift, on his accuracy, now depended the success of all bombers in the group formation.[8]

As Demitropoulos concentrated and watched the lead ship closely the *Moonbeam* rocked and shook violently as heavy flak blasts exploded all around her. Shards of white hot metal tore through the aluminium skin of the *Moonbeam* at numerous locations causing varying degrees of damage. Even above the din of the B-17 and the flak bursts outside, the crew could always ascertain when flak found its mark on their bomber from its distinctive noise. It sounded just like gravel thrown on tinfoil.[9] As the lead bombardier concentrated, through the flak smoke in the otherwise clear morning light the crosshairs of his Norden bombsight edged closer to the target now 13,000 feet below. Steady…Steady…. Finally, the crosshairs were over the DuNord Works of Villacoublay – the final map pin.

At 8.13 hrs, he flicked his bomb release toggle and one by one his bombs started to fall. Demitropoulos did the same and it was also *Bombs Away* on the *Moonbeam*. With a clank of steel and aluminium each 500 pounder fell free of its rack on both sides of the catwalk. McGovern filmed the bombs as they fell free and followed them down as he felt the *Moonbeam* immediately rise up momentarily suddenly free of its payload. As always at this point the relief throughout the aircraft was palpable. All B-17s in McGovern's formation had released. He continued to film as finally, the carpet of bombs exploded all over the target below. He explained: "That was Bomb Spotting. It was part of the job to film the bomb hits so that intelligence could use that footage."

A photo taken from a 305th B-17 over the River Seine near Paris. Other B-17s are in formation below. This may have been taken just prior to the bomb run when the larger formation had already broken into its various group components. **Photo: The Ken Snyder Collection/Eric Barko.**

Bombs fall away at bottom of shot towards Villacoublay airfield, workshops and assembly plants as bombs dropped just ahead detonate. **Photo courtesy of the United States Air Force Historical Research Agency (AFHRA).**

He pointed out one photography problem which frequently arose capturing bomb spotting footage. "If it was overcast then frequently the bombs could not be easily seen falling away. As a result, when the film was developed, the bombs were hard to see in the film footage too."

As Dan filmed, Demitropoulos appeared for an instant just forward to quickly check that no bombs had been hung up. "All away!" he exclaimed to the pilots as he passed behind them on his return to the nose. Once there, Demitropoulos flicked a lever to his left and closed the bomb bay doors to restore some measure of the protection they provided to the interior of the *Moonbeam McSwine*. The overall bombing of the target was excellent with many enemy aircraft destroyed and with severe damage to hangars, workshops and assembly plants.[10] Kney now swiftly banked and peeled the *Moonbeam* away after the bombers ahead of him as they headed towards the *RP* – the Rally Point, were all the bomb groups would regroup once again into one massive formation for the run home. As the B-17s now climbed away to the north-west the flak began to ease. Then they came.

The pilots saw them first. The line of little black dots way in the far distance. "Bandits!, Bandits! at 12 O'Clock!" The wolves, as the airmen often referred to the enemy fighters, where gathering for the attack. Many crew members now turned up their individual oxygen flows on their regulator gauges to *Full*. It had been learned among the bomber crews since the first American daylight raid almost a year before in August 1942 that, once in the heat of battle and with adrenaline flowing, the greatly enriched oxygen supply helped to keep them sharper and better able to concentrate on the dangerous job at hand.

BANDITS AND BROWNINGS

The German fighter pilots would attack the formations from all angles but they had learned that head-on attacks, often from slightly above the highest lead elements of the formation, were the safest way to approach the mass formations given the lack of forward facing guns on each B-17. Big Mack recalled: "We learned by trial and error that the Germans would attack the B-17s head-on as they had little or no forward armament. We had waist guns, a gun turret on the top, a ball turret in the belly of the B-17 and guns in the rear in what we called the *stinger* position but little or no armament in the front so eventually they did put a gun mount there."[11]

For now though, as the groups of B-17s once again merged together over the Rally Point, the crews just had to combat the terrifying German frontal attacks as best they could with the guns they had. The 305th now tightened up its group formation as much as possible in the interests of mutual defence. The approaching line of black dots became bigger and bigger to the lead B-17s until the clearly defined front profiles of the oncoming sleek German Messerschmitt 109 fighters were clearly visible to the Americans. As the fighters made their final approach on the lead bombers the flak ceased. Without the weight of their bombs the B-17s were flying now at between 170 to 180 miles per hour[12] and the German fighters coming at them at well over 300 miles per hour – resulting in a closing speed in excess of 500mph. The fighters came on in what was the first of many head-on attacks that day often with up to six fighters, line astern, one after the other as they attempted to blast the bombers out of the sky.

Frequently, the German fighters continued to fire to within only 200 yards of the oncoming B-17s before peeling off. For a few fleeting seconds the pilots of the opposing planes were clearly visible to each other before the German fighters flew past the lead B-17s and into the main body of the American formation at tremendous speed.

On the *Moonbeam* all the gunners opened up on the intruders as they flew through so fast that Dan had to do some quick adjustments to his camera to capture the German fighters which followed. He remembered: "24 or 32 frames a second was normal but the German fighters were moving so fast through the formation that the best thing to do to always capture them was to use 48 frames a second." When firing on enemy planes from B-17s in combat boxes well inside the formations, American gunners had to be careful not to inadvertently fire on their own aircraft. As Dan would soon find out this was not always averted. As he filmed he now experienced the intermittent staccato of machine gun bursts and the corresponding dings of the empty cartridges as they continued to fall on the bomber's deck fused with the excited intercom traffic chatter in his ears. Underlying it all that was one constant noise – the drone of the bomber's engines.

A German fighter levels off to attack an American B-17 formation. **Image: A film frame from 'The Cold Blue' courtesy of Erik Nelson.**

In addition to their terrifying full frontal high-speed attacks, now German fighters came at the formation from all points of the sky and attacked individual B-17s at every opportunity. Crew members screamed out the positions of the hostile fighters over the intercom as soon as they were seen, often three or four abreast as they fired at the mass of B-17s in front of them. More and more frequently now the Messerschmitts and also Focke Wulf 190s, came at the Americans out of the glare of the sun where they could not be clearly seen by the American gunners until the very last minute. Most vulnerable, of course, were the trailing bombers at the rear of the formation, the Tail End Charlies in Coffin Corner where the least American machine guns could be brought to bear.

Despite McGovern being located well inside the formation the oncoming fighters still got through and many frequently latched onto his B-17. As German 20mm cannon and machine guns blazed at the *Moonbeam* and other bombers around her the big fifties of the fortresses tried to counter the onslaught. Rounds of German cannon and machine gun fire soon tore through the *Moonbeam* inflicting more jagged tears and holes in her aluminium skin but luckily no damage occurred yet to seriously threaten the bomber or any of her crew. Then, the left waist gunner, Sgt. Lewison, yelled out over the intercom that bandits were now closing fast straight out in the distance from him.

From the radio room hatch McGovern was tracking a damaged Messerschmitt with his camera when seconds later a burst of cannon and machine gun fire again tore through the *Moonbeam*. Lewison suddenly shouted out that he had been hit but almost simultaneously a round struck the steel helmet on Mack's head, snapping the chinstrap and hurling the heavy helmet onto the deck of the radio compartment where it rolled around continuously such was the force of the strike. McGovern instinctively froze and grimaced as he took stock of what had just happened. Lt. Kney meanwhile, yelled over the intercom for Mack to render assistance to Lewison. As he moved to put down his camera he noticed two bullet holes in the interior radio hatch fairing at chest height. These two had missed him by only an inch but Mack realised that the holes were too big in size and were on the wrong side of the radio room to have come from the attacking German fighters.

He now moved quickly to get to Lewison and rendered him First Aid. He remembered: "Waist gunners were frequently hit as that was the most exposed position on the B-17. When that happened I applied tourniquets or bandages. I always tried to make myself useful whenever I could." Lewison had sustained some minor cuts about the eyes when a series of three cannon rounds from the oncoming German fighter exploded to his left tearing chunks out of the B-17 and cutting the ammunition feed chute of the Browning clean in half. Luckily, though Lewison was not seriously wounded and soon got back to his gun. He rigged up a makeshift ammunition feed and soon continued his sweeping vigil of the skies before him. Mack got back to his filming duties too but he now contemplated just how close he himself had come to serious injury or even worse.

McGovern had almost been killed by friendly fire from another B-17. "One of the problems with flying in B-17s was that the waist gunners had a tendency to shoot at our own planes." This was in the excitement and fear during combat against German fighters and coupled with the up and down bobbing motion of all the planes in the formation. Between fifteen to twenty German Messerschmitt 109 and Focke-Wulf 190 fighters[13] had pounced and began to ferociously attack and harry the American bombers – relentless, determined. The combined fire from the bomber combat boxes including the five YB-40 gunships was effective, however.

Many German fighters were shot down in flames or had been damaged but Dan now witnessed American bombers starting to go down too. Close by another German fighter with all guns blazing now came at one of the five B-17s of the 365th squadron in which McGovern was flying. The gunners on the *Moonbeam* and in the other surrounding 305th bombers desperately fired at the attacker. However, they could only watch helplessly as, after the German fighter passed, smoke and fire started to billow out of both the Number 3 inner starboard engine and then from the cockpit area of the *Windy City Challenger*. She quickly fell back out of formation and started to go down, spinning out of control as it plummeted towards the ground crashing just south of Villacoublay. Many crewmen on the other bombers kept a watch for parachutes, to count them to see how many, if any, of the stricken crew members would get out. Once a ship started to go down crewmen had no more than thirty seconds to grab a parachute and snap it onto their parachute harness and jump – if they could jump. Only four parachutes were seen.[14] Seven of the crew were killed in action. Three parachuted to safety. Suspended under a fourth parachute was Chelveston stills Photographer/Observer George Friend,[15] who, with the three surviving crew members of the *Windy City Challenger*, became a prisoner of war.

Another bomber in the formation from the 384th Bomb Group was shot down and another severely damaged.

THE RUN FOR HOME

McGovern continued to film anything that interested him as the B-17 formation continued on its return leg home. This now included several bombers at varying distances away from the *Moonbeam* which were now trailing smoke having been damaged by either flak or fighters or both. Intermittent but heavy to moderate flak and fighter attacks continued to threaten the bombers all the way to the English Channel. Once the formation was over the water the flak abated and the enemy fighters peeled off and returned to base. The 305th crews that day estimated that their group alone had been set upon by between forty to fifty enemy aircraft. The attacks had been unrelenting for forty five minutes.[16] That other menace, the flak, all the way to the target and all the way back to the channel, had been much heavier than expected and particularly over eight well defended towns along the route. A severely damaged B-17 from the 303rd Bomb Group ditched in the channel.

In addition to the loss of the *Windy City Challenger* over Paris, thirteen of the twenty Chelveston based B-17s on the raid had sustained battle damage. The formation reached the welcome site of the English coast and countryside beyond just before 10.00 hrs. Fifteen minutes later the B-17s of the 305th were circling Chelveston. Some returning bombers fired flares over the airfield. Red flares signified wounded on board. Yellow, mechanical trouble usually arising from battle damage. Several of these priority bombers would land first to be met with a fleet of ambulances containing several AAF flight nurses.[17] Fire and maintenance crews also stood by.

By 10.30 hrs the *Moonbeam* had touched down and Lt. Kney had taxied the B-17 to her hard stand once again. He swung the bomber around and brought her to a halt. The crew chief and his maintenance crew were already waiting nearby surveying the B-17's visual damage and wondering what other unseen damage would have to be repaired before the next mission. They would soon be briefed on everything that needed to be done. One by one, Kney then shut down his engines.[18] Every man paused for a few moments just relishing the sudden silence and the fact that somehow, he had managed to return safely yet again.[19] For now at least, nothing more than shards of strong sunlight penetrated the peppered battle scarred fuselage of the *Moonbeam McSwine*. For this crew it had been their toughest raid so far.[20]

Then they started for the hatches. With his ears ringing somewhat from the constant noise on the five hour round trip mission, Big Mack, once again burdened with his equipment, made his way down to the rear hatch from the radio room very carefully now through a deck littered with spent brass .50 calibre cartridge cases. They were strewn everywhere. "It was a mess. There were spent cartridges all over the place and boxes here and boxes there," McGovern remembered. As he eventually appeared at the rear hatch, a Detachment B colleague, who had arrived with a USAAF Public Relations man and a photographer, rushed over to take his camera box and other items of equipment to allow Mack to exit the B-17 a little easier. All three had been anxiously waiting. McGovern thanked both Major Normand and Lt. Kney for having him on board and for getting him back safely and told them about his close shave with friendly fire.

He was then filmed and photographed with the crew in front of the *Moonbeam*. The crew then made their way hurriedly to the latrines and then to Interrogation where they were debriefed and questioned about all aspects of the raid. Mack, however, remained at the bomber thankful to be down safe. As he was filmed peeling off his heavy shearling leathers, the PR man asked questions about his experience on the raid.[21] Eventually, Mack also got around to telling the three men that, in the middle of one onslaught of German fighters, he had been narrowly missed by friendly fire from another B-17. That got their attention.

Dan McGovern (rear left) and Major Normand, (front row, second from left), with the Kney crew by the 'Moonbeam McSwine' immediately after the Villacoublay raid. **Photo: The Ken Snyder Collection/Eric Barko.**

Dan peels off his leather shearling protective flying suit beside the 'Moonbeam McSwine' after filming on the B-17 during his first combat mission. A frame taken from film footage. A USAAF photographer colleague can be seen in the background. **Image: The Nagel Collection/AFHRA.**

Dan points to where several rounds of friendly fire struck in the radio room narrowly missing him. A frame taken from original film footage shot after the Villacoublay mission. **Image: *The Nagel Collection/AFHRA.***

As a result, Mack briefly returned to the *Moonbeam's* radio compartment where he was filmed pointing to where two of the three rounds of friendly fire had lodged having narrowly missed him. The Public Relations man took notes. It had been a close call, but McGovern had at least completed his first combat mission safely. A little later, he filmed other B-17s as they returned from Villacoublay, some of which were badly damaged and with wounded aboard. Already an experienced aerial photographer, he had learned some valuable new lessons in high altitude aerial cinematography in the combat environment that day.

For his next mission he already had a few fresh ideas which would hopefully, help resolve the challenges of high altitude combat filming. Of his first experience of aerial combat Dan recalled: "We were fighting a battle. We fought our way there and we fought our way out to get back home." He recalled also the fear he experienced on his first mission. "Sure I was scared but I could not become a spectator up there." Dan went on: "I was so busy that I wasn't thinking about a battle. I was thinking about filming and about taking care of other members of the crew up there in the event that I was needed." Big Mack McGovern had survived his first combat mission – only just. He had also filmed some fantastic footage and he knew it, but it had certainly been anything but the milk run it was expected to be. Within days, the other cameramen of Detachment B would start to fly combat missions from Chelveston too.

---

1. American Air Force Museum in Britain archive.
2. 305th Bomb Group Navigation Reports via Steven Quillman, 305th BG Historical FB Group.
3. At around the same time that McGovern was going on his first mission the USAAF was standardising the use of more efficient and safer *demand* regulator oxygen systems for its aircraft. In or around the end of the summer of 1943 all bombers would be either factory or retro-fitted with the much improved *Demand* oxygen regulator system. Unlike the *Freeflow* system the demand regulator released oxygen only when it was needed and was less wasteful. The new regulator was incorporated into an indicator panel which displayed 2 separate mechanical gauges – one indicating oxygen pressure and another either a moving red *bounding ball* in a clear tube or the later white *blinker eyeball* dial which blinked continuously indicating normal oxygen flow when in use. The upgraded higher pressure oxygen system regulator also incorporated an Automix system which automatically compensated the crew with the correct percentage of oxygen needed to breathe normally at various altitudes and dispensing with the need for manual adjustments. However, an adjustment knurled knob was retained and could be used to override the Automix oxygen setting. With both oxygen systems wounded crew members on board were usually given a greatly increased oxygen supply to help keep them conscious. Before missions or whilst in the air crew members also frequently availed of 100 percent oxygen hits as a quick fix for hangovers.
4. As recorded in the mission account of waist gunner Ken Snyder via Eric Barko.
5. Walter Swanson, *Lady Luck,* 360th Squadron.
6. Around this time the US Army Air Forces were undertaking extreme temperature testing with a new camera for aerial filming to address the challenges of filming at up to – 60 degrees at altitude. The electric motor driven Cineflex A5 35mm movie camera was a clone copy of the finely built but rugged and reliable German made Arriflex 1A camera which was, of course,

no longer available to the Americans. The Cineflex later entered service with a separate magazine storage case which contained 6 X 35mm 200 foot magazines to facilitate easy reloading at altitude temperature extremes.

7. In the extreme freezing temperatures at altitude it was considered a frostbite risk to have mittens removed for more than two minutes.

8. The pilot had temporarily transferred full control of the bomber to the lead bombardier during the run in to the target from the Initial Point. This was to achieve maximum accuracy with the Norden bomb sight. It was common practice for the lead bombardier of the group to drop first which was the signal for other bombers behind to do likewise. Tight formation flying was therefore crucial to achieve the tightest bombing pattern possible.

9. Tail gunner's recollection to Brian Bateman, 8th Air Force Historical Society.

10. 367th Bomb Squadron mission report.

11. A chin turret with twin .50 calibre machine guns was eventually factory fitted to Flying Fortresses produced from July 1943 but these would not reach the 8th Air Force until near the end of the year. – Joe Baugher, USAF Bombers (.com). Prior to this, additional single and twin machine guns were retro-fitted mounted on special brackets in the nosecone plexiglass of the B-17 which greatly improved its frontal protection.

12. 305th Bomb Group Navigation Reports via Steven Quillman, 305th BG Facebook Historical Group.

13. Walter Swanson, *Lady Luck,* 360th Bomb Squadron.

14. The average evacuation from a B-17 was 5 out of the crew of 10. (Doug Morrell, Combat Cameraman, 15th Air Force, *Shooting War*, Dreamworks Video.)

15. Sgt. George Friend, was an 8th Air Force Photographer/Observer already at Chelveston before the arrival of McGovern's detachment. He was not on assignment with McGovern's 8th CCU.

16. 369th Squadron, 306th BG Combat Diary.

17. With the exception of the wounded it was common practice for the flight nurses to give each crew member a single shot of whiskey on his return. It helped to calm nerves. – USAAF Flight Nurse, Ethel Cerasale, Oral History, IWM.

18. Often after landing pilots would frequently shut down at least two of their four engines and taxi from the runway to their hardstands on the remaining engines only. Taxiing in this manner required very little engine thrust and particularly with no bombs on board. It also immediately reduced engine noise and saved fuel.

19. Due to the constant noise to which they were exposed during multiple bombing missions, many air crew members suffered from various degrees of deafness both during and after their military service.

20. As recorded in the mission account of waist gunner Ken Snyder via Eric Barko.

21. The *PR man* may, in fact, have been an army reporter. During WW2 McGovern was profiled in two articles in *Stars & Stripes*, the newspaper of the US Armed Forces.

13

FILMING INNOVATION AND THE BELLE OF THE BALL

SNAFU'S Disappointment

MACK MCGOVERN now knew that he had to find a better camera solution for filming at the extreme temperature altitudes at which the B-17s flew. Given the dangers faced from enemy activity as well as the environment extremes on man and machine on every raid, camera malfunctions had to be avoided at all costs. It was clear that the extreme cold could affect the standard Filmo 16mm spool feed and spring wound cameras at altitude. The Eyemo 35mm camera would also be similarly susceptible. It was the fine oil in the mechanism which was freezing causing the very opposite effect for which the oil was intended. One answer was to completely remove all trace of the oil from the camera mechanism. This would work but might not be totally ideal.

McGovern needed to be able to film continuously and trouble free at any altitude. The cassette camera he carried on his first mission had proven to be much easier to both handle and reload but, like the Eyemo and Filmo, was also similarly susceptible to the extremes of cold. It also had of course, the disadvantage of that greatly reduced film capacity. Mack soon came up with a solution – multiple cassette cameras and an electric thermal bucket. Although still spring wound, if he used these much handier compact and lighter cameras in conjunction with the electrically heated thermal bucket, he could keep them warm at any altitude.

The trade-off was less footage captured between reloads given the smaller capacity magazines. The thermal bucket had a dry central storage core which was surrounded by water heated by an electric element. The bucket would be plugged into the B-17's 24 Volt power supply in the radio compartment where McGovern was based. An insulated lid kept the inside storage core warm at a pre-set temperature.

The Kodak 'Model B' cassette movie camera. Dan McGovern would pioneer the innovative use of such cassette cameras for high altitude extreme cold filming.
Photo: ©Richard Bennett, cinemagear.com.

He had several cassette movie cameras for his own personal use and having made enquiries, soon acquired several more and an ample supply of 16mm colour film magazines. Mack now also put another innovative idea, another fresh camera angle, into practice in order to maximise the footage obtained on each mission – Gun Sight Aiming Point cameras or GSAP cameras. Back at Fort Roach in Culver City he had taught his trainee cameramen about these small sleek and robust electrically powered cameras and about the value of the unique actual combat footage they captured when installed in the wings or fuselage of fighter planes.[1] Crucially, GSAPs were readily available to photographic personnel and were obtainable in quartermaster stores particularly within the 8th Air Force's support escort fighter squadrons. Mack would now press GSAPs into service but in a hand-held capacity on combat missions in addition to his own Bell & Howell and Kodak cassette cameras. Unlike the original models, more recent GSAP cameras had now started to arrive in theatre with a factory fitted rudimentary but useful foldaway peep sight viewfinder. "I set up a batch of 6 GSAP cameras with both 15mm or 35mm lenses attached," Mack recalled. Six GSAPs would run a total of 300 feet of film – equal to three standard Filmo spools but, even when run at the faster 48 frames a second to film the swift oncoming enemy fighters, the resulting footage captured would be more than adequate and quite remarkable. The GSAPs, however, were not intended directly for his own use.

By now, a few weeks after Mack's first mission to Villacoublay, the photographs he had sent had been gratefully received in the mail by the crew members' loved ones back Stateside. Each of the ten men soon let McGovern know that at the first opportunity. "They'd tell me: 'Hey Mack, Mom got the picture, Thanks!' or 'My gal received the photo!' or whatever. Anyway, in this way word soon got around." Indeed word did get around. Not only had McGovern sent pictures to the crew's loved ones back home but he had taken the time to also print off copies of dozens of still photographs which he had taken on his first mission.

These photos captured all aspects of the crew, the *Moonbeam McSwine*, the action as it had unfolded around them and in addition, scenes of everyday life on the ground at their Chelveston air base. He made it a point to give each crew member in essence, enough photographs to fill a small album for posterity – a permanent record of their wartime service in England. This was his *Eleventh Man Plan* in its totality and Mack would do the same for every crew member with whom he would fly.[2] In this way he became an asset to the crews as he filmed on their B-17s.

Very soon McGovern had the chance to test his new camera innovations. For his second aerial filming mission it would be fresh eggs[3] for breakfast just prior to the mission briefing as he would film on the 8th Air Force's deepest penetration raid to date into Germany itself on 28th July 1943. This would be a mass formation raid to attack the Fieseler Flugzeugbau aircraft factories in Kassel. Like Villacoublay, this was another Focke Wulf

190 fighter assembly plant. 302 B-17s in total would participate – at least initially. The 8th Air Force's mission number 78 was a two pronged attack. 21 B-17s from three squadrons of the 305th Bomb Group at Chelveston flew in formation as the lead group at 27,800 feet with the 92nd Bomb Group also in formation above it and the 306th Bomb Group in formation below it in the larger V shaped provisional combat wing.

For this mission it was planned that three such provisional combat wings comprising 182 bombers would form up and fly one behind the other to the target at varying altitudes as the larger 1st Bombardment Wing. A second attack force with 120 B-17s comprising six groups in two provisional combat wings set out simultaneously to attack yet another Focke Wulf assembly plant at Oschersleben, 125 miles to the north-east of Kassel. This second force was designated as the 4th Bombardment Wing. This raid was to be part of what became known as *Blitz Week* with raids flown against German key targets for six out of the week's seven days. On this mission McGovern would film on a B-17 called *Lallah V* skippered by Lt. Martin E. Willson of the 364th Bomb Squadron.

On the morning of the raid he introduced himself to the *Lallah V's* crew members and just as prior to his first mission, he gave an undertaking that he would take a photo of each man and send it back to whomever they wanted in the States. Now he asked a favour of co-pilot, Lt. Sam Johnstone. "I asked the co-pilot would he mind taking footage of what he saw with the GSAP cameras if he had a chance and he agreed." Once in the radio room of the bomber, McGovern plugged his electric thermal bucket into the spare power socket. He placed his four cassette cameras inside its dry core and replaced the lid. Once the bomber's engines were running, the water would start to properly heat up.

Mack then made his way forward to the flight deck where he handed Lt. Johnstone the six loaded electric GSAP cameras for what was basically a point-and-shoot situation. To film, the co-pilot would simply plug a GSAP into the power socket on the panel to his right and when film ran out he would simply plug in another one. Apart from being the deepest penetration raid into Germany to date, it was also the first time that P-47 Thunderbolt fighters were deployed as long range escorts to the bombers with 105 dispatched with drop tanks for the first time.[4] Once aloft, McGovern started to film amongst the formation and its reassuring fighter escort with his new and innovative temperature controlled camera set up. The heated box remained warm and it was working fine. "I used both Bell & Howell and Kodak 16mm cassette cameras which I kept in the thermal bucket. I'd take one camera out, shoot with it, return it to the thermal bucket and then take another out and so on and so forth," he explained. Heavy cloud at altitude resulted in many groups being unable to assemble safely into their formations.[5] The result was that the majority of B-17s had no choice but to either return to base or bomb other targets of opportunity elsewhere.

Of the original 182 bombers of nine groups comprising the 1st Bombardment Wing which had taken off for Kassel, only one third of it – the three groups of McGovern's provisional combat wing plus four stragglers from the 4th Bombardment Wing,[6] now made up the formation after the attempted assembly over the North Sea. The depleted formation flew on lead by the 305th leaving heavy persistent contrails in its wake. Once the formation crossed the enemy coast in northern Holland intensive German flak barrages commenced. The enemy fighter attacks on the formation started at 9.50am and the B-17s of the 305th were constantly harassed by an estimated 100 to 125 German fighters for over two hours. As sporadic fighter dogfights ensued all around the formation, many German fighters got through often coming to within 250 yards of McGovern's 305th B-17s and despite being exposed to their own flak.[7]

As the formation crossed the German border its fighter escort, for the first time, crossed into German airspace too but all too soon they reached the additional limit of their range permitted by their drop tanks and had to turn for home. Now, as many as twenty-three enemy Messerschmitt 109 fighters were counted in just one of the enemy fighter formations sighted. They came at the B-17s of the leading 305th group with ferocious mostly head-on co-ordinated attacks often six or even twelve abreast[8] before peeling off or flying on through the American combat wing formation.

Many German fighters did not need to come in so close. They were equipped with a brand new rocket powered air-to-air mortar which they now used for the first time firing the rockets from a range of over 900 yards. As many as five of these specially adapted fighters attacked in unison and often from much closer range. In contrast to the black puffs of flak exploding in and around the B-17s, when air mortars were fired into the American formation they exploded in a huge burst of white smoke which often momentarily obscured as many as three B-17s.[9] Meanwhile, the flak continued all along the route to the target over Germany.

All the time McGovern filmed the action from the radio room top hatch and elsewhere throughout the bomber, frequently exchanging cameras from his heated thermal box. Co-pilot, Sam Johnstone, had managed to film with the GSAPs too and through the flight deck windows, had caught many of the relentless oncoming attacks on film. Now and again Mack made his way up to Johnstone on the flight deck to make sure he had a fresh camera plugged in and also to reload the GSAPs if needed. *The Lallah V,* with McGovern filming on board, was one of only 43 B-17s of the 1st Bombardment Wing to reach the target. On the bomb run with the three individual groups now approaching the target in column formation, one behind the other, the fighters disappeared only for intense and accurate flak to start again on approach to and over Kassel itself.

The groups arrived over the target exactly on schedule just before 10.30am and at altitudes of between 27,000 and 23,000 feet. The 305th attacked first and after running the gauntlet of a

90 second bomb run through the heavy flak, it was *Bombs Away* at 10.53am despite a thick haze over the target. Behind, the other groups started their bomb runs too as McGovern filmed the 305th drop for intelligence purposes through the bomb bay doors. The bombs of the 305th landed right on the nose.[10]

With many B-17s now damaged to varying degrees due to the intense and accurate flak on the bomb run, the B-17s at last now banked away sharply and headed for the Rally Point for the journey home. The German fighters now returned and were tenacious in their attacks. Suddenly, as McGovern filmed, a waist gunner roared over the intercom that the other waist gunner had been hit. Mack quickly returned his camera to the thermal box with its comrades and quickly made his way aft. Immediately, he saw a waist gunner on the deck with the other one desperately trying to divide his attention between his buddy and the ongoing onslaught of German fighter attacks.

A MESSERSCHMITT LEVELLED OFF

Just as Mack got to the unmanned waist gun he glanced out the open window. "I saw a Messerschmitt coming straight at us with all his guns firing," he recalled. The German fighter was levelled off and closing fast. Now, all Dan's gunnery training back on the range in Nevada kicked in. It had been intended for emergencies just like this. "I grabbed the machine gun and got it into action." With his clumsy leather mittens he aimed the .50 calibre Browning at the closing silhouette and pushed the trigger. In fear of his life and with adrenaline now pumping through his veins he kept the trigger depressed. Rat-a tat-a tat -a tat -a tat -a tat a tat tat....! "I saw my bullets hitting home," he remembered. "There was a sudden plume of black smoke from the Messerschmitt which finally swung off and went down in flames."

All this happened in a matter of seconds. Five enemy fighters had been shot down by the fortresses of the 305th and a further two damaged but, as a cameraman, Mack would never officially be credited with his kill. The waist gunner whose gun Mack had manned had not been hit by enemy fire but had passed out due to lack of oxygen. Either battle damage had severed his oxygen feed somewhere, or the hose of his mask had detached from its socket in the heat of battle. In either case this was a common occurrence amongst the mass bomber formations of the 8th Air Force. The unconscious waist gunner was quickly put on emergency oxygen and made as comfortable as possible.

Then a 365th Squadron B-17 close to McGovern was hit and started to go down. Tail number 42-29970 had not been given a name and the colourful nose art which adorned most of her sisters. She was gone and her place in the formation was quickly filled as the bomb groups reformed at the Rally Point. As they withdrew many of the American crews in McGovern's formation reported seeing German fighter pilots machine gunning bailed out B-17 airmen as they hung helplessly under their parachute canopies. Dan continued to man the gun through what remained of two hours of relentless fighter attacks after the bombs had been dropped. As the B-17s approached Rotterdam and the Dutch coast the formation's fighter escort of P-47s appeared somewhat later than scheduled but McGovern stayed at his gun for the remainder of the flight home.

Intriguingly, just as his battered formation reached the English Channel many of its pilots and crewmen reported a strange B-17 with no markings weaving in and out among the other bombers, forcing the American B-17s out of formation. The strange bomber remained until ten minutes from the English coast when it abruptly left the formation and headed back towards the enemy coast.

There were also reports of another strange *dirty brown* B-17, unusually with all its windows closed at this point in a mission which, on the homeward leg, fell into a tail position in the formation. This B-17 spent some time there before it also dropped out of formation at 10.44am and made a 180 degree turn before also heading back towards enemy air space. These were B-17s captured and repaired by the Germans to closely observe and disrupt the American formations. Over occupied Europe they were often used to relay a formation's speed and altitude to the German flak batteries further ahead or, later in the war, to jam the radio signals of navigational blind bombing and ground scanning radar systems.[11]

Twenty-two B-17s had been lost in total on this raid, 114 crewmen killed in action. Another 102 became prisoners of war. 26 crewmen were seriously or slightly wounded. Seven of the lost bombers were from McGovern's formation of which 15 had been seriously damaged whilst another 48 sustained minor damage. Fifteen B-17s had been lost from the Oschersleben formation which had another 11 seriously damaged and 44 with minor damage. The raid had only been partly successful. The bad weather had resulted in 155 bombers from the two large attack wings abandoning the mission. Despite the accuracy of the bombs of the 305th, bombing overall had been only fair and this necessitated another mission against Kassel two days later.[12]

On a more positive note, McGovern's innovative combination of multiple cassette cameras and heated thermal box, in conjunction with the electrically powered GSAPs, had coped well with the extreme cold at high altitude and had greatly increased the mission footage shot by McGovern on and from the *Lallah V.* It would be with this technique that *Big Mack* would film much of his aerial combat footage on his future missions. It would be a filming technique soon adopted by the other cameramen of Detachment B and eventually by countless other combat cameramen of the 8th Air Force as they too captured the action in the freezing hostile skies of wartime Europe. However, McGovern's aerial filming innovation would not merely stop there as he went about capturing his combat footage.

———

Five days after the Kassel mission and on August 2nd 1943, a high-profile VIP delegation of five United States senators visited Station 105 at Chelveston which kept McGovern busy. This special committee of senators met the officers and men and inspected the B-17s and the base facilities. The delegation had set out from Washington only a week before on 25th July on a sixty-five day inspection tour of United States overseas military bases, not just in Britain, but also throughout the Middle East, North Africa, Australia and China. McGovern filmed and photographed Senators Henry Cabot Lodge Jr. of Massachusetts, James M. Mead of New York, Benjamin *Happy* Chandler of Kentucky, Richard R. Russell of Georgia and Owen Brewster of Maine who were also accompanied on their tour by a number of high-ranking Army Air Force officers.

When the senators gathered around it, McGovern was confident that *We The People* and its crew were about to be chosen for both the bond tour and William Wyler's documentary. "We thought *We The People* was going to get it when the senators[13] came up there in August of 1943. *We The People* was out there in the field and the senators came around. We thought that it was going to be the plane that was going back to the United States to sell war bonds but we were sadly mistaken," Dan recalled.

Much to the disappointment of Dan and his cameramen and to the crew of *SNAFU/We the People*,[14] another B-17 had already been chosen for the war bond tour in the United States and it was not *SNAFU/We the People*. The B-17 chosen was the *Memphis Belle* of the 91st Bomb Group which had been based at nearby Bassingbourn.

Furthermore, by the time McGovern and the crews of the other contender B-17s heard about it, the *Memphis Belle* had already been flown back to the United States where it had commenced its war bond tour on 16th June. It was a bomber on which Wyler himself had actually filmed during several missions and he had an existing rapport with the crew members who usually flew it.[15]

However, the *Memphis Belle* only completed its 25 missions on 19th May 1943. Looking back on it Mack said: "We had never heard of the *Memphis Belle* until then and it certainly wasn't in the running. It was way out in left field."[16] He went on to explain: "The *Memphis Belle* was not the first bomber to complete 25 missions over German occupied Europe. Far from it. The *Belle* was in the 91st Bomb Group but by then we had as many as five cameramen flying in all the actual bombers which were very close to completing 25 missions in different bomb groups all over Southern England." All five cameramen frequently flew together on single missions and spaced throughout the mass formations of B-17s.

On May 1st 1943 another 91st Bomb Group B-17, *Delta Rebel 2,* actually became the first to complete 25 missions eighteen days before the *Memphis Belle.*[17] Another B-17, *Hell's Angels* of the 303rd Bomb Group, completed 25 missions on 13th May 1943 six days before the *Memphis Belle*[18] and twelve days after *Delta Rebel 2. SNAFU/We The People* had completed her 25th mission having returned from a raid against Kiel, Germany, on 14th May 1943 – five days before the *Memphis Belle.*

Despite it being apparently only the *fourth* B-17 to reach 25 missions it was the *Memphis Belle* that flew back to America on her 26th special mission on 9th June 1943. There, on 16th June, to great fanfare, her bond tour commenced to raise public funding for the American war effort. Subsequently, it would be the *Memphis Belle* and her crew which would also eventually star in Wyler's documentary.

Of the *Memphis Belle* and her subsequent fame, Dan put it this way: "One bomber could not do everything but the *Memphis Belle* represented all the bombers. There were thousands of *Memphis Belles* that were doing the same terrific job. I think Wyler figured that the *Memphis Belle* was a bit more sophisticated. It was the boy at war and the girl back home – the romantic approach and all that jazz but anyway that's how the *Memphis Belle* became famous."

With the US senators gone, Technical Sergeant McGovern and his fellow crewmen got back to work on what was now known to be William Wyler's *Memphis Belle* documentary filming additional material on the ground and combat footage in the air for the production. "Wyler was always after our footage," he remembered. Then, almost one month after Mack's first combat mission, combat cameraman, Sgt. George Gamble, flew off on a B-17 from Chelveston on 12th August 1943 to film during a mission to bomb synthetic oil refineries in the industrial Ruhr Valley area of Germany.

During that mission over Oberschleven a 20mm cannon round from a German fighter entered the radio room where he was filming and exploded wounding Gamble in the arm. He returned and was awarded the Purple Heart medal for being wounded in action. During the time McGovern was on assignment with the 8th Air Force in England in 1943 Gamble was Detachment B's first casualty.[19] He would not be the last.

---

1. Once the GSAP fighter footage had been viewed by USAAF officials for intelligence purposes it was then circulated to USAAF bomber bases where it was eagerly viewed by the crews. – John H. Day, B-17 Ball Turret gunner, 100th BG via Raymond McFalone interview, YouTube.

2. This is how many 305th veterans came by their collections of Chelveston photographs. Whilst McGovern did indeed take a large proportion of these photographs himself it is a fair assumption, however, given that he was the NCO In Charge, that he may have included others taken by other cameramen/photographers in the photos he gifted.

3. Multiple 8th Air Force B-17s flew west to Dan McGovern's home country of Ireland from Britain every Saturday during the war. Having landed at Casement Aerodrome outside Dublin, the bombers were filled mainly with fresh food including bacon, eggs, milk, cream, butter and other items which were more plentiful in Southern Ireland than in wartime Britain. The fresh Irish produce was more than likely destined merely for the top officer tier of the 8th Air Force. This was a reciprocating arrangement with the Americans providing the Irish with other items in exchange which, ironically, included cases of whiskey. As Ireland was a neutral nation, this arrangement was kept quiet and a stipulation that the B-17s have their guns removed was observed by the Americans.

4. *AAF: The Official Guide to the Army Air Forces*, New York: Special Edition for AAF Organizations, Henry H. Arnold p334.

5. This and many other details and statistics of the Kassel mission gleaned from the official 305th Bomb Group Report of Operations from 28th July 1943, AFHRA, as well as from American Air Museum in Britain mission archive.

6. All four were from the 303rd Bomb Group. They were the only B-17s of the aborted groups/combat wings to fly on. – Official 305th Bomb Group Summaries of Operations from 28th July 1943 courtesy of AFHRA.

7. At least one attacking FW190 fighter was seen exploding having been hit by German flak. – 305th Official Report of Operations, AFHRA.

8. 305th Bomb Group Summaries of Operations, AFHRA.

9. As recorded in the Kassel mission diary entry of *Old Reliable's* waist gunner Sgt. Ken Snyder via Eric Barko. This was the Werfer-Granate 21 rocket launched air-to-air mortar designed to negate the combined offensive fire-power of the American formations. It is often stated that these weapons were used for the first time against American bombers during the Schwein-furt/Regensbruck raid of 17th August 1943. However, from research, an account in the Combat Diary of the 369th Squadron of the 306th Bomb Group records them being fired at a formation *from a considerable distance* during the raid to Hannover on 26th July 1943. Snyder's account records the aerial mortars being used during the Kassel raid two days later. The projectiles were lobbed from tubes attached externally underneath the wings of the German fighters into a formation from a safe distance of over 1000 yards away. They were, however, largely inaccurate. Two of these aerial mortars could be installed on single engine Focke Wulf 190 and Messer-schmitt 109 fighters and four on twin engine fighters. They were often fired at a single formation by an entire staffel or squadron. The crews of the 4th Bombardment Wing bombers attacking Oschersleben also reported this weapon being used against them the same day as the Kassel raid.

10. 1st Lt. John O. Booker of the 92nd Bomb Group behind the 305th saw its bombs fall *right on the nose*. 92nd Bomb Group archives.

11. Official 305th Bomb Group Summary of Operations from 28th July 1943, AFHRA. Later in the war, even when a target was obscured by thick cloud cover rendering optical bomb sights virtually useless, navigational *blind bombing* and ground scanning radar systems could direct bombers to their target and assist with accurate bomb release.

12. American Air Museum in Britain archive.

13. In his oral History, McGovern refers to the politicians as *congressmen* but only the delegation of senators visited Station 105 in August of 1943.

14. Whether McGovern had anything to do with it or not, *SNAFU/We the People,* perhaps as something of a consolation prize, was shipped back to the United States and to the FMPU studios of Fort Roach where it was installed on a sound stage. It was used in a static role to film many studio segments of B-17 related training films and documentaries. By then she had completed a staggering 76 perilous missions.

15. Dr. Harry Friedman in his presentation *Memphis Belle, Dispelling the Myths* at the National Museum of the US Air Force, April 18th 2018, makes the case that the choice of the *Memphis Belle* was already a *done deal* for the bond tour for a number of reasons. He points out that Wyler had already filmed it for his movie, that pilot Bob Morgan completed his twenty five

missions on May 17th 1943 with the *Memphis Belle* completing its twenty fifth mission two days later on 19th May. Dr Friedman adds that General Eaker's memo of 1st June directing that a bomber approaching 25 missions be chosen, gave the appearance at least, that the choice of bomber was open to discussion and also that the bomber would be chosen in consultation with group commanders. Yet, just over a week after Eaker's memo was circulated, the *Memphis Belle* was flown back to America on 9th June. According to the book *Five Came Back* by Mark Harris, the bomber arrived back in the United States on 16th June 1943.

16. Much is open to interpretation but McGovern certainly met with William Wyler in person before the director returned to the United States certainly by July of 1943. McGovern gave Wyler a Mitchell camera. However, it appears that Mack was left unaware that the *Memphis Belle* and her crew had been chosen for both the bond tour and to star in Wyler's documentary. Apart from McGovern's recollection, the most compelling evidence of this comes from the combat diary of waist gunner Ken Snyder of Lt. Jack Kney's crew. McGovern flew his first mission with this crew on the *Moonbeam McSwine* to Villacoublay on 14th July 1943. Snyder's entry in his diary after this mission reads: *"We had a photographer (McGovern) along and many pictures were taken of fighters and flak and of ourselves. A story is to be written based around our crew from the movies taken."* This indicates that, even at this late stage, Kney's crew also thought that they too might be in the running to be the subject B-17 and crew, at the very least, for Wyler's documentary if not the bond tour. There seems little doubt that by the end of June 1943 Wyler had already secretly chosen the *Memphis Belle* and her crew to be the subject matter for what was then still his original twenty minute short documentary. With a view to future content he had arranged that the King and Queen of England be filmed with the *Memphis Belle* at Bassingbourn during a royal visit there earlier in 1943. However, the huge ongoing success of the *Memphis Belle's* war bond tour all across America by early July 1943 appears to have been the deciding factor for Wyler to, only then, reveal that the *Memphis Belle*, now familiar to the American public, would be the subject of his now to be extended documentary film. Another reason Wyler may also have delayed naming the bomber to star in his documentary was as an incentive to ensure enthusiastic co-operation from the bomber crews until the cameramen flying with them, such as McGovern, had gathered sufficient footage for the production. The final title of the documentary which would reflect the name *Memphis Belle* would not be chosen until much later.

17. American Air Museum in Britain.

18. *Hells Angels, The True Story of the 303rd Bomb Group in World War 2*, Jay Stout p97. After flying 48 missions this bomber also returned to the US for a war bond tour but later in 1944. – National Museum of the United States Air Force.

19. McGovern's account as recorded in *History of the First Motion Picture Unit, Army Air Forces, California, 1944* James Scanlan.

SCHWEINFURT

The Most Terrifying Mission

FIVE DAYS later on the anniversary of the 8th Air Force's first mission from England against Nazi targets to Rouen, France a year before, *The Mighty Eighth* flew its deepest ever penetration raid into the heart of Nazi Germany. This was mission number 84 which was over 500 miles from the English coast. It would also be the most complex mission to date. This would be Dan McGovern's third combat mission and it was conceived as a simultaneous double strike against the Schweinfurter Kugellagerwerke ball bearing factories at Schweinfurt as well as the Messerschmitt fighter plane factories at Regensburg, both in Bavaria in central Germany on August 17th 1943. This was the same day that Sicily fell to the Allies. For the crews at Chelveston it had been fresh eggs for breakfast yet again that morning.

This mission, like McGovern's previous missions to Villacoublay and Kassel, was also devised as part of the overall *Operation Pointblank* campaign. The mission to Schweinfurt and Regensburg would also be the largest attempted up to that time in the war. The raid was carefully planned and would have to be carefully choreographed in order to achieve the element of surprise and the best bombing results with the least losses. It would, however, be notorious. This combined raid involved a total of 19 bomb groups comprising two massive strike force formations of 376 bombers in total.[1] The 4th Bombardment Task Force, comprising 146 B-17s from seven bombardment groups from bases in East Anglia in Southern England, would take off at 5.45am and fly the deepest penetration mission yet into Germany to attack the targets in Regensburg. Instead of returning to England having dropped its bombs, this wing would continue on and land instead at bases in North Africa. Due to the long flight, the bombers of this element of the mission would be fitted with Tokyo drop tanks for increased range.

This strike force would be led by the 305th Bomb Group's former Commanding Officer, Colonel Curtis LeMay. Meanwhile, twenty nine B-17s from the 305th would fly in a larger force of 230 bombers which comprised the 1st Bombardment Task Force to bomb targets in Schweinfurt. The 305th would again fly in combat wing formation with the 306th and 92nd Bomb Groups as one of four combat wings drawn from 12 bomb groups. This second and larger task force would fly from Chelveston and other bases throughout the English midlands, taking off 9 minutes after LeMay's force.

As Schweinfurt was 75 miles closer than Regensburg, it would follow a similar route but only deviate off its course northeastwards towards Schweinfurt after passing the city of Frankfurt. This strike force would be led by Brigadier General Robert Williams. The plan was for both strike forces to fly from England almost simultaneously on not dissimilar courses and to bomb their respective targets at approximately the same time. With this strategy it was envisaged that German flak and fighter controllers would be confused and that the larger, slightly later, B-17 force would run a considerably lesser risk from attack from the menace of German fighters. It had been concluded that, with LeMay's slightly earlier force having been already attacked by the German fighters, they would be on the ground refuelling and re-arming by the time the Schweinfurt bound force would pass into their area of operations thus allowing the second larger B-17 formation to slip by unmolested. That, at least, was the plan.

On the Schweinfurt/Regensburg mission there would be fighter escorts but they would only go as far as easternmost Belgium where the P-47 Thunderbolt fighters, having taken over escort duty from the shorter range British Spitfires, would reach their maximum range before having to peel off and return to base. Allied escort fighters would pick up the returning bomber formations of the 1st Bombardment Task Force again over eastern Belgium on their homeward flight. Mack McGovern would fly to Schweinfurt with the 305th but this time on board the B-17 *Louisiana Purchase* of the 422nd Bomb Squadron skippered by Lt. Harvey Rodgers.

On the morning of the raid, the co-pilot of the *Louisiana Purchase*, Lt. Dwight K. Anderson, agreed to work the GSAP cameras for McGovern at any opportunity he could. This was going to be a tough mission and everybody knew it and before kitting up and going to their fortresses that morning most crewmen took the blessing offered by their chaplains after the main briefing. However, thick fog covered their B-17 bases. As a result LeMay's task force for Regensburg was ordered to delay its launch which it did for a full 90 minutes.

LeMay and many of the pilots in his task force had been well trained in the art of instrument flying and despite conditions being far from ideal, his 146 bombers took off from their bases at 7.15am. General Williams and his pilots of the Schweinfurt bound task force were not as proficient at instrument flying. The crews of these 230 B-17s stood down temporarily and waited instead for the weather to improve. Dan McGovern stood down too. The plan was starting to unravel. Meanwhile, after a four and a half hour flight, Colonel LeMay's formations appeared over Regensburg and started to bomb the Messerschmitt factories below at 11.43am. Seventeen minutes later, at noon, the General Williams led 1st Bombardment Task Force finally started taking off from their airfields and making for the Assembly Points four hours, rather than the planned nine minutes after LeMay's task force had done the same.

A FORMATION TWENTY MILES LONG

The various groups in their high, low and centre combat boxes formed into the larger mass formation combat wings before setting course, one after the other, for the continent cruising at altitudes of between 23,000 and 26,000 feet. Above, 96 British Spitfires flew as escort. From the very front lead ship to Tail End Charlie, the Schweinfurt bomber formation with its 230 B-17s, including McGovern and the *Louisiana Purchase,* was all of twenty miles long. However, the precise take-off timing of both task forces, so crucial to the planned confusion of the German air defence plotters, had just evaporated as had the fog which had caused the timing of the plan to go awry in the first place. Gone too was the element of surprise for Schweinfurt and a price would be paid for that. Such numbers of bombers were soon picked up on the German radar. Now, one and a half hours into the mission and on crossing the Dutch coast, the B-17 mass formation had already lost 8 bombers which had returned to base due to mechanical problems.

Intense German flak barrages had come up almost immediately and would be encountered at no less than eighteen locations along the route to the target. The remaining 222 B-17s were forced to descend to 17,000 feet and below dense unexpected cloud banks. With such tight formations being flown, losing visibility between the bombers was considered just too risky. On the *Louisiana Purchase* McGovern had already taken a cartridge camera from his thermal box and shot some footage of the mass formation as it passed through the first bursts of exploding flak. The thermal box was again working fine so Mack would again exchange warm cameras from it as he prepared to shoot the aerial combat footage which he now felt certain was about to unfold.

However, by now McGovern had also employed other new and novel ways of capturing that footage at altitude. Instead of just filming from the radio room and other positions as he had on his two previous missions, Mack had fashioned a strong but long and lightweight extension monopod to one end of which he securely fixed not one, but multiple cassette cameras from his heated thermal box. Each camera was secured in its own cradle but faced a different direction. He started each camera rolling inside the B-17 before raising the business end of the monopod out into the slipstream above the bomber.

There was always some film exposure wastage until he secured the monopod vertically to minimise shake and the length of footage captured in this way was short. However, when this footage was intercut with that captured in the more conventional way, the result was spectacular offering an additional unparalleled filming perspective. Once reconfigured and with the cameras having been interchanged with warm ones from the thermal box McGovern's unorthodox multi-camera monopod could also be used in a similar manner when extended horizontally out through the waist machine gun ports.

However, this filming technique was only employed at times when it did not interfere with the effectiveness of the waist gunner.[2] Big Mack had also come up with another idea. He designed and fashioned a cradle into which sat an Eyemo Type 71 Bomb Spotting movie camera which was secured externally below the bomb bay and out of the way of both crew and bombs. He devised a way to press the *shoot* button remotely from just above. This captured spectacular unimpeded footage of the bombs falling away towards the ground but Mack's bomb bay cradle could also be pivoted to adjust the camera's shooting angle in any direction thus offering numerous perspective possibilities.

As McGovern operated his camera systems, over 2400 Browning .50 calibre machine guns on the B-17s throughout the Schweinfurt task force continuously scanned every part of the sky for the appearance of the enemy fighters. All in their

bombers on their way to Schweinfurt now awaited the inevitable
onslaught. Not ten minutes had passed when the hostile black
specks appeared in the far distance and the cry of *Bandits!* rang
out. McGovern braced himself for what was to come. Already on
high alert and with LeMay's task force having already hit Regensburg hard less than two hours before, the Germans put up every
single fighter they could muster to blunt the second American
attack. It was the largest German fighter force to ever attack an
American formation. The crews of the 305th alone would record
150 German fighters sighted.

Hundreds were scrambled from 24 bases to intercept the
Schweinfurt bound formations and the result was carnage. The
Spitfires broke off to deal with them. Dogfights ensued. In the
few fleeting seconds in which the duelling fighters would appear
before him McGovern filmed what footage he could of the
clashes between the Spitfires and either the German Messerschmitt 109 or the Focke Wulf 190 fighters. These duels usually
ended in one or the other trailing smoke and going down and
McGovern sometimes managed to be in a position to film that
too and even the pilot as he bailed out with his parachute from
his stricken plane. However, there were so many German fighters
that they got through to the bombers again and again, sometimes
attacking in swarms of over twenty at a time.

In McGovern's three group combat wing the lead group of
B-17s just ahead of the 305th took the brunt of the head-on
attacks whilst other German fighters picked out and engaged B-
17s at will throughout the rest of the mass formations. Again, B-
17s on the flanks were vulnerable but bombers at the tail end of
formations the most vulnerable of all. In the German fighter
strategy adopted, it was the less manoeuvrable twin engine
Messerschmitt 110 fighters, in addition to the 109's and
FW190s, which would also engage the American Tail End Charlies but approaching from the rear where less guns could effectively be brought to bear on them. In all it was relentless. All the
time McGovern filmed conventionally from the best vantage

points on the B-17 and also using his innovative multi-camera monopod to best effect.

The Spitfires shot down eight German fighters until they reached the full extent of their fuel range and had to peel off in Eastern Belgium and head for home leaving the B-17s to their fate as they approached the German border. 88 longer range American P-47 fighters now took over escort duties from the Spitfires but, having arrived late, engaged the German fighters for only a short while before they too broke off the fight and headed for home. Now the B-17s still had 90 minutes flying time to the target and another 90 minutes back out until they could avail of fighter protection once again.

Now the enemy fighters came at the B-17s with an increasing ferocity and from all angles. More enemy fighters now appeared than at any other point during the mission so far and by now, a force of 300 from eighteen different bases across Germany and the Netherlands came at the formation. McGovern filmed more and more bombers getting hit, going down and starting to spin out of control. Many more had started to lag behind trailing smoke and with engines out all the way across the Netherlands and Belgium. Now the mass formation was about to enter Germany itself. McGovern continued to pull warm cameras from his thermal box and to return the freezing ones as he continuously filmed the events unfolding before him.

Many of the Focke Wulf 190s, Messerschmitt 109s and twin engined Messerschmitt 110s now started to let loose at the American bombers with air to air rocket mortars. Despite the German rockets being largely ineffective the flak and relentless cannon and machine gun fire from the German fighter onslaught resulted in more and more American bombers going down. McGovern remembered: "Jerry was coming at us in droves and planes were falling all around. It reminded me of a free-for-all fight in a beer hall with the place crowded and everybody throwing stuff."[3] It was now, two and three quarter hours into the mission and fifteen miles out from Schweinfurt.

B-17s of the 1st Bombardment Task Force with which Dan McGovern flew pictured over Schweinfurt on 17th August 1943. **Photo: AFHRA.**

On approach to the Initial Point the 1st Bombardment Strike Force on which McGovern was filming had already lost twenty four B-17s since it was first engaged shortly after crossing the Dutch coast. Eighteen German fighters had been shot down[4] and the enemy staffels now broke off their attack to return to base to refuel and rearm. Their relentless continuous attacks on the B-17 formation on which McGovern filmed had lasted one hour and eighteen minutes. They would attack the Americans again after they turned for home. "When it was over it was peaceful all of a sudden. It seemed we had been fighting for hours," McGovern recalled. However, now the flak ground fire intensified even more. The bomber wings, down to a total of over 180 B-17s, had by now separated into individual groups and now began their staggered run-ins at the Initial Point. All the time McGovern filmed. Finally, shortly before 3.00pm the first wing released its bombs over the ball bearing factories. Each subsequent wing then did the same at time staggered 20 second intervals. Over the city another bomber fell out of formation and started to go down and then another and then another, all three hit by flak. With *Bombs Away* each bomber group turned and headed for the Rally Point over the town of Meiningen almost fifty miles to the north. 424 tons of high explosive and 125 tons of incendiary bombs were dropped continuously for 24 minutes on the five ball bearing factory targets of Schweinfurt below.

At the Rally Point the groups assembled once again into the mass mutual defensive formation of their combat wings for the long and treacherous journey home. Twenty minutes later the German fighters returned and the onslaught resumed. They now concentrated their fire on the damaged and trailing bombers but also on the main body of the formation. Frequently, the attacking enemy fighters dived down onto the American formation as they attacked out of the sun, often flying through the American bombers and only pulling out of their dive well below the formation. By the time the formations had again reached the Belgian border the Luftwaffe fighters were still coming at the Americans bombers in swarms.

On the route out from the target the German fighters continuously harassed the returning formation for another half hour before a large joint force of P-47 Thunderbolts and Spitfires started to show up close to Rotterdam to escort the battered formation back to England. By now the *Louisiana Purchase*, like so many other B-17s in the formation dispatched to Schweinfurt, was peppered with flak shrapnel and shot full of holes. Still she flew on. Despite the escort intercepting the German fighters and blunting their attacks Messerschmitts and Focke Wulfs still managed to get through to the American bombers and a further eight B-17s were lost before the formation even reached the North Sea where another three aircraft ditched in the water. When they eventually peeled off the German fighters had continuously attacked the formation on its perilous journey home for

This photo shows some of the damage to the B-17 'Louisiana Purchase' on which McGovern filmed on the first Schweinfurt raid on 17th August 1943. Battle damage to the rear fuselage can be seen near the port horizontal stabiliser. Rounds appear to have exited at this location having struck the fuselage on the opposite side.
Photo: 305th USAAF Archive/Chris Coffman.

an hour and seven minutes. The remaining B-17s at last made landfall and crossed the English coast before landing at their respective airfields. They had continuously flown over German occupied territory for three and a half hours and over Germany itself with no fighter escort whatsoever. "I think Schweinfurt was the most terrifying mission I was on," Dan McGovern remembered. "We were heavily hit. We lost a tremendous amount of planes on that one."

In fact, on the Schweinfurt/Regensburg raid a total of 60 B-17s were lost to enemy fire, ditched in the sea or crashed in Switzerland. It had started out as an ambitious plan to strike a killer blow at Hitler's aviation and ball bearing industries. Instead, it was of limited success and the 8th Air Force had received its worst mauling at the hands of the German Luftwaffe to date. The Americans had lost 552 men, half of whom were killed in action with most of the remainder becoming prisoners of war. Twenty were interned in Switzerland. Five crews were rescued from the North Sea.[5] Of that 60 ship overall loss figure from both strike forces McGovern's Schweinfurt 1st Bombardment Task Force had faired the worst having lost 36 bombers. When the remaining B-17s landed back at their various bases in England, 7 dead crew members were taken from the battered bombers and 21 wounded. Five of the American P-47s and British Spitfire escort fighters, sent to protect the Schweinfurt Task Force, had been shot down in their clashes with

German fighters.[6] Of Colonel LeMay's 4th Bombardment Regensburg strike force 24 bombers were lost and 122 B-17s out of 146 made it to North Africa. Of these, 60 had suffered battle damage and a great many were never returned to service due to lack of facilities and parts at the bases on which they had landed. This was more than double the highest figure of losses up to that time and more costly in terms of men and aeroplanes lost than in the first six months of the American bombing campaign over Europe combined. This mission was thereafter referred to as *Black Tuesday*. More than any other mission it had also clearly demonstrated the need for fighter escort protection for the bombers *all* the way to the target and back.

––––––

THE MOONBEAM GOES DOWN

Ten days later, on 27th August 1943, Mack McGovern flew his next mission once more back with Lt. Jack Kney and his crew of the 365th Bomb Squadron. This time, however, he was on board yet another different *B-17. Old Reliable,* was one of eighteen bombers from the 305th which set out with another eight groups in a mass formation of 159 B-17s and a Spitfire escort.

The Mighty Eighth's mission number 87 was the first against the new German V2 rocket launching sites then still under construction at Watten in the Pas De Calais in Northern France. In addition, another force of 65 B-17s from seven other groups would also attack the rocket sites separately.[7] Mack would continue to film at altitude using his thermal bucket and cassette cameras conventionally but often deploying the camera monopod. For this mission he would adopt yet another innovative filming practice aimed at maximising the footage captured – two combat cameramen would fly with the 305th but on different B-17s. In addition to McGovern on *Old Reliable,* his Detachment B colleague, Technical Sgt. Bill Wood, would also fly on the

Moonbeam McSwine. The target was located just inside an edge of the Forest of Éperlecques near Watten which offered the V2 launch sites a measure of concealment.

For this mission *Old Reliable* was the lead plane of the 365th Squadron in the 305th element of the overall larger formation. The V2 launching sites incorporated hardened concrete block-houses. The bombers and their escort flew across France between Calais and Boulogne at 16,000 feet and encountered heavy flak but were not engaged by enemy fighters.[8]

In the 305th combat box formation *Old Reliable,* with McGovern aboard, flew in the same 3 plane V element as the *Moonbeam McSwine* which was positioned to starboard, slightly behind and slightly below *Old Reliable*. It was the first mission in quite a while that Kney's crew had not flown the *Moonbeam* – their usual B-17.

With considerable haze over the ground below, the formation broke into its various groups. The 305th soon arrived at the Initial Point where its B-17s opened their bomb doors to start the bomb run into the late evening sun.[9] *Old Reliable* and the *Moonbeam McSwine* were flying close together when the lead 305th B-17 started to drop its bombs as did all the bombers behind it. As McGovern filmed the fall of the bombs on the target below the V2 site resembled a hole in the ground surrounded as it was by dense forestry.[10] As they flew through it the flak remained unrelenting and very accurate.

With *Bombs Away* at last the 305th B-17s peeled off flying a slightly looser formation as they headed for the Rally Point to reform into their mass formation for the run for home. Having filmed and photographed throughout the mission so far McGovern now raised his Baby Speedgraphic stills camera and framed the *Moonbeam* through the starboard machine gun port as she flew above the northern French countryside close to St. Omer. Only seconds after the camera shutter closed Mack witnessed a terrific explosion. A flak burst caught the *Moonbeam* and she immediately caught fire.[11]

The 'Moonbeam McSwine' as photographed by Dan McGovern seconds before it was hit by flak and went down over St. Omer, France. **Photo: The Ken Snyder Collection/Eric Barko.**

German soldiers inspect what remains of the 'Moonbeam McSwine' at its crash site at St. Omer, France. **Photo: The Nagel Collection/AFHRA.**

He now watched in horror as, almost in slow motion, the blazing *Moonbeam McSwine,* billowing and trailing smoke, now started to lag behind the formation. The stricken B-17 flew on for some distance before it spun out of control and went down in flames crashing in a fireball.[12] Some parachutes were seen by other passing crewmen but the *Moonbeam* and her crew, along with combat cameraman Sergeant Bill Wood, were gone. To rub salt into the wounds, the lead 305th B-17 dropped its bombs too early resulting in the entire group's bombs mostly falling short of the target leaving the crews very bitter indeed.

1. Archives of the American Air Museum in Britain.
2. The author discovered a vague reference to one of these filming techniques in one of McGovern's accounts. However, the additional details used in the narrative were made known to the author by Gary Boyd, Director, AETC History and Museums Program at Randolph Air Force Base, Texas. Mr. Boyd knew Dan McGovern but heard details of his innovative firming techniques directly from Dan's great friend 422nd Bomb Squadron Flight Engineer and Top Turret Gunner, the late David Nagel.
3. Quote to the *Buffalo Evening News*, March 1944.
4. *The Schweinfurt-Regensburg Mission of the 8th Air Force – Animated, The Operations Room*, You Tube.
5. Freeman, *Mighty Eighth War Diary*.
6. Wikipedia.
7. American Air Museum in Britain archive.
8. The Summary of Operations/Combat Diary of both the 305th Bomb Group and the 369th Bomb Squadron, 306th Bomb Group, state that no enemy fighters were encountered.
9. From the combat diary of 369th Bomb Squadron, 306th Bomb Group. Unusually, the 306th bombed by squadron rather than by group that day and from only 15,000 feet, factors which the crews felt were unnecessarily dangerous. It is unknown if the 305th and the 92nd Bomb Groups did likewise but it appears that the bitterness recorded resulted from dropping too early. The change in bombing tactic may have been due to the importance of the target.
10. Combat diary of 369th Bomb Squadron, 306th Bomb Group.
11. Account gleaned from the official 305th Bomb Group Summary of Operations from 27th August 1943, AFHRA; the mission diary of *Old Reliable's* waist gunner Sgt. Ken Snyder via Eric Barko and also from the accounts of the *Moonbeam's* navigator that day, Lt. Jim Meade and photographer Bill Wood in *Collection of 305th BG Stories* Vol. 1 – Chris Coffman. Chris's father, Robert Coffman, was the *Moonbeam's* co-pilot on the Watten raid

and became a POW. McGovern later gave Snyder the print of this photograph which is reproduced here along with many others in his keepsake collection now in the careful possession of Eric Barko.

12. The *Moonbeam's* pilot, Lt. Don *Pappy* Moore, perished that day but managed to hold the B-17 straight and level long enough for his crew to bail out before the bomber went down. Four were killed and the remaining crew members of *Moonbeam* taken as prisoners of war. Another B-17 was also hit by flak on the same mission and also crashed in St. Omer. This was *Shangri La Lil* of the 303rd Bomb Group based close to Chelveston at Molesworth USAAF Air Station – American Air Museum in Britain.

15

THE GERMAN ESCORT HOME

Bomb Racks and Searchlights

BACK STATESIDE, the *Memphis Belle's* war bond tour was a great success. For two and a half months the bomber and her crew criss-crossed the nation flying in and out of 31 airfields in American cities and towns raising the profile of how the American bomber boys and their aeroplanes were, day after day now, striking a blow right in the heart of Nazi Germany itself. Everywhere the *Belle* went the bomber and her crew were cheered by welcoming crowds and lauded by dignitaries and celebrities. The newsreels, newspapers and radio stations had a field day and together made sure that, for both propaganda and morale purposes, the story of the *Memphis Belle* and her brave crew was seen, heard of or read about in every home in America. Millions of dollars had been raised as had the profile of the Army Air Forces much to the delight of its top brass including Commanding General *Hap* Arnold and 8th Air Force commander General Ira Eaker.

All the while Dan McGovern and his Detachment B team continued to gather actual combat footage for what would be the documentary focusing on the *Memphis Belle* which would follow and on which William Wyler was now working towards completion. Now, Mack's fifth mission on Wednesday 15th September 1943, would be a strike against the German Luftwaffe servicing and repair depot and airfields at Romilly Sur Seine eighty miles south-east of Paris.[1] This time he would fly aboard B-17 *Hell-Cat* of the 365th Bomb Squadron.

The crew of the *Hell-Cat* were no strangers to McGovern. He had flown on his previous mission to Watten with Lt. Jack Kney and his crew aboard *Old Reliable* and also with them on the *Moonbeam McSwine* for his first combat mission to Villacoublay now two months before. Kney's co-pilot for this mission though, was Squadron Commander, Major Normand. The navigator was Lt. Jack Edwards but apart from that the crew remained the same. Still there were Demitropoulos, Kiefer, Lane, Lyons, Hill, Snyder and Lewison. However, the crew's usual navigator, Lt. Edward S. Child, would also be on board as a twelfth man. He would fly as a passenger/observer.[2]

EXPERIMENTAL BOMB RACKS

The target of the 8th Air Force's mission Number 90 was important because German reserve aircraft of all types were stored there to supply, re-equip and repair the Luftwaffe in France as well as the Low Countries. In addition to his photographic duties for Wyler's B-17 documentary, McGovern was given an additional assignment for this mission. *Hell-Cat* and several more of the B-17s attacking Romilly Sur Seine had been retro-fitted to increase the bomb load.[3] "This was an experimental trip with a heavier than usual bomb load," Mack recalled. "They had decided to install 1000 pound bombs on racks under the wings of the forts and to carry this load in addition to the bombs in the bomb bay. I went along to photograph the experiment." It was to be an evening mission.

A total of 87 B-17s took off just before 3pm at which point the problems started immediately. The crews of *Hell-Cat* and the bombers fitted with the additional bombs under the wings found that, due to the increased weight, their bombers could not climb at the same rate as the other B-17s. Therefore, the various groups including the 305th were late to form up into their formations. When they eventually did, even on approach to the French coast Lt. Kney noticed an alarming drop in the reading of *Hell-Cat's* gasoline gauge. The pilots on all the experimental bomb rack B-17s noticed the same. Some there and then, having consulted with their flight engineers and navigators, elected to abort their missions having calculated that, with that increased rate of fuel consumption, there was no way they could make it back to base. *Hell-Cat* flew on but even before it reached the French coast McGovern's bomber experienced another problem. Perhaps due to the increased payload, a turbo supercharger, which boosts engine power by increasing air supply, started to malfunction and then stopped working altogether. "So we couldn't reach altitude at all," Dan remembered.

Having already flown some considerable distance into France under fire from flak batteries Kney and Major Normand made the decision to leave the formation and to drop their bombs on another designated enemy target of opportunity close by instead. As *Hell-Cat* then swung for home, alone and vulnerable, quite remarkably still not a single German fighter had appeared. As darkness fell they were reasonably close to the relative safety of the English Channel but Dan's lone B-17 continued to be rocked by heavy flak. It sustained considerable battle damage. Now though, the needle on the ship's gas gauge had Kney extremely worried. In order to conserve enough gasoline to make England he began to throttle back the four engines – a little at first and then a little more. Mack recounted the concern of all on board. "The skipper started to reduce our speed to conserve gasoline and pretty soon we were down to 120mph." Still no German fighters had materialised to intercept *Hell-Cat* but the flak continued along the route home and even with the protective cloak of darkness, there was always the ever-present danger of being detected by German night fighters.

At last *Hell-Cat,* eventually drew away from the coast of France and the flak stopped. They were now over the channel and miraculously still not a single enemy fighter had appeared. Lt. Kney's concerns, however, that there might not be adequate gas to get *Hell-Cat* back to England, continued to grow. Ten minutes later the first of the Wright Cyclone engines, starved of fuel, stopped as Flight Engineer Charlie Kiefer, worked frantically to get the last drop of fuel in the bombers gas tanks to the remaining engines.

Lieutenant Kney passed the word to dump everything possible out of the B-17 and to get ready for a crash-landing in the channel in pitch darkness. Everything had to be dumped to lighten the B-17 and to keep her in the air as long as possible. This was also to minimise the possibility of injury to the crew when the force of the crash-landing would send everything in the fortress flying forward when it ditched in the sea at speed. Anything not secured in the aeroplane had to go and the crew quickly set to their task. Even the waist machine guns were thrown out the side windows into the channel below.

What happened next was a difficult pill for Dan to swallow after surviving that day and filming some great footage. He now realised that he would have to jettison his heavy cameras, his monopod and other gear. "I took most of what I had and threw it out the bomb bay." However, given their light weight he retained a single loaded 16mm cassette camera as well as a small compact stills camera. Then all but the pilots joined Dan and the radioman in the radio compartment where they assumed crash positions on the floor with their hands behind their heads in preparation for ditching at sea. They inflated their Mae West life preservers. Now another engine stopped.

A GUIDING LIGHT

Still gradually losing altitude the bomber continued to limp even closer to the English coast. Dan recounted that then, all of a sudden, Kney announced that they were not now going to ditch in the sea after all. "The sky in front of us was lit up like day with British searchlights."

A formation of German Heinkel He 111 bombers. It was in the middle of such a formation, but at night, that Mack and the crew of 'Hell-Cat' found themselves as they returned over the English coast from the Romilly Sur Seine raid on the night of September 15th 1943. Searchlights and flak bursts would have only intermittently illuminated such a night formation.
Photo: Bundesarchiv, Bild 1011-408-0847-10.

At last the crippled bomber left the real threat of the icy channel water behind it as it crossed over the English coast but into more trouble. "It was then that the British started to throw everything up at us. We could almost walk on the flak. Our radioman frantically tried to contact the base but the radio was closed out. I noticed him leaning over his desk towards me and all the time he was sending out the aircraft's code in morse with his code key. We didn't know it at the time but in the darkness we were riding in with a large formation of German bombers which was raiding the English coast!"

The crew could not see the enemy bombers all around them and the Germans, distracted with the thick British flak, probing searchlights and concentrating on the ground ahead as they approached their targets, were blissfully unaware of the B-17 now in their own formation. Now though pilots Kney and Normand frantically scanned the darkness below looking for somewhere, anywhere, to put the bomber down. With the exception of the searchlights everything was blacked out.[4]

Then, at last, a British searchlight crew noticed the lone B-17 in trouble in the middle of the German bomber formation. Mack: "I think there were three cones of light but then they all went out except for one which caught our plane, circled it and then the big searchlight beam flashed from us several times across the sky to a westerly direction over England. That cone of light in the darkness was our signal of where to go!" With two engines out and the B-17 not responding properly Kney grappled with the controls of the big bomber and managed to turn her in the direction the searchlight had indicated.

Within minutes, yet another engine went out. Now though, with *Hell-Cat* rapidly losing altitude, the pilots could at last see a flashing red beacon light[5] indicating the location of Hawkinge RAF fighter station which was located 8 miles south-west of Dover. However, the landing gear was only partially down. "Lt. Kney knew we'd have to crash-land and asked the crew if they wanted to bail out but everybody decided to stick with him," Mack recalled.

Soon after that the unmistakable silhouetted features of an airfield could be seen not far below and just ahead. There was no time to waste. The pilot warned Mack and the crew as they braced in the radio compartment to get ready for impact. The crippled B-17 was approaching at the wrong angle to use the grass landing strip but Kney and his commander, Major Normand, both knew anyway that they could not risk blocking it with their downed and damaged aeroplane. They would be crash-landing on open ground on the periphery of the airfield.

Almost immediately the B-17 ploughed into the ground and skidded at great velocity some considerable distance in the darkness. They were down. The careering *Hell-Cat* came to an abrupt stop only when it impacted an embankment[6] on the very edge of the airfield so heavily that a portion of one of the bomber's wings and several engines were torn off. The B-17 came to rest on top of the embankment and just short of a precarious drop-off some 30 feet to a farmland below.

McGovern's heavy shearling leathers had provided some bodily protection but he had struck his head and had been knocked unconscious by the force of the impact.[7] He woke up in hospital ten hours later. "All I remember was a British officer coming over to me and asking could they take the remaining machine guns off the bomber! I told him I was a cameraman, that it wasn't my airplane and that I couldn't care less what he did." Apart from one of the crew sustaining a broken arm there were no other injuries but *Hell-Cat* was a total loss.

Mack was released from hospital after a few days and filmed and photographed *Hell-Cat* and her crew as she was being recovered from the crash site. He went back to Chelveston and back to work but his crash-landing on *Hell-Cat* was to have something of a delayed effect on him in the months ahead. Remarkably, this would not be his last crash-landing in a B-17 starved of fuel but it clearly demonstrated, yet again, that the cameraman of the United States Army Air Force put himself in harm's way every bit as much as any other USAAF serviceman on active service.

Mack McGovern had by now completed five dangerous combat missions into German occupied Europe and all without the benefit of an electrically heated suit in temperature extremes of up to − 60 degrees at altitude. He was subsequently awarded the USAAF Air Medal and Flight Wings which were presented to him by the commanding officer of the 8th Combat Camera Unit, Major Ted Tetzlaff. By now, regardless of which B-17 on which he had flown, he had always given the crew members a collection of photographs taken on the mission and around the base. He had also continued to send photographs to the loved ones of the crew members back home.

B-17 'Hell-Cat' at the crash site on the edge of Hawkinge airfield near Dover. What appears to be the runway and parked aircraft are to the right of shot. **Photo: The Ken Snyder Collection/Eric Barko.**

The crew and RAF personnel inspect the damaged 'Hell-Cat' at Hawkinge airfield. **Photo: The Ken Snyder Collection/Eric Barko.**

A front view of the crashed B-17 'Hell-Cat' showing the substantial damage to the aeroplane. **Photo: The Ken Snyder Collection/Eric Barko.**

The bomber came to a halt just yards from the drop-off visible in this photograph. **Photo: The Ken Snyder Collection/Eric Barko.**

The days of Big Mack being regarded as *that nuisance bastard cameraman* were long gone. Apart from his crash-landing, he had completed his missions to date relatively safely and his innovative filming methods, utilising his own system of keeping his cassette cameras warm and protected from the extreme cold at altitude, had performed well – most of the time. Once, to his annoyance, the water in his thermal bucket had frozen solid at altitude for a portion of the mission but, despite this, Mack had identified the problem and overcome it to get the job done. McGovern continued to concentrate also on filming interesting subject matter on the ground wherever he saw it.

By now much of his footage was also being used regularly in newsreels not just back in America, but in Britain and all across the world, in *Army Air Force Combat Weekly Digest* and particularly in many First Motion Picture Unit produced 8th Air Force documentaries. One was *Combat America*, (1943), which was narrated by Hollywood actor Clark Gable[8] who also starred in the production which focused on the B-17 tail gunners – the *stingers*. Gable was stationed with the 351st Bomb Group at Polebrook where the film was shot and only eighteen miles from Chelveston. At the time, Gable had already actually flown several missions into German occupied Europe on a B-17.

McGovern knew Gable. "I worked on footage for *Combat America*. It was a gunnery film." Other 1943 produced films in which Mack's footage was used are *Learn and Live,* an instructional film for pilots and *A Gal Called Stella* which deals with the repair and fly-out of a crash-landed B-17. Another, released in 1944 is *Target for Today*. "That was all shot in England and all in black and white. It was done with real people. There's no actors in it." Much of the footage taken by Dan and his unit for *Target for Today* went on after the war to be used in a commercial movie called *Twelve O'Clock High* starring Hollywood great, Gregory Peck. Another production to which *Big Mack* McGovern contributed would be released in 1945. That was *Target Germany*. "That one was all about the modifications which were

made to future B-17s. *Target Germany* also showed Service
Command – the story of the supplies, the bomb dumps and
things of that sort. It didn't glorify any particular bomber type
either as it had B-17s and B-24s, as well as P-38 and P-51
fighters in it. It told the overall story in greater detail." Mack
captured footage that was used in many more productions.

With the considerable losses of cameramen already incurred
by the 8th Combat Camera Unit on missions over occupied
Europe, Technical Sergeant Mack McGovern, in consultation
with his superiors, now also set about re-organising the unit to
make the best use of the cameramen still available to him.
However, as effective as his filming techniques were, both on the
ground and in the air, the frequency in which they were now
filming in the dangerous combat zone that was German occupied
Europe had begun to take its toll on McGovern. The fear, the
intense combat and the close shaves coupled with the loss of
cameramen colleagues, air crew members and indeed B-17s that
he had come to know well, all began to have something of a
negative effect on him. This was about to come to a head.

The second week of October 1943 saw the USAAF 8th Air
Force undertake a series of maximum effort missions against
Nazi targets in continental Europe. On October 8th targets were
hit in the Breman and Vegesack areas. Then the following day
Marienburg, Danzig, Anklam and Gdynia were all bombed. The
day after that, on 10th October, Mack McGovern boarded a B-17
at Chelveston called *Nobody's Baby* of the 365th Bomb Squadron
for what would be his sixth and final combat mission. This
bomber had been so named before it even left America because,
just like *SNAFU* due to its negative idiosyncrasies, no pilot
wanted it.[9] This was 8th Air Force mission number 114 against
the railroad facilities and waterway canals of Münster in Western
Germany. However, it would turn out to be another bad day for
the 8th Air Force and also for Dan McGovern. It had taken some
time to gather them up, but Mack filmed on board *Nobody's Baby*
using replacement cassette and GSAP cameras, working from a

replacement thermal bucket and with a replacement camera extension monopod and bomb bay camera cradle system. This time the 305th was positioned as the high group behind the 92nd Bomb Group in the lead and with the 306th Bomb Group in the low element of the V shaped combat wing formation.[10]

Mack filmed from the centre of the second combat wing formation to arrive over the target of 139 bombers comprising what was by now collectively called the 1st Bombardment *Division* sixteen B-17s of which were from the 305th Bomb Group. The initial attack on Münster had been made by the 3rd Bombardment Division comprising 133 B-17s which was intercepted by hundreds of German fighters over the city scattering the attacking force. Twenty nine B-17s of this division were shot down and over fifty sustained battle damage.[11]

Once McGovern's 1st Bombardment Division reached the Initial Point and broke up into its individual groups for the bomb run the 305th was attacked by enemy fighters for a full ten minutes before they broke off the attack. They took a mauling but no Chelveston B-17 was shot down. However, by the time the 305th eventually did arrive over the city, so thick were the palls of smoke and haze that it obscured the targets below resulting in many of the bomber groups diverting either to secondary targets or other targets of opportunity.[12]

Apart from the smoke cover resulting from the initial bombardment from the first wave of bombers, the Germans were also deploying experimental smoke screens for the first time that day. Then, quite suddenly at the last minute, McGovern's 305th Bomb Group and its 16 bombers were forced off its bomb run over Münster to avoid colliding with another group also on its bomb run.[13] The 305th now joined 17 B-17s from the 379th Bomb Group. On the return leg home they bombed German airfields at Enschede in the north-east of the Netherlands and close to the German border.

In the course of the day, of the two formations comprising 307 bombers sent out, a total of 30 were shot down. Three B-17s in McGovern's formation had sustained battle damage and *Nobody's Baby* was about to have troubles of her own. McGovern was in the nose of the bomber where he had anxiously watched the approaching English coast and shared the relief of all on board when they had finally crossed it. Now, through one of the two navigator's windows to his left, he filmed the silhouette of the B-17 cast by the sun onto the English countryside below as it kept pace with the bomber which now approached its landing field still some distance ahead. However, just like *Hell-Cat* on her return from Romilly on McGovern's last mission, *Nobody's Baby* was now dangerously low on fuel.

Within minutes the B-17's Number 3 engine, the closest inboard engine on the starboard wing, started to miss and splutter and then stopped starved of fuel. Realising they were almost out of gasoline the flight engineer and top turret gunner Carl Brunswick worked feverishly on his fuel line taps trying to spread the feed of the few remaining gallons of gasoline in the gas tanks evenly between the remaining three engines. With Brunswick busy, co-pilot Ray Bullock feathered the propeller on the stopped engine to minimise the air resistance by turning its three blades away from the onrushing wind. Now, everybody on board was getting nervous. Skipper, Jim Oakley, managed to get the landing gear down and warned his crew to prepare for a possible crash-landing. The gunners, navigator and bombardier joined the radioman in his compartment and assumed brace positions. McGovern, however, had other ideas.

A CRASH-LANDING FILMED

This time, unlike prior to his last crash-landing on *Hell-Cat*, he had not been ordered to jettison any of his movie cameras and filming gear and it was also daylight. He immediately set about filming the potential crisis as it began to unfold around him. He filmed the starboard stalled engine through the navigator's window. All was fine for a minute or so until the Number 4 engine on the outermost starboard side also started to cough and splutter. Mack filmed it as it stopped too. The tension mounted.

At about six hundred feet and with the bomber losing height rapidly co-pilot Bullock was feathering the second stalled engine when a third, Number 1 engine, on the extreme left port side of the B-17 also stalled starved of fuel. All the time Mack continued to film, but sparingly, to make sure he had ample unexposed film ready for what he now suspected was to come. "The two engines on the right side were out and one on the left so with my camera rolling I cut to the right and cut to the left. We had one engine."[14]

A frame from McGovern's footage from his second crash-landing on approach to Chelveston showing the two starboard engines out on B-17 'Nobody's Baby' on return from the Münster mission of 10th October 1943. **Image: US National Archives.**

Another frame showing the stalled #1 engine on the port wing of B-17 'Nobody's Baby' as filmed by Dan McGovern low on approach over Chelveston on 10th October 1943. Seconds later the remaining fourth engine would also stop. **Image: US National Archives.**

The B-17 now approached Chelveston[15] with the propeller feathered on the third stalled engine. The pilots started to struggle now as they tried to control the lumbering bomber which was now very rapidly losing height. Oakley called out over the intercom for all crew members to brace for a hard landing. At least now they were on final approach to one of the runways and there was a chance that, even with only one engine, the B-17 might land at least somewhat normally. Mack wanted to capture this unorthodox landing on film and moved further forward in the nose of the B-17. He too now braced for impact but pointed his camera through the plexiglass just in front of him. With virtually no power and now on a precarious glide path McGovern filmed as Oakley managed to keep the rapidly descending bomber straight and level. Both pilots were still desperately attempting to make some last second adjustments when the wheels of the B-17 violently impacted the runway. Everybody inside braced even harder now and McGovern somehow managed to continue to film as he instinctively braced even harder too.

The force of the impact on the undercarriage and the excessive landing speed was a dangerous combination. "The B-17 skidded off the runway and ended up in a gully," McGovern remembered. "I figured that if I was going to die I would go down doing what I do best so I filmed that crash-landing.[16] You don't think about it in the excitement. You're not really scared. It's afterwards that you're scared." Mack continued: "When you have time to think about what you've just gone through. It's then that you get scared and I was shaking like a leaf."[17] Again he sustained some injuries and was removed to the nearest hospital for treatment but returned to duty.

A FIELD COMMISSION

Five days later, on 15th October 1943, Technical Sergeant Dan *Big Mack* McGovern travelled to 8th Air Force Headquarters at Bushy Park, Middlesex south of London. There he received a field commission to the rank of Second Lieutenant in the United States Army Air Forces, in no small part because of the work he had undertaken to obtain his combat footage. The achievement however, was tinged with considerable sadness. The previous day, as part of the latest maximum effort bombing campaign, the four squadrons of the 305th Bomb Group had set out on a second mission to bomb the ball bearing factories of Schweinfurt. This second Schweinfurt raid, as with many other missions that week, had resulted in a terrible price in US servicemen and aircraft.

Of 291 bombers dispatched from the various bomb groups for Schweinfurt, 257 had entered German airspace. 60 were shot down, just over 20% of the number dispatched. 229 bombers reached Schweinfurt and dropped their bombs and 197 returned to England. McGovern learned that his own 305th Bomb Group was the worst hit group of the entire mission. It lost 13 of its 15 B-17s and 130 crewmen of which 36 were killed. The group's 364th Bomb Squadron was totally destroyed that day within thirteen minutes and before it could even cross the Rhine.[18]

Thursday 14th October 1943 was the 8th Air Force's worst day in Europe and infamously became known as *Black Thursday* in the annals of the United States Army Air Forces. The second Schweinfurt raid had occurred within what would become known as *Black Week*. The gloom that hung over Station 105 was not hard to comprehend. In the late evening of October 14th the crew chiefs and maintenance teams, always the first to welcome back the returning bombers and crews, had remained on the empty hard stands refusing to leave as they vainly waited for the return of *their* B-17s from Schweinfurt.

Over the previous months McGovern had filmed many of these men at their work, focused and industrious, as they brought to bear their own particular skills, expertise and often creative innovation in a combined dedicated effort to keep their designated B-17s airworthy. However, even as dusk fell that fateful October evening these ground crews still constantly scanned the skies above the Northamptonshire countryside harbouring the dawning realisation of the catastrophe that had befallen their ships and crews. The maintenance men were eventually ordered to stand down and did so only reluctantly. Mack too had known the lost crews and their bombers well.

Now, all around the dispersal areas on the peripheries of Station 105, all but a few of the concrete hard stands remained empty as throughout scores of barracks in the communal areas the personal possessions and the bedding of the lost crew members were being gradually but reverently cleared. The mood on the base was one of stunned resignation. In yet another testament to the sheer scale of the projection of American air power, these lost crews and their aeroplanes would, however, all be replaced within days.

Dan had not been seriously injured in his October 10th crash-landing but the trauma of two crash-landings, the head injury he had sustained in his first one and the terrible events of October 14th had exacerbated other psychological factors. Given these factors, his own considerable combat experiences and with his continued determined efforts to re-organise the 8th Combat Camera Unit, McGovern had just pushed himself too far. Consequently, some time afterwards, 2nd Lieutenant McGovern collapsed and was later found in convulsions. He was rushed to a local hospital but was soon transferred to the 2nd General Military Hospital in Oxford. This was St. Hugh's College, one of the four colleges of the University of Oxford, which had been requisitioned as a specialist head injury military hospital for the duration of the war.[19] He was suffering from Combat Fatigue.[20] Dan elaborated on the condition: "When you're a cameraman you're trained not to become a participant in what you're photographing because, if you do, you're going to lose the action. Then, after its all over, you become aware of what you have just done and you replay that action. It's like the person that will run over to a burning car to pull people out. It's an instinct. They don't realise they've done it until it's all over."

Big Mack reflected on some of his own harrowing experiences during his time with the 305th Bomb Group. "Combat men don't like to talk about what they did. You go through recollections of airplanes crashing, of pulling headless bodies out of airplanes and heads with helmets still on, limbs here, limbs there. You say to yourself – 'There for the grace of God go I' and you relive it in your sleep. It's an experience you will never forget. So you get nervous. You're all shook up and I think that's what happened to me. I think I was just plumb worn out and as it turned out, that was to end my work with Detachment B."

Meanwhile, exposed colour film totalling 20,000 feet shot by Wyler and William Clothier from the original team augmented by the footage shot by Dan McGovern and other cameramen of the 8th Combat Camera Unit would eventually be edited down into the finished film for director William Wyler's *Memphis Belle* documentary. Filming was now virtually wrapped and back in America Wyler now moved into post-production mode to turn all the exposed footage into what he had now planned to be a substantial and ground breaking documentary.

Now hospitalised in Oxford, Big Mack found himself at the start of what would be a long road to recovery. His predicament was tempered to some degree at least by several positive developments. The first came in a letter from home. Dan learned that his first child, a son, had been born. He and Virginia would name the baby boy Daniel Junior. The second positive development occurred a month after the second Schweinfurt raid and in mid-November 1943. It was then that a thin, somewhat gaunt and dishevelled figure turned up to visit Mack in hospital with a big smile on his face. Mack could not believe who it was. Standing in front of him was none other than Sergeant Bill Wood who had been posted missing and presumed dead after Big Mack watched in horror as the *Moonbeam McSwine,* on which Wood was filming, was shot down by flak right in front of him over St. Omer, France back on August 27th.

Sergeant Wood told McGovern the amazing story of how he had managed to get back. Mack related it. "Bill had been sitting in the waist of the B-17 with his camera watching and waiting for action. When the flak got especially heavy he looked out at the engines." It was around 7.15pm. Suddenly, a flak round exploded very close and caught the bomber on its belly between the ball turret and the left waist gunner's position knocking out the B-17's oxygen and interphone systems. Almost immediately another round exploded at full force just beneath the port wing between its two engines. Another flak burst blew the wingtip off. The bomber, now on fire, started to vibrate violently before it slowly started to spiral and fall. The pilot, *Pappy* Moore, realising the bomber was doomed, hit the bailout alarm button which sent every crew member scrambling for their parachutes.

The flames very quickly spread from the front portion of the B-17 all the way back to the tail. Avoiding the flames, Wood, having quickly donned his parachute, crawled desperately along the deck of the bomber to get to the waist hatch on the starboard side just aft of the waist gunner's window. In quick succession Wood saw the waist gunners jump. He then saw the wounded ball turret gunner scrambling out of his turret inside the *Moonbeam* in an attempt to get to his parachute and jump too. "With the fort on fire Wood then grabbed his parachute and jumped from 14,000 feet." He fell out backwards. As he fell he saw the *Moonbeam* engulfed in flames.

McGovern recalled: "Somehow, Bill Wood had known instinctively not to pull his parachute immediately. This was to make it more difficult for the Germans to follow him and pick him up where he would land but also to avoid the burning material falling above him onto his parachute canopy from his own stricken B-17. Mack added: "He told me that the fall gave him the sensation of falling from a high diving board. He turned over and over, falling through the barrages of flak. He was falling too fast to be a target. When he opened his chute at 2,000 feet he felt like his body was being pulled apart. He only saw two other parachute canopies and then he briefly saw the *Moonbeam* again. It was back in level flight but burning furiously and quickly losing altitude as it made a slow sweeping 180 degree turn over the target area. Wood landed safely and his only injury was a twisted ankle."[21]

Once on the ground he had made it to a French farmhouse where the occupants fed and sheltered him and then passed him on to another French farmhouse. Interestingly, as he tried to light a cigarette inside the house, the farmer forbad it, took his American cigarettes and gave him some local tobacco instead, explaining that the Germans could distinguish the difference in the distinct smell of American cigarettes to French tobacco – a fact which would give the game away that an American had been sheltered there. Wood was then passed on to the French Resistance. He was given a kayak and told to paddle in a particular direction on a canal.

At one stage he had been challenged by the Germans and thinking he was out of options, indicated that he was surrendering by raising his paddle which was then shot out of his hands. He quickly grabbed it again and paddled away. Somehow, he had narrowly escaped being captured by the Germans and eventually made it to Paris. Having been passed from one Resistance group to another they eventually got him over the Pyrenees into Spain where he was interned. Dan added: "After being bonded out by the American embassy he soon arrived back at our unit." Remarkably, Wood was not the only one who had bailed out of the *Moonbeam* and managed to evade capture. Tail gunner, Jim King, had also managed to evacuate the doomed *B-17* through the rear hatch just forward of his gun position and had landed safely. He had managed to evade the Germans too and with the help of the Resistance, had eventually been smuggled out of France by sea. He returned to Chelveston in or around the same time as Wood.

CAMERAMEN CASUALTIES

By the end of 1943 and including Sgt. Wood's return and McGovern's hospitalisation, of the 9 officers and 23 enlisted men of the original 8th Combat Camera Unit who had arrived at bases in England seven months before, only six remained. The remainder had either been killed in action or hospitalised like Mack, or been transferred. McGovern's unit had suffered its first fatality when Lt. Tony Edwards[22] who was the liaison man for the 8th CCU's commanding officer, Major Tetzlaff, was reassigned to the unit's medium bomber bombardment group on B-26 twin engine Marauders. The group had flown 80 support missions without anybody being killed or wounded. Dan remembered: "That was Edwards' first mission." It was also his last. "Over the target his bomber was completely blown up."

Sergeant Irving Slater from Tennessee subsequently reported to the 8th CCU at Chelveston from the USAAF replacement centre in England. "We sent him out to cover the B-24 Liberator heavy bombers. He went on a few missions and then he was killed." Another cameraman, Sgt. Robert Hussey Jr., went out one day to film a mission on a B-26 Marauder. Dan remembered what happened to him: "He had his glasses shot off. He had double vision and couldn't see what he was doing. He groped around and nearly fell out through the Marauder's bomb bay. A gunner pulled him back. He was later hospitalised and was returned to the US where he was discharged."

Another casualty was Sgt. David Barker from New York City. "His first missions were uneventful but he then went on a routine mission and his ship was hit and burst into flames. Several men jumped free but he wasn't one of them. He was officially listed as Missing In Action." Barker had particularly impressed McGovern with his actions and coolness under fire during a mission to Stuttgart on September 6th. Barker had been filming from a waist window on B-17 *Big Moose* with Lt. Kney and his crew when, with his camera rolling over Germany, Barker faced down a German fighter that was diving straight at him with all guns blazing. "He never moved," Mack said of Barker, "he wanted that footage."

Barker wasn't wounded by the German fighter but nor was he finished going above and beyond the call of duty as he filmed that day. *Big Moose* ran out of fuel on return to Chelveston and had to crash-land at RAF Heston outside London. Mack takes up the story which was very similar to his own second crash-landing. "Barker went into the bombardier's compartment, the most dangerous position on the ship, aimed his camera out through the plexiglass nose, started the camera rolling and braced himself on the floor. He got sensational pictures of the ground rushing up at the fortress and the actual impact of the crash. That footage has been used hundreds of times since."

An illustrated profile of Dan McGovern which accompanied one of the two 'Stars & Stripes' articles which featured him during WW2. **Image: 'Stars and Stripes' and courtesy of the McGovern family.**

Lt. Dan McGovern was discharged from the 8th Combat Camera Unit on medical grounds on 18th December 1943 after almost seven months with the 305th Bomb Group. After almost three months of medical treatment he was discharged from hospital on 31st January 1944[23] and sailed on a hospital ship for the United States where he would undergo further specialist treatment at a rehabilitation hospital there. Thus ended his tour as a combat cameraman in Europe.

Only three days before, back at the First Motion Picture Unit Headquarters at Fort Roach in Culver City, William Wyler finally completed *Project 114/25 Missions*. Only in December had he given the film its final title – *The Memphis Belle – A Story of A Flying Fortress*. The core of the film captured the Memphis

Belle's 91st Bomb Group base of Bassingbourn with some scenes also having been filmed at air bases at Polebrook, Molesworth, Alconbury, Hardwick and Bovingdon.[24] However, a very large percentage of the documentary footage is of the 305th Bomb Group and features a large proportion of Dan McGovern's footage shot at Chelveston. Wyler was also particularly happy with the ground and aerial shots taken by McGovern[25] so much so that it was to Big Mack that Wyler gifted at least some if not all of the B-Rolls – the reels of out-takes of the finished film. This may also have been in return for McGovern providing Wyler with one of Detachment B's Mitchell cameras in the course of filming in England and before Wyler returned to the United States in July 1943.[26] "That particular Mitchell camera had a great assortment of lenses," Mack recalled.

Of his aerial footage used in the *Memphis Belle* documentary McGovern referred to his innovative handy cassette cameras and thermal box combination which he also used in conjunction with his monopod extension and bomb bay camera cradle systems. "Much of the footage in the *Memphis Belle* documentary was shot in that particular way," he said.

---

1. According to a statement taken by Scanlan from McGovern in his *History of the First Motion Picture Unit, 1944* McGovern's last mission was to Romilly Sur Seine on 15th September 1943. However, based on information obtained in the US NARA archives this was only McGovern's *fifth* mission but it did end in his *first* crash-landing but it occurred at night. The crash-landing he filmed was during the day. Mack flew one additional mission after 15th September 1943.
2. This may have been in a training capacity along with mission navigator Lt. Jack J. Edwards.
3. McGovern's account as recorded *in History of the First Motion Picture Unit, Army Air Forces, California, 1944,* James Scanlan.
4. The 305th Bomb Group mission report for the 15th October 1943 filed by the crew of *Hell-Cat* during their debriefing later states the following: *Due to failure of field lighting at home base and shortage of gasoline several aircraft landed away from base.* This report also states that there were no enemy fighters encountered during the mission – AFHRA via Steve Quillman, 305th Bomb Group Historical FB Page.

5. At night every RAF aerodrome displayed a flashing red navigational beacon called a Pundit. These were a portable self-contained generator powered unit which flashed a two letter morse signature code unique to each air station.

6. *Hell-Cat* came to rest on the embankment inside the perimeter of Hawkinge aerodrome and adjoining Terlingham Farm.

7. In his USAF oral history the sequence of Dan McGovern's two crash-landings and the one in which he sustained his head injury are not clearly defined. Dan states that his first crash-landing, which was certainly on *Hell-Cat* on 15th September 1943, resulted in ending his tour with the 8th Air Force in England. However, this cannot be correct as he is documented as flying another mission on 10th October 1943. The author has concluded that he was released from hospital possibly the following day and having returned to duty photographed the recovery of the crash-landed *Hell-Cat* at Hawkinge. He was hospitalised again after his second crash-landing on his next mission which only then resulted in bringing an end to his 8th Air Force tour. The author has therefore written the narrative to reflect this conclusion.

8. Gable was still grieving the loss of his wife actress Carole Lombard in a plane crash in Nevada in January 1942.

9. American Air Museum in Britain archive.

10. Deduced from 369th Squadron Combat Diary, 306th Bomb Group.

11. 305th Bomb Group Summary of Operations, 11th October 1943.

12. Blind bombing radar systems do not appear to have been in use by the 305th Bomb Group at this point.

13. 305th Bomb Group Summary of Operations, 11th October 1943.

14. Quote taken from McGovern's *Shooting War* interview. Dreamworks Video (2000).

15. Via Brad Markell, California. Dan McGovern told him in conversation that he crash-landed at Chelveston on 10th October 1943.

16. Some of the *engines out* footage taken by McGovern as well as the daylight footage of the *Hell-Cat* crash site filmed following his earlier September 15th 1943 first crash-landing were both used in *A Gal Called Stella* (1943) albeit with one stalled engine scene which appears to have been reversed. The film focuses on the repair of a crash-landed B-17 called *Stella* on farmland and the building of a temporary runway to fly the repaired B-17 out and back to service. It is also possible that Dan McGovern filmed additional scenes for this production. Some scenes used in *A Gal Called Stella* also appeared in the Steven Spielberg produced and Tom Hanks narrated documentary *Shooting War /Dreamworks Video* (2000). In this documentary, focusing on the combat cameramen of WW2, McGovern, speaking about the crash-landing he filmed, explains how he shot it. The author believes, however, that the final few seconds of actual impact footage used in *A Gal Called Stella* which also featured in the *Shooting War* sequence is actually that shot by McGovern's Detachment B colleague David Barker when he crash-landed in the field of oats on B-17 *Big Moose*. This was with Jack Kney's crew at Heston, England on 6th September 1943. McGovern's own actual footage which captured his B-17 touching down heavily and veering off the runway before coming to rest in a gully was most likely simply

replaced by 1943 film editors with Barker's earlier footage for more dramatic effect.

17. From McGovern's *Shooting War* interview, *Dreamworks Video*.

18. American Air Museum in Britain. Major Charles Normand, with whom Dan McGovern had flown twice, was Mission Commander for the 305th Bomb Group for this, the equally infamous second raid on Schweinfurt. He was among the crews of only two B-17s to return to Chelveston out of fifteen sent out that fateful day.

19. *WW2 People's War* Online Archive BBC, Deborah Quare.

20. Given his combat experiences and recollections McGovern was more than likely suffering from what today we call Post Traumatic Stress Disorder (PTSD).

21. The parachutes with which B-17 crews were equipped were, for the large part, exactly the same reserve parachutes used by American paratroopers. Two spring loaded snap hooks on the back of the parachute pack attached it in seconds to two D rings on the front of the parachute harness which was donned by each crew member before take-off. These reserve canopies had a smaller than normal 28 feet diameter which resulted in harder landings and injuries. Backpack parachutes were also used but to a much lesser extent.

22. McGovern's recollections of combat cameraman casualties drawn from his accounts recorded in James Scanlan's *History of the First Motion Picture Unit, Army Air Forces, California*. 1944. Edwards was killed the same day *Delta Rebel 2*, one of Wyler's original B-17 contenders, went down in flames in a raid over Gelsenkirchen, Germany on August 12th 1943.

23. *History of the First Motion Picture Unit, Army Air Forces, 1944*, James Scanlan.

24. *Memphis Belle, Dispelling the Myths*, Presentation by Dr Harry Friedman, National Museum of the US Air Force, April 18th 2018.

25. *305th BG Stories*, 6th Collection – Chris Coffman.

26. This was confirmed to Gary Boyd, Director, AETC History and Museums Program at Randolph Air Force Base Museum, Texas, by 422nd bomb Squadron Flight Engineer and Top Turret Gunner, the late David Nagel – a great friend of Dan McGovern. Mr. Nagel also stated that it was Dan who subsequently placed the out-takes in the US National Archives. Whilst a considerable amount of Wyler's completed *The Memphis Belle – A Story of A Flying Fortress* contains 305th Bomb Group footage shot by McGovern and his team the out-takes also contain a considerable amount of this material. Wyler may also have omitted it for continuity reasons given that the *Memphis Belle* was based at Bassingbourn. These out-takes have been used in many productions. Most recently, the footage has been meticulously restored and used to make the Erik Nelson directed *The Cold Blue* (2017). In the book *Five Came Back*, Mark Harris states that Wyler arrived back in the United States on 26th June 1943. However, in his biography *William Wyler, the Life and Films of Hollywood's Most Celebrated Director*, Gabriel Miller refers to a letter from Wyler to Asst. Secretary of War for Air, Robert Lovett, in which he indicates that he is, only at that point, leaving for the United States.

PART 3

Japan and the Post War Years

16

PRESIDENT TRUMAN'S DECISION

Into Japan 1945

Lt. Daniel McGovern disembarked a ship in New York Harbour in early February 1944. He was glad to be home. Dan was now scheduled to spend some time at a US military rehabilitation facility in Utica, New York until he was fully recovered but first he would call to the McGovern apartment in The Bronx to visit his father and sisters. "My eldest sister Margaret had by now married and moved to Ohio, but my other three sisters Ann, Betty[1] and Genevieve, were all living in the apartment with Dad at the time." Having visited the apartment and having been given a big welcome home by his sisters Dan asked after his Dad. He was surprised to learn that the former RIC sergeant had decided to come out of retirement.

As a wartime necessity, Dan Sr. was back at his old job as a policeman at the New Haven and Hartford Railroad station. "So I went down to see my father," Dan remembered. Both father and son were delighted to see each other and during their conversation Dan Jr. asked his father why he was back working at the railroad station. The old RIC sergeant pointed out that, as so many men were away fighting for the United States in the war, he too had to do his bit for the duration.

Dan pictured with his father in New York on his return
from Europe in January 1944. The old RIC sergeant passed
away two weeks after this photograph was taken. **Photo**
courtesy of the McGovern family.

"I came back to take care of the boys," he explained. "Sure,
there's nobody else to take over," he told Dan in his Irish Cavan
brogue." After a long conversation and much catching up, Dan
Jr. had to be on his way to Utica and he and his father embraced.
"Well Dad, you take care of yourself." There was a short pause
before the old police sergeant replied: "Ohh….. I've a feeling you
won't be seeing me again, Danny." Two weeks later the elder Dan
McGovern was preparing to shave in the bathroom of the family
apartment. He always left the door open when shaving and was

having a conversation with his daughter, Ann, who was sitting in a nearby room. Meat had become rationed in the United States at the latter end of 1943 and now required a certain amount of *red points* in addition to money to buy. Old Dan enquired of his daughter: "Ann, how many points did you pay for the meat?" Ann was about to answer when she heard something metallic fall on the tile floor in the bathroom. A little worried, she got up and made her way hurriedly towards her father. "Dad?" She found him lying on the bathroom floor with one arm outstretched and his razor close by. He was dead. Dan Jr: "He had a heart attack and that was it. He was 74."

Meanwhile, *The Memphis Belle – A Story of A Flying Fortress,* was distributed by Paramount Pictures under the auspices of the US government's War Activities Committee and had its general release on 21st February 1944. Five hundred Technicolor prints had been distributed right across the United States so that the documentary would be seen in cinemas by the American public. It was a smash hit with press reviews lauding in particular its B-17 flight and combat scenes all shot in brilliant colour. Meanwhile, only days later, the six remaining men of the original 8th Combat Camera Unit were rotated home. This was once a replacement unit comprising fresh personnel arrived in England from the First Motion Picture Unit's Cameramen Replacement Pool in Culver City.[2]

Having first attended his father's funeral, Dan then spent several more months in rehabilitation in Utica. After some excellent care, rest and relaxation, he was soon back to himself. "They put me through a whole series of tests and I thought that I would be released from the service but I was a doer. I didn't feel sorry for myself. I'd always work by writing articles or something. I became useful. I think that was my salvation." Lt. Dan McGovern went back on duty to one of the major US Army Air Forces Bombardment Training Centres in the United States. "They sent me to Will Rogers Field in Oklahoma City to join the reconnaissance squadron there and I became a Public Affairs

Officer." However, pretty soon Dan was gravitating back towards his chosen area of expertise – motion picture camera work. "Through pure persistence and determination I got back into film production and I was transferred out of the reconnaissance squadron." Dan was going back to familiar ground as a Cameraman/Director. "I went back to the First Motion Picture Unit in Culver City and Captain Reagan was still there as adjutant." By now Dan and Ronald Reagan had a great mutual respect for each other, both at a professional and personal level and had become good friends. Also by this time, the First Motion Picture Unit had been renamed the 18th Army Air Force Base Unit, although many associated with the unit would always refer to it fondly by its original name.

US National Archives.

THE COOK'S PART IN *THREE CADETS*

Straight away Dan was assigned to work on a training film called *Three Cadets*. This was more of a warning film explaining how promiscuous social behaviour by young officers could undermine the war effort. Dan recalled the production: "That was a picture on venereal disease. I filmed the ugly side of the disease and what it looks like in both the female and the male." Dan approached an Air Force cook at Fort Roach and said he needed him for a part in the film and asked him if he would volunteer. The cook agreed but was somewhat bewildered when his *part* turned out to be filmed being correctly covered with a rubber prophylactic for the cameras! Dan added: "We took the finished picture up to the Santa Ana Army Air Force Training Centre over thirty miles away where we screened it for the first time to about 4000 to 5000 cadets."

Dan pictured as a 2nd Lieutenant. This is the photograph which accompanied his letter to his baby daughter, Patricia, in 1945. **Photo courtesy of the McGovern family.**

Over the ensuing months, Dan worked on many other productions at the 18th AAF Base Unit/First Motion Picture Unit and this sometimes called for him to be away filming on location. A year after returning from England in February 1945,

Dan was away once more from Virginia and his toddler son when the couple welcomed their second child, a daughter they called Patricia. The day after Patricia was born Mack penned a letter to her and enclosed with it a recent photograph of himself dressed in his officer's uniform. She would read and understand it when she was old enough. In the letter he explained his absence but the following excerpt perhaps best sums up the reason Dan and so many others like him were away serving in the United States Armed Forces during World War 2.

It read: ... *My present absence from home will not be for long, for you see Patricia I am doing just a little so that you and Danny and your children when the time comes, can live a normal life and not be troubled with wars and dictators. I just don't want you to be denied the happiness that America offers all people, regardless of race, color or creed.*" In the years ahead, Dan and Virginia, would go on to have two more sons, Mike and Tim.

On 12th April 1945 President Franklin Delano Roosevelt passed away and his Vice President, Harry S. Truman, became the 33rd President of the United States. Less than a month later, on 7th May 1945, Germany surrendered to the Allies and the war in Europe at least, finally ended. Within weeks, Dan's brother, Lieutenant Malachy McGovern, travelled from England to Ireland.[3] A photograph of him in his full US Navy uniform along with another Irish-born American officer, was taken on Dublin's O'Connell Street and appeared on the front page of *The Irish Press* newspaper on 31st May 1945. Within days Malachy was back in Carrickmacross. He was the first of the McGovern family to return to his boyhood hometown.

At around the same time and given his considerable experience, Dan McGovern was promoted to First Lieutenant and sent on another cinematography assignment overseas. This time he was assigned to be part of a special production team of the 11th Combat Camera Unit, based mainly on the Pacific's Mariana Islands, to make a documentary being produced by Warner Brothers called *The Last Bomb*. On this assignment, Mack was under the command of producer/director Major Frank Lloyd who, back in 1935, had directed *Mutiny On the Bounty* with Clark Gable and Charles Laughton. The movie had won an Academy Award for *Best Picture*.

US National Archives.

Of Lloyd's latest production Dan remembered: "*The Last Bomb* was a big production being filmed in 35mm Technicolor Monopack, a very unstable son-of-a-bitch of a colour film. It was a new *colour reversal* film that sometimes had a bad habit of turning magenta if not stored properly." In fact, for stability purposes, the original raw stock Monopack film had to be stored in a special container with dry ice. Dan said of it: "When you needed a roll of Monopack you had to take it out of the box and get it back to room temperature before using it. Apart from that, it was really good stuff." Kodachrome was another popular colour reversal film by then which, like Technicolor Monopack, was processed directly into a positive print eliminating the negative altogether.

In the 1940s virtually all movie film stock in use, regardless of brand, was what was called *nitrate* based. It was highly flammable and had to be carried and stored in special containers. It decomposed slowly but continuously and was prone to shrinkage over its lifetime. During the war years it had only started to be gradually replaced by Cellulose Triacetate or simply *acetate* based *Safety Film* which was a much more stable film.[4]

Despite its title, *The Last Bomb* focuses mainly on the conventional bombing of Japan by the USAAF operating B-29 bombers from the islands of Tinian, Saipan and Guam. These islands had been either captured or recaptured by the Americans and air bases built or extended on them. Guam was now the headquarters of the 20th Air Force. The tenacity of the Japanese in fighting the Americans in their advance towards Japan had been demonstrated in the Marianas campaign. McGovern now found himself working on the islands of Iwo Jima and Okinawa where a heavy price in American lives had been paid for that advance. In *The Last Bomb* documentary the former Commanding Officer at Chelveston, Curtis LeMay, is featured now promoted to Major General. He is filmed with staff members planning a daylight B-29 mission to bomb industrial targets on one of the home islands of Japan. The film focuses on all aspects of the effort needed to undertake the subsequent mission which involves up to 15 hours in the air and on the mission's demands in human and aircraft terms. Iwo Jima is featured as a fighter base for escorting the B-29s from the Marianas to and from their bombing missions to the Japanese mainland.

However, the Americans soon found out that ground defensive flak and Japanese fighters were still more than capable of intercepting their B-29s and inflicting considerable damage either during their high-flying day missions or their lower altitude night missions. This resulted in B-29s being shot down and with many more crippled and limping back to their bases. Many crash-landed on their return and were so badly damaged that they could never be returned to flight status. McGovern thought that this would be interesting material to film for that aspect of the story for possible inclusion in *The Last Bomb*.

On Tinian, Big Mack also found himself photographing the disposal of beyond repair B-29s which had crash-landed on the island. A large crane suspended the written-off bomber fuselages which were underslung at their centre of gravity. Then a large guillotine cut the fuselage in half. The sections were then dumped over the cliff edge into the ocean below. Dan filmed the dumped bomber sections from the clifftop and then broke down his tripod and camera before hauling the cumbersome filming equipment on foot carefully down to a vantage point closer to sea level. From there he then filmed additional footage of the still visible B-29 sections protruding from the water. When he made his way back up to the top several hours later, he was surprised to find several military policemen waiting for him. "Lieutenant, you've been filming here!" said one of the MPs. "Yes, what's the problem?," Dan enquired.

"General O'Donnell wants to see you," came the reply. The general who wanted to see Dan was Brigadier General Emmet *Rosie* O' Donnell Jr. who, in November 1944 with a mass formation of B-29s, had led the first bombing mission on Tokyo since the Doolittle Raid in 1942.[5] Dan soon found himself standing in front of the general. O'Donnell opened the conversation.

"Lieutenant, I understand that you've been photographing the dumping of these crashed bombers into the sea over there."

"Yes, Sir. That's true," replied Mack.

"What possessed you to do that?" asked the general.

"It's a good historical reference," Mack replied. The general then took on a somewhat more serious demeanour and looked Big Mack squarely in the face before stating a little more sternly: "Do you realise the trouble that I'm already in with the media people? They're accusing me of not salvaging this particular material or that particular material and then here's you, an officer in the Army Air Force, documenting things like that." The general pointed out that such footage was potentially damaging to him on the home front. "Did you photograph that, Lieutenant?" asked the general.

"I sure did," replied McGovern, at which point there was something of a pregnant pause during which the general still continued to look his subordinate officer straight in the face. Mack had to think fast. He reached down and detached his external 400 feet film magazine from his 16mm Mitchell camera, cut the film at the midway point between the magazine's two spools and opened one of the two circular doors of the magazine's *light traps*[6] or spool compartments. He carefully pulled a spool of film from the magazine and handed it to General O'Donnell whose stern expression immediately started to soften. "There you are general. There's the whole thing." General O'Donnell thanked Mack for what he had just done. "McGovern, the MPs will now take you over to the quarry over there where you will see where we, in fact, salvage what we can."

A quarry on Tinian Island containing sections and spare parts of scrapped B-29 bombers. It is likely that this is the quarry to which McGovern was directed by General O'Donnell after he had incurred the general's wrath for filming other scrapped B-29s being thrown into the sea. **Photo: AFHRA.**

Dan was taken by the MPs to the quarry which was close by. It was full of wrecked B-29s in various stages of disassembly with sections for individual parts. He recalled: "I was amazed when I got down there to see that they had everything laid out meticulously with signs for aluminium, copper, silver and platinum.

There were even buckets of mercury. I went around it and filmed the whole thing." However, all was not lost either with Dan's earlier footage of the bomber sections being dumped over the cliff edge. "I'm sure the general didn't know just which side of the magazine was the exposed side and which was the unexposed side. In any case I saved that particular footage!" Dan had in fact handed General O'Donnell the unexposed spool of his magazine and the general and his MPs were none the wiser. In any case, production of *The Last Bomb* was nearing its end as indeed was the war itself.

On 26th July 1945 President Truman and the Allied leaders demanded that the Japanese government surrender unconditionally under the terms of the Potsdam Conference. Truman received no answer. With the Japanese refusing to surrender and the bombardment of their homeland continuing, the United States and its Pacific allies now faced the likelihood of an amphibious invasion of the Japanese mainland scheduled for December 1945.[7] That though, was judged by the Americans, to result in a catastrophic and unacceptable loss of American and Allied lives.

TRUMAN'S DECISION

As Mack McGovern was undertaking film work on Guam towards the completion of *The Last Bomb*, President Truman made a decision. On August 6th 1945, three B-29 bombers of the 509th Composite Group, 20th Air Force, took off from the island of Tinian 120 miles north of Guam, for a six hour flight to Japan. One of the three bombers was called after pilot, Paul Tibbets' mother – *Enola Gay*.

The 3 bombers appeared over Hiroshima in clear weather at 31,000 feet. At 8.09am Tibbets started his bomb run and shortly before 8.15am the *Little Boy* atomic bomb was released over the city. When the bomb fell to 1900 feet it detonated causing an atomic chain reaction that released an unprecedented cataclysmic swathe of death and destruction on the city below. A huge mushroom cloud rose into the sky and beneath it, Hiroshima lay flattened.[8] 70,000 to 80,000 people were killed instantly and hundreds of thousands more injured as a result of this single atomic blast.

It is estimated that within months between 90,000 and 166,000 people died in Hiroshima from the excruciating heat and flash burns and from the acute radiation.[9] American President Harry S. Truman then again called on the Empire of Japan to surrender warning that it could now expect a *rain of ruin from the air* if it did not. Still no offer of a Japanese surrender came.

Then, just after 11.01am on the morning of August 9th, three days after the first atomic bomb was dropped on Hiroshima, another USAAF B-29 called *Bockscar* dropped a second American nuclear bomb called *Fat Man* on the industrial city of Nagasaki which lay at the end of a long bay on the island of Kyushu. It exploded 47 seconds later resulting in another mushroom cloud under which Nagasaki was laid waste killing over 35,000 people instantly and injuring over 60,000. Within months 60,000 to 80,000 people would die in Nagasaki.[10]

The Americans were ready to drop a third atomic bomb on a Japanese city yet to be ascertained on 19th August, but then, finally, on August 15th, Emperor Michinomya Hirohito intervened and the Empire of Japan finally surrendered. "We were on Guam shooting B-29s for the last sequence of *The Last Bomb* when we heard that Japan had capitulated," McGovern recalled. Almost immediately Dan received new orders from the United States War Department informing him that he had been chosen for an important new assignment.

In any case, just after the Japanese capitulated, all mainstream productions that were being made by the 18th AAF Base Unit/First Motion Picture Unit were cancelled within weeks. However, *The Last Bomb,* being produced by Warner Brothers, was completed and it incorporated colour footage taken from the B-29s of the mushroom cloud over Nagasaki in the final scenes.

THE CORRESPONDENTS

On August 28th 1945 the United States occupation of Japan commenced at the Japanese naval air base at Atsugi which would become the main entry point to Japan for the occupying forces.[11] Atsugi was just over 35 miles from Tokyo which lay to the northeast. "There were certain troops, paratroopers and other groups that had got in very early because these groups had to arrange the protocol to get the Japanese peace groups onto the *USS Missouri* for the official surrender ceremony on September 2nd," Dan explained. Among this first contingent into Japan at this time was a delegation of as many as twenty high profile and seasoned American and Allied newspaper and broadcast journalists who were there as guests solely of the United States Army Air Forces.

As the Air Forces at the time were part of the US Army, many among the army top brass felt that army representation at the surrender ceremonies should suffice. The Air Forces' press delegation was led by Colonel Tex McCrary.[12] McCrary was working for the top brass of the USAAF which, intent on gaining its independence from the army at the time, did not want to be left out of the Japanese surrender ceremonies after all it had contributed to ending the war. Good publicity for the Army Air Forces was imperative.

In addition to McCrary the Air Forces press delegation included William H. (Bill) Lawrence[13] of the *New York Times*; Homer Bigart of the *New York Herald Tribune*; Wilfred Burchett of the *Daily Express* in London; Clark Lee of *International News Service*; Vern Haugland and photographer Jim Hutchenson of *Associated Press*; John Bockhorst of MGM's *News of the Day*; James McGlinchey of *United Press*; photographers Bernard Hoffman[14] of *Life* magazine and Stanley Troutman of *Acme War Pool*. Several prominent US radio correspondents including Bill Downs of *CBS News*, NBC's Guthrie Janssen, Fredrick Opper of *ABC News* and Bob Brumby of *MBS News* as well as a press officer attached to General Douglas MacArthur's staff, Captain

Joe Snyder, were also part of McCrary's Air Force press delegation.[15] All stayed either at Tokyo's plush *Imperial Hotel,* at the equally plush *Grand Hotel* where MacArthur himself would stay when he arrived in Japan,[16] or at the *Radio Tokyo* Building.

The correspondents had arrived at Atsugi from Okinawa on board a plush customised and converted B-17 bomber which they called *The Headliner.* The bomber had passenger seats fitted and it also had special high-powered short wave radio communication capabilities via which the correspondents could file their stories directly to the United States.[17] The correspondents were allocated their own dedicated army censor who would scrutinise the content of their stories on *The Headliner* prior to them being transmitted from the aircraft Stateside and elsewhere. This was Lieutenant Colonel Hubert Schneider.[18] Several days later on 30th August General Douglas MacArthur, now designated as Supreme Commander of the Allied Powers in Japan, duly arrived at Atsugi. He established his headquarters in the Meiji Building in Tokyo as the occupation of Japan got under way and took the official Japanese surrender aboard the *USS Missouri* in Tokyo Bay ending World War 2.

Many of McCrary's correspondents, had initially covered MacArthur's arrival in Japan and most, but not all of them, the official surrender ceremony on the *Missouri* which had also included a noisy mass flyover by a formation of 462 B-29s.[19] The bigger picture, of course, was the devastation wrought by the atomic bombs in Hiroshima and Nagasaki and McCrary's correspondents now continuously pressed MacArthur's administration for permission to visit both devastated cities. However, the journalists had several problems. The first was that MacArthur had confined all press representatives to areas only where the advance American troops were in occupation. The second problem was that the general had also issued strict orders that Hiroshima or Nagasaki were off-limits to the press until he said otherwise.[20]

However, on the very day of the surrender ceremony McCrary,[21] leading a party of at least eight correspondents, had managed to get into Hiroshima having flown on their converted B-17 to an airfield at Kure twelve miles away.[22] The visit to Hiroshima was totally unauthorised and in direct contravention of General MacArthur's directive. Two of McCrary's reporters filed uncensored stories directly with their papers against MacArthur's press directives. Bill Lawrence, having flown there with McCrary's party, filed a story on the effects of radiation in Hiroshima with the *New York Times*. Australian correspondent Wilfred Burchett, however, had decided to act entirely alone.

On the same day, September 2nd, he had simply taken a train from Tokyo to Hiroshima and filed his uncensored story with the *Daily Express* outlining what he had seen there.[23] However, neither Lawrence nor Burchett were the first to file a story describing the destruction on the ground resulting from the atomic bombs. Japanese Hawaiian born *United Press* journalist, Leslie Nakashima, had already filed a detailed story in the west on 22nd August. He had arrived into Hiroshima after the bomb was dropped frantically looking for his mother. Miraculously, Mrs. Nakashima had survived.[24] Some days after the official surrender ceremony Mack McGovern boarded a C-47 transport aircraft on Guam which had been specially assigned to him with its pilot, co-pilot, navigator and crew chief and also flew into Atsugi for his new temporary special duty assignment. Lt. McGovern was now the Air Force cameraman supporting a new newsreel pool which was a group of specialised individual branch of service teams now entering Japan which included US Army and US Navy cameramen. As in Europe, these newsreel pools had been formed to support the media with news articles, features, film footage, photographs and any other additional information useful to them as they went about reporting their stories from Japan in surrender.

His initial assignment now was to provide movie and stills photography support to McCrary and his high profile Air Force correspondents. His title was *Chief of the Newsreel Pool*. "I was like a hired camera as I was at the mercy of Tex McCrary who was hosting these people. I provided picture and sound back-up. They went around getting the stories and if they wanted photographic coverage they had to let me know in advance. We took enough pictures to satisfy everyone." Mack had also been instructed to get film footage of the devastation in both Hiroshima and Nagasaki.[25] He would be amongst the first to film it. McGovern did not realise it then, but he was about to embark on a ten-month journey that would become something of a personal quest in which he would travel many thousands of miles across that country by aircraft, train and jeep.

He would film an invaluable record for posterity of what he saw in the broken country that was now Japan in defeat. His orders also instructed him to film Tokyo which had been severely damaged by USAAF conventional bombing. He was to film in both colour and black and white formats. Also part of Dan's team was sound man, Sergeant John Drane and a Japanese American soldier, or Nisei, called Staff Sergeant Michio *Mitch* Shimomura. Mack's assignment with the correspondents would in fact last for a month and he was well prepared. "Inside the airplane I had a jeep and trailer and we were loaded with cameras, film and supplies." In the early days of the occupation of Japan transportation, even for the occupiers, was a problem. Atsugi to Hiroshima was over 470 miles away whilst Nagasaki over 700 miles distant. "We were practically stampeded by other people who wanted to get on board our airplane but we couldn't take them. We were limited by our weight control policy." Mack remembered seeing Medal of Honor winner and pioneering US Navy aviator, Rear Admiral Richard Byrd at Atsugi that day and said of him: "Even he couldn't get a flight anywhere!"

With at least most of the correspondents having covered the official surrender ceremony on the *USS Missouri* in Tokyo Bay on 2nd September, one aspect of Japan that MacArthur wanted covered by the press was the release and evacuation of Allied prisoners of war. McCrary's press delegation was officially cleared to undertake such coverage. 20,000 POWs were held in scores of

camps on Kyusho and on the western portion of the neighbouring Honshu island.[26] Several such POW camps were somewhat conveniently located in, or on the outskirts of Nagasaki.
Mother McCrary, as Mack and the correspondents soon took to
calling Tex, had considerable sway and he decided that, yet
again, the bigger picture could not be ignored. He decided to
flout MacArthur's orders once more and to make an unauthorised visit to Nagasaki. However, some semblance of legitimacy
to this visit would actually be observed by virtue of the fact that
the delegation would visit one of the city's POW camps which
was located just over a mile south of Ground Zero. Technically
speaking, of those in Tex McCrary's press delegation, Big Mack
McGovern and his team of USAAF motion picture specialists
and support crew, would be the only ones authorised to be in the
city. McCrary, his correspondents and Mack and his team,
comprising a party of fourteen in total, set out for Nagasaki from
Atsugi on 8th September 1945. Perhaps buoyed up from accounts
of their journalist colleagues who had been in Hiroshima on 2nd
September, some other members of McCrary's press delegation
decided to travel there instead.[27]

In order for McCrary's main group of correspondents to get
into Nagasaki the destination was Omura naval air base some 20
miles from the city. However, the runway at Omura had been
heavily bomb damaged and cratered. Lt. McGovern now took
the press delegation aboard, not his designated C-47 Dakota
aircraft, but a C-46 Commando transport aircraft which had
been assigned for this journey as it was more rugged than the C-
47 and better suited to where they were going. The C-46 took
off, banked slightly and headed, not immediately for Omura, but
for Nagasaki. The plane made multiple passes over the city from
as low as 75 feet[28] allowing the correspondents to get a bird's eye
view of the devastation below.

McGovern and the photographers captured aerial footage
and still shots before the C-46 banked again and this time
headed for Omura. When they got there, only the combination

of the ruggedness of their aircraft and the skill of their pilot, got Dan, his team and the press delegation down safely. This had been after three overflights. When they clambered down, one by one, from their aeroplane they were welcomed by the Japanese naval commander of the base.

Because of their change of aircraft they now had no ground transport with them, so the Japanese base commander informed them that he was providing them with a bus, a car and two drivers for their journey into Nagasaki. He also informed them that they should expect a rough two to three hour journey to get there. As it was already pretty late and getting dark, the decision was taken to spend the night in Omura. Dan remembered: "We had to stay on the C-46 overnight. There was no place else."

1. The youngest of the McGovern girls, Elizabeth was by now being referred to by the diminutive form of her given name.
2. *History of the First Motion Picture Unit, Army Air Forces, California, 1944* James Scanlan. The camera school may have relocated to the former Pacific Military Academy by then. All the original *Memphis Belle* footage was silent. Wyler added the soundtrack and narration later. He took the crew of the *Memphis Belle* to Hollywood where they recorded typical mission chatter for their mission scenes.
3. Lt. Malachy McGovern may have been hand-picked by the American military authorities to be part of a delegation of Irish-born American servicemen to return to Ireland. As the war was over, they were now permitted to wear their uniforms anywhere in the Irish Free State. During the war, however, uniformed Allied servicemen, American or otherwise, entering Southern Ireland for a visit exchanged their uniform for rented civilian clothing at the port of entry. The military uniforms were returned to the visiting servicemen at the same port just prior to their return sailing to Britain. The author is aware of several occasions where American servicemen crossed the land border from Northern Ireland to Southern Ireland in uniform and travelled to Dublin.
4. *The Care of Motion Picture Film*, a paper, Francis W. Decker, USAF Motion Picture Film Depository, 1961.
5. Also on that first B-29 raid were pilot Lt. Col. Robert Morgan and bombardier Capt. Vincent Evans who had been crew members of the *Memphis Belle* B-17 which had also dropped the first bombs on Germany. Back in England on completion of their 25 missions on the *Belle,* Evan's was asked by Air Force commander, General *Hap* Arnold, what he would most like to do now. Not withstanding General Jimmy Doolittle's exploits over

the city in 1942, Evans replied that he wanted to be the first to bomb Tokyo. General Arnold made sure Evans got his wish. He was the first to drop his bombs on the first mass B-29 raid over the city. A contingent of Air Force combat cameramen were also assigned to fly and capture film footage of this significant raid. Among them was Bill Wood, now a lieutenant, the Chelveston cameraman who had evaded capture by the Germans after being shot down in France and who had made his way back to his base in England.

6. Light trap compartments permitted the removal of one spool without contaminating the other.

7. In July 1945 the Japanese military expected the Allies to invade Japan sometime in November of that year. – Fukuoka #14 POW Sidney Lawrence Oral History, IWM.

8. On 7th August, the day after the atomic bomb devastated Hiroshima, a team of top Japanese scientists visited the ruins of the city and confirmed to the Japanese High Command on 8th August that the destruction had indeed been caused by an atomic bomb. – *Radioactivity: Introduction and History from the Quantam of Quarks p 235* by Michael F. Annunziata. The Japanese had been studying an atomic bomb since 1941. On May 15th 1945 a US destroyer, the *USS Sutton*, captured German submarine U-234 which had been sailing from Norway to Japan. The American sailors discovered the submarine was packed with state-of-the-art weaponry, but they also discovered that over 1200 pounds of German produced fissionable Uranium Oxide and two Japanese scientists were also on board. The wartime head of the Top Secret American *Manhattan Project* developing the atomic bombs, Dr. Robert Oppenheimer, ordered that the uranium be sent to the project's facility at Oak Ridge, Tennessee. *U Boats – Hitler's Sharks. Part 3, The Sound of the Drum.* This uranium was later used in the *Little Boy* atomic bomb that was dropped on Hiroshima. – *The Sensational Surrender of Four Nazi U-Boats at Portsmouth Naval Dockyard,* New England Historical Society.

9. Japan/US Radiation Effects Research Foundation.

10. iBid.

11. Atsugi was the first place in Japan that an American flag was raised by the occupying American forces.

12. McCrary was already an accomplished journalist and publicist. With his wife, Jinx Falkenburg, he would go on to pioneer the format of the talk show first on radio in the late 1940s and later on early television.

13. William (Bill) Lawrence is not to be confused with his *New York Times* colleague William L. Laurence who had flown with the B-29s which had dropped to atomic bomb on Nagasaki. William *L* Laurence had been co-awarded the Pulitzer Prize for his reporting in 1937. He would win the prize in his own right for his coverage of the atomic bombings but having never visited Nagasaki in the bomb's aftermath. The other William *H* Lawrence, who was part of McCrary's delegation with McGovern, had also managed to get into Hiroshima on the same day as journalist Wilfred Burchett. William *H* also had an article on the effects of radiation published in the *NY Times* on 5th September 1945.

14. *Life* magazine's Bernie Hoffman claimed to have been the first photo-journalist on the ground in both Hiroshima and Nagasaki when other press members were attending the official ceremonies ending WW2 on the *USS Missouri* on 2nd September 1945 – *Photographer recalls LIFE on run*, article, *New Jersey News Tribune*, August 20, 1977. Similarly, according to a news article in the *Los Angeles Times* owned *Daily Pilot* newspaper on February 16th 2020, Stanley Troutman also gave up an opportunity to photograph the ceremony on the *USS Missouri* in order to take a flight to Nagasaki to photograph the devastation there. American correspondent George Weller also claimed to have been the first outsider on 5th September 1945 to reach Nagasaki and like Wilfred Burchett, had travelled by train – *First Into Nagasaki*, George and Anthony Weller. Dan McGovern filmed in Nagasaki during his first visit there with Hoffman and Troutman. The author believes that Hoffman and Troutman at least joined McCrary's Allied correspondents' delegation to get into Nagasaki for the first time. However, according to McGovern the correspondents' delegation only got into the devastated city on September 9th.

15. Partial list of the media organisations and correspondents gleaned from Dan McGovern's own accounts, from *Six Presidents, Too Many Wars* by Bill Lawrence, Chapter 12, pages 137-140 and also *From the Stinko to the USSBS Motion Picture Project* essay, Atsuko Shigesawa. *As many as twenty correspondents*, as stated, derived from multiple additional sources.

16. *Tex McCrary – Wars- Women-Politics An Adventurous Life Across the American Century* by Charles J. Kelly and *Para(graph) Trooper for MacArthur*, Joe Snyder.

17. *Six Presidents, Too Many Wars*, Bill Lawrence, Chapter 12, pages 136-140.

18. iBid and not to be confused with MacArthur's Press Officer Joe Snyder.

19. *Para(graph) Trooper for MacArthur*, Joe Snyder and also Smithsonian Air and Space Museum.

20. iBid.

21. iBid.

22. In his book *Six Presidents, Too Many Wars,* Chapter 12, pages 136-140, Bill Lawrence alludes to MacArthur threatening to court-martial journalists having heard of their entering Hiroshima contrary to his off-limits order. Lawrence points out that for MacArthur to do so would have meant court-martialing the representatives of eight powerful media organisations which he names, thus indicating that at least that many journalists had been in Hiroshima on September 2nd contrary to the general's orders. The group flew to Hiroshima on their converted B-17 bomber *The Headliner*. In his book *Tex McCrary – Wars- Women-Politics, An Adventurous Life Across the American Century,* Charles J. Kelly states that Tex McCrary himself took the journalists to Hiroshima that day. At the time flights to and from Hiroshima and Nagasaki were also tightly monitored by MacArthur's administration.

23. *Para(graph) Trooper for MacArthur*, Joe Snyder.

24. Details sourced from *The Case of Leslie Satoru Nakashima and His Breaking News Dispatch*, Crystal Uchino; *First News Dispatch From Hiroshima*, Part 1, Masami Nishimoto, Hiroshima Peace Media Centre and *Three Lives Tethered to Hiroshima*, Carl M. Cannon, Real Clear Politics.

25. Presumably, McGovern had been ordered to get the first ground film footage of the devastation for USAAF purposes and in case it would be needed for the news pool.
26. *Marines in World War 2 Commemorative Series*/Park History Online.
27. *Para(graph) Trooper for MacArthur*, Joe Snyder. Possibly this was due to having heard accounts from some of their colleagues after their unauthorised September 2nd visit. Bill Lawrence and possibly other journalists who had visited Hiroshima appear not to have travelled to Nagasaki. This may have been due to the fact that they had previously overflown the city on a correspondents flight on August 27th – *Six Presidents, Too Many Wars*, Bill Lawrence p131.
28. Nagasaki overflight details gleaned from *Para(graph) Trooper for MacArthur*, Joe Snyder.

NAGASAKI

Filming the Devastation

On the morning of Sunday 9th September 1945 all on the C-46 arose at 5.00am and had breakfast. Then, at 5.45am, with a bus, a car and drivers provided by the Japanese Navy, Mack and his team, as part of McCrary's correspondents party, drove off across the mountains for Nagasaki. It would be a difficult journey as, apart from bad roads, it had now started to rain. For assignments such as this Mack had by now taken to carrying two personal Eyemo cameras - one loaded with black and white film and the other with colour, as well as a 16mm colour Filmo and a stills camera. When he set out for a day's filming all four cameras were always locked, loaded and ready for action.

Dan remembered the unfolding scenes of the aftermath of the atomic detonation as they began to approach Nagasaki: "Every village we passed through was deserted with not a soul in sight." Gradually the roads began to improve. Closer to Nagasaki they passed through a series of tunnels. "We saw large amounts of heavy machinery, aircraft engines, propellers and aircraft tyres," he recalled. As the party got nearer the city, among the hills and valleys they began to see the physical evidence of the atomic bomb's awesome power. "Everything that was in front of a hill was destroyed but anything that was on the leeside was intact. It wasn't even touched. Now, as we approached the city, we had a panoramic view of the valley below – naked and bare and almost lifeless." This was the Urakami Valley to the north of Nagasaki city centre and above which the atomic bomb had detonated. This city, which had been the setting for Puccini's opera, *Madame Butterfly*, now looked like a moonscape. When they finally reached the outskirts of the city at 10.00am the Americans had a welcoming committee waiting for them which included a man dressed in a morning suit and a top hat. "Maybe he was the mayor but he had a table there with a flower in a little vase and there was also some sake."[1]

Mack and his team along with the correspondents' party were amongst the very first outsiders into the city as no American of Allied occupation forces had yet reached it. For information and advice they made for police headquarters and the Superintendent of Police. Dan recounted: "He was happy to see us and after some tea we sat down for a conference." They were informed by the police superintendent that, as far as the local police were concerned, occupational forces led by the 2nd US Marine Division would not take over the city and its environs until September 23rd – fifteen days away.

In keeping with the official reason for their presence in Nagasaki, Lt. McGovern and McCrary's party first set out with their police escort to Fukuoka #14, a POW camp which had been established both in and adjacent to a disused Mitsubishi warehouse[2] in the heart of Nagasaki's industrial area and only 1.15 miles south of Ground Zero. This was a relatively new camp housing mostly British, Australian and Dutch POWs. The warehouse had been remodelled to facilitate the prisoners, most of whom were used as forced labour in Mitsubishi's production facilities nearby which included factories, foundries and shipyards.[3] In his early months in Japan, McGovern always sought out former prisoners of war in the camps. "We wanted to get to the POWs wherever we could find them because we wanted the first hand accounts. It was always very interesting." Upon arrival at Fukuoka #14, the buildings of which were all but obliterated by the bomb, McGovern and the correspondents were informed that the American prisoners had already left and set off for harbour areas in order to try and get home to the United States. One reason for this swift departure was that, after the atomic bomb attack, a rumour had abounded in the camp that General MacArthur had sailed into Tokyo Bay with a fleet of American ships and was taking POWs out of Japan as fast as possible.[4] Mack pointed out: "The Americans in particular wouldn't stick around. They'd just get up and walk. They wanted to get the hell out." Toyko was over 750 miles away.

A TONIC BOMB

Another rumour which had filtered through to the POWs in the camp in advance of the McCrary party's arrival was that the special bomb used to attack Nagasaki was called a *tonic* bomb.[5] Mack heard also how most of the prison camp camp guards just suddenly disappeared when the surrender was announced. Those guards who had remained refused to be interviewed. "They were timid and afraid," he remembered. The majority of the prisoners of war now remaining at Fukuoka #14 were Dutch merchant sailors. McGovern and the correspondents interviewed many of them and Drane and he listened intently and filmed and recorded everything they said. It was often harrowing. They heard of the brutality of the POWs' incarceration at the hands of the Japanese, about the lack of food and medical attention and other stories. Then they heard the first-hand accounts of the atomic bomb explosion. They learned that whilst most prisoners had been working inside the Mitsubishi production facilities, many were on a work break back at the camp at 11.00am when the bomb exploded exactly a month before. Other prisoners had been working in open fields on flat ground closer to the camp and at various levels on neighbouring hillsides further way.

Pictured is a view of Nagasaki after the atomic bomb taken from the surrounding mountains. **Photo: USSBS/US National Archives.**

Fukuoka POW Camp #14 in Nagasaki's industrial area as seen from the air in 1945. The arrow shows the site where the camp's wooden buildings were situated outside the main quarters in the converted warehouse. The bomb swept away the wooden structures. **Photo: Anonymous source.**

Many of those prisoners described seeing a white parachute[6] float down to earth over the camp and the train station. They recalled hearing a strange sizzling sound before seeing an enormous blue light of great brilliance like a giant welding flash which totally eclipsed the sun. Then, seconds later, the all engulfing heatwave passed overhead searing everything and everybody in its path.[7] Anybody lucky enough to have been standing in the leeside of hills or any natural or manmade barrier in the path of the blast and heat surge had some measure of protection. Many were even untouched.

Minutes later the choking dust and smoke started to abate. This gave many POWs for the very first time glimpses of the death and destruction just visited on Nagasaki. What they saw defied comprehension. At this point very large grape size drops of muddy rain started to fall[8]– the *Black Rain*. Mack and the correspondents heard that anyone caught by the blast on higher ground, for example, was burned to a greater degree compared to those working at lower levels. People who had the presence of mind to drop prone to the ground had also been relatively untouched. Such was the power of the bomb that the POWs gave accounts of witnessing strongly built buildings crumble before them and of lesser mainly wooden structures, such as those in their own prison camp, being swept away.

Of the several hundred or so POWs held at Fukuoka #14 four were killed instantly by the atomic explosion and thirty, mostly Dutch prisoners, were seriously wounded.[9] With their prison camp all but gone in an instant both the POWs and Japanese guards were for once united – in terror. Many thought that the atomic explosion was simply the end of the world. "There were several interviews made but we couldn't dwell on what they had experienced for too long," McGovern remembered. The POWs of Fukuoka #14 would board a ship and leave Japan to return home six days later on 15th September.[10]

Once finished their interviews at the POW camp outside Nagasaki McCrary took his charges back to the office of the

Chief of Police. They were now about to enter the city itself. Dan recalled:"The Chief of Police continued to give us help in locating some of the atomic bomb victims." The American visitors were also given an escort of several police cars in addition to their own vehicles. With their bus and now plenty of cars, the press party decided to break into several groups and to visit different sites as they would go about documenting the horrible effects of the atomic bomb in Nagasaki. "We were advised not to stay too long in any one area because of the radiation," McGovern remembered. With each convoy led by a police car they drove carefully through the rubble strewn streets. Dan now travelled with his soundman John Drane, his Nisei interpreter Staff Sergeant Shimomura, photographer Stanley Troutman from *Acme* magazine and *Life* magazine photo-journalist Bernie Hoffman who had his camera wrapped in a film of lead foil to protect it from radiation.[11] Mack filmed but he also took still photos too. "I shot both 35mm black and white and 35mm Technicolor Monopack colour film plus black and white and colour stills." Lt. McGovern's smaller group made its way to the centre of the desolation and alighted from their vehicles in what had been largely an industrial area.

Just like his late father the RIC sergeant, some years before, Mack McGovern had taken to smoking a pipe. Now, the rich tobacco aroma from it helped to block out somewhat the pungent smell of death and destruction which hung in the air. With his camera already in hand Dan was in awe at what he was witnessing. As Hoffman and Troutman went about their work in their own way he too started filming. The bomb had detonated just above where he stood now and had wiped out half the city.[12] Mack explained: "It exploded downward and about ten seconds later the base surge occurred which went out sideways from the explosion in a circle on the ground for a couple of miles. It came back in again and moved upward into the air to form that big characteristic mushroom cloud. It was like a tidal[13] wave before it hits. It went out and then it came back in again."

It was here, as they surveyed the desolation at the location known then simply as Point Zero, that Mack gave Bernie Hoffman some spare colour film. "I gave him a folder of colour film as I had plenty," Mack remembered. In return Hoffman took a photo of Mack, Eyemo camera in hand, as he gazed out over the sea of rubble which surrounded him and with the destroyed Urakami Cathedral in the background.[14] "Everything was just complete devastation in Nagasaki. The streets were in ruins. They were just flat and rubble strewn as if a massive anvil had fallen down and destroyed their buildings. Everything was a scene of rust, grey and black." He added that there wasn't a speck of green vegetation anywhere and that fields seven miles out from the blast epicentre were bleached white. There was very little transport. "You might find the odd trolley car[15] running or you might see an Ox and cart but that was about it." What he had witnessed on approach to Nagasaki regarding the blast damage on the exposed side of a hill with the leeside unaffected had been repeated throughout the city. Some of the buildings in Nagasaki therefore survived.

FUNERAL PYRES

Death was everywhere. There had been no firestorm as in Hiroshima but Dan and his group noticed many small fires burning at street intersections throughout the city. "We learned that these were in fact funeral pyres for burning corpses. I filmed the burning bodies of children. I remember the Shiroyama Primary School.[16] One side of it was just hundreds and hundreds of skulls and other bones piled up in stacks – what remained of schoolchildren. Hundreds of kids had been sucked out through the windows. We were always finding bones."

There was affliction everywhere too. "You would find people in hovels, in shelters, in lean-tos and in what had once been their homes. People were living in caves." Mack remembered those who had nowhere to go or who were just too badly injured or too sick to move. "People were lying by the wayside like sick animals. They lay there until somebody got to them. They were all alone. If they were dying they died," – and died they did in their thousands. The Japanese had sacred tributes for their departed if and when they found them and regardless of the condition of whatever was left of their loved ones. Mack elaborated: "Some people would be picking up the remains of family members and reverently taking that material and putting it into little boxes with white covers on them."

Many of the walking wounded were to be found wandering about the devastation, whimpering as they walked. Those unable to walk but who had been lucky enough to get to a hospital for treatment, did so by the most rudimentary means."There was no such thing as an ambulance with sirens flashing to take people to hospital. All across the city that all had to be done by manual labour and all the time litter[17] bearers were rushing somewhere."

With the constant stream of the terribly injured and suffering arriving there, McGovern and his companions also found themselves at Nagasaki Hospital. They first entered the operating amphitheatre which had once been completely tiled inside. "The blast had sucked all the tiles and the roof completely away." They were led inside the damaged hospital. There, Dan encountered many of the worst of Nagasaki's atomic bomb victims. An overwhelmed medical staff treated men, women and children of all ages for varying degrees of pain and suffering caused by severe burns, blistering, disfigurement, broken bones, blindness and all manner of cuts and lacerations. There were physical wounds of all kinds to be seen brought about by the cataclysmic explosion which had engulfed their city. "The Japanese are very orderly but it was nothing to go into a hospital room and find complete and utter disarray. There was cleanliness, of course, but there was also no light and no power. There was no penicillin to speak of." The only heat available was by using traditional Japanese heating devices called hibachis which were round or box shaped containers which used charcoal as a fuel source.

A section of the Shiroyama Primary School in Nagasaki showing some of the destruction caused there by the atomic bomb on 9th August 1945. **Photo: USSBS, US National Archives.**

There were bones everywhere McGovern recalled from his first visit to Nagasaki. A frame from film footage. **US National Archives.**

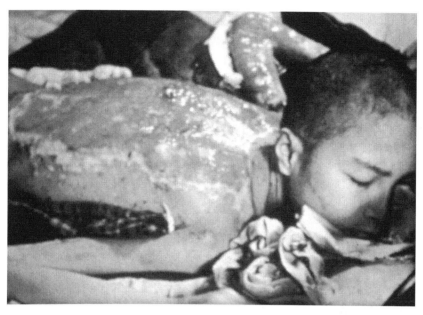

18-year-old Sumiteru Taniguchi was the boy whose horrific back and arm burns Dan likened to 'bubbling tomatoes'. He would survive and live to old age. A frame from USSBS film footage. **US National Archives.**

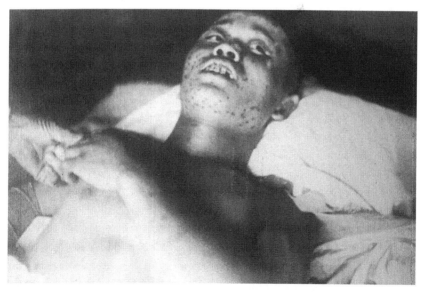

This victim of the atomic bombs displays skin blotching – one of the many symptoms of radiation sickness which were all too apparent in Hiroshima and Nagasaki. A frame from film footage. **US National Archives.**

Dan remembered the injuries of one particular patient who, like so many other people, had severe burns over much his body from the atomic blast. "He couldn't have been any more than 18 years old and his whole back just looked like a bowl of bubbling tomatoes.[18] It's only when you see that in dramatic colour that you begin to realise the suffering," he remarked. Dan noticed also that many burn victims had the fabric weave pattern of the clothes they were wearing when they were caught in the explosion permanently burned into their skin just like a tattoo. There were, of course, other types of illnesses. Scores of people, unable to grasp or cope with the reality of what had befallen them and their city, simply lost their wits. They had struggled also with the scale of material and acute personal loss.

A STRANGE SICKNESS

Japanese doctors also frequently approached the members of McGovern's five strong party asking if they had a cure for another malady they did not understand which had started to afflict their patients. This strange sickness had first manifested itself approximately four days after the bomb had been dropped. Many people were dying as a result of it and doctors had no idea how to treat those afflicted with it. This mystery malady manifested itself with the presence of red or purple spots on the skin, with brown liquid thrown up by the patients, with dehydration and diarrhoea, accelerating hair loss and with uncontrolled bleeding from the nose and mouth. Dan and his party were witnessing the results of acute radiation sickness which would go on to become the single most disturbing legacy of the atomic bomb and its after effects. Dan said of it: "Radiation is a horrible invisible thing that can hurt an awful lot of people."

He remembered one particular medical professional whom he photographed that day. "I saw a man in a dark Japanese Kimono type robe who was standing overlooking the ruins of the Urakami Valley below. I couldn't figure out what was wrong with him. "He had a wooden staff that he was holding on to and he reminded me of Jesus Christ with that staff. That was Mr. Nagai and he was a radiologist at the medical college and I took a picture of him. He told me he was suffering from radiation sickness. He had lost his entire family and he was the last." Dan added: "That picture to me is rare because a couple of days later he was gone too."

Mr. Nagai overlooking the ruins of his city as photographed by Dan McGovern in Nagasaki. The radiologist died a few days after this photograph was taken. ***Photo: US National Archives.***

Further down the valley Dan also filmed the ruins of Saint Mary's Catholic Cathedral in Urakami which had been run by the Jesuits. "It was completely destroyed. Nagasaki had been the centre of Catholicism in Japan for centuries." Nagasaki was a scene of misery and chaos on a grand scale and of deep pity and helplessness by anyone beholding it. Dan filmed and photographed it all, shocking and striking as it was. Similar scenes were being played out at several other hospitals in Nagasaki and in Hiroshima too with both cities now engulfed in an all-consuming wave of grief, mental anguish and hysteria amid the material destruction. Mack recalled: "We had a certain compassion for the people and they had no animosity towards us. We always carried things and we had plenty so we shared what we had with them – some quick soups, maybe an apple or an orange or some candy and they were always very thankful for anything we gave them."

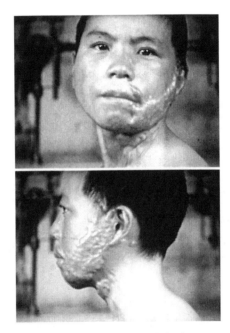

A Japanese boy displays severe facial keloid scarring. This excessive scar tissue resulted anywhere on the body where severe flash burns were sustained when the atomic bombs exploded. Thousands were so afflicted and Dan McGovern filmed many. Frames from USSBS film footage. **US National Archives.**

Throughout the city, Mack had already noticed that green, yellow and red flags were to be seen at various sites amid the rubble. This was where very early advance parties of American scientists had used rudimentary geiger counters to record radiation levels. Red flags signified *no go* areas whilst yellow flags signified *moderate* radiation and the green flags *safe* areas. There were no warning signs, checkpoints or controlled areas at all. Knowledge of radiation and its effects on the human body was only in its infancy. In fact, in the course of all his visits to both Nagasaki and Hiroshima, Mack would work without any form of personal radiation protection. Looking back on it he said: "I think we were just too ignorant to be aware because we were not too well briefed in that regard."

ODDBALL THINGS

Apart from the obvious devastation and suffering all around him in Nagasaki, McGovern also observed a great many strange things which resulted from the nuclear explosion. "There were all sorts of oddball things. I remember many times seeing a shadow where a person had been sitting, standing or walking just before the explosion occurred." These victims had been atomised. When the bomb exploded their shadows were etched onto solid buildings and roadways either where they had been or close by. This was known as Atomic Shadow and was caused by the radiant heat of the nuclear explosion. Where it had caught human beings the phenomenon soon became known to the Japanese as the Shadow of Death. Atomic Shadow, human or otherwise, was to be seen everywhere.

Dan pointed out: "This all happened in the first four seconds of the blast. It was as if a thousand suns had come down to earth. That first four seconds, that burn, was the most devastating thing." As he filmed the phenomenon Dan was struck by the unusual angles of the atomic shadows which were cast.

"I also saw the shadow of a ladder against one building which had been transposed onto another across the way and also the shadow of a large vial container cast onto the pigmented paint of another structure." He went on: "Another thing that struck me was the atomic shadow cast by plants. I remember once I moved a plant and behind it, on a cedar wood panel, was the shadow of the plant."[19]

The eerie image of a man and his ladder etched onto a wall in Nagasaki.
This was caused by the radiant heat of atomic bomb when it exploded.
Photo: Getty Images.

Within days of the first atomic explosion in Hiroshima Japanese scientists had worked out the exact location of Ground Zero there. This had been through a process of triangulation[20] from various points in the city. The same science had been applied in Nagasaki. The Japanese called both Ground Zeros the *Hypocentres.*

Meanwhile, some of the concrete or stone buildings in Nagasaki which had not been damaged in the blast had been designated to house the approaching American occupation forces. Now with an Eyemo camera on its tripod outside one of these buildings, Dan filmed the Japanese as they threw masses of paper from the building's windows.

As the paper floated to the ground he filmed others quickly gathering it up and taking it away to be used for heating and other purposes. He asked his Nisei interpreter what was going on. Sergeant Shimomura explained that they were dumping all paperwork out the windows in case the Americans should find anything incriminating pertaining to written evidence of Japanese military atrocities against Americans in the course of the war.

Mack then recalled one humorous incident which occurred just as he finished filming the paper sequence. He remarked a group of a dozen or so young girls across the street sniggering amongst themselves and they seemed to be sniggering at him! "These were solid well built young ladies whom we called Bloomer Girls because they all wore navy blue bloomers and white jumpsuits." One of them was being dared to do something by the others and came over and bowed to Sergeant Shimomura who spoke with her in Japanese. Shimomura started to smile. "Lieutenant Mack," he said, "don't get mad. They're having some fun over there and she's not going to do you any harm, ok?"

The girl then walked over to Dan who takes up the story: "She bowed down, lifted up the leg of my pants, grabbed a bunch of the hairs on my leg and pulled them. 'Ouch! What did you do that for?' Dan enquired of the girl as she quickly ran back across the street to her friends. All the girls were now giggling loudly. "What the hell was all that about?" asked a bewildered Dan having turned to Shimomura. The sergeant replied: "They've never seen a man as tall as you, Mack. She was checking to see if you had stilts on is all."

Dan pointed out the broader significance of that little incident. "That was the Japanese people. Even amid all this devastation and disaster around them they still had a sense of fun." After a harrowing day in a desolated city Lt. McGovern and the two contingents of press correspondents converged back at the Nagasaki police chief's headquarters. "We thanked the police chief for the outstanding help he had given us and then shared some snacks, hot tea and sake."

Tex McCrary, Dan and his support crew and the correspondents then got back on their bus and car. The Japanese Navy drivers started out on the slow and tedious drive back to Omura Naval Airfield. There, after everybody had boarded the C-46 and settled in for take off, there was total silence. Nobody said a word – each man alone with his thoughts. The impact of what they had just experienced throughout the day had a profound effect on all of them and even on those who had previously been in Hiroshima just over a week before. At this point McCrary broke the silence. Given that their visit to Nagasaki was unauthorised he suggested, rather than ordered, that none of the correspondents should write and file anything of what they had just witnessed – at least for now.[21] They all agreed. The C-46 took off from Omura and landed back at Atsugi naval air base. It was just starting to get dark.

---

1. Traditional Japanese alcoholic spirit drink distilled from rice.
2. *Medical Services of the R.A.N.* (1961) P84. According Bill Lawrence in his book *Six Presidents, Too Many Wars,* a previously unknown POW camp in Nagasaki's harbour area was spotted from the air during a flyover of the destroyed city from Guam by McCrary and his correspondents on 27th August. This camp was in the middle of the Mitsubishi arms works. It is highly likely that this was in fact Fukuoka #14 and that, as a result,

McCrary decided to visit the camp with McGovern and the correspondents later on September 9th 1945. Research indicates that Dan McGovern may also have filmed on this 27th August correspondents' overflight.

3. From an un-named inmate's report courtesy of Fukuoka #14 Historical Group and also from recollections of Fukuoka #14, POW Sidney Lawrence, RAF, Oral History, IWM. The other main POW camp in Nagasaki was Fukuoka #2 located on Kouyagi Island further south from Fukuoka #14 and over 6.5 miles from Ground Zero.

4. Fukuoka #14 POW Sidney Lawrence, RAF, Oral History, IWM.

5. POW's recollection, Oral History, IWM.

6. This was more likely a pod dropped from one of the two other aircraft containing technical instruments to record aspects of the explosion. The *Fat Man* atomic bomb did not use a parachute deployment system.

7. The wall of heat was up to 4,000 degrees Celsius.

8. Details comparing the atomic bomb's detonation light to a welding flash eclipsing the sun, the grape sized raindrops and the description of the destruction of Nagasaki defying comprehension is from British Fukuoka #14 POW Geoffrey Sherring.

9. *Australian POWs and the Nagasaki A-Bombing*, Mick Broderick. *The Asia Pacific Journal/Japan Focus.*

10. According to Dutch POW Claude Belloni.

11. *Tex McCrary – Wars- Women-Politics, An Adventurous Life Across the American Century* by Charles J. Kelly. p97.

12. *Six Presidents, Too Many Wars*, Bill Lawrence p132.

13. A tsunami.

14. The caption accompanying this photograph of Dan McGovern taken on 8th September 1945 at the spot above which the detonation occurred in Nagasaki states: *the spot is now called "zero".* The photograph was likely taken by Hoffman with one of McGovern's cameras.

15. A tram.

16. 500 metres from Ground Zero. 1400 primary school children perished there.

17. A stretcher in Europe.

18. This was Mr. Sumiteru Taniguchi who survived his horrific injuries. He died from cancer in August 2017 aged 88.

19. The outline of the plant's leaves were clearly defined.

20. *Encounter with Disaster*, Dr. Averill Liebow, p117.

21. *Tex McCrary – Wars- Women-Politics, An Adventurous Life Across the American Century* by Charles J. Kelly. p82.

Lt. Dan McGovern, pictured with his Eyemo camera, at Point Zero in Nagasaki on 9th September 1945 This is the photograph taken by Bernie Hoffman. *Image: US National Archives.*

18

TOJO AND THE EMPEROR'S WHITE HORSE

The First Fleeting Visit to Hiroshima

ON ARRIVAL AT ATSUGI, Dan, his sound man and the correspondents, headed for Seoul, the capital of Korea, aboard their usual *Headliner* B-17. They would be back the following day. The purpose of this journey was to take part in special Korean independence celebrations which were to be held there as a way to thank representatives of all countries which had helped to liberate Korea from thirty five years of Japanese occupation. However, the celebrations were to honour the Americans in particular. Dan and the delegation spent just one night in Korea before returning to Japan. He remembered. "It was there that I had my first hot bath in a long time. I stayed at the Chosun Hotel.[1] Everything was provided." Everything that is, except beds. "There were no beds available so, like ten other correspondents, I slept on the floor."

All the time though, McGovern was being drawn back to Japan and back to Nagasaki and he had yet to get to Hiroshima. The fact was he was not too impressed with many of the visiting press contingent to whom he would be attached for several weeks yet. "They were a hard-drinking group. I don't know how the hell they did their stories. They were under the influence half the time. Every time you would find them they would be in the bar. I was more interested in seeing what Seoul was like and documenting it."

Meanwhile, Leslie Nakashima's story *Hiroshima As I Saw It* had been published in the *New York Times* on August 31st. Wilfred Burchett's uncensored story which he had filed after visiting Hiroshima on 2th September had appeared on the front page of the *Daily Express* in Britain. Similarly, Bill Lawrence's story, also from Hiroshima, had appeared in the *New York Times* the same day. Joe Snyder, a MacArthur press officer travelling with the delegation at the time and referring to Burchett's story in particular, stated that such stories *broke the blockade.*

With the cat out of the bag as far as they were concerned the remaining journalists now started to file stories and photographs to their respective publications and broadcasting outlets based on what they had witnessed in Nagasaki and Hiroshima.[2] However, MacArthur and his CIC – Counter Intelligence Corps staff in Tokyo, had by now gotten wind that McCrary had taken the correspondents into Hiroshima in direct contravention of the general's orders. MacArthur and the CIC would also soon find out about Nagasaki. The Supreme Commander was furious and now even considered court-martialing McCrary.[3] However, if Burchett and Lawrence's stories had *broken the blockade* it was only temporarily so. The correspondents would soon find out that the stories they would file and the photographs they would take from here on in would be heavily censored by MacArthur's new occupation administration in Tokyo. In fact, many stories and photographs would be suppressed completely and many for decades to come. As it would turn out, Mack McGovern would later have his own problems in that regard too.

On the morning of 11th September 1945 Dan and the correspondents returned from Korea to Atsugi at 11am. Dan was barely off the plane when McCrary approached him for a special job. Since the occupation had commenced, both the US military and the American press had been desperately attempting to track down Japanese former premier, General Hideki Tojo, who had held that position when Pearl Harbor was attacked. Tojo was by then known to be living in seclusion somewhere in Tokyo. One of McCrary's correspondents, Clark Lee, had not travelled to Korea. Instead, he had been working his sources in Tokyo and along with another journalist, Harry Brundidge, had tracked down the former Japanese premier. They got the scoop and interviewed him the day before. They were now again at Tojo's house to complete their interview and McCrary had dispatched Mack to assist Lee and Brundidge in case they needed him to film the Tojo interview with sound. Mack now found himself on the grounds of Tojo's suburban Tokyo property and standing near a window outside the terracotta bungalow which stood on an elevated site. Always prepared for the unexpected, he set up a Mitchell camera on its tripod. It was early afternoon and he was waiting for Brundidge and Lee to call him inside.

Earlier, the two reporters had received a tip-off that General MacArthur was about to issue orders that Tojo was to be located and arrested for war crimes along with other alleged Japanese war criminals. Now, inside the house, they remonstrated with the former Japanese prime minister to accompany them in their car to MacArthur's Tokyo GHQ in the Meiji Building rather than be taken there by the military police. Tojo, however, refused stating that he preferred to be taken by the appropriate military authorities. By now MacArthur's arrest order had been issued several hours before. Whilst GHQ had in fact, no idea where Tojo's house was, more and more reporters were hot on his trail. Always ahead of the military, they had found the house and had started to gather outside waiting to get the story.

Mack too continued to wait. Then, at 4pm a large arrest party led by Major Paul Kraus and Lt. Jack Wilpers[4] of General MacArthur's Counter Intelligence Corps, the CIC, finally arrived. They banged on the front door demanding entry but there was no reply. Then something unexpected happened. Somebody close to where Mack was standing shouted: "There's

Tojo at the window!" Tojo had opened a window and now stood there waving at McGovern and the reporters gathered outside.

Former Japanese Prime Minister General Hideki Tojo appears at the window of his bungalow in suburban Tokyo moments before his attempted suicide. Dan McGovern was among the group of journalists and photographers present when this photograph was taken. **Photo: Charles Gorry, Associated Press/Shutterstock.**

Several still cameras flashed as reporters jostled to get closer firing a torrent of questions upward towards the former Japanese premier who was now no more than ten feet away. Dan quickly tilted his camera upwards at the bald-headed Tojo at his window and let it roll. The former premier appeared twice at the window within several minutes. However, when he realised he was being photographed, he became somewhat irate.[5]

Through an interpreter Tojo asked if the soldiers who had arrived were from MacArthur's headquarters and if they were there to arrest him. At the behest of Major Kraus, Lt. Wilpers produced his credentials and confirmed that they were indeed there to arrest him. They again demanded entry stating that they initially intended to question the former Japanese prime minister. Mack remembered what happened next: "Then Tojo closed the window[6] and a short time after that there was a shot!" Dan went on: "All hell broke loose!" Kraus and Wilpers gained entry by kicking in the doors of the house followed by almost the entire press entourage. In a room inside Tojo now lay slumped in an armchair. He had tried to commit suicide by shooting himself in the chest but had been unsuccessful.

Among the many reporters on the scene was another Irishman who witnessed the pandemonium which erupted. This was Cornelius Ryan who would go on to write such classic accounts of World War 2 as *The Longest Day* and *A Bridge Too Far*. "The whole thing," wrote Ryan of Tojo's suicide attempt in the *Daily Telegraph*, "was a cross between a Marx Brothers movie, *Hellzapoppin*[7] and an Irish wake!" Mack, however, did not film inside the house as by then additional cameramen had arrived. "The Army Pictorial Service was there in force," he said, "so why duplicate it?" Tojo was rushed to a US Army Medical Centre where he was given a blood transfusion. Dan pointed out: "I followed Tojo there and filmed him on a gurney. It's not generally known but it was a blood transfusion from an American army sergeant that saved Tojo's life that day. All that is in the National Archives." The former Japanese premier was subsequently remanded in Sugamo Prison in Tokyo to await his trial.[8]

MACARTHUR'S UNDERSTANDING

McGovern was now interested in getting out and about into Tokyo to document the Japanese capital which was also in ruins as a result of General LeMay's conventional bombing strikes. He locked and loaded his cameras, put his tripod and camera box in the back of his jeep and set out to film the considerable bomb damage in the city but also some human interest angles of Tokyo and its inhabitants. From the outset MacArthur adopted a passive approach towards the Japanese people now under Allied occupation and warned Allied servicemen under his command that they were to treat the native Japanese people as they would expect to be treated themselves.

Mack was always of the opinion that, with the Japanese in defeat, General MacArthur perhaps understood their mindset better than anybody else. "General MacArthur gave specific orders that American troops were, under no circumstances, to carry weapons in Tokyo." Dan didn't have much dealings with MacArthur but he did see him quite regularly and met him on one occasion. "He was in an entirely different orbit to me but he was soon hugely popular with the Japanese. They would have made him emperor only for he was American.' MacArthur was an egoist to a certain degree. He would always play for the cameras and you would always have to photograph him from a certain angle. You certainly never intentionally photographed his side profile."

MacArthur also gave specific orders that there was to be no fraternisation between American servicemen and the Japanese. However, particularly with so many lonely Allied servicemen so far away from home, that was going to be unworkable. Dan recalled: "I observed many young US soldiers, sailors and marines walking hand in hand with pretty young Japanese maidens and I filmed that." There had been many American bombing raids on Tokyo including the famous Doolittle Raid in April 1942. However, none was more infamous than that of 9th and 10th March 1945 when General LeMay had unleashed a fire-bombing raid on the city. It was the most destructive conventional air raid in human history in terms of the number of people killed and buildings destroyed.

Sixteen square miles of central Tokyo was flattened, at least 8,000 people killed and millions left homeless. During the war years much of Tokyo was a city comprised largely of traditional Japanese wooden buildings. Nevertheless, many other buildings including the Imperial Palace and the Meiji building in which MacArthur now had his headquarters, as well as the American embassy did survive. This was mainly due to the fact that the bombers purposely targeted the wooden buildings in order to start a firestorm to destroy the city centre.

LeMay's B-29s had approached Tokyo at the very low altitude of only 2000 to 2500 feet where greater accuracy in their bombing could be achieved. Dan was amazed at the contrast in Tokyo in that regard. "All you needed to do was to get up to the top of some of these buildings that were still intact and look out. All you could see all around you was complete devastation." A great many of Tokyo's roads were still impassable and its bridges had been destroyed which meant that, even in his four wheel drive jeep, getting around the city could be a challenge. Mack McGovern filmed everything of interest that he came across.

THE IMPERIAL PALACE

Four days later on September 16th Mack found himself on a street close to Emperor Hirohito's Imperial Palace when suddenly he heard sirens. "Six black limousines were coming towards me with flags flying led by MPs on motorcycles. I didn't know what the hell it was." The convoy turned into the palace. Dan immediately drove into the palace grounds by another entrance where he approached a large cluster of white canvas US Army tents by which many US military vehicles were parked. A big sign declared that this was the command post of the 1st US Cavalry Division. In the centre of the tents was a large spacious area of grass on the periphery of which quite a large crowd of mainly military personnel was starting to gather. Dan drove up to a 1st Cavalry Division sergeant who was holding the reins of a beautiful white horse.

"What the hell's going on?" he asked the sergeant.

"It's Admiral Halsey. He's going to ride this here emperor's white horse," came the reply.

"Where's Halsey?" asked Dan.

"He's coming down now with General Chase," replied the 1st Cavalry sergeant. The sergeant was referring to something which had been widely reported in the American media seven months before. At a press conference, US Navy Admiral William *Bull* Halsey, had been asked if the emperor's palace was a military objective. Halsey had said it wasn't and that, in any case, he would hate to kill the emperor's white horse in any assault as he wanted to ride it himself! The sentiment was widely reported and became a rallying cry right across America – *to remove Hirohito from his high horse.*

Now the admiral was finally going to do it but General Chase had arranged it as a surprise for the admiral. This was something very symbolic for which the American people had long waited and Dan McGovern was there to record it in moving pictures. Sure enough Admiral Halsey and 1st Cavalry commander Major General William Chase soon appeared and made their way over to the horse which now stood in front of the large 1st Cavalry Division sign. Both were enjoying cigarettes and in great spirits. There were other news media representatives there too but McGovern was the only one with a movie camera. He set up an Eyemo on its tripod where the admiral and the emperor's white horse best filled his viewfinder.

General Chase and Admiral Halsey walked over and firstly stood for photographs with the *emperor's* white horse. "It was too bad I didn't have sound because Halsey suddenly said: 'How the hell do I get on this damn thing?' Admiral Halsey had a word in the horse's ear before a certain Lt. McGovern walked over and helped the cavalry sergeant to get Halsey onto the horse before rushing back to his camera viewfinder. He pressed the button on his Eyemo......Whirrrr.... "Halsey had never been on a horse before in his life but he gets on it, sits there and laughs. Then, under the careful eye of General Chase, Halsey, cigarette still in his mouth, managed to ride the horse around for the benefit of the cameras present and everybody applauded."

*Admiral William 'Bull' Halsey rides a white horse in the Imperial Palace grounds in Tokyo as General William Chase of the 1st Cavalry looks on. Dan McGovern filmed the event. **Main Photo** courtesy of 1st Cavalry Division, Fort Hood, Texas. **Inset Photo:** Dan McGovern's production slate from the footage. **US National Archives.***

Dan decided that he would use the film of Admiral Halsey and the emperor's horse for the correspondent's newsreel pool. He divulged one little aspect of that particular story though. "Well, it wasn't the emperor's horse at all. It was just a white horse. There's 200 feet of silent film of that in the National Archives." Dan added: "It was a fun thing for them to do to satisfy the news media. Of course the correspondents were nowhere to be seen but they still got their scoop and they loved it." From 21st to 24th September 1945 Dan next travelled with the correspondents delegation to the cultural centre of Japan – Kyoto. "It was one of the few Japanese cities not touched by the war," he recalled. As the correspondents still tended to gravitate towards the nearest bar, Dan always made himself scarce. He had more important things to do. "Technically I was going AWOL but I was more interested in seeing what Kyoto was like and documenting it with my cameras. I covered everything from Shinto weddings to other ceremonies of all types. There was always a celebration of something or other going on in Kyoto." Among those McGovern interviewed and captured on film in Kyoto was renowned Belgian missionary priest, theologian and writer, Father Joseph Spae, who had remained in Japan for the duration of the war but with his freedom curtailed considerably by the Japanese military authorities.

In the final days of September 1945, Tex McCrary offered Dan the chance to continue his camera work with the correspondents newsreel pool. As they had already visited Seoul in Korea and Shanghai in China before that, McCrary had now planned for the delegation to be the first American correspondents into other now liberated major cities of Asia.[9] Dan politely declined the offer. "No, Colonel," he told McCrary. "There's a story that has to be told here and I would like to stay here and do it. I'm doing this damn thing myself." With McCrary and the correspondents now departed, Mack McGovern was a free agent with several free days on his hands. Now, working solely with his own Air Force team, he undertook some additional filming in Nagasaki before finally flying to Hiroshima in the C-47 Dakota to film there.

———

HIROSHIMA – A FLEETING VISIT

"In Hiroshima the devastation was greater than in Nagasaki to a certain degree because there are four or five rivers there and it's all flatland," Mack recalled. He added: "There was nothing in Hiroshima to resist the blast. Everything was gone. The only thing left standing was the Industrial Promotion Centre which is

the domed shaped building that is still standing today. That was
the epicentre. The hospital next to it was completely gone."

*The devastation that was Hiroshima after the atomic bomb destroyed the
city. The stronger concrete buildings which survived the blast can be seen.*
Photo: US National Archives. Inset: *A public clock in Hiroshima frozen
in time a few minutes before 8.15am when the atomic bomb 'Little Boy'
exploded. A still from American film footage.* **US National Archives.**

With little resistance to dissipate its power, such was the
force of the atomic blast in Hiroshima, that trees in the neighbouring coastal town of Kure, some fifteen miles away, bent over
to such a degree that they almost touched the ground.[10] A
firestorm had also raged through Hiroshima in the immediate
aftermath of the bomb. Mack remembered one particular
example of Atomic Shadow in Hiroshima which struck him. The
Japanese back then commonly wore traditional rubber or
wooden clogs called *geta*. "I saw the outline of geta on the granite
steps of a bank building where a person had been sitting when
the explosion occurred and also the impression of his buttocks
and of his back." That person had been atomised by the atomic

detonation. Only the shadow was left. "In order to demonstrate this for the camera I had a person sit there and then I had them get up as I filmed."

However, as much as he wanted to continue his film documentation in Hiroshima, Mack McGovern now had an urgent problem to address that would necessitate putting his film documentation of Hiroshima on hold for a while. With his temporary duty assignment of 30 days now all but over and with his outfit, the 11th Combat Camera Unit, getting ready to return to the United States, Dan's time in Japan had almost run out. Somehow, he needed to either get his existing orders extended or to get new orders which would allow him to stay in Japan and crucially, to continue filming what he knew would be highly significant historical footage in the ruins of Hiroshima and Nagasaki. He had to return to Tokyo.

---

1. One of the most luxurious hotels in The Orient.
2. The author believes that the news that Nakashima, Burchett and Lawrence had already scooped them signalled the go ahead for the remaining correspondents and photographers to start filing their own stories of the devastation in both cities.
3. *Tex McCrary – Wars- Women-Politics, An Adventurous Life Across the American Century* by Charles J. Kelly.
4. In an interview with the *Times Union* newspaper on 11th September 2010 Wilpers, of Saratoga, New York, said that they eventually located Tojo's house by following the trail of the American newsmen. Additional information gleaned from the account of *Yank* Magazine Correspondent George Burns, October 19th 1945.
5. According to correspondent Harry Brundidge.
6. Harry Brundidge stated that Tojo slammed the window shut.
7. 1941 musical comedy film and earlier Broadway show.
8. Tojo would be tried and executed in December 1948.
9. *Tex McCrary – Wars- Women-Politics, An Adventurous Life Across the American Century* by Charles J. Kelly.
10. *Six Presidents, Too Many Wars*, Bill Lawrence, p137.

19

GENERAL ANDERSON AND THE USSBS

The Japanese Film Crew

ONCE BACK IN the Japanese capital, McGovern made for General MacArthur's new permanent headquarters in the imposing Greek revival style eight storey Meiji Building. Officially, this was known as General Headquarters of the Supreme Commander for the Allied Powers or GHQ/SCAP. It was early October. There, Dan was firstly directed to the office of General Thomas Farrell who was Deputy Commander of the *Manhattan Project* having been appointed to the position in December 1944 as second-in-command to Major General Leslie Groves.[1] As a senior officer in the Army Corps of Engineers, it was Groves who had directed the *Manhattan Project* to develop the atomic bomb working closely with nuclear physicist Robert Oppenheimer.

On Tinian Island, from where the atomic bomb B-29s had taken off, General Farrell had been one of the informally named Joint Chiefs along with Rear Admiral William R. Purnell and Rear Admiral William S. Parsons. However, it was Farrell who had had the decision-making powers regarding the missions to drop the atomic bombs. Farrell had arrived in Japan several days after McGovern and had already lead a research team out on the ground in Hiroshima and Nagasaki inspecting damage and monitoring radiation which had resulted from the atomic bombs.[2] Of his discussion with General Farrell Dan said: "The general told me that General Anderson wanted to see me and that an appointment had been made for me for the next day."

Major General Orvil A. Anderson had been Deputy Commanding General of Operations for the 8th Air Force in England for its bombing offensive against targets in Nazi Germany between 1944 and 1945. Anderson though was now the military adviser to Franklin D'Olier who was Chairman of the United States Strategic Bomb Survey – the USSBS. Anderson had previously been Chief of the Military Analysis Division of the USSBS in Europe.[3]

General Orvil A. Anderson – Dan McGovern's great supporter. **Photo: AFHRA.**

The United States Strategic Bomb Survey was comprised of specialist military and civilian technical personnel charged with compiling a broad but impartial assessment by way of a finalised written and visual report on the effectiveness of Allied and American bombing. The USSBS had been set up by a directive from President Roosevelt and had undertaken surveys in Germany following the end of the European war. Now, on the direction of President Truman, the USSBS was in Japan to undertake its surveys there.

The following day Mack met with General Anderson and after some pleasantries were exchanged, the meeting got down to business. Mack informed Anderson that his temporary duty assignment with Tex McCrary and the correspondents was now over. "I told him what I had seen down in Nagasaki and Hiroshima, that I was doing newsreel coverage for the news pool and that I was also filming the same thing for historical reasons in 16mm and 35mm colour. I told General Anderson that I wanted to show the world what the atomic bomb had done to a nation and what it had done to human beings." The general enquired as to the type and quantity of equipment he had. McGovern had actually secured all the film resources that were left over from *The Last Bomb* production on the Mariana Islands which had now wrapped. He gave the general a quick outline of the cameras and associated support equipment to which he currently had access. He added: "General, I've got plenty of film too. I've got enough for the next year."

BEFORE THE GRASS TURNS GREEN

On hearing this, General Anderson informed Dan that he would be transferring him to his United States Strategic Bomb Survey stating: "This story must be told of the Japanese people and before the grass turns green. They're beginning to reconstruct. Get the people now in defeat, their despair, their education, their medical services, their transportation. Anything you need McGovern by way of equipment, logistics and manpower let me know and you will get it." Dan remembered: "The main thing I had to do was to document the Japanese before they started reconstruction." General Anderson told Dan to arrange a flight back to 20th Air Force Headquarters on Guam as soon as he could to get all the photographic and production equipment he needed and to pick up his new orders transferring him out of the 11th Combat Camera Unit to the USSBS.

The general said that he would arrange everything else. "When I got to Guam my orders were already waiting for me. They put me down as a technical analyst type which was the sort of thing I could do anyway as, by now, I had a tremendous background. I could be an evaluator, I could read maps, I could find targets and I'd learned all this the hard way but that all stood me in good stead." Dan was given the title *Photographic Equipment Engineer* and along with that he was issued an *Access All Areas* military pass for all of Japan which covered his entire team. This pass was printed in five languages and made out to *Lt. Daniel A. McGovern, United States Army Air Forces.*

With General Anderson's authority Dan now set about gathering everything he was going to need from among the inventory left over from *The Last Bomb.* He would spend nearly a week on the island. "I took everything from Guam from *The Last Bomb* inventory and that included the jeeps, generators and production lights." He arranged to have the bulk of this equipment shipped to Japan as a priority. For now though, he returned to Japan on a transport plane with 1000 lbs of what photographic equipment the plane could carry.[4] He had just taken the first steps in establishing a USSBS film unit for an assignment which would be ongoing throughout Japan for the next nine months.

General Anderson greatly supported McGovern as he now set about the professional film documentation of Hiroshima and Nagasaki and the wider aspects of Japan and its people in the wake of hostilities. Dan recalled: "He was our godfather. He instilled in me the determination to see it through and to do it. He was a great believer in air power and he talked about it endlessly." General Anderson was also just as determined to see the film documentation of the physical damage caused by conventional American strategic bombing. He would be briefed regularly on what Mack's USSBS team was documenting on the ground in Japan. Lt. McGovern would make sure of that. Anderson also informed Mack that in order to augment his film documentation work for the USSBS, he would need the services of one of its physical damage experts. The general introduced Lt. McGovern to the 20th Army Air Force's Colonel Dan B. Dyer who was the target analyst for General Curtis LeMay. In total the USSBS would eventually have a 1150[5] strong survey team operating throughout Japan but split up into many separate teams each undertaking different types of survey work throughout the country.

McGovern and Dyers' visual and scientific team would indeed concentrate mainly on the effects of the various types of air attack undertaken by American land based air power. The dropping of the two atomic bombs had, however, added a new and extraordinary dimension to their work. Dyer's findings would be greatly aided by McGovern's photographic images and film footage. All would be included in the broader USSBS survey report which would be published at a later stage. With both of them now working for the USSBS, Mack and Dan Dyer started to put a plan together – a filming and analysis itinerary and timeframe for the future colour film documentation of Japan after the surrender. However, a problem had started to become apparent. Dan had hoped that he could retain the services of many of the specialists with whom he had worked during the correspondents' three week visit and that he could also get them reassigned to his fledgling USSBS team.

However, with the war now over, many long-serving American servicemen had amassed the required points based on length of war service and other factors to enable them to go home and get out of the military. Many were opting to do so. It had been a long war. Lt. McGovern too had also amassed the required points. "However, I wasn't even thinking of going home but many of the enlisted men were." This was particularly apparent with many technical specialist non-commissioned officers. Many of these had been on special assignment with Mack and attached to the news pool. "I would find little notes in my room from so and so saying that a ship is in the harbour, that they had the points and that they were gone home. They just left, went down to the docks and walked onto a ship that was going to the States. That's how things were. Even my sound man, John Drane, left me," he remembered.[6] As a result and after further discussions with his new boss, General Anderson now gave Mack the authority to second specialist production personnel wherever he could find them.

Then, in early November 1945, Dan returned firstly to Nagasaki and continued his initial dedicated colour filming there alongside Dan Dyer's analysis work throughout the city but this time for what was now officially called the USSBS Motion Picture Project. Apart from his title of *Photographic Equipment Engineer*, McGovern was by now officially designated as *Director of Photography and Production* and *Officer in Charge* of the project.[7] The project in fact had now two official aims. The first was to bring to the public an objective picture of life in Japan as it existed at that point and the second was to record the physical damage inflicted upon Japan and to document certain important technological aspects of the Japanese war economy.[8]

A film frame of a production slate used by Lt. Dan McGovern for a scene in Nagasaki filmed on 15th November 1945. This was when Mack first started filming for the USSBS with Dan Dyer who undertook the physical damage surveys. **Image: USSBS, US National Archives.**

"We stayed aboard the *USS Barr* in Nagasaki harbor," McGovern recalled. Despite being a full colonel and possibly for security reasons, for this assignment Dyer only wore a US uniform devoid of all rank insignia and more akin to that of a war correspondent. As such, he was still afforded all the privileges of the officer class. Possibly as a result of the USSBS team's close daily contact with the US Navy on the *Barr* the US Naval Tactical Mission in Japan now began to take an interest in what Big Mack and his team were undertaking. The navy now decided that it wanted Mack and his team to document all aspects of the Japanese Navy in defeat such as its ships, naval facilities and any relevant naval technological advancements they had. The navy request was facilitated by the USSBS. As a result a US naval officer with a background in intelligence and the Japanese language, Lt. Commander A. Nicholas Vardac,[9] was also assigned as liaison officer to Dan's USSBS team. However, he soon flew to the United States to take up his new position there.

Vardac would be based at an office at Consolidated Film Processing Laboratories in Hollywood, California. This was one of the most prominent film processing facilities in Hollywood and was capable of processing large volumes of exposed negative movie film on an industrial scale into positive movie prints ready for projection. There, Vardac would oversee the processing of the colour motion picture project footage on Lt. McGovern's behalf as it arrived from his team. It was also agreed that Vardac would return periodically to liaise with McGovern in Japan. "Vardac was soon also working a deal with the studios Stateside to try and sell the concept of a movie given our historical documentation. We wanted the world to know about it and General Anderson encouraged that too."

Among other studios in Hollywood it was hoped that Warner Brothers in particular might be brought on board to produce a film based on the colour footage Mack and his team would produce. At this point also, McGovern's team was assigned an American liaison man between the United States and Japanese governments called Dr. Ernest M. Hall. Before the war Dr. Hall had taught at Kyoto University and was fluent in Japanese. He would be based mainly at the USSBS office in GHQ at the Meiji Building in Tokyo. This brought Big Mack's USSBS Motion Picture Project team to four.

THE JAPANESE FOOTAGE

It was whilst he was filming amid the ruins of the Mitsubishi arms factory in Nagasaki that McGovern first came across leading members of a Japanese film crew.[10] This chance meeting would prove significant. Their producer, Akira Iwasaki,[11] introduced himself to McGovern in perfect English and Mack listened intently to what he had to say. Iwasaki made it known that he and a team of cameraman from the Japanese newsreel service Nippon Eigasha, also commonly referred to in Japan as Nichiei, had also been previously filming amid the devastation of both Hiroshima and Nagasaki since 15th August and before anybody else. This was mere days after the atomic bombings. The Japanese cameramen had been working alongside research scientists from the Japanese Ministry of Education. Nippon Eigasha was a film production company formed by combining cameramen and other production staff drawn from various Japanese newsreel companies.

The purpose of the Japanese footage had been intended for propaganda purposes but later, on the same day filming had commenced, Emperor Hirohito had made his surrender broadcast to the Japanese people negating the original purpose of their filming assignment. However, filming had still continued, albeit now for scientific and historical purposes at least. Dan raised an eyebrow when Iwasaki then informed him that over 26,000 feet of 35mm Nippon Eigasha footage had already been shot amid the ruins of both Nagasaki and Hiroshima. Dan: "I saw the potential there. These cameramen had been filming weeks before I got there and with Mitchell cameras." Mack learned that, of the 26,000 feet of footage captured by the Japanese cameramen in both cities, 20,000 feet was of the devastation. However, the remaining 6,000 feet had focused instead on the harrowing graphic medical injuries and on the suffering the atomic bombs had inflicted on the survivors. As far as McGovern and the USSBS were concerned, this chance meeting with Iwasaki was an important one.

The Nippon Eigasha team comprised a total of 33 production professionals broken down into five individual film units to undertake their documentation task throughout the devastated cities. They had been sent firstly into Hiroshima with one lone cameraman choosing to commence filming in Nagasaki instead on the same day as his colleagues on August 15th 1945. Then, by early October 1945, the Japanese research and camera teams in Hiroshima had gradually started to relocate to Nagasaki where they joined their colleague to commence the main bulk of their work in that city.[12]

However, a problem had arisen with the arrival of the American occupation forces. With the Nippon Eigasha cameramen having commenced their filming assignments in both Hiroshima and Nagasaki, advance elements of the 2nd Marine Division had initially landed in Nagasaki on September 16th 1945 – over a month after the dropping of the atomic bombs. The main contingent of the division then landed in Nagasaki harbour on 23rd September just as the Mayor of Nagasaki had expected.

The general plan was for the division to occupy Nagasaki itself but also to fan out and occupy the administrative areas called prefectures of Kumamoto, Kagoshima and Miyazaki south of Nagasaki city. The 2nd Marine Division would eventually occupy all of the home island of Kyushu within a month.[13] However, having landed and once organised ashore, one of the division's first duties was to assist the 9000 Allied prisoners of war who had been designated a priority by MacArthur's occupation administration. With this task finally complete, the division then gave its full attention to its occupation duties in the ruins of Nagasaki. Iwasaki told McGovern, that shortly afterwards on October 24th 1945, one of his cameramen had been confronted by military policemen from the American 2nd Marine Division.

After an argument at the scene of this confrontation, film had been confiscated by the MPs and the cameraman instructed to clear out and leave. Later that same day the Nippon Eigasha photography had been suspended by order of MacArthur's occupational forces in Tokyo. Three days after that, on October 27th, their assignment was, officially at least, cancelled altogether when MacArthur formally banned all filming in both devastated cities.[14] This was with the Nippon Eigasha film crew, having wrapped filming in Hiroshima but with only 60% of the required filming completed in Nagasaki.[15]

An exception to the rule would be sanctioned filming for official US military purposes such as that being conducted by McGovern and the United States Strategic Bomb Survey. The Japanese production team had subsequently stood down its film crews greatly fearing now that it was about to lose its precious footage forever. However, they had not stood down completely. When McGovern encountered them in the first weeks of November 1945, Iwasaki and his small team was all that remained in Nagasaki. They had been filming in direct contravention of MacArthur's filming ban.

As a result of what he learned when he met Akira Iwasaki, McGovern could see little point in the USSBS spending considerable time and expense in essence duplicating the same footage already ably captured by the Nippon Eigasha cameramen. Despite the fact that the footage was not colour, Mack now wanted access to it. He had immediately realised its potential possibly for another unique production opportunity – but in black and white. Iwasaki now also informed Mack that his small film crew was about to exhaust its last reserves of black and white film. "They were down to their last 1000 feet of 35mm film so I gave them 5000 feet of Kodak BGX and more if they wanted it so that they could finish the job." McGovern now told Iwasaki to continue filming and that if the American MPs challenged them again, to say that they were now working for him. "I had the authority," he pointed out.

OTHER DESIGNS

However, as it turned out, Dan McGovern had not been the only American to come into contact with the Japanese film makers as they went about their work. A pathologist with the United States Surgeon General's Office had earlier observed a production crew as they filmed the terrible suffering in a Hiroshima hospital and spoken with them. Dr Averill Liebow[16] had soon realised the potential of the Japanese footage from a medical point of view.

Liebow had been in Hiroshima as part of a specialist commission surveying the medical consequences of the atomic explosions and he too now wanted the footage – but for the Surgeon General's Office. As Liebow negotiated with Nippon Eigasha management to obtain the film, he also successfully petitioned MacArthur's GHQ through official channels via memoranda to confiscate the footage from Nippon Eigasha and for it to be handed over to the Surgeon General's Office. The footage was seized on 18th December 1945 with a view to being shipped to the United States.[17] It soon also became apparent that there were others at General Headquarters who had seen the most graphic segments of the Japanese footage.

GHQ/SCAP Civil Information and Education Section, the CIE, had also wanted the film seized by the Counter Intelligence Corps because it *might be inflammatory if shown to the general public* and as it was *objectionable from a security or public safety viewpoint to have the film completed by the Japanese*.[18] Dan now feared that there was an intention to destroy the 26,000 feet of Japanese footage. He was already of the opinion that, now in the possession of the Surgeon General's Office, it would be unlikely to ever see the light of day again anyway.

McGovern had no doubt as to the reason for the American authorities' opposition to the footage ever being seen by the American public. "6,000 feet of that Japanese material was dreadful and sickening with burned and maimed bodies and skeletons all over the place in piles. It included footage of autopsies performed by Japanese doctors demonstrating the effects of radiation on deep internal organ tissue. They just squeamed at anything of that sort and they just did not want that footage to get out." Such opposition from inside MacArthur's headquarters could also potentially have serious ramifications for the USSBS colour film documentation on the ground in Hiroshima and

Nagasaki and elsewhere throughout Japan which had now commenced in earnest.

A tussle for control of the footage now intensified.[19] A series of memoranda were exchanged between MacArthur's GHQ, the Surgeon General's Office and the United States Strategic Bomb Survey with several of the latter memos being penned by Lt. McGovern himself. McGovern, by way of strongly worded correspondence, stressed to his superiors the importance of all the original Japanese film footage being turned over the USSBS. Then, a conference was arranged at General MacArthur's headquarters in the Meiji Building in Tokyo on the morning of January 2nd 1946 and at which all American interested parties could stake their claim to determine the future of the Nippon Eigasha footage.

Mack was determined to fight for it and by now he had an idea how he could use it if he could only get possession of it. He needed some leverage. In advance of the conference McGovern arranged to meet with representatives of the United States Navy who would also be present at the conference table. "We worked with them and told them the story," he recalled. Present at the hour long conference was a four strong United States Strategic Bomb Survey delegation which included Lt. McGovern and Dan Dyer. The Office of the Chief Surgeon of the United States was represented by a senior medical officer, Col. Walter H. Schwichtenberg. Two representatives of the United States Navy Technical Mission in Japan were present – Commander W.S. Heston and Captain A.L. Dunning.[20] Major John Cook, a Technical Intelligence officer with MacArthur's administration, took the minutes of the meeting. A strong case was made for the original Japanese film footage to be turned over to the USSBS by both Dan McGovern and Dan Dyer.

Mack now put a proposal to the conference delegates. "If you give me the same men who shot the material and the Japanese scientists who worked alongside them, that material could then be translated into English and their production finished under my direction. I will accept responsibility for that." McGovern stressed that the Japanese who shot the material were the best qualified to edit down the mass of exposed film material into the finished documentary. The finished film, he pointed out, would also be captioned and narrated in English. McGovern's pitch was greatly strengthened by Dan Dyer's bomb survey analysis contribution, aspects of which it was stressed, would also be included in the final production which would evolve from the Japanese footage from Hiroshima and Nagasaki.

McGovern's pitch to the conference was then also strongly supported by the representatives of the United States Navy.[21] They had earlier recognised the potential of what he was attempting to achieve and sided with Mack and the USSBS. Overall, a much stronger case was made for the continuance of the Japanese production than for its cessation and also against any confiscation of its footage. McGovern had got his way. It was agreed at the conference that the Surgeon General's Office would return the Japanese footage to the Nippon Eigasha production team which would now resume its remaining location filming activities in Nagasaki. This was towards the overall completion of the black and white documentary, but crucially, now under Dan McGovern's direction and supervision.

It was also agreed that no material would be shipped to the United States until after the documentary was completed. Furthermore, no other agency was permitted to confiscate or remove material.[22] It was also decided that the documentary crafted from the Japanese footage would comprise three main segments – *Hiroshima*, *Nagasaki* and a third *Medical* segment with footage centring mainly on the topics of physics, structural damage, botany and biology in the aftermath of the atomic bombs. Official orders outlining what had been agreed at that conference were immediately ratified by MacArthur's GHQ and issued to the USSBS and the Surgeon General's Office officially outlining the new status quo. As a direct result of this conference contracts were also drawn up ensuring that the Japanese cameramen and production staff were paid for their ongoing services. McGovern remembered: "I was granted all that I asked. We won the right to finish that particular picture thanks to General Anderson, Dan Dyer and the United States Strategic Bomb Survey. The Nippon Eigasha footage already shot was saved and its film documentation allowed to be finished."

However, there was yet another important reason why Dan was given the go ahead to finish his production. Despite the obvious rivalry between the USSBS and the Surgeon General's Office as to which organisation should have control of the footage, its seizure and possible destruction by elements in GHQ would be of no benefit to either organisation. "We even had allies in the Surgeon General's Office in Washington DC and also in the Institute of Pathology there and they won out and got around General MacArthur to not destroy the material."

It was also agreed at the conference that a 26,000 feet positive workprint would be produced from the negative footage. This was subsequently viewed by the US Surgeon General's Office representatives in Tokyo who then decided that, rather than wait for the entire documentary to be completed, it would be happy with a new 8,000 feet print copy of just the medical footage. There was agreement that the remainder of the workprint and the entire original Japanese negative would be handed over to the USSBS. Under Mack's direction Nippon Eigasha manager and producer Akira Iwasaki and his crew would now resume filming for their separate 35mm Black and White film documentary.

This would run parallel to the USSBS colour filming activities. The Japanese cameramen were now officially working for the United States government and would be supplied with everything they needed including ample film, rations, living quarters and logistical support. With the Nippon Eigasha issue now resolved and with the threat of any further interference removed, the way was now clear for McGovern to get back to his team on the colour Motion Picture Project. He had, by now, an idea in his head for an eventual full colour movie which he had decided to entitle *Japan in Defeat*.

Concurrent to his work on the Motion Picture Project he would now oversee the remaining Nippon Eigasha location filming in Nagasaki and then that film's post production to completion. McGovern knew that both his projects, when finished, would represent highly scientific and highly technical productions and perhaps more than anything else, a very valuable historical resource for posterity. However, General Anderson had given McGovern and Dyer a deadline to have the colour movie and bomb analysis documentation completed. That was the spring of 1946. With just himself undertaking the filming and given that Dan Dyer, Ernest Hall and Sergeant Shimomura were all on other duties for the project, the deadline to complete its filming was going to be tight and Dan knew it.

The general had given McGovern the authorisation to increase his personnel as well as to make whatever logistical arrangements he thought necessary to get the job done. Dan needed additional cameramen. Furthermore, he knew too that the team's C-47 transport aircraft, swift as it was but packed to capacity with USSBS personnel, their single jeep and trailer and their existing photographic equipment and supplies, had limitations. Transport in general was proving to be a challenge and a better logistical arrangement was required.

---

1. Before starting work on the *Manhattan Project* in September 1942 the then Colonel Leslie Groves had overseen the early phases of construction of the Pentagon building in Virginia. *Fine & Remington 1972,* pages 659 to 661.
2. It may have been Farrell's research team which had planted the green, yellow and red safety flags denoting radiation levels which McGovern had seen in Nagasaki.
3. From General Anderson's military citations, USAF.
4. Incoming message from COMGEM USASTAF to USASTAF ADVON ATT G-4 USSASB, Tokyo, undated, Folder: 664 - Outgoing message (USASTAF) October 1945, Box 151, RG 243. *From the Stinko to the USSBS Motion Picture Project* essay, Atsuko Shigesawa, p116 footnote #49.
5. *Surveys of Hiroshima and Nagasaki,* Atomic Heritage Foundation website.

6. Drane had been ordered back to Guam.

7. Personnel Order No. 16, Dec. 7, 1945, Folder: 300.4-F Personnel Order, Box 12, RG 243. *From the Stinko to the USSBS Motion Picture Project* essay, Atsuko Shigesawa, p117 footnote #56.

8. *Aims* source: Function of PDD #10, memorandum to G-2 Section, USSBS, Nov. 17, 1945, Role No. 53, USSBS RSR via *From the Stinko to the USSBS Motion Picture Project* essay, Atsuko Shigesawa, pages 117-118.

9. A. Nicholas Vardac would later himself become a film producer and writer.

10. In his oral history, Dan McGovern recollects that he came across the Japanese film crew during his first visit to Nagasaki with the correspondents. However, this is unlikely as that was only on 9th September and no filming ban was yet in place. McGovern was certainly filming in Nagasaki in the first days of November and only within days of GHQ's filming ban being introduced. The author believes that this was when the chance meeting with Iwasaki's small film crew actually took place.

11. Iwasaki went on to become a prominent Japanese film critic, producer and film historian.

12. The lone cameraman/director was Ito Sueo. *The Body at the Centre – The Effects of the Atomic Bomb in Hiroshima and Nagasaki* Abé Mark Nornes, pages 124 and 125.

13. *Marine Corps Historical Reference Pamphlet*, Occupation of Japan, pages 17 and 20.

14. Memo Major John Cook Army Technical Intelligence, 3rd January 1946 following resolution Conference on 2nd January.

15. Hibakusha Cinema, *The Body at the Centre – The Effects of the Atomic Bomb in Hiroshima and Nagasaki* Abé Mark Nornes p127.

16. Like McGovern Dr. Liebow had emigrated to the United States as a young boy but from his native Austria.

17. Hibakusha Cinema, *The Body at the Centre – The Effects of the Atomic Bomb in Hiroshima and Nagasaki,* Abé Mark Nornes, p129.

18. From *The Stinko to the USSBS Motion Picture Project* essay, Atsuko Shigesawa, p117.

19. Much of what actually transpired regarding the confiscation/seizure of the Nippon Eigasha black and white footage in Tokyo is complex and open to interpretation. The author has chosen to impart a simple but factual narrative based on the documentation and oral accounts available.

20. Memo Major John Cook Army Technical Intelligence, 3rd January 1946 following resolution conference on 2nd January. The United States Naval Technical Mission in Japan, NAVTECHJAP, was a special navy group charged with ascertaining the extent of Japanese technical knowledge pertaining to all naval matters in comparison to the United States.

21. McGovern recalled that the US Navy contribution at this conference was an important factor to its outcome.

22. Memo Major John Cook, Army Technical Intelligence, 3rd January 1946 following resolution conference on 2nd January.

20

FILMING JAPAN FROM THE EMPEROR SPECIAL

The Return to Hiroshima

ONCE BACK IN Tokyo Dan set about commandeering a fully equipped train which he located in Yokohama but which was going to take some time to prepare. By now the film production equipment and the vehicles Mack had shipped from Guam had arrived. In the meantime, he now set about looking for the additional cameramen and support staff he needed. However, Mack soon found that, with the continuing rush Stateside from all branches of the service since war's end, suitably qualified cameramen in particular were proving difficult to find for the job at hand.

Eventually, by December, he managed to secure the services of five additional USAAF NCO cameramen who now joined the team but only on loan from the 5th Combat Camera Unit now based in Yokohama. These were Corporal Raymond V. Wizbowski, Corporal Henry Wischoofer Jr., S/Sgt. Olaf. A. Bolm, Sgt. Benjamin R. Potts and Sergeant Wallace G. Hoover. Hoover was also a qualified sound technician and had the designation of *Sound Cameraman*. Then, a twenty-four-year-old second lieutenant whom Dan had met back at Fort Roach in Culver City, also showed up looking for a job. Dan needed a scriptwriter so Lt. Herb Sussan also joined the team. Sussan had been a clerk sergeant at Fort Roach prior to being selected for officer training on 22nd February 1944 after which he was commissioned as a 2nd Lieutenant.[1] Mack said of Sussan: "I took Herb on as an adjutant or administrative type to take care of scriptwriting and captions and to work out logistics. Things of that sort.[2] I was glad to have him because he knew how to write. He was a great poker player who was sometimes more inclined to play poker and deal on the black market but he did his job."

A third Fort Roach officer now also joined the team. First Lt. Robert H. Wildermuth, like Big Mack, had a background in aerial photography. With navy liaison officer Lt. Commander Vardac by now back Stateside in support at Consolidated Laboratories, McGovern's team on the ground in Japan to continue work on the USSBS Motion Picture Project comprised: Lt. McGovern, Dan Dyer, Lt. Herb Sussan, Lt. Robert H. Wildermuth, Dr. Ernest Hall and Staff Sergeants Olaf A. Bolm and Michio *Mitch* Shimomura; Sergeants Wallace G. Hoover and Benjamin Potts as well as Corporal Henry Wischoofer Jr. and Cpl. Ray V. Wizbowski.

This new enlarged USSBS Motion Picture Project team now included no less than six cameramen. Their C-47 Dakota transport aeroplane would by no means be redundant. It would be still available and regularly used to obtain aerial footage of the areas they were documenting on the ground.[3] The C-47 would also be utilised for return flights to Tokyo from filming locations. With the majority of rail links to city centres and towns throughout Japan still largely intact, or at least repairable, Dan and his team now had the means to get practically anywhere they needed in Japan. With their train they were also self-sufficient. Dan: "We called it the *Emperor Special* and code-named it *Casper*.[4] I had an engineer and all the people who go with a train and even a cook." The train consisted of locomotive #48635 and coal tender behind which was pulled an eighteen berth Pullman wagon, a lounge car and a dining car complete with stewards.

Most of the USSBS team pictured with their four jeeps and the locomotive of the 'Emperor Special'. This photograph was probably taken by Dan McGovern. **Photo: Japan Peace Museum.**

The 'Emperor Special' train with the 'Casper' Pullman carriage to the rear. This train gave Dan and his USSBS team an ideal portable base as they went about their documentation of Japan. **Photo: Japan Peace Museum.**

Another view of Nagasaki with its surrounding hills and the destruction visited upon it. **Photo: US National Archives.**

A view of Nagasaki taken from street level. What remains of the city's once ordered streets and blocks is evident. **Photo: US National Archives.**

The lounge car doubled as a work base and it was also from there that the main business of any given day was organised and conducted. The team's cameras and its fresh film stocks were also stored there. For their documentation of Japan, the USSBS cameramen would predominantly use 16mm Kodachrome colour film. They would also use stocks of the good, but unstable, 35mm Technicolor Monopack.[5] Also added to the train was a baggage car and an enclosed wooden bodied reefer cargo car which carried the team's large cumbersome items of equipment sometimes needed to augment filming. This included production lights and stands, electrical cabling and other associated paraphernalia. Three flatbed wagons were added which carried the team's four jeeps and trailers and the electrical generators. In essence, the train was now a mobile base on which Dan and his men could work, eat and unwind at the end of a busy day.

The *Emperor Special* would now propel McGovern and his USSBS team to a wide variety of filming and survey locations right across Japan. They boarded their train in Tokyo Central Station for the first time on January 6th 1946. Even then, the rush Stateside struck again. Cameraman Sergeant Benjamin Potts failed to show up. Potts was already aboard a ship bound for the United States.

The USSBS team, depleted as it was, set out regardless on its nine hour train journey to return firstly to Nagasaki where filming and bomb survey documentation soon recommenced.[6] It appeared as if little had physically changed there since McGovern had first entered the devastated city with the correspondents back in September. By now, the tens of thousands of dead bodies, which had been so visible throughout the city when he had first arrived there, had largely been taken care of, but they continued to be gradually replaced by thousands more. The will to survive could be seen throughout the city and sometimes pitifully so. Starving, many poor people scavenged for morsels of whatever food they could find amid massive piles of refuse on garbage barges tied up throughout the city.

*Dan McGovern behind a Mitchell 35mm camera as caught
on film by a USSBS cameraman colleague in Nagasaki in
January 1946.* **Image: US National Archives.**

On closer inspection, however, some semblance of normality
was being observed by the survivors of that shattered city. They
filmed the children – those innocent youngsters of various ages
in the sea of death and destruction around them, often bewildered, often laughing and always curious. They were the future
of whatever could be salvaged from this calamity. McGovern and
his cameramen filmed it all and helped where they could.
Temporary housing had appeared and here and there, attempts
were being made to restore infrastructure. Dan himself initially
concentrated on filming the human medical aspects of the
atomic bomb in Nagasaki. The terrible suffering continued.

He filmed the many terrible heat flash burn cases now being
cared for, often in hospitals which were slowly starting to become
operational again or in other makeshift medical facilities. The
team used their strong electric lights to sometimes illuminate
what they were filming. However, the direct heat on many of the
patients, given the sensitivity of their terrible seared injuries,
frequently only caused additional agony. "When we would turn
on these lights it would hurt the poor burns patients to such an
extent that we had to subdue our lighting to cut down the heat."

A PILOT'S LAMENTATION

During filming in Nagasaki Mack also remembered seeing one particular USAAF crewman busy distributing hundreds of boxes of penicillin. What Mack found out about him was interesting. "I was told that he was one of the pilots of the B-29s that dropped the second atomic bomb. He flew hundreds of pounds of penicillin into Nagasaki. He was so overwrought with what he had seen that he came there prepared as if offering lamentation to the people for their suffering. That penicillin was a godsend to the Japanese."

To obtain the variety of colour footage required for their task, Mack came up with the concept of *roaming cameramen*. Rather than his remaining four cameramen filming different scenes in any given area, better use would be made of them. He sent them out, often with an interpreter, on multiple assignments considerable distances away by jeep and trailer, usually filming with one group or another himself. With the team now having four jeeps and with the cameramen dispatched in this way, considerable footage was recorded in and around Nagasaki. This was a system which would be largely used for the remainder of their assignment throughout Japan. This worked particularly well with the four borrowed 5th Combat Camera Unit cameramen Wischoofer, Hoover, Bolm and Wizbowski. Dan remembered: "They were young cameramen and very good. I told them what I wanted – footage of a community somewhere or maybe a farming family somewhere else and they just went out and did it."

Permanently painted prominently onto all USSBS production slates now was *Director – Lt. D.A. McGovern.* "I'd tell them to come back when they felt like it but to make sure to always *put a slate on the footage.*" Given the very large volume and variance of footage being shot by his cameramen and to avoid mistakes, Dan was simply re-stressing the importance of always filming a few frames of a production slate prior to shooting.

Often as not a colleague might take over this responsibility from the cameraman during location filming.

THE APPROACH TO LEADERSHIP

Dan always felt that the approach to leadership on his part was the right one. In keeping somewhat with the informal approach to rank adopted at Fort Roach, Dan was frequently simply referred to by his subordinates as *Lieutenant Mack*. This had been carried on by Sgt. Shimomura from in or around the Bloomer Girls episode with the correspondents back in September.

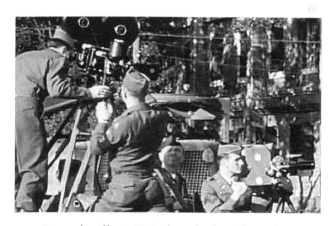

Captured on film in Nagasaki in this frame from USSBS footage shot in January 1946 are, the author believes, the four 5th Combat Camera Unit cameramen who joined McGovern's team, namely Wischoofer, Hoover, Bolm and Wizbowski. **Image: US National Archives.**

"You take care of your men first which is one of the attributes of a good leader. This was one of the reasons I feel that I was so successful in getting things done. There was nobody on their tail all the time." However, one new member of the team had anything but this approach. "1st Lt. Robert H. Wildermuth was a problem because he had a nasty disposition. He treated the men like dirt. I told him to show them a little kindness and consideration but even I had a difficult time trying to stop him being abusive towards the men. He'd make them walk while he'd ride and things of that sort."

As Mack and his cameramen filmed their respective filming assignments Herb Sussan concentrated on his writing assignments which also included writing captions for the footage shot. Dan Dyer meanwhile, focused his attention on the effect of the atomic bomb detonation. Dyer gathered bomb survey analysis on oil refineries, aircraft plants and any structure or installation which had been designated as a possible target or which had previously been bombed conventionally. He had target folders which held technical data, schematics and aerial photographs of what these previously designated targets looked like.

On one occasion Dyer was particularly interested in a large 110 feet high brick smokestack for instance. When studying reconnaissance photographs of structures in advance of bombing missions, counting the bricks in the smokestack under magnification would give an idea of the true height of such a smokestack in advance of a strategic strike. "So we counted the number of bricks in that particular structure and made comparisons," McGovern recalled. The team discovered that tall round chimneys and fire watchtowers in both Hiroshima and Nagasaki had demonstrated a high resistance to the atomic blasts and had remained largely intact. Mack: "We photographed the physical damage aspect of everything under the sun in both cities. Fortunately, we had some pretty good weather."

Every evening at the end of their work day and having double checked content labels, the cinematographers turned in their exposed spools of 16mm colour film footage to McGovern. Mack carefully filed the canisters away in one of several storage footlockers in the lounge car. The crew then usually had dinner and relaxed afterwards with a few beers and watched feature films with their screen and projector. They then retired to their Pullman carriage for a good night's sleep in preparation for another busy day's filming and surveying the following morning. On his regular return flights back to Tokyo for GHQ briefings and other purposes, Mack always returned with as many essential supplies as he could carry. To help while away the evenings this included as many feature films as he could get his hands on at GHQ which were always in demand. Some films of course, were better than others, but even mediocre movie entertainment was better than none at all. Sometimes he would give his charges their assignments for the following day before they would retire for the night but other times just after breakfast in the morning.

Dan McGovern (seated) is served cake during dinner in the dining carriage of the 'Emperor Special' by Herb Sussan and a Japanese waiter. **Inset:** *Andy, the team's cook.* **Photos: USSBS/Japan Peace Museum.**

To assist their efforts the USSBS team now also received a substantial boost in the form of filming equipment and other additional resources from the United States Navy. McGovern wasted no time in putting it to good use. "I refurbished all my existing equipment and I also got new additional equipment which was a great help."

At the end of January 1946 and with the USSBS Motion Picture Project just starting to get into its stride, Mack received a setback. The 5th Combat Camera Unit was requesting its cameramen be returned and with the ever-increasing flow of servicemen going back to the United States and getting out of the service, they were now going to be even harder to replace. Subsequently, the team now lost the services of cameramen Wischoffer and Hoover and also Lt. Wildermuth. In any case the lieutenant in particular had found the death and destruction on a magnitude of this scale just too difficult to deal with.

McGovern had also observed similar traits in Lt. Herb Sussan but, despite Sussan's abhorrence of what he was witnessing around him, he had remained with the team. McGovern managed to retain cameramen Wizbowski and Bolm who were keen to continue their secondment with the USSBS given the historical significance of the footage they were shooting.

NICHIEI DOCUMENTARY FILMING WRAPS

Also at the end of January, Dan got word that nine Nippon Eigasha cameramen who had also been in Nagasaki filming the concluding scenes for the Japanese black and white documentary film, had completed their location filming in the city. Thousands of feet of black and white film now had to be edited into a finished narrated documentary. It was time to leave his own crew for the time being to fly the Japanese production crew and all their equipment and footage to Tokyo and Allied GHQ. There, he had set up a movie editing suite on the seventh floor of the Meiji building.

Under Big Mack's direction, the Nippon Eigasha team would now undertake Post Production. "I supervised them to edit and finalise the new film which was now entitled *Effects of the Atomic Bomb on Hiroshima and Nagasaki*."[7] The documentary would be produced in line with what was agreed at the January GHQ conference which had paved the way for the continuance and completion of the production. Within those parameters however, Dan McGovern would largely leave Iwasaki and his team to their own devices to produce what would, in essence be, a production of Nichiei scientific findings about the atomic bombs and their aftermath. Before returning to his team in Nagasaki though, Dan needed to find replacement cameramen to help finish the USSBS Motion Picture Project on time. After a considerable search he eventually managed to employ the services of a top Japanese civilian film producer who had been a cameraman in Hollywood and who was a member of the Association of Cinematographers of America. When McGovern found him he was working for the Toho Studios in Tokyo from where he came on loan. He would be vital to the team getting all its photographic tasks completed. His name was Akira *Harry* Mimura.

Harry returned to Nagasaki with McGovern where he shot a significant amount of colour footage to ensure that filming wrapped there. Dan said of Mimura: "Harry was an outstanding man to have. He was a Japanese citizen and was delighted to come work for me. He did alot of work for the team." There were now four cameramen instead of five but Harry Mimura's wide experience and expertise would go a long way to make up the difference. In addition, a Japanese American public relations specialist, Sam Okimoto, now also joined the project team as an interpreter to assist the other production members.

Operating with what would be its final complement of personnel, McGovern's USSBS team now turned its attention to surviving Japanese industry and its workers. They filmed and photographed everyday life in and around many smaller industrial cities in which industry had remained undamaged including Yawata, south of Kyoto, Kudamatsu, Ube and Tokuyma, south of Hiroshima and then in Korosue on the outskirts of Osaka. Throughout these cities they filmed massive surviving industrial complexes and the people who worked them including steel mills and smelting furnaces, coal mines and miners and other more traditional Japanese industrial processes.

Accomplished cinematographer Akira 'Harry' Mimura pictured on his berth on the 'Emperor Special'. **Photo: USSBS, Japan Peace Museum.**

Harry Mimura and an assistant having just completed filming a scene watched by a local Japanese boy. **Photo: USSBS, Japan Peace Museum.**

Typically, Mack would usually send a minimum of 10,000 feet of exposed film in sealed canisters[8] of various spool sizes to Lt. Cmdr. Vardac at Consolidated Industries in robust standard issue US Army wooden footlockers. These would usually be flown from the nearest air base from which an aircraft was departing for the United States. Vardac went about his work diligently and methodically and much to McGovern's satisfaction and he kept his boss well informed of progress from his end. He oversaw the transformation of the exposed colour film received from Japan into the processed footage which could then be viewed prior to the editing process. This raw footage was now ready for the next crucial step – editing into the final movie cut. Dan pointed out: "At Consolidated Labs the footage was properly processed and duplicated.[9] Companies like that had the film processing contract for the United States government." Dan wanted to get the processing done before any of those government contracts expired given that the war had ended.[10]

One early cable Big Mack received from Vardac informed him that some of the footage from Nagasaki had been processed and had turned out great. However, he also learned in a later cable that some reels of the 35mm Technicolor Monopack film stock was still up to its old tricks. It was turning magenta during processing due to its unstable chemical make-up. However, thankfully as time went on, this only affected a small percentage of the exposed film. Meanwhile, back in Tokyo, the black and white footage shot by the Japanese Nippon Eigasha cameramen was still in the process of being edited into the final film. "Every so often I'd leave the USSBS team and fly back to Tokyo to supervise the Nippon Eigasha team," Mack recounted.

THE DEFEATED ARMIES RETURN

Mack and his team now travelled several hours to the south-west and the harbour city of Otake where one of several demobilisation centres had been set up to process returning Japanese servicemen. It was here that they would film mainly soldiers of the Imperial Japanese Army returning to their homeland in their thousands from their now liberated reaches of conquest. Mack: "That was one of the most moving things that I saw. They were coming from Manchuria, from China and from all sorts of far flung places and it was the Australians who were in charge of that whole operation so I had to work with them." He added: "We spent days filming that and I think it is the only record that has ever been made of the Japanese armies coming home."

Ship after ship came in. The returning troops disembarked and entered a massive demobilisation area where they were deloused with DTT. "They had already given up their weapons someplace else and they all carried their packs on their backs. They had no rank markings on them at all," Dan remembered. He also remarked that there existed a sense of humiliation among those returning soldiers but he always kept in mind what General MacArthur had said about treating the Japanese as you would like to be treated yourself. "I'd pass them some cigarettes, pieces of candy or a Hershey chocolate bar and the interpreters would reassure them and settle them down."

With the help of his interpreters, Nisei Staff Sergeant Shimomura and Sam Okamoto, Dan interviewed and filmed many of the returning servicemen. "I interviewed generals to private soldiers and I put them on camera. It was cold at that time of year. We would often call them over to our campfire and they would sit and chat." Japanese staff officers who had been on the staff of the more senior Japanese commanders were always that bit more obstinate and surly. "You paid respect to them. You could always tell them," Mack recalled, adding that the wives and children of Japanese officers were also coming through the demobilisation centre. "The American forces are the best fed forces in the world and we had loads of food. We had apples, oranges, peaches and candy. We even had cans of Coca Cola before cans of Coke even came on the market. These were the things we used to gain the confidence of the Japanese people."

*Defeated and dejected Japanese troops disembark from their ship at the port of Otake in March 1946. As many as six million Japanese military personnel, officials and civilians were repatriated. **Inset:** A Japanese general pictured at Otake. **Photos: USSBS/US National Archives.***

*Huge numbers of defeated Japanese troops arrived home to Japan at the port of Otake and through the demobilisation centre there administered by Australian occupation forces. **Photo: USSBS/US National Archives.***

Japanese Army officers returning to their homeland at Otake. Many had served the Empire for years in its far flung conquered colonies throughout Asia and the Western Pacific. **Photo: USSBS/US National Archives.**

Returning Japanese troops at the Otake processing centre just over twenty miles to the south west of Hiroshima. McGovern remembered their overall sense of humiliation. Nearly all are wearing masks presumably in advance of delousing with DDT. **Photo: USSBS/US National Archives.**

BACK TO HIROSHIMA

By early March 1946 the USSBS film documentation and survey specialists briefly found themselves filming in Japan's second largest city, Yokohama in Tokyo Bay. There, Mack came across what he remembered was the most tear-jerking moment of all concerning his film documentation of prisoners of war. He recalled: "We saw American POWs lined up on the dock near Yokohama just waiting for a ship to come to repatriate them. They were just emaciated little skeletons."

Shortly afterwards the team travelled over four hundred miles east to Hiroshima or *Hiro* to which they frequently referred to it. What was left of the city was cameraman Harry Mimura's home-town. On board the train Mack and the team were now preparing for what would be nearly a month's filming and bomb surveying in Hiroshima, capturing similar footage and target analysis information to that of Nagasaki. Only three of Hiroshima's 45 hospitals had remained partially functional after the atomic bomb exploded over the city the previous August. Now, in the remaining hospitals or in subsequent makeshift medical facilities as in Nagasaki, the suffering continued.

Mack and his cameramen now filmed doctors and nurses as they cared for the thousands of bomb survivors who continued to suffer from a myriad of complaints including radiation sickness, flash burns and cuts and lacerations often as not caused by flying glass. The cameramen also filmed operations being carried out on bomb victims. In the Red Cross Hospital in Hiroshima even now they continued to film blood splattered walls. There was some degree of irony experienced in that hospital as they filmed stores of hospital X-Ray film which, despite been carefully stored in cabinets, had all been rendered useless by the radiation emitted when the bomb exploded. Elsewhere throughout Hiroshima the cameramen filmed the effect flash burn had on bamboo trees, on granite tombstones, wooden posts, iron chains and on various surfaces such as concrete and asphalt.

By March 1946 considerable temporary housing such as that pictured had been constructed throughout Hiroshima and also in Nagasaki. A film frame from the USSBS footage. **US National Archives.**

A linesman filmed in Hiroshima working to restore essential power supplies. A frame from USSBS film footage. **US National Archives.**

A woman in solemn prayer at a Hiroshima shrine containing the remains of atomic bomb dead. A USSBS film frame. **US National Archives.**

A resident of Hiroshima tills a small piece of ground as some semblance of normality returned to the city after it was destroyed by the atomic bomb. Similar scenes were also being played out by survivors in Nagasaki. A frame from the USSBS footage. **US National Archives.**

Mack and his cameramen filmed the inhabitants of Hiroshima as they attempted to piece their lives back together in a city which itself lay in pieces around them. Whilst further out from Ground Zero many main roadways into the city had now been cleared, once bustling city centre streets near Ground Zero still remained mere pathways in a sea of rubble. Through these pathways the city's inhabitants now made their way on foot, sometimes on bicycles or often pulling humble handcarts in what was some attempt at the resumption of daily life in Hiroshima.

As in Nagasaki, large numbers of temporary prefabricated wooden houses had by now started to be erected in an attempt to at least re-house some of the city centre's inhabitants. Men, women and children were filmed picking through the rubble searching possibly for personal effects and useful rebuilding materials. Elsewhere, others continued to persevere in their frantic but vain search for the remains of loved ones who, often as not, had simply been atomised in the explosion. By now, plants had started to grow again, breaking out through the heat seared earth. As a result, perhaps, striving for normality amid all this abhorrent abnormality, some city residents now carefully raked small patches of brown earth here and there as they attempted to coax once again what greenery they could from what had once been proudly kept gardens and lawns. All around them the lifeless stalks of charred, limbless and sometimes partially uprooted trees protruded regularly through the mass of desolation in Hiroshima. Burned out, crushed and rusting vehicles of all shapes and sizes littered the city. McGovern and his cameramen filmed it all.

Unlike in Nagasaki a few tram cars had resumed running some services in the days immediately after the bomb, ferrying passengers from one rubble strewn neighbourhood to another. During his first brief visit to Hiroshima, McGovern had filmed that in the first days of October. Now, in March, he noticed that considerably more trams were running. Overhead, electricians and linesmen were filmed perched high up on wooden electricity poles as they attempted to repair or replace burned out transformers, cracked ceramic insulators and electric cables to ensure that power was at hand in the city whenever it was available and needed again. Dan and his cameramen also filmed the remains of many of Hiroshima's badly damaged concrete and brick buildings. Most were largely destroyed, structurally cracked, hollow and even askew with entire sections sometimes shunted sideways. This was due to the sheer power of the atomic blast and these sections now overhung precariously to one side. Complete sections of other buildings had either collapsed or were missing altogether. Through fractured concrete, many of these buildings and other deformed structures such as concrete bridges and walls now also bared their internal steel reinforcing.

Other buildings at varying distances away from Ground Zero had retained their structural integrity but were now largely devoid of rooves, windows, doors and internal fixtures and fittings to various degrees – all blown away by the force of the bomb. Here and there among the rubble, numerous public clocks were also filmed their hands frozen forever on that infamous moment in time which was just minutes before 8.15am – the exact time the bomb had exploded on the morning of August 6th 1945. In Hiroshima the team also filmed aspects of Shinto and Buddhist funeral rites or memorial services of just a tiny fraction of the many people that had died since the bomb was released over their city. Yet, despite the suffering, the mourning and the destruction, most significantly of all perhaps the cameramen also filmed the first tentative steps of the people of Hiroshima as they started to clear the mass of rubble all around them and to begin to rebuild their city anew.

THE AIMING POINT

The Aioi-Bashi Bridge in Hiroshima, with its distinctive T configuration, had been used by Tibbets and the crew of the *Enola Gay* as the aiming point for the first atomic bomb. Lt.

McGovern now found himself standing on it. He noticed that the bridge's railings on either side were all gone but that their atomic shadow had been projected onto the tarmac asphalt of the bridge's pavement. Dan noticed the faint image of something else. "We had the bridge cleared and washed down and we filmed what was the faint image of a farmer's ox and cart. It was almost like a film negative transposed onto the asphalt. You could even see where the halter lines were coming down from the ox." Also visible was the shadow of what had been the farmer.

It was at this point that Mack commandeered an intact German-made fire truck which had a very long extending rescue ladder. "It was a beautiful job. There were few buildings left standing in Hiroshima from which to get elevated shots to shoot downwards. Hiroshima didn't need the fire truck as there was nothing left to burn. In exchange we kept the fire house going with food." Dan pointed out that, despite the terrible suffering and plight of the Japanese, he never encountered any animosity towards him as he filmed. "They knew they had been wrong. They were ready to pay the price and they did but that's the spirit of the Japanese people." Of the considerable misery he witnessed in both Hiroshima and Nagasaki during his filming visits Dan recalled: "There was a lot of misery but the strange thing was that I rarely ever saw the Japanese cry. They took their pain with them. There was a certain character to the Japanese in that they were embarrassed to a certain degree."

Then, on 20th March 1946, the Mount Sakurajima volcano on the south-western tip of Japan's home island of Kyushu erupted. Lt. McGovern left the team in Hiroshima for several days when he received a telegram assigning him to film it for the newsreels. This would be done from their C-47. "We had the capability to do that so we flew down there for what turned out to be a terrifying experience." Neither Dan nor his crew expected such severe turbulence flying so close to an erupting volcano. "Boy were we bounced all over the sky. I thought we were going to crash." Eventually, however, they landed safely.

*The Atoi-Bashi Bridge in Hiroshima as photographed by Dan McGovern
and his crew from the rescue ladder of their borrowed German fire truck.*
Photo: USSBS, US National Archives.

*This eerie atomic shadow is all that remained of the person who had been
sitting on these bank steps in Hiroshima.* **Photo: Getty Images.**

Atomic shadow on the Yorozuya Bridge in Hiroshima. What the Japanese refer to as the 'Hypocentre' of the explosion was just over a half mile away to the right of shot. **Photo: US National Archives.**

Once finished their film and survey documentation work in Hiroshima Mack and his USSBS team returned their trusty German fire engine to the city's Fire Department. It had enabled them to get the best elevated shots of the desolation. They then boarded the *Emperor Special* once again. It was now early April and as the train sped through the Japanese countryside to their next filming location, the cherry blossoms were in full bloom and looked resplendent.

1. *The history of the First Motion Picture Unit, 1944* – Scanlan.
2. Other narratives have Herb Sussan as a cameraman. However, McGovern is clear regarding the capacity in which Sussan joined the team.
3. Dan and his USSBS Motion Picture Project team adopted a filming and bomb survey itinerary which largely criss-crossed Japan rather than simply filming at new locations based solely on convenience.
4. This was the name already painted on the side of the pullman. However, above that was now stencilled, if somewhat more roughly, – *US Army*.

5. McGovern would film many USSBS colour scenes in both Nagasaki and Tokyo in all totalling 16 exposed reels, with a Mitchell 35mm camera and using Technicolor Monopack film. Some scenes were filmed with sound. This information is recorded on a detailed six page USAF *Atomic Bomb Special Film List* dated 12th March 1964 provided to the author courtesy of Wayne Weiss. Given that *The Last Bomb* was shot with this 35mm film and that there were considerable stocks left over from that production, it is likely that McGovern made use of it, albeit in a very limited way, in addition to his stocks of 16mm silent Kodachrome.

6. Prior to attending the January 2nd conference at MacArthur's headquarters in Tokyo to decide the future of the Japanese B&W footage, it appears that McGovern made a brief return visit to Nagasaki over the holiday period. He filmed Midnight Mass amid the ruins of Nagasaki's Catholic Urakami Cathedral on Christmas Eve/Christmas Day, 1945.

7. The film is most commonly referred to as *The Effects of the Atomic Bomb on Hiroshima and Nagasaki*. Dan McGovern also referred to it as such. However, in Japanese the word *the* does not exist – *Japanese Language Stack Exchange* website. As director, McGovern may simply have permitted producer, Akira Iwasaki, to omit the prefix from the actual English film title. This may have been in the belief and rightly so, that not all effects of the bomb were yet known at that point. The film will be referred to in this narrative by its actual title without the prefix.

8. Canisters containing exposed film spools were usually sealed with *black* adhesive tape.

9. It was US military practice when processing such historical 16mm colour footage to immediately duplicate it and to archive the camera original.

10. The contracts were terminated in 1947.

21

CLIPPED WINGS AND SUNKEN HULKS

Reagan's Kamikaze Gear

THE USSBS TEAM frequently filmed whatever they found of interest regarding Japanese military aviation. They filmed intact, destroyed or partially destroyed airfield installations and aircraft in many parts of Japan. Earlier, back in Tokyo for example, Mack had filmed a record of those Japanese airmen who had terrorised approaching American and Allied shipping with their *Divine Wind,* one way trip suicide missions in their high speed, high explosive-laden single seat fighter planes – the Kamikaze pilots.

Most intact aircraft on Japanese air bases, in keeping with pre-occupation instructions, now stood largely abandoned with their propellers removed. At Chofu airfield just west of Tokyo, McGovern however, had assembled fully intact Japanese fighters and pilots for his film shoot. "I also came across kamikaze flying outfits complete with headgear, jackets, goggles and hachimaki headscarves." He re-created four kamikaze pilots offering their last prayers at a Shinto Shrine and then drinking a farewell toast at a small table. When he and Sgt. Bolm had finished filming, Mack thought of his friend, the adjutant back at Fort Roach. "I sent Ronald Reagan[1] a complete kamikaze outfit. He sent me back a letter thanking me for doing that." It's a letter Dan kept.

A production still of a re-enactment of Kamikaze pilots at a Shinto shrine in Chofu, Tokyo. After this shoot Mack sent Kamikaze flying gear to Ronald Reagan back at Fort Roach. **Photo: USSBS, US National Archives.**

Hundreds of disused Japanese warplanes as photographed by Dan and the USSBS team. They filmed and photographed at many such locations and military airfields all across Japan. **Photo: US National Archives.**

ILLNESS AND RECUPERATION

Mack next found himself just south of Hiroshima in the city of Kure. During World War 2 Kure was Japan's most important naval facility and dockyard. "I was documenting the occupation there by British Forces with their pomp and circumstance when I fell ill." After six months intensive documentation and survey work Lt. McGovern was exhausted. "I was so worn out from doing all the things I had to do that I was down to 175 pounds in weight."

Dan was taken by the British authorities to a private family home to recuperate. "I was looked after by a *mama-san,* an older woman of the house and stayed there for ten days. I was really sick and I slept on a tatami mat. I think I was just worn out again. I got the determination and stamina to keep going though from my heritage and background." When he had recovered, Dan and his team then filmed and surveyed Kure Harbour. One of the things which General Anderson had stressed to McGovern to concentrate on where he could find it was the results of aerial mining. One way the US Army Air Forces had waged war on Japanese shipping was to drop large numbers of anti-shipping mines from the air into Japanese shipping lanes. This had resulted in considerable numbers of ships being sunk or damaged. This was something in which the United States Navy also had an interest.

Dan and his crew now filmed the shallow sunken, partly sunken, beached or damaged Japanese naval and civilian shipping which had struck American laid mines or which had fallen victim to American bombing. "This was all part of documenting the prelude to the defeat of Japan and how we defeated them in their inland waters through aerial mining." However, unexploded mines were still in Kure Harbour. That presented a problem for getting the film footage needed as no wooden boats were available which represented less of a risk of exploding the magnetic detonators on the aerial mines. A solution was soon found. "With the help of both the US and Japanese navies we were eventually able to get an old mine-sweeper that we used in the harbour to get the footage we needed. We filmed aircraft carriers, destroyers and super destroyers all either beached, sunk or damaged," Mack remembered.

A partly sunken Japanese battleship in Kure harbour as photographed by McGovern's USSBS team in 1946. **Photo: US National Archives.**

The Japanese aircraft carrier *Ryuho* was by this time being broken up in Kure and Dan had an opportunity to go aboard to film it being taken apart. "Her guns were being taken down and things of that sort but when I went on the bridge I found a massive pair of three foot long marine binoculars mounted on a pedestal." Dan asked the shipmaster could he have the binoculars which were gladly given but Dan gave some cigarettes and candy from their stores in return. "I shipped the binoculars back to the

Pentagon but that was the last I ever saw of them as they were stolen there."

The team next travelled to the city of Okayama which had been firebombed and largely destroyed. Here Dan and the team filmed many wasteland scenes as well as focusing on burned and collapsed ruins which had once been military installations, textile factories and other manufacturing facilities. At Okayama aerial footage was also taken from the team's C-47. At every filming location where they came across bomb damage Dan Dyer also recorded the damage analysis information.

Dan and the team next boarded the *Emperor Special* bound for their 80 mile journey to Japan's commercial shipping centre – the port of Kobe just west of the city of Osaka. "We had noticed by then that, more and more, Allied military rule had begun to be imposed. If anybody left a military vehicle unattended and it was not properly identified it would be impounded." In Kobe, Lt. McGovern grabbed his camera gear and along with Dan Dyer and Sam Okimoto, climbed a very high fire watch tower where he filmed the city below including areas that had been bombed by the Americans. "Those towers were typical of the big cities in Japan. Fire towers were strategically located throughout cities so that, if a fire broke out it could be seen, the alarm raised and the fire dealt with quickly." When he eventually got back down to the ground Dan had a nasty surprise. "Our jeep had been impounded by the military police. We had a heck of a time getting it back again but we eventually did because officially we were there on the direction of President Harry S. Truman. The military police had no bearing on us whatsoever."

THE JAPANESE FILM COMPLETED

It was at the end of April that Dan finally received the good news from Tokyo that *Effects of the Atomic Bomb on Hiroshima and Nagasaki,* on which the nine Nippon Eigasha cameramen had been working under his direction, was finally completed – all 2 hours 45 minutes of it. Bad weather had hampered the film's completion which was over a month behind schedule, but now at least, over 30,000 feet of raw black and white 35mm footage had been edited down by Akira Iwasaki and his team to the finished article 14,914 feet long. McGovern quickly returned to Tokyo as he now had several matters pertaining to the finished documentary to attend to. He arranged the first preview of *Effects of the Atomic Bomb on Hiroshima and Nagasaki* at MacArthur's Headquarters on 4th May 1946[2] with the general himself and other senior military personnel.

The opening title of the Japanese made 'Effects' documentary.
Image: US National Archives.

However, MacArthur failed to attend. McGovern though, ever mindful of a future general public release of the film back in the United States, arranged another preview three days later. This time he invited members of the international press. This was a much shorter preview and the screening costs this time, were paid out of McGovern's own pocket.[3] Now, in compliance with what had been agreed at the January 2nd conference six months before, McGovern supervised the Japanese filmmakers as they reluctantly started to gather all footage and associated production material of the film they had just completed for transfer to the United States.

All 19 reels of *Effects of the Atomic Bomb on Hiroshima and Nagasaki* which had been used for the two previews – the first positive print, were carefully placed in sturdy US Army issue wooden footlockers. In addition, all other production film materials associated with the documentary were also similarly boxed and the seven footlockers in total numbered and labelled for the attention of the USSBS Headquarters, Gravelly Point, Virginia, USA. This included the film's preprint[4] material – the original cut negative print and soundtrack, hundreds of production still photographs, caption material, research material as well as every scrap, long or short, of the remaining 15,000 feet of unused footage which had ended up on the cutting room floor. McGovern secured the footlockers for the time being. They would be going back to the United States with him.

The Japanese film makers were not happy that the fruits of their efforts which were, initially at least, funded by Nippon Eigasha, were now, in their view, being confiscated to be spirited away to the United States possibly never to be seen again. However, from the American point of view the arrangement brokered with the Nippon Eigasha team had been on a contract basis for which they had been employed and duly reimbursed. This was something which Dan McGovern always went to great pains to stress, pointing to an invoice furnished by Iwasaki Akira of Nippon Eigasha to the USSBS. There was also a subsequent receipt signed by McGovern for Supply and Service dated 30th March 1946 after Nippon Eigasha had been paid over $20,000 for its services up to that point.

However, the *Effects* film prints in the wooden footlockers were not, in fact the only prints of the film in existence. Feeling hard done by given the film's graphic content and fearing that it might be suppressed once it got to America, producer Akira Iwasaki and the Japanese filmmakers secretly made another silent but incomplete copy under the noses of the American military police guards permanently posted outside the door of their editing room.[5] This was done before they had gathered together all the material which McGovern was to collect and send to the United States. Big Mack was well aware of what the Japanese production team had done. He chose however, to turn a blind eye. This film print was carefully hidden by the Japanese production team above the false ceiling of a colleague's workroom.

Several weeks later on 11th May, McGovern was back in Tokyo and the Meiji Building. On reaching the third floor he encountered some unusual commotion. On investigation he discovered that General MacArthur was receiving quite a distinguished visitor that afternoon. This was none other, than General Dwight D. Eisenhower who had been the Supreme Allied Commander in Europe. *Ike* had commanded the D-Day Landings in Normandy, France which, within a year, had ended the war in Europe.[6] His visit was a big news story but McGovern, since his transfer to the USSBS, was no longer concerned with news stories. "I would have been the first one to do a story like that but I had an entirely different mission now." Dan, however, did at least meet Eisenhower and shake hands with him in what was only a brief introduction.

On the following day, 12th May 1946, Dan flew back from Tokyo and rejoined his film documentation and bomb survey colleagues over 280 miles away in Japan's cultural city of Kyoto. Dan had been there before with the correspondents, of course, but this time the cameramen filmed cultural and arts related subject matter. This included Japanese gardens and shrines, water painting, Japanese martial arts and colourful Geisha girls. They also captured on film Buddhist processions, Noh ceremonial plays and the various manufacturing processes involved in the production of traditional Japanese lacquerware and decorative cloisonne vases in Japan's sacred city. "We photographed the everyday life of the Japanese people," Dan remembered.

The team filmed the bustling city centre with its densely packed traditional wooden housing, its retail stores, civic buildings and public squares and its population going about its everyday business. The team also took their cameras into ordinary Japanese homes where they filmed typical mealtimes and family members going about their mundane household chores.

Also filmed were aspects of the black market in the city as well as the Kyoto Fire Department drilling and undertaking exercises with its fire truck. Filmed too were stores of over 300 two-man submarines as well as tunnels and underground cities which contained kamikaze piloted Ohka flying bombs.

McGovern (Left) pictured on set as he oversees filming of a domestic scene of everyday life in Kyoto. **Photo: USSBS, Japan Peace Museum.**

The day after that on May 13th 1946, as a result of the press previews of the documentary days before, many articles started to appear in newspapers throughout the United States. They carried considerable detail pertaining to the Japanese produced film's graphic content and informed the American public at large that *Effects of the Atomic Bomb on Hiroshima and Nagasaki* would be soon on its way to the United States for public release. The May 16th edition of *Stars & Stripes*, the newspaper of the US military community, carried a report that *a valuable film* had been sent to Washington in advance of planned nuclear tests on Bikini Atoll in the Marshall Islands.[7] There were others who doubtless read the reports of the Japanese film's impending arrival in the United States with some concern. At the end of May the team filmed and surveyed additional maritime centres including the ports of Miazuru and Tsuruga on the coast of the Sea of Japan. "Those areas were also littered with sunken, semi-sunken or beached shipping of all shapes and sizes," Dan recalled.

Meanwhile, back in the United States, work had been progressing on the preparation of the United States Strategic Bomb Survey report pertaining to Japan. It was now nearing completion. By June 1946 Dan and his team knew that their assignment in Japan for the USSBS Motion Picture Project which they had undertaken so diligently was nearing completion too. It was now almost nine months since Mack had been transferred to the USSBS by General Anderson and ten months in total since he had first landed at Atsugi naval air station from Guam to support the press correspondents. It had been planned that the USSBS team might travel to China to undertake similar work there but by then, pressure was being brought to bear from Washington to disband the United States Strategic Bomb Survey of Japan and for the team members to return to the United States. In any case General Anderson was himself now back in Washington. Dan and his team now travelled further east to what would be their final filming location. This was the city of Nagoya. Here they filmed and surveyed scores of bomb damaged weapons, arsenals and explosive ordnance factories. These factories too now lay in ruins having been pounded relentlessly by American B-29s.

ALL FILMING WRAPS

It was in Nagoya on 7th June 1946 where Mack McGovern and the USSBS team completed their colour documentation filming for the USSBS Motion Picture Project. This was a month or so after the completion of the Nichiei black and white documentary. Dan and his team members then took a week-long well deserved period of rest and relaxation. Then, on June 14th 1946, Lt. McGovern received a cable from Washington DC. It was from General Anderson directing the team to return to Washington at once. The general was no longer involved in a managing capacity with the USSBS. "It came as a surprise but then again it was a relief to know that we had done our job well," Dan recalled when he got the news. "I was glad it was all over because I was worn out and tired."

It was in the city of Nagoya, having filmed the destruction of what had been one of the largest centres of aircraft production in Japan, that Dan and his USSBS colleagues boarded their special train for the last time before returning it to its base at the railyards at Yokohama. They said goodbye to the *Emperor Special* from which they had documented so much of Japan and to all its personnel who had served them so well. He recalled: "The remaining days were devoted to removing equipment from the train and turning it in." They unloaded whatever equipment they could fit aboard their four jeeps and trailers in Yokohama and made arrangements to have the heavier items of equipment still on board the train collected by Air Force personnel. Mack and his team members now made their way by road north to a United States Army Air Force depot outside Tokyo to which they had been told to report. Here they would turn in all their equipment and support vehicles.

"By then we had all sorts of photographic and sound equipment – 35mm Eyemo and Mitchell cameras, tripods, stills cameras, the *RCA* double synch sound systems and the specialist lighting equipment etc. All just fantastic items. I would have loved to have brought home one of those lovely cameras in my footlocker but imagine me getting to the States and being accused of stealing government property." After all, US military items such as cameras and sound equipment were still clearly marked: *Property of the US Army Air Forces* or *Property of US Navy*. Dan turned in all the equipment which had to be returned at the Army Air Force depot. He remembered what happened next: "I was instructed to put all this stuff on a pallet inside a shed but the shed had no roof. It was open to the elements!" Worse was to come. "They took all that fantastic equipment, dug a hole and buried it. They never took it back and I heard they did the same thing on all the islands! There was so much surplus equipment after the war that our American industrial leaders thought that if we brought it back they'd go bankrupt!"

Lt. Dan McGovern and the remaining members of his team now made their way to Tokyo to make final preparations to leave Japan to return to the United States. There, McGovern sent on the final undeveloped colour *Japan in Defeat* exposed film spools to Vardac on the first available transport aeroplane. With its arrival, all the *Japan in Defeat* raw colour footage taken in Hiroshima, Nagasaki, Tokyo and in so many other cities and rural areas for survey and historical purposes, would be safely back with Consolidated Labs in Hollywood, California. There it would be processed and as far as Dan was concerned, soon edited into its final colour print.

Several days later Dan and the remaining members of his team settled into their spartan green canvas seats on the C-54 for the series of flights home. With them on the plane, securely fastened down for the long journey back to the United States, were the seven footlockers full of material from the production of *Effects of the Atomic Bomb on Hiroshima and Nagasaki*. In keeping with the terms of the agreement for which McGovern had fought so hard at the January 2nd conference, the completed Japanese made film and all its associated material was now, finally on its way to the United States.

McGovern, as the director of the *Effects* film as well as *Director of Photography and Production* and *Officer in Charge* of the USSBS Motion Picture Project, was now personally and solely responsible for the delivery of the *Effects* film to the Pentagon in Washington. In total during their time on assignment in Japan and in addition to the black and white footage taken by the Japanese cameramen, Mack and his team had shot 100,280 feet[8] of colour film for *Japan in Defeat*. One by one the four engines of the C-54 started up. As Lt. McGovern closed his eyes and settled back for the start of what would be a long sequence of flights home, he looked forward to the day when both films would be finished and shown to the world.

---

1. The former First Motion Picture Unit adjutant would meet the wartime Japanese Emperor Hirohito as President of the United States in Tokyo during an official visit to Japan in November 1983.

2. Details of this screening taken from *Japanese Documentary Film – The Meiji Era Through Hiroshima*, Abe Mark Nornes, p202.

3. *Japanese Documentary Film – The Meiji Era Through Hiroshima*, Abe Mark Nornes, p202.

4. McGovern refers to *Preprint* material as being the original cut (edited) negative and its soundtrack. However, the term was often used in a broader context during editing to encompass any film production element utilised to arrive at the final cut of a film.

5. *Japanese Documentary Film – The Meiji Era Through Hiroshima*, Abe Mark Nornes, p201.

6. Ironically, according to journalist Bill Lawrence in his book *Six Presidents, Too Many Wars*, p72, MacArthur hated Eisenhower.

7. *The Chigoku Shugoku*, Hiroshima Peace Media Centre, History of Hiroshima 1945 -1955 by Masami Nishimoto, Staff Writer. (Originally published 1995.)

8. The exact length of colour footage shot is stated in a letter to US National Archives archivist, Dr. Wayne C. Grover from William R Boucher of the Department of the Air Force dated 15th September 1961. This letter offered the now declassified films, on 186 reels, to the National Archives.

22

THE SUPPRESSION OF THE FOOTAGE

Disappointment and Realisation

EFFECTS of the Atomic Bomb on Hiroshima and Nagasaki gives us a fascinating and meticulously detailed insight into the world's first wartime atomic bomb detonations. The bombs destroyed Hiroshima and Nagasaki and killed or injured the inhabitants of those cities in their tens of thousands. Importantly, it also documents in detail the aftermath. The film draws on the data compiled in the bomb survey aspect of the overall documentation. Hiroshima is called the *city of water* and is the seventh largest city in Japan. It was built on delta flatlands and has no less than six rivers flowing through it. The Chūgoku Mountains lie far in the distance to the north.

As we view the film we learn that four square miles of the centre of Hiroshima contained three quarters of the total inhabitants of the city which, at the time, was a slightly greater concentration than that of Brooklyn, New York. We learn also of other population densities in Hiroshima and the film gives an overview of the city's layout, its building structure make up and its industrial and residential composition before the blast occurred. We also learn that some, but not all, peripheral parts of the city were beyond the effective limits of the atomic bomb which wrought such havoc upon it. In short, just before 8.15 am on 6th August 1945, Hiroshima was already a largely progressive modern city with a vibrant population of 350,000 with an excellent and well developed modern infrastructure. It had, for example, a good police force and a well-trained fire service with modern equipment. As well trained as they were and as modern their equipment, they would never have a prayer in dealing with the fires that were about to befall Hiroshima. The film urges the viewer to bear all these aspects of Hiroshima in mind when considering what came afterwards. It then shows the wasteland that was central Hiroshima after the atomic bomb laid it waste. With overlay graphics it demonstrates the area of desolation in the city and superimposes this over a similar land mass of Washington DC just to drive the point home.

HEAT, BLAST AND RADIATION

The Dan McGovern directed film then focuses on when the bomb detonated above the city centre at what the narrator now refers to as *Ground* Zero – one of the first ever references, at least on film, to the term. We are then informed that the atomic bomb's energy was released in three forms: *Blast, Heat* and *Radiation.* The result must first, of course, deal with the human cost which, by the end of 1945 alone, was estimated at 140,000. Hundreds of thousands more were terribly injured. We know now, of course, that the radiation factor would be adding to the death toll for decades after the film was made.

The film tells us about the uncontrolled terror of the survivors who subsequently, devoid of medical attention and indeed attention of any sort, often fled the city to avail of it elsewhere as well as food and shelter. With so many so badly injured, grieving, suffering, homeless and often witless due to the calamity which had befallen them, self-preservation became the priority. In the aftermath, others returned though, often within days to try and pick up the pieces of both their shattered lives and their shattered city. They would now try to rebuild both. In their terrible plight they cried out only when they could bear the pain no more. Otherwise, they suffered in silence and suffer they did as help was far from at hand. We're informed that all but a few non-military hospitals and other medical facilities in Hiroshima were destroyed in the blast.

Anybody in these hospitals within three thousand feet of the detonation was killed or injured and this included all the city's doctors and nurses. All dead. All laid waste. A segment on autopsies shows the effects the radiation had on the eyes, heart, liver, the skin and the bone marrow. The film also clearly shows the bleaching effects of the atomic bomb on many forms of vegetation.

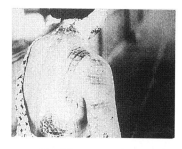

The fabric weave pattern from clothing has been seared onto the skin of this woman. A frame from the Nichiei 'Effects' film. **US National Archives.**

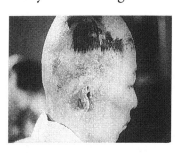

This man sustained severe flash burns and disfigurement to the head as featured in the 'Effects' film. **US National Archives.**

It depicts rice paddies destroyed by the explosion seven miles from Ground Zero. Atomic Shadow is also featured. The viewer is shown the shadow of what had been a man with an oddly shaped hat painting a large tank from a ladder and carrying a paint bucket with one arm outstretched. All this detail etched onto the tank exterior by the intense light and radiation emanating from the source of the nuclear explosion which atomised the painting man in an instant. In addition, in Hiroshima 62,000 buildings in total, the film informs us, were destroyed in the urban area of the city and another 6,000 severely damaged. Approximately fifty re-enforced concrete buildings, some of which were earthquake resistant in one peripheral area of Hiroshima, remained standing and structurally intact despite most being gutted by fire. Multi storey brick buildings were extensively damaged. Single storey buildings to a lesser extent.

We see too once ornate building pillars two feet thick just snapped like twigs by the force of the atomic blast. All streets and roads in the greater Hiroshima area were rendered impassable due to the massive amounts of debris hurled onto them in seconds resulting from the atomic explosion. All destroyed. All laid waste. Fires were immediately ignited as far away as a mile from Ground Zero.

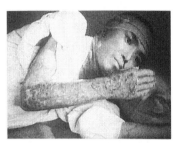

A patient with severe flash burns to the head and arms filmed for the 'Effects' documentary. **US National Archives.**

Surgery is performed in a damaged and windowless operating theatre in a Hiroshima hospital. A frame from the Japanese 'Effects' film. **US National Archives.**

However, we learn that the majority of subsequent fires were caused as a result of secondary sources of ignition arising from the atomic blast such as short circuits and kitchen fires when the blast energy collapsed buildings, often on top of their unsuspecting occupants. Hundreds of fires erupting at once ultimately resulted in a firestorm engulfing central Hiroshima. The heat of the fire sucked air into its vortex at a speed of 30 to 40mph fuelling the massive inferno. The firestorm almost completely burned out a 4.5 square mile radius of the city. All destroyed. All laid waste. *Effects of the Atomic Bomb on Hiroshima,* as directed by Dan McGovern, incorporates considerable damage facts, figures and percentages in relation to their location to Ground Zero. We learn that Hiroshima's telecommunications network was 85% destroyed but service was restored about ten days later to those buildings which survived. Hiroshima's reinforced concrete water reservoir was located two miles to the north-east of the city centre and was undamaged.

However, there were 70,000 ruptured water pipes mainly in damaged buildings arising from the blast and subsequent fires throughout the city. Six sewage pumping stations were knocked out as were gas storage facilities. The city's electricity generating plant and distribution network was also badly hit. Somehow, the Japanese had managed to get power restored to most parts of the city within 24 hours.

The mangled remains of a metal structure in Hiroshima. A frame from the Japanese 'Effects' film. **US National Archives.**

Blast damage which resulted to a window in a Hiroshima building from the atomic bomb explosion. A frame from the Japanese 'Effects' film. US National Archives.

Most large industrial plants were located on the outskirts of Hiroshima. The film informs us that machinery in wooden industrial buildings was rendered unusable but that only 25% to 30% of machinery in reinforced concrete buildings was seriously affected. Interestingly, it informs us too that it was the ensuing weather exposure which rendered much of this machinery unserviceable rather than the atomic blast itself. Steel and concrete bridges remained intact throughout Hiroshima and usable despite some structural damage, but wooden bridges were destroyed not always by the explosion itself but by the subsequent fires. Whilst all cars, trucks buses and trams were largely destroyed by the atomic explosion, damage to trains and rolling stock was light as these were mostly on the perimeter of the city. Most rail services resumed within two days after the atomic bomb fell on the city. Amid the devastation throughout Hiroshima the film shows us solitary electric trams frequently rolling amid the backdrop of the destruction.

This service did improve considerably over the following months but the footage of those lone trams hinted even then of a regeneration of the city's infrastructure. Whatever life was left in Hiroshima still had to go on – somehow. Then the film's focus of attention turns to Nagasaki.

The *Fat Man* atomic bomb dropped on Nagasaki was more powerful than the *Little Boy* device

Atomic Shadow cast from a valve wheel onto a metal storage tank in Hiroshima. A frame from the Japanese 'Effects' film. **US National Archives.**

used against Hiroshima. The desolation we see is similar to that of Hiroshima but we are informed that the area of destruction was in fact smaller. This was partly due to the typography consisting of more hills and valleys than the flat delta terrain of Hiroshima. The area devastated was two square miles compared to Hiroshima's four and a half miles. Like Hiroshima, there was the human cost. However, this would be approximately 50% less than Hiroshima. As many as 80,000 may have died in Nagasaki as a result of the atomic bomb before the end of 1945. One small microcosm demonstrating the loss of life in the film is that, of 115 employees of the tram car company in the city, only three

This tree in Hiroshima snapped in half just like a twig such was the force of the atomic explosion on August 6th 1945. A frame from the Japanese 'Effects' film. **US National Archives.**

survived the blast. Unlike in Hiroshima, even after two months there were still no trams running in Nagasaki although a single train did run in the city on 13th August – a mere week after the bomb was dropped.[1] However, unlike Hiroshima Nagasaki's rail network was severely hit with rail lines and stations being completely destroyed.

Such was the force of the blast in Nagasaki that wooden rail sleepers or *ties* were thrown 7,000 feet into the air and railway carriages were hurled down embankments. Radioactive sand was blown into water wells over three miles from the blast.

A building in Hiroshima driven sideways with the force of the atomic explosion. A frame from the Japanese 'Effects' film. **US National Archives.**

This resulted in anybody who drank from those wells being inflicted with chronic diarrhoea. As the bomb's power was stronger, the reinforced concrete buildings throughout the city were damaged to a far greater degree than in Hiroshima but this, the film informs us, was also partly due to those buildings being of inferior construction quality than those in Hiroshima. Nagasaki was a city in which many factories producing war materials for the Japanese military were located. Three Mitsubishi factories were located there which, along with the military dockyards,

A Torri or Shrine Gate in Nagasaki which withstood the atomic bomb and as it appears in the Japanese film. **US National Archives.**

produced 90% of the total military production of the city. The epicentre of the blast was in close proximity to these factories. As a result factory damage in Nagasaki was greater than in Hiroshima. We see what is left of these factories with their cladding completely blown away and their steel frameworks grotesquely twisted out of shape by the force of the blast. Like Hiroshima, Nagasaki's hospitals were all located within 3,000 feet of Ground Zero. 80% of them along with their patients and staff were simply obliterated. All destroyed – all laid waste. It is pointed out to the viewer that if the typography of Nagasaki had been more akin to that of Hiroshima with flat ground and less hills, the death toll and material destruction in and around the city would have been far greater.

The Industrial Promotion Hall, today the Genbaku Dome, as filmed by the Nippon Eigasha cameramen weeks after the atomic bomb was dropped on Hiroshima. The damaged building has been preserved and is now the centrepiece of the Hiroshima Peace Museum. A frame from the Japanese 'Effects' film. **US National Archives.**

The film concludes with additional footage of the desolation of Nagasaki and with the following narration: *We have seen what took place at Hiroshima and Nagasaki. What happened to homes and factories, to schools and hospitals, to transportation and commu-nications and to public services of all kinds and to the people them-selves. From these scenes we have some measure of the magnitude of disaster that would befall an American city under an atomic bomb attack.* A warning perhaps to governments everywhere and to the general public of all nations as to the possible climax of war in the then fledgling post-war modern Atomic Age.

Given its scientific nature, the *Effects* film also contains scenes of Japanese scientists tentatively measuring the angles of Atomic Shadow. From these angles, in addition to their examination of blast damage, they calculated quite accurately, the height above Ground Zero at which the bombs had exploded. According to McGovern, they had not, however, been the first Japanese to deduce this technical information, but the *Effects* film also incorporates scientific graphics demonstrating their professional findings with regard to both Hiroshima and Nagasaki. However, for McGovern, right there would lie the crux of a problem he was about to encompass.

Having arrived back in the United States, Big Mack met with General Anderson in his office at the Pentagon. "I briefed the general and explained to him what the situation was as far as all the documentation was concerned. I asked him if it might be possible for us to work up an arrangement with the public affairs people of all the services so that we could have a public release of the material for the newsreels and to the commercial interests involved and especially Warner Brothers." When Mack and the team were in Japan it was Lt. Commander Vardac in Hollywood who had been working to this end. Correspondence had already been exchanged.

THE USSBS REPORT

Meanwhile, the United States Strategic Bomb Survey's Summary Report was published in July 1946. The report held the view that air power and land based air power in particular, had insured Japan's defeat and had actually done so as early as the spring of 1944. The Japanese had been unable to counter America's growing domination in the air which soon amounted to freedom of the skies over Japan. Significantly, the USSBS report also stated – *certainly prior to 31ˢᵗ December 1945 and in all probability prior to 1ˢᵗ November 1945, Japan would have surrendered even if Russia had not entered the war* (against Japan on August 8ᵗʰ 1945) *and even if no invasion had been planned or contemplated.*[2]

Arrangements were eventually made to screen *Effects of the Atomic Bomb on Hiroshima and Nagasaki* at the United States Naval Support facility at Anacostia, three miles from the Pentagon building in Washington DC. This was with a view to releasing the documentary to the public. The screening was attended by representatives of the US Army Air Forces, the United States Army, the US Navy, representatives of the US intelligence community and crucially, also by other US Army representatives of what was known as the *Manhattan District*[3] which had been involved in the development of the atomic bombs. The screening of *Effects of the Atomic Bomb on Hiroshima and Nagasaki* lasted two hours and forty minutes.

Dan remembered what happened next. "After the screening I was told that the material could not be released to the news media or to the general public as a whole." By way of an explanation it was pointed out to him by the Manhattan officials that this was because certain sequences of the film just viewed depicted technical information including the altitude at which a bomb had detonated. This, he was informed, was sensitive information.[4]

He was then asked how he had found out the detonation height of the atomic bomb over Nagasaki which had been disclosed in the film. Dan told them truthfully how he had learned of this information. "I told them that a bunch of Japanese boy scouts had first figured out the triangulation measurement from three different points with these angles being correlated to plus or minus a few feet."[5] Then came the clincher. "I was then told that the material was to be classified *Secret RD*." Dan was gutted. Now the film on which he had worked so hard, was being suppressed by the American authorities.

A Japanese scientist in Hiroshima filmed by a Nippon Eigasha cameraman in a makeshift laboratory at what the Japanese called the 'hypocentre' of the atomic bomb shortly after the blast. He was one of a team of scientists on the ground in both cities very early before the war ended. Relatively quickly they had worked out the detonation height and other aspects of the bombs, but according to McGovern, only after a group of boy scouts in Nagasaki at least, had done so first. **Image: US National Archives.**

On top of this disappointment a realisation came to McGovern regarding the future of what he knew was significant historical footage. "After all the effort that went into documenting it I knew what the consequences would be once this footage got out of my hands. It would be classified and buried and possibly destroyed and lost forever." Dan added: "The fact is that they simply did not want those films to get out. I was told afterwards that they didn't want the American public seeing the horrors and the devastation of Hiroshima and Nagasaki." Dejected, McGovern returned the film he had just screened to its footlocker and drove it back to the Pentagon building where he made sure it was secure. He now needed some insurance.

The day after the Anacostia screening and before the military authorities moved to seize and classify *Effects of the Atomic Bomb on Hiroshima and Nagasaki,* Dan took it upon himself to remove the original 35mm film master negative and soundtrack – the preprint of the film, from its footlocker at the Pentagon. He discreetly made two smaller format 16mm copies in the film processing laboratory there.[6] This was before any *Restricted Data* classification markings were spliced onto the original film reels' leaders and tails and also put on all the film's storage canisters. Once films of a sensitive nature were classified, they were so marked and then segregated to be stored away from general film collections in secure vaults.[7]

An actual 'Secret' classification frame added to the 'Effects' film after the Anacostia Naval facility viewing. These were added to the film's reel heads and tails. **Image: US National Archives.**

Mack then returned the master negative to its footlocker back in the Pentagon. Of his actions to copy the *Effects* film he recalled: "Why I did that I have no idea but I didn't want to let that terrific footage go until I knew it was saved for posterity." He then took one of the two copies and drove it almost five hundred miles to the United States Army Air Forces Motion Picture Film Depository at Wright Field Army Air Force Base[8] in Dayton, Ohio. "I told the curator there that I wanted this material to be set aside and preserved for posterity – for it to be accessioned and that it was not to be opened without contacting me."[9] It was accessioned and given a United States Army Air Force accession and file number. It was to remain there, hidden away in those vaults, for decades. The second copy Dan kept safely and securely himself. The powers that be at the Pentagon were none the wiser.

THE ATOMIC ENERGY COMMISSION

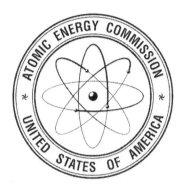

On August 1st 1946, the Atomic Energy Commission was established and took over control of the peacetime development of atomic energy in the United States. It was now also in charge of developing America's nuclear arsenal. The new atomic authority would soon also commence regular atomic bomb tests at its Nevada test site in the western United States and also at a number of remote test sites in the Pacific.[10]

Subsequently, it was the Atomic Energy Commission which classified McGovern's Japanese *Effects* film.[11] The original 35mm projection print and preprint material was stored away securely also at the Wright Field Motion Picture Film Depository but in the Classified vault and once *Secret* and *Restricted Data* frames were added to the beginning and end of its film reels. The film's storage canisters all now also bore Atomic Energy Commission Classified/Restricted Data cover labels. The material would after all, if needed, surely be easily located and retrieved in the future. McGovern was technically still responsible for *Effects of the Atomic Bomb on Hiroshima and Nagasaki,* but under the circumstances, he could do nothing more with it. "So I just decided to forget about that film and just get on with my Air Force career," he remembered. However, by now all the remaining USSBS *Japan in Defeat* colour footage had been processed in California, – all 100,000 feet of it.

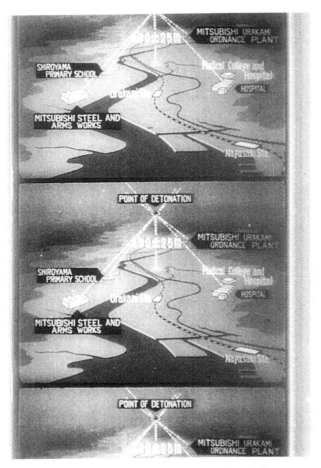

Actual frames of 'Effects of the Atomic Bomb on Hiroshima and Nagasaki' technically explaining how the height at which the bomb exploded over Nagasaki was determined. Such data caused concern amongst the Manhattan representatives who viewed it at the Anacostia Naval facility. **Image: US National Archives.**

Unlike the Nippon Eigasha black and white finished documentary film, the colour material was still just raw unedited footage. It had not been *annotated* – edited and produced into any semblance of a finished film with narration similar to *Effects of the Atomic Bomb on Hiroshima and Nagasaki*. "It was just a whole lot of visuals," as Dan put it. Therefore it did not fall within the criteria to be officially classified as *Restricted Data*. "Many people tried to say at the time that this footage too was *Classified* and *Restricted Data* but it certainly was not."

Navy Lt. Commander Vardac, who had earlier been appointed to Dan's USSBS team and based in California, had overseen the processing of this material which had been sent in batches to Consolidated Laboratories. Like many US servicemen, he too was now leaving the military and had arrived in Washington on August 21st 1946 where he had delivered all 100,000 feet of the processed colour footage to McGovern. "General Anderson was still interested in it but by now was Commandant of the Air War College at Maxwell Army Air Force Base in Alabama." General Anderson though came to Washington for a conference with the Commanding General of the Army Air Forces, Carl Spaatz, to try and get something done with the colour material.

However, any hope of even it being used in a commercial movie production by the likes of Warner Brothers for public consumption as Mack had discussed with Colonel Anderson, was also quickly dashed. "I was told that the war was now over and that it cost money to produce things and that the idea of Warner Brothers doing a documentary of *Japan in Defeat* was now out of the question." Dan now felt compelled to generate interest himself in the historical colour film footage that had been taken in Hiroshima and Nagasaki. He set about promoting it in the hope that it would be picked up and used now for other appropriate historical, medical and scientific purposes.

He now started what would be four days of work in the Pentagon's film processing laboratories printing off a series of high quality production stills from the *Japan in Defeat* footage. These prints he compiled into three spiral-bound pictorial books of *Japan in Defeat* with striking images of the aftermath of the atomic bombs. The books contained the *horrible stuff* as Dan called it, the human cost – the bodies, the bones, the flash burns and the blistering and resulting suffering, misery and grief. These spiral-bound books displayed in graphic detail the devastation that was wrought on Hiroshima and Nagasaki as well as the oddball things such as the shadow of the farmer and his ox and cart cast onto the pavement on the bridge in Hiroshima. Surely somebody would be interested? He was shocked at the response.

"Even that went nowhere. The amazing part of this whole thing is that with all this historical material there was such a lack of interest. I was dumbfounded. I was fighting a stone wall." He then took all the promotional production still material he had, including the three spiral books and went to the offices of the most senior military and civilian medical officer in the United States – the Surgeon General. Surely he would want it? "I was told.. 'Oh…we don't want those.' "They couldn't care less," Dan remembered. "Nobody was interested in it. That was the attitude of the people in Washington at that particular time." Dan then took his production stills across Washington to the Armed Forces Institute of Pathology. "I turned the books over to them and I've never seen them since."

By the end of 1946, a frustrated Lt. McGovern also transferred the 100,000 feet of colour *Japan in Defeat* footage and all its associated materials and records to the film depository at Wright Field in Ohio. Here, the colour footage now joined the original but classified 35mm *Effects of the Atomic Bomb on Hiroshima and Nagasaki* film and its preprint and all other associated material as well as Dan's separately accessioned black and white 16mm *Effects* insurance copy. At least all the footage was now stored in the one location but McGovern was the only one who knew the full extent of what was accessioned there.

Given the graphic and sensitive nature of some of Dan's USSBS colour material and pending its evaluation in that regard, it was also placed in the depository's Classified vault along with the *Effects* documentary materials. The colour material was simply being stored there and had been given a designation, but it had not been classified as *Restricted Data*. However, as it would turn out, the *Japan in Defeat* colour movie production envisaged by Dan McGovern would never be made. In any case McGovern would soon be taking up a position at Wright Field but working for and reporting directly to General Anderson in Alabama. Mack would therefore be able to keep a watchful eye on all the footage. The move would also allow him to start cataloguing the colour material whenever he had a chance in order to get it safely archived for future reference. "General Anderson now wanted me to do research regarding the type of pictures that would be needed for the new United States Air Force. Independence for the Air Force as a branch of service was by now on the horizon and in that regard McGovern would assist General Anderson in other ways too.

---

1. Fukuota #14 POW Sidney Lawrence Oral History, IWM.
2. *War in the Air, USSBS – Effects of Bombing on Japan*, Keystone Press, London (1977).
3. The US Army Corps of Engineers has traditionally been organised into geographic divisions and districts. The *Manhattan District* was established in June 1942 as a cover to hide the development of the atomic bombs. – US Army Corps of Engineers Headquarters website.
4. By early 1946 the US authorities were aware that Soviet espionage activities in the United States and Canada were directed toward atomic energy information. *Security Classification of Information*, (Under the Atomic Energy Act) Vol. 1, Chapter 4, Arvin S. Quist, Federation of American Scientists, (fas.org).
5. The boy scouts may indeed have worked this out for themselves before the scientists by also using the Atomic Shadow triangulation alignment method. Alternatively, they may simply have been privy to the findings of the scientists. In any case, this information was passed onto the *Effects* production team, McGovern became aware of it and it was included in the production.
6. When only a few 16mm reduction print copies were required from a larger 35mm original film it was general practice back in 1946 to reduce the original 35mm film frame size using what was called an *Optical Slit Aperture*. This was in a process called *35/32*. This firstly reduced the 35mm frame size using the original 35mm negative print. The frame size was optically reduced by projecting it down to 16mm. Then all the film's reduced sequential frames were printed or *struck* onto one half of the same side of a new unexposed 35mm reel of film. This process was then repeated so that another 16mm positive print was also stuck but this time onto the other remaining side of the 35mm print which was them physically split in two

along its length to produce two 16mm reduction prints in this instance of five 16mm reels each. McGovern would then have added the soundtrack of *Effects of the Atomic Bomb on Hiroshima and Nagasaki* to each new 16mm reduction print. As nineteen 35mm reels were being reduced down to five 16mm reels Mack had to have taken significant care to remove the film leaders, which were also reprinted and to carefully re-splice the reels together in order to maintain the film's soundtrack synchronisation from beginning to end. Having deposited one copy in the Wright Field Film Depository he retained the second 16mm reduction print himself for safekeeping but also to reduce the chance of somebody stumbling upon what was, in essence, culpable evidence of his own personal actions to save the footage contrary to direct orders.

7. In the US military classified film receives special handling during all phases of production and post-production. Only persons cleared to the level of classification of the film ie: *Confidential*, *Secret* or *Top Secret*, are permitted access. All film elements are marked accordingly and stored in a controlled access *Classified* vault. Similar clearance rules applied in 1946 regarding the earlier classification of *Restricted Data*. Then, as now, any security classification of a film after it is completed is highly irregular. – Classification details courtesy of Wayne Weiss.

8. Later Wright-Patterson Air Force Base. A section of the base contains the original site where Wilbur and Orville Wright made the first ever powered flight in history on December 17th 1903.

9. McGovern wrote his contact details and his signature on the canisters.

10. American atomic bomb testing would, in fact, continue for the next forty seven years until 1992.

11. *From the Stinko to the USSBS Motion Picture Project* essay, Atsuko Shigesawa, p120.

23

THE POST WAR YEARS

The Roswell Connection

FOR THANKSGIVING DAY on 28th November 1946, Dan took some well deserved time off with Virginia and their two children, Danny and Patricia. The couple had just bought a new Spartan Manor trailer caravan which they were pulling through the hills of West Virginia behind their 1942 Hudson Terraplane. "The brakes seized on the trailer which meant that the car was pulling dead weight." Dan pulled over, detached the trailer and asked his wife to take the car and the kids to a motel and to then call the American Automobile Association. Dan was now on the side of the road with his new trailer/caravan waiting for the *AAA* to pick him up.

Then a brand new Packard car came along and the driver offered to help out and insisted on pulling the trailer to the nearest garage. Dan was glad of the offer of help and agreed. However, by the time they approached the city of Grafton, the combination of the seized brakes, the hills of West Virginia and the dead weight of the trailer/caravan had resulted in the new Packard overheating. This was to such a degree that the heat from the manifold and exhaust pipe caused the front of the wooden floor of the vehicle to catch fire. Flames started to appear inside. "Stop the car. We're on fire!," demanded Lt. McGovern. "Ahh, let it burn." replied the driver.

It was only at this stage that Dan realised that the driver was well intoxicated but he eventually complied and pulled over. Dan managed to get the fire out. By now it was starting to get dark. Dan removed the safety chains and screwed down the jockey wheel on the front of the trailer/caravan. He warned the driver not to pull away until he had something in place behind the wheels of the trailer and walked back a little distance to gather some rocks for this purpose. "I turned around and to my shock my trailer was rolling back. It quickly struck me, knocked me to the ground and rolled on top of me." The drunken driver had driven off regardless of Mack's warning. McGovern now found himself on his back with the trailer over him. Before he could extricate himself the jockey wheel collapsed pinning him to the ground by his head. Dan screamed in excruciating pain. He had come through six combat missions over Nazi occupied Europe only to be severely injured by a rolling house trailer thanks to the blatant irresponsibility of a lousy drunk driver.

His screams were heard as they echoed among the West Virginia hills until a local hotel owner finally went out to investigate, found Dan and rendered him First Aid before calling the emergency services. "I was told I was dying and I got the Last Rites." He was so seriously injured in fact, that he was removed in a critical condition to hospital in Pittsburgh ninety miles away. He had five compound skull fractures and a broken nose and was unconscious for 12 days. When General Anderson heard what had happened he ordered a C-47 transport aircraft to medivac Lt. McGovern to Walter Reed Military Hospital just outside Washington DC where he could receive the best care. Mack recalled: "That made me feel pretty good and yet again it was General Anderson coming to the rescue."

At Walter Reed the lieutenant was operated on. He received facial reconstruction and a titanium plate in his skull. "Fortunately, there was not too much damage to the brain area but I was lucky to be alive." Between hospitalisation and recuperation Mack McGovern was out of commission for a period of six months. As always, General Anderson was very supportive. "He was so dedicated to my particular interest in preserving the Japanese footage. He told me nothing would be done with the material until I was up and well and he was true to his word." When he did get back to work Dan eagerly spent long dedicated hours at the Wright Field film depository cataloguing and accessioning the *Japan in Defeat* colour material to get it identified and into the archives. "I was the only person to do it and I was glad to be doing it," he remembered.

Meanwhile, Dan, Virginia and the family rented a 160 acre farm in Xenia, Ohio. "It was owned by a Greek who had a restaurant in Dayton but he was going back to Greece for a year." He rented the farm to Dan and Virginia for $50 a month. "We just had to take care of the pigs and chickens whilst he was away and as it turned out, it was one of the most wonderful experiences we ever had." Big Mack McGovern then became something of a troubleshooter for General Anderson based at the Pentagon in Washington. He was frequently sent as something of a personal equerry for the general to various Air Force establishments all across the United States.

ROSWELL AND PROJECT BLUEBOOK

In June 1947 strange looking debris was discovered on a farm 30 miles north of the town of Roswell close to which a US Army Air Force base had been located since 1941.[1] What did or indeed what did not occur there has since captured the imagination of people the world over. It would become known as the *Roswell Incident*. This was just over 100 miles away from Holloman Army Air Force Base. The Army Air Force dispatched a field investigation team to Roswell from Washington DC to look into the crash.[2] The debris was initially described in an Army Air Force press release as that of a crashed flying disc. The AAF, however, quickly retracted this story and explained that what had actually crashed had been no more than a weather balloon which had fallen to earth. Almost immediately the rumours commenced and continue to persist. Roswell has since become the most famous UFO town in the world. All sorts of conspiracy theories began to abound and it was increasingly claimed that one or more alien spaceships had crashed there with their alien occupants which had resulted in an Air Force cover-up.

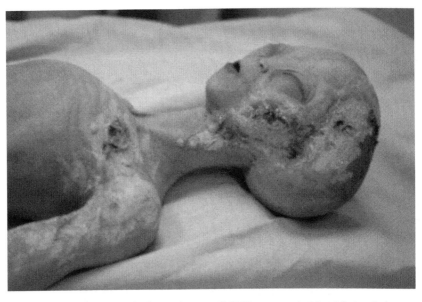

A re-created static display at the Roswell UFO museum in New Mexico. It depicts alien remains on which an autopsy was purportedly performed in 1947 and following a UFO crash claim. The image is purposely out of focus as was much of the original Santelli film. **Photo: Alamy.com**

Dan McGovern recalled the Roswell Incident and his thoughts on it were frank. "I will admit that the Air Force was flying some unusual objects between 1947 and 1950 but no damned UFO crashed at Roswell! There was no spaceship and little men. That's a load of crap! I worked on *Project Bluebook* for a couple of years and the blue book was nothing more than a registration of the people who had observed unusual objects."

Public speculation about what did actually happen at Roswell, however, continued to grow. Years later, in 1995, a shaky seventeen minute black and white film surfaced in England having been released by London based businessmen Ray Santelli and Gary Shoefield. This grainy film was purported to be footage from an autopsy of a dead alien which had been taken from the crashed UFO at Roswell. The *Santelli film*, as it became known, showed the autopsy being undertaken on a small humanoid figure with elongated fingers by two pathologists in fully protective suits. It showed another similarly suited individual taking notes and a fourth peering out from behind a window.

This film was sensational but controversial for many years after its release. Santelli claimed in 1995 that he had acquired the film from a retired military cameraman who wished to remain anonymous. The cameraman, it was claimed, had been flown in from Washington DC and having filmed the autopsy, had developed the film himself.[3] Dan McGovern and two other highly experienced World War 2 veteran cameramen film experts were consulted and asked to look at the film. McGovern had already filmed several autopsies and soon made known some observations. He pointed out that the US military had proscribed procedures for everything which had to be strictly adhered to. Mack was positive that all autopsies were shot in colour rather than back and white and that two cameras were used from fixed positions rather than being hand-held as was the case in the Santelli alien autopsy film. One camera would be on a tripod and the second in the *riser* position overhead.

In addition, McGovern also pointed out that, in important medical procedures, it was policy that a stills photographer also had to be present, yet no evidence of any still photographs of this autopsy had ever come to light. Unlike the high quality footage always recorded by United States military cameramen, the quality of the Santelli alien autopsy footage he concluded, was dismal. It was badly shot, it was sometimes shaky, frequently out of focus and poorly lit. Dan was of the opinion that the film was deliberately blurred so that nothing is visible in any detail. He added also that there were already adequately qualified cameraman on Air Force bases much nearer to Roswell than Washington DC and that Top Secret film footage would, in any case, never have been developed by the cameraman himself as had been claimed.

Eastman Kodak had offered to physically verify and date the *Santelli film* but to do that, they would have to be able to physically test at least several frames. Despite his strong opinions about the film's dubious origins and given the divided public opinion on the *Santelli film,* Dan offered to do some verification work of his own perhaps in an attempt to confirm his own deductions about the film. McGovern was still considered one of the best cinematographers in his field. In conjunction with the Eastman Kodak offer he said he could attempt to authenticate the cameraman who supposedly shot the film and nobody would be better placed to do that than Dan McGovern as he knew them all. He offered to take a fifteen minute phone call from the alleged cameraman promising only to reveal if this individual was at least authentic or not. As it turned out a sample of the film was never passed to Eastman Kodak for testing and Dan never received that phone call from the cameraman.[4]

However, in 2006 Santelli finally came clean. He revealed that he had viewed the original autopsy film. However, the version he had released in 1995, had been *reconstructed* from an original set of 22 reels of autopsy material which had been received from the retired military cameraman. He added that these original reels had by then degraded to such an extent that only a few frames of original material had been used in the reconstructed film. Later, in a report also during the 1990s, the US Air Force stated that what had crashed in Roswell was not a weather balloon but in fact a secret Cold War nuclear test surveillance balloon from *Project Mogul.* Apart from its photographic capabilities, the sophisticated balloon could also detect sound waves at high altitude emanating from Soviet atomic

THE POST WAR YEARS

bomb tests on sites similar to that which the Americans were conducting in the Nevada Desert and on Pacific atolls. Dan worked on many such balloon projects. One was a constant level photographic reconnaissance balloon designed to fly over Russia to take pictures of their sites.

Dan explained that another possible explanation for the flying saucer theories might have resulted from high altitude parachute tests. These were undertaken from specialised capsules at Holloman with Air Force personnel bailing out from 80,000 feet, falling back to earth and landing by parachute. "They went up to 100,000 feet for survival tests in the capsules and these were saucer like vehicles. When people saw these things they figured they were from outer space. They were just test vehicles but all these tests were a prelude to what we have today in the American space programme."

Mack, however, did recall one genuinely strange UFO phenomenon in the late 1940s which he and others did see from the photographic aircraft at altitude on which he was filming. This was at a time when there were UFO reports in an area of New Mexico between Holloman and Kirkland Army Air Force Bases. "These UFOs were transparent," he recalled. "The objects were not flying from the heavens down. They came from below the horizon at high speed at an angle of some 45 degrees and at an altitude of 70,000 or 80,000 feet. They then changed their direction from a vertical climb to horizontal and then the brilliant white light emitted from these UFOs disappeared in the skies. We didn't get anything on film of that particular movement. I was never able to film them."

Dan explained that the negative plates on the still cameras they were using should have recorded it as there was plenty of room to capture the phenomenon. "You could tell for how long the shutter on the camera was open as Polaris, the North Star, left a white trace. That proved that what we had seen was transparent. These were objects made out of matter and composed of gases that were flying upward."

A NEW AIR FORCE

On September 18th 1947, under the auspices of the Department of the Air Force, the *United States Air Force* was formally established finally giving the service independence from all other branches of the US military. This had been sought for many years by many senior officers and exponents of the United States Army Air Forces and of the Air Corps before that. A month or so later Lieutenant McGovern was posted to work directly with General Anderson at the new Air Force's Air War College in Montgomery Alabama. "That was to manage the making of highly technical films on the effect of the atomic bomb." $72,000 had been allocated to produce five training films which were to be used for training purposes at the college. "That particular effort was the result of General Anderson's foresight. He was teaching the new staff officers new concepts and new strategies." When completed these five films would finally incorporate at least some of the raw colour footage of Hiroshima and Nagasaki documented by or under the direction of Dan McGovern from the footage he accessioned in Dayton. However, as these training films were being produced for the USAF, all but one would be classified *Confidential* or *Top Secret.*

As 1947 came to a close McGovern was content that the *Japan in Defeat* colour footage was now at least safely archived to his own satisfaction in the secure film depository of what was now Wright-Patterson Air Force Base in Dayton. He had also drawn some solace from the fact that at least some of the material was now being used in the training films. It was a start and hopefully with time, the classification on the Japanese *Effects* film might be lifted. Given his vast experience, Dan continued to be sent by General Anderson to address problems wherever they were found. "That sent my career into a whole different orbit. The general told me that a good staff officer has got to have the ability to understand various problems in various functions of command." Firstly, he addressed problems only within combat camera units, but later this would encompass a wider scope within the Air Force. "I would be called in to find out what the problem was. I was the troubleshooter. I could see what was wrong and fix it."

Soon promoted to Captain, one of the Air Force facilities to which Dan was sent in early 1948 was Holloman Air Force Base and range in the desert region of Alamogordo, New Mexico. Ironically, it was on the White Sands Proving Ground adjacent but remote from Holloman where *Trinity* - the first test detonation of the Manhattan Project's atomic test device, had taken place. This had led to the atomic bombs being used against Hiroshima and Nagasaki, the aftermath of which Dan had filmed in such detail in Japan. On this assignment to Holloman, Captain McGovern had carte blanche to investigate problems. Dan made his substantial report, a staff study, citing personnel problems and equipment shortages which needed to be addressed and subsequently changes started to be implemented. Holloman was about to enter a new phase for a new Air Force. Dan remembered: "Little did I realise then that the staff study I had prepared for General Anderson was part of the future of the new US Air Force." Holloman Air Force Base and the adjoining White Sands Proving Grounds were soon merged to become the New Mexico Joint Guided Missile Test Range which would eventually become the headquarters of the largest military facility in the United States – the White Sands Missile Range.

Captain McGovern's specialist photographic expertise, however, was always very much in demand. In early 1948 he was posted permanently to Holloman Air Force Base as *Chief of Technical Photography*. The vast remote desert typography of Holloman and its surroundings had long been identified as an ideal site for testing a new generation of military aircraft and weapons. This had really begun in earnest towards the end of 1945 with the start of the covert *Operation Paperclip* with captured rocket powered German *V2* ballistic missiles complete with former top Nazi scientists led by Wernher Von Braun.

These particular German scientists were now in the employ of
the US government. Others were working for the Russians. Now
McGovern was filming Von Braun's ongoing V2 tests.

These missile flights were the very first attempts to launch
payloads into space using rocket propulsion before attempting to
return them safely to earth using parachute systems. They were
the precursors of the American space programme. Dan recalled
one particular series of four V2 launches on which he worked in
early 1948 in what was called *Project Blossom*. "The nosecone of
the *V2* would frequently have a test capsule installed in which a
monkey was placed for experimental purposes." This was the tiny
Rhesus monkey. The rocket was launched and its nosecone
would separate in space with the test capsule supposed to return
to the ground via parachute. "It often ended up 40 feet down in
the white sand," Dan remembered. Unfortunately, none of the
monkeys survived[5] but in the valuable film footage recorded, the
scientists could see the effects of altitude and space on the
animals when the footage was retrieved. It was Dan who had
installed the 16mm camera in the nosecone. Mack was involved
in several other *V2* filming experiments. "There was another shot
we made to get the curvature of the earth where we put cameras
on the rocket. We got about 30 to 40 seconds of footage showing
the actual curvature."

Mack also worked with medical research doctor Colonel
John Paul Strapp who was then also an Air Force captain. Strapp
was referred to as *The Fastest Man In The World*. He was a pioneer
in the field of acceleration and deceleration on the human body.
He had earlier pioneered automobile impact testing in America
and was now at Holloman where, with the use of his purpose
built Rocket Sled Decelerator, he undertook a series of tests
pertaining to rapid acceleration and deceleration on pilots in the
aircraft environment. In one series of tests he successfully proved
that pilots could survive high speed cockpit ejections at high altitude. The footage of a great many of Colonel Strapp's pioneering
tests were filmed by Captain Dan McGovern.

Dr John Strapp pictured just before one of his pioneering tests on a Rocket Sled Decelerator at Holloman Air Force Base. **Photo: Air Force Test Centre History Office.**

A frame of very high speed footage taken during a test on one of Dr. Strapp's Rocket Sled Decelerators. Dan McGovern filmed many such tests at Holloman Air Force Base during what was a period of intensive technical testing there. **Photo: Air Force Test Centre History Office.**

THE KOREAN WAR AND LOOKOUT MOUNTAIN

Despite his many areas of expertise within the Air Force Mack McGovern was still a highly experienced and highly sought after combat cameraman. In 1950 the Korean War broke out and Dan was again sent overseas to document that war with his cameras. "What was called a *Direct Name Request* arrived at Holloman for me," Dan could remember. Including his boyhood experiences in Ireland this was his third war. He had been handpicked as *Photo Operations Officer,* this time with the 5th Combat Camera Unit. He was going back to familiar ground. "I was based at Yokosuka, Japan and also in Seoul in Korea. I was still determined to do the job and to do it right for the benefit of the Air Force."

However, it was around this time with Mack overseas that something occurred regarding his carefully catalogued and archived colour *Japan in Defeat* footage that was to inadvertently suppress that material for over 3 decades. "Somebody classified the whole damn batch of 100,000 feet of material, but all that preprint and unedited material should never have been classified."[6] Dan remained in Korea until after hostilities ended returning to the United States in 1954 when he was then assigned as *Motion Picture, Producer/Director* and *Project Officer* at Lookout Mountain Air Force Station in Laurel Canyon, Hollywood, California. Lookout Mountain was only seven miles north of his former wartime First Motion Picture Unit base at the Hal Roach Studios in Culver City. "Lookout Mountain station was a highly classified Top Secret facility for the production of motion pictures and documentary and technical photography pertaining to the Atomic Energy Commission tests at Nevada, Bikini and Eniwetak atolls in the Marshall Islands." The 100,000 square foot facility had walls three feet thick, underground parking facilities, 17 storage vaults and a helicopter pad. 6,500 films were produced there most of which, at the time, would only be viewed by a select few military, government, scientific and intelligence personnel. The location had been chosen because the very top technical talent needed to man the facility was readily at hand in Hollywood. Dan wore only civilian clothes on that posting. "We were always afraid of Russian spies getting a hold of us to find out what we knew."

Dan McGovern (right) with his Lookout Mountain Documentary Photographic Element cameramen colleagues pictured on a filming break during 'Operation Hardtack' on Eniwetak Atoll in 1958. These cameramen filmed atomic bomb tests on the Pacific atolls often for months on end. **Photo: Defence Special Weapons Agency/DTRA.**

People living in the Hollywood area thought that atomic bombs were being manufactured there as twice a year a major movement of staff and equipment in trucks would preceed an atomic explosion later. This was either on Bikini or Eniwetak atolls or at the remote Nevada Test Site. Regardless as to where the nuclear tests were taking place, McGovern was always there with his movie cameras to document the detonations. This was often for several months at a time. Dan filmed many detonations during *Operation Plumb Bob* – a series of 29 nuclear tests conducted at the Nevada Test Site between May 28th and October 7th 1957.[7] "I was even on one of those tests where they had troops located in trenches in the test area. After the detonation they had them get out of the trenches and walk towards the mushroom cloud[8] which was stupid. I filmed that. Why subject people to all that radiation with the knowledge that was made available after Hiroshima and Nagasaki?" Dan knew more about that than most people around him.

He was of the opinion that scientists and engineers were always striving to make a *safe* bomb. "This is one of the peculiar things. They were trying to control the fallout." Then, between April 18th and August 28th 1958, the United States conducted a further 35 nuclear tests, this time as part of *Operation Hardtack* at its Pacific Proving Grounds which was more than all prior Pacific nuclear detonations combined.[9] Promoted to the rank of Major during 1958, Dan McGovern filmed many of those test detonations too. The bigger the atomic device the further away the cameramen had to locate themselves to film the detonation. The smaller atomic detonations were filmed from relatively close by.

After this and with the Cold War warming up, Major Daniel A. McGovern was again handpicked by his superiors for his next job. This was a posting as commander of the 1369th Photographic Squadron at the newly established Vandenberg Air Force Base. The base was located on the coast of California roughly half way between Los Angeles and San Francisco. Formerly Camp Cooke, Vandenberg had been chosen from over 200 locations as a remote combat ready site for ballistic missiles and also as a missile training base.

Given his experience, McGovern had been chosen to set up a photographic facility to support Strategic Air Command and its 1st Missile Division in testing its Atlas and Titan missiles on their launch pads or hardened missile silos. It was an important job with considerable responsibility. "We were the Photo Instrumentation and Technical Documentation specialists." This was only a year after the Russians had launched Sputnik 1 and 2, the first artificial satellites in space, causing concern in the United States.

*A frame taken from an original film showing US Marines in their trenches during an atomic test detonation as part of 'Operation Desert Rock' at the Nevada Test Site. Dan McGovern filmed many such tests on assignment at Lookout Mountain. **Image: US National Archives.***

*The same marines filmed as they walk towards the atomic mushroom cloud simulating future assaults. **Image: US National Archives.***

The result had been an acceleration of the US missile programme. The job of McGovern and his photographic squadron was to photograph every aspect of test launches. "We did continuous coverage of all missile launches. We even had ignition cameras on the nacelles of the engines I remember, set at 400 frames a second to capture the action. We always started the cameras a few seconds before ignition because sometimes *Golden-fingers*, the guy on the controls, might not launch at the exact time he was supposed to."

Mack remembered one delayed launch. "General Curtis LeMay was there. He sacked the colonel responsible on the spot and put his deputy in charge. I even saw them testing missile detonations at altitude hung from balloons. Today that photographic squadron has twelve officers and over 400 enlisted men.[10] When I started that in early 1958 I had two officers and four non-commissioned officers. I built that particular photographic squadron up." Today missiles are still tested at Vandenberg missile base and it has also become an important space launch facility. During his time there McGovern also filmed and produced training and information movies on the SM-62 Snark missile system which was the first long range surface-to-surface missile produced by the United States and the forerunner to Intercontinental Ballistic Missiles – the ICBMs. Much of the filming for the Snark productions was undertaken over 800 miles away from Vandenberg back at Holloman Air Force Base in New Mexico which was, of course, a base Dan knew well.

At Vandenberg, one day in 1961, Dan received notification that he had to attend an Air Force medical inspection which, on the surface of it, seemed routine enough. "It was my annual physical. It was particularly intensive due to the titanium plate in my head from the accident with the car trailer back in West Virginia in 1946. I had never had so many tests done on me in my life." Major McGovern then appeared before an evaluation board and was evaluated at 60% disability. "Well, I had no idea that I was being evaluated for disability but that went up to the board in the Air Force and came back as a 50% disability. The result was that I had to leave the Air Force." After twenty one year's continuous service it was time for Dan to retire. He would not, however, retire a major.

Dan McGovern pictured during his retirement parade which took place at Vandenberg Air Force Base, California on 15th October 1961. The combat cameraman retired as a Lieutenant Colonel after twenty one years full-time service. **Photo courtesy of AFHRA and the McGovern family.**

On 15th October 1961 and exactly eighteen years since he was first commissioned as an officer, the 1st Missile Division held a big retirement parade for the popular Big Mack at Vandenberg Air Force Base. "I had my family there which was just great." Dan now stood and reviewed his own retirement parade with silver oak leaf insignia pinned to his epaulettes. He was now *Lieutenant Colonel* Daniel A. McGovern. Reflecting on that achievement Dan said: "For a former enlisted man to retire as a Lieutenant Colonel was just something else."

Dan was always very proud of the fact that he had come to the United States through Ellis Island as an immigrant from Ireland and worked his way up the hard way. "That is one reason why the United States is such a good country. We know what America is and what it stands for and I won't see anybody beat it down. It has its faults but so have other countries. Look at Britain and Ireland. I was only wishing the day of my retirement that my wonderful father, Daniel Senior and my mother Margaret had been around to see that." Just like his father before him back in 1922, the next day following his retirement he was Daniel McGovern, *civilian*. For many, their working lives might have ended right there, but not for Big Mack. He was about to enter yet another phase of his remarkable career.

---

1. The 509th Bomb Group and its B-29 bombers which had dropped the atomic bombs on Hiroshima and Nagasaki was stationed at Roswell Air Force Base in 1947 following its return from the Pacific Theatre of War after WW2.
2. In an informal conversation following an interview in 1999 Dan McGovern told the author that he was present in Roswell at the time of the crash there. He was certainly based at the Pentagon at the time. However, whether he was part of the Air Force investigation team sent to Roswell from Washington DC could not be ascertained.
3. *Alien Autopsy: The True Story* (British Sky Broadcasting, 2006).
4. Details of McGovern's observations on the alien film taken from Santilli's Controversial Autopsy Movie, Comprehensive Review by Kent Jeffrey.
5. McGovern helped bury the monkeys. "I remember *Albert 1*, *Albert 2* and *Albert 3*. We put up little crosses for them," he recalled.
6. The exact level of classification the colour footage received at that point is vague. It is possible that this resulted simply due to a routine audit of the Classified vault and in order to justify its presence there.
7. Also in 1957, the Hal Roach Studios – that peacetime *Laugh Factory of the World* which had so seamlessly adapted to its wartime role as the FMPU's Fort Roach in 1942 until war's end, went bankrupt forcing the studios to close temporarily. They would close permanently in 1962.– *Remembering the Hal Roach Studios,* Marc Wannamaker, Reel Culver City, Articles, Culver City Historical Society website.
8. Among the tests conducted during *Operation Plumb Bob* were many which sought to determine how US troops would perform both physically and psychologically on the nuclear battlefield. – *Operation Plumb Bob 1957,* Atomic Heritage Foundation. Large numbers of US servicemen participated

in these tests with many filmed just as Dan described, emerging from trenches shortly after detonation and walking towards the mushroom cloud. These tests simulated a combined air and ground attack against an enemy objective.

9. *Operation Hardtack* Fact Sheet 1/Fort Belvoir.
10. Based on a 1999 interview.

24

THE FOOTAGE DECLASSIFIED

The XB-70 Incident

FOLLOWING HIS AIR FORCE RETIREMENT, Mack would, however, continue his illustrious photographic documentation career in a civilian capacity. You can take the man out of the Air Force but you can't take the Air Force out of the man. Within twenty four hours of his retirement he was offered a civil service position in photographic management at Edwards Air Force Base in California as *Photographic Division Civilian Chief* based at the Air Force Flight Test Centre Laboratory.

Geographically, Mack was back to his photographic roots because Edwards AFB was in the centre of what was formerly Muroc Dry Lake where he had honed his aerial mapping skills and photographed the *Muroc Maru* as a lowly USAAF corporal back in the 1942. Now though he was out of the military but still working for the United States government. He was now Dan the civil servant. Thirty five years since taking his first full-time job as an eighteen-year-old rookie photographer back in New York, Dan McGovern was now in charge of photographic planning and photo coverage of all test flights at Edwards.

The photographic senior management there were so anxious to get someone with Dan's experience and qualifications that they offered him a house on the base to sweeten the appointment. Somewhat ironically this was just at a time when Dan and Virginia were already starting to build their new family home in Northridge, California. "When I told my wife about the job offer she replied, 'You're going back into the military again, aren't you?' Technically, her husband was not as he was now a civil servant, but he was taking a high profile, high paying job with a high military security clearance on the most highly classified military air base in the United States. "I pointed out to Virginia that it was good money and that I still had to provide for my family." The McGoverns subsequently moved to Edwards.

At that particular time there, intensive flying was being undertaken by America's top test pilots including Chuck Yeager who had been the first man to go supersonic and break the sound barrier in the very first of the experimental or X planes, the Bell X1, in 1947. Among other aircraft being tested there at the time was the North American X-15 rocket powered hypersonic aircraft and the Lockheed U-2 spy plane. Five years into his job as Photo Chief at the Photography Division at the base one of the latest aircraft being tested there was the North American XB-70 Valkyrie bomber. This was a sleek six engine, delta winged aeroplane with smaller distinctive canard wings near the front of the fuselage. It resembled the Concorde airliner.

The aircraft had been envisaged as a deep-penetration strategic bomber for USAF's Strategic Air Command to carry nuclear devices. Only two had been built and were being tested when, in early June 1966, XB-70 #2 was about to be turned over to the Flight Test Centre of NASA – the National Aeronautical and Space Administration. Before the aircraft was transferred the manufacturers of the Valkyrie's engines, the General Electric Corporation, wanted aerial publicity photographs of the experimental bomber.

A formation flight was arranged for 8th June 1966 with the XB-70 taking centre stage surrounded by other jets which also used General Electric engines – a McDonnell Douglas F4

Phantom fighter bomber, a Lockheed F-104N Starfighter, a
Northtrop T038A Talon and a Northtrop UF-5A Freedom
Fighter. A Chicago based public relations company had been
hired to do the aerial photography and their photographers were
also joined by several others representing many high profile
American publications. A private Learjet, owned by singer Frank
Sinatra, had been hired as the camera ship for the photoshoot.

However, before the civilian photographers would be
permitted to photograph the spectacle, clearance had to be
obtained from Edwards ground staff to allow them to do so. The
man they were sent to see was Mack McGovern. "Part of my job
involved issuing passes to photographers who wanted to undertake technical photography on or over the base." However, he
was unable to accede to their request. "I denied them accredita-
tion because what they wanted to do was not technically orien-
tated photography and they did not have mission support
functions to undertake." Dan suggested that they pursue other
public relations channels on the base. The civilian photographers
eventually got clearance elsewhere and early the next morning
were high in the sky aboard Frank Sinatra's Learjet with cameras
pointed to starboard photographing Valkyrie #2 flying in formation with the other aircraft slightly below them at 30,000 feet.

The sleek XB-70 bomber was being piloted by North American test pilot Al White and co-pilot Major Carl Croft who was
flying his very first XB-70 mission. The formation flew on for
twenty uneventful minutes being shadowed by the observing
Learjet. The formation was about to disperse when suddenly the
F-104 Starfighter veered unexplainably and collided with the
Valkyrie bomber, sheering off its twin vertical stabilisers. The
fighter burst into flames and exploded moments later. Its NASA
test pilot, Joe Walker, was killed instantly. The bomber, having
flown on for some seconds, pitched to the left and started to go
down in a spin bellowing smoke. Pilot Al White ejected but co-
pilot Carl Croft did not and was killed when the massive bomber
disintegrated when it hit the ground.

The General Electric promotional flight in formation as photographed from Frank Sinatra's Learjet over Edwards Air Force Base moments before disaster struck. **Photo: US Air Force Test Centre History Office.**

The F-104 Starfighter engulfed in flames after colliding with the XB-70 which flies on minus her two vertical stabilisers. It too would crash killing its co-pilot. **Photo: US Air Force Test Centre History Office.**

Two pilots were dead and two cutting edge aircraft were lost within a matter of seconds. The collision, the fighter's explosion and the Valkyrie's descent to her doom had all been filmed by civilians in the skies above one of America's most Top Secret facilities. There was hell to pay and somebody had to pay it. "Many senior officers were affected for allowing that to occur," Dan remembered. There was a congressional and military enquiry and Dan was one of many people to appear before it. The enquiry wanted answers about the cause of the crash, but also about who had issued passes to civilian photographers who had not only witnessed the whole disaster, but who had recorded it too. For many weeks anybody at Edwards who had even the slightest association with the civilian photographers were interviewed and closely scrutinised for their involvement to ascertain just who was responsible for issuing the passes.

Eventually, though Dan's professional judgement in refusing the passes to the public relations photographic crew was recognised by the enquiry and by his superiors. "I came out smelling of roses from that one but many high ranking and good officers I knew, did not. In the eyes of certain people and for their own petty reasons, as a civilian I became persona non grata."

Dan had done everything right but these few people started to make life difficult for him in his work. He felt that he could not work in that environment. "That incident made me get out of Technical Photography at Edwards Air Force Base. First I got another job in production photography which was much more creative. Then I left. It didn't hurt my career." Dan McGovern next took up a highly sought after position with General Dynamics Aerospace and Defence Corporation based at Wright Patterson Air Force Base in Dayton, Ohio which, of course, was a base he knew very well. This was as *Chief Special Project Officer* for training film contracts. It was a job in which he would remain for many years.

————

SENATOR KENNEDY'S COMMISSION

One day in 1967 and only a year or so into his new position at Wright Patterson, Mack received an urgent phone call. On the other end of the line was Mrs. Hermine Baumhofer who was the chief archivist at the base's central film depository. McGovern had deposited and accessioned all his colour and black and white Japanese atomic bomb film footage in its vaults over twenty years before.

Mrs. Baumhofer had been requested to retrieve a film called *Effects of the Atomic Bomb on Hiroshima and Nagasaki* following interest shown in it by a high profile US Congressional Committee which included Senator Robert Kennedy.[1] "Mack, you were responsible for the Nippon Eigasha film. Where is it? Where's the preprint material?" she asked. "We can't find it anywhere!" Big Mack replied that it should be somewhere in the vaults of the depository but was informed by the chief archivist that the original positive print of *Effects of the Atomic Bomb on Hiroshima and Nagasaki* and all its associated preprint material were nowhere to be found. Dan was not surprised.

He then reassured a concerned Mrs. Baumhofer that all was not lost. "Mrs. Baumhofer, you will find a 16mm print of that film in your archives," he declared. Mack gave the chief archivist a USAF accession number. "Go back in there and under that number you will find what you're looking for." Several hours later the telephone rang again and it was a greatly relieved Mrs. Baumhofer. "We found it, Mack! We found it!"[2] She had found Dan's 1946 16mm *insurance* copy.

THE NICHIEI FILM DECLASSIFIED

The fact was, however, that of the original *Secret* and *Restricted* 19 reels of *Effects of the Atomic Bomb on Hiroshima and Nagasaki*, produced by Akira Iwasaki and his Nippon Eigasha cameraman under McGovern's direction, 12 had been quietly declassified as far back as 9th October 1950. The remaining reels, due to their graphic and sensitive medical content, were at that point reclassified as *Restricted*.[3] Furthermore, since 1950, all 19 reels of the production had, in fact, remained deep in the vaults of the Wright Patterson Film Depository – somewhere.

An actual declassification frame added to the 'Effects' film in 1967. **Image: US National Archives.**

In any case, the last seven reels of the film were eventually declassified on or before September 19th 1967 but, even then, with the proviso that the film not to be released to the public without Department of Defense approval. It was only at this point that the entire film was finally transferred to the US National Archives.[4] Also in 1967 the US government returned a 16mm print copy of the complete Nippon Eigasha produced film to the Japanese government. That year also, the Air Force began moving its Central Film Depository from Wright Patterson AFB to Norton AFB, California, where, over the next few years, the Department of Defense established a centralised Motion Media Records Center (MMRC), consolidating the film and video archives of all the military services.[5]

Twenty-seven years later in 1994, Wayne Weiss, a Department of Defense contract film producer at Norton Air Force Base, stumbled onto the largely forgotten story of McGovern's efforts to save *Effects of the Atomic Bomb on Hiroshima and Nagasaki*. By then the entire base including its film depository was being permanently closed in the wake of the Cold War. Just as had been the case at Wright Patterson, only designated archived films were selected for retention and relocation with the remainder marked for various means of disposal.

However, such was the scale of destruction that Weiss became alarmed. Of the thousands of films consigned to oblivion his attention was drawn to three 16mm film cans on the disposal queue which had very distinctive and personalised labels. This was highly irregular for US Department of Defense films. He decided they deserved closer scrutiny. "I found the reels in their original cans. They were among thousands of other archived military films. The canister labels had Dan McGovern's name, rank and also his signature on them. That's what drew my attention to them in the first place and why I pulled them off the destruction queue," he explained.

TANGIBLE EVIDENCE

Weiss had stumbled across parts of McGovern's 16mm insurance copy of the *Effects* film. Edge codes on the celluloid was dated 1966. However, surprisingly, Weiss also discovered that the leaders of these film reels – the heads and tails, were old and discoloured and contained then Lt. Dan McGovern's handwritten notations. They were Mack's original leaders from his 1946 *Effects* copy. They had been repurposed and spliced onto the reels of a later safety film copy of the film. The vintage leaders definitely state that the original 35mm preprint negative which McGovern had brought back from Japan was indeed the source of his unauthorised 1946 copy.

These original leaders and canisters with McGovern's notations and signature were tangible evidence of his little known act of personal defiance in order to save the film the Japanese filmmakers had produced from the obscurity of bureaucratic classification. "McGovern had left instructions with this 16mm copy of the *Effects* film to contact him should anyone question its presence. He may have done this to establish provenance or in the hope someone would eventually take notice and look into it further. I saw Dan at the Norton Air Force Base Film Depository frequently during the 1980's," Weiss remembered.

Weiss said of McGovern's 1946 decision to copy the Japanese film: "In this act of defiance as a mere Army Air Force lieutenant he cleverly skirted security protocols." He added: "As somebody who has personally chaffed under classification impediments myself I find this breathtakingly bold." Weiss went further adding: "McGovern was counting on military bureaucracy to not make the connection. His plan worked better than he could have imagined." The partial film copy discovered by Weiss, including its important original 1946 leaders and personalised canister labels linking them to Dan McGovern, were also subsequently accessioned to the United States National Archives.

THE FIRST PUBLIC VIEWING

In February 1970 a film called *Hiroshima Nagasaki – August 1945* was screened at New York's Museum of Modern Art. This was a sixteen minute documentary short produced by Erik Barnouw and Columbia University. It was compiled from segments of the 160 minutes of *Effects of the Atomic Bomb on Hiroshima and Nagasaki* which Barnouw had located in the National Archives in 1968. There had been no objection from the Department of Defense to the release of the Nippon Eigasha film into the public domain.

This New York screening represented the first time that at least some of the often harrowing footage shot by the Nippon Eigasha cameramen was seen by the general public.[6] The auditorium was jammed. Such was the impact of Barnouw's film that, at the end, the audience sat in stunned silence.[7] To this day *Effects of the Atomic Bomb on Hiroshima and Nagasaki* remains the most comprehensive audiovisual record of the aftermath of America's decision to use the atomic bombs against Japan. Much, if not all of the film, is readily available via modern digital storage and viewing media.

Three film canisters containing reels of the 16mm copy of the Japanese made 'Effects of the Atomic Bomb on Hiroshima and Nagasaki' found by Wayne Weiss at Norton Air Force Base in 1994. **Photo: ©Wayne Weiss.**

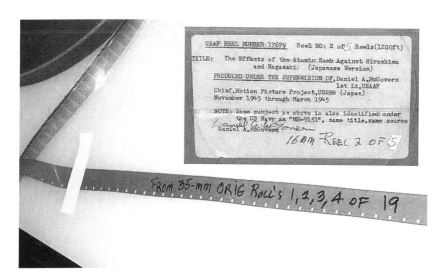

Leader ends from the original 1946 'Effects' copy made by Dan McGovern had been spliced onto the reels of the later safety film found by Wayne Weiss at Norton Air Force Base. The leader pictured explains that this film has been copied from the original 19 reels of 35mm footage of 'Effects' taken from Japan. **Inset:** *Labels signed by McGovern also appear on all three reels found by Weiss.* **Photos: ©Wayne Weiss.**

THE COLOUR FOOTAGE DECLASSIFIED

But what of the colour *Japan in Defeat* footage? The 100,000 feet
of this footage was declassified on or before 15th September
1961[8] – six years earlier than the remaining Japanese black and
white *Effects* reels and in the same year that McGovern had
retired from the Air Force. It was transferred to the US National
Archives on 21st February 1962.[9] Fittingly, this unedited
100,000 feet of footage is known as *The McGovern Film*. It was
discovered by Japanese researchers by chance only in the early
1980s. Over the years it too has been gradually transferred onto
more stable film material and can also be accessed via digital
storage and viewing media.

Both the complete Japanese made *Effects* documentary and
the unedited colour footage were, at last, now known to exist and
being in the public domain, they were accessible by anybody.
This finally ensured that the world was left a comprehensive
visual record of the aftermath of the atomic bombs on
Hiroshima and Nagasaki – the only time atomic weapons have
been used in anger. These films and indeed a considerable
number of McGovern's often overlooked still documentation
photographs, have subsequently been incorporated into TV and
film productions as well as into newspaper, magazine and online
articles etc. all across the world.

Perhaps more than anything else, the footage McGovern
either personally shot or supervised and then saved, despite the
odds stacked against him, have provided subsequent generations
with what is now their definitive impression of nuclear devastation. To that end Dan McGovern never forgot the contribution
of US Air Force General Orvil A. Anderson who had stood by
him through thick and thin. Without Anderson's support that
footage might never have been recorded in the first place.

Having remained at Maxwell Air Force Base in Alabama the
general died aged 70 from lung cancer in August 1965 and
almost four years after Lt. Col. McGovern's retirement. Recalling

the general Dan fondly said of him: "He was a wonderful man and a wonderful leader who died way ahead of his time." Just three years before, despite attempts to revive its fortunes, the Hal Roach Studios had closed permanently and the entire studio complex was totally demolished a year later in 1963.[10] Mack would spend the next fifteen years of his civilian career working with General Dynamics based at Wright Patterson making many training films essential to the safe operation and maintenance of the aircraft produced by General Dynamics such as the F111 Aardvark all-weather attack aircraft.

Dan would finish out his civil service career much closer to his home as a film producer and director at Norton Air Force Base in San Bernardino, California. This was firstly with the Defence Audio Visual Agency, (DAVA) and then with the Aerospace Audio Visual Services (AAVS). By then the AAVS was the umbrella agency which provided all audiovisual services, including combat cameramen and women, to the Air Force and other branches of US military service.

Dan and Virginia raised their family of three boys and a girl typically at homes on or near Air Force bases right across the United States, but whenever possible Los Angeles was home. Dan McGovern was a founder member of the International Combat Cameramen's Association and never tired in his quest to get the work of combat cameramen and combat camerawomen recognised and credited whenever their resulting footage was used. Finally, Dan retired altogether at the age of 71 in 1980. This was with the exception of some part-time consultancy and media work. This included contributing to the Steven Spielberg produced *Shooting War* (2000) which was narrated by actor Tom Hanks. This acclaimed documentary focused on the American combat cameramen of World War 2. Dan was but one of many combat cameramen interviewed. He told the story of filming one of his two B-17 bomber crash-landings in England. As McGovern relates it in *Shooting War* we see segments of the film he shot as he explains to us what happened and we're there with him – there's the actual footage – two engines out to starboard and one out to port starved of gasoline before the big bomber belly lands – down roughly but down none the less. For one of only several times throughout his remarkable career Dan himself had become part of the story.

In 1994, the same year that Wayne Weiss discovered the three copied reels of the *Effects* documentary, Dan McGovern returned to Japan. He saw for himself the flourishing democracy the country had become since those terrible early days after the end of World War 2 when he had first arrived there. "I was amazed to see how beautiful and green the cities were," he remembered.

He was particularly impressed also by the Peace monuments in Nagasaki and Hiroshima, both of which had been built on sites over which the atomic bombs had exploded. The Peace Park in Nagasaki contained its *Point Zero,* to the Japanese the *Hypocentre* – the spot beneath which the *Fat Man* atomic bomb had detonated. It was right there, right on that spot, where McGovern himself had been photographed by *Life* magazine's Bernie Hoffman back in September 1945 as he went about documenting the devastation that had just been visited on the city.

Now, close by during Mack's return visit, stood the rebuilt Urakami Cathedral set on a hill overlooking a rebuilt and thriving city. During that return visit Dan appeared on *Nippon TV* and gave interviews recalling his experiences during the ten months he filmed in Japan in the aftermath of the atomic bombs. Dan McGovern returned to Japan several times and often as a guest of the Japanese government who rolled out the red carpet for this tall Irish-American who filmed among them in darker days but always with compassion and understanding. The Japanese will always hold Dan McGovern in very high esteem indeed because it was, after all, his persistence that brought the horrors of the atomic bombings to a world audience.

———

During the 1980s a movement in Japan called the *Ten Feet Film Movement*, having raised money from donations from all across Japan, managed to purchase from the United States copies of all the USSBS colour footage as well as a copy of *Effects of the Atomic Bomb on Hiroshima and Nagasaki*. Also in the same year that Dan McGovern returned to Japan, 1994, further fundraising efforts by the *Ten Feet Film Movement* resulted in a Japanese language version of the *Effects* film being made which was finally broadcast throughout Japan.[11]

From an early age and right throughout his life Dan McGovern had experienced war and conflict. In his later years he said of it: "I hate war but its kill or be killed. It would be wonderful if we had peace all the time but as long as there's the human race in this sorry world of ours you are, unfortunately, going to have wars."

---

1. This may have been in order to return a copy of the film to the Japanese government which occurred that year. However, it may have been for another reason. Senators Robert Kennedy and George A. Aiken tabled a bill to the US Senate in 1967 to have a number of amendments made to the Atomic Energy Act. One of the aims of the bill was the protection of public health and safety. The thermal and effluent effects of domestic atomic power on the environment was debated. The overall Bill failed. – *Prelicensing Antitrust Review of Nuclear Powerplants, Joint Congressional Committee on Atomic Energy*. US Congress, 1970. Given its high scientific content the Japanese *Effects* film may have been requested by Senators Kennedy and Aiken in the course of research for these hearings.
2. Mack gives this account of his 1967 phone call with Mrs. Baumhofer in his 2003 *Library of Congress* Veterans History Project interview. He mentions the Congressional Committee's involvement and that the original material was accessioned in a US Navy log rather than in that of the USAAF. As yet, this has not been substantiated because those US Navy records have yet to be inventoried by the National Archives. They are presently stored in limestone caverns in Lenexa, Kansas.
3. This information is stated in a then broadly circulated Department of the Army/Office of the Adjutant General announcement memo, *AGAD 312.1/Security (0379)*, dated 9th October 1950 pertaining to film *USAF 17679*. Surprisingly, the film is listed as *Signal Corps Project 13393 -19 reels*. *Effects* was not a Signal Corps production. This memo confirms that the film's 19 reels had been classified *Secret* and all reels are individually listed with roll numbers, reel title and revised classification. The document was

unearthed in the US National Archives by Wayne Weiss in the course of research for this biography.

4. H.M. Baumhofer, Department of the Air Force letter to NARA 19th September 1967.

5. The new Department of Defense Motion Media Records Centre at Norton AFB was over two thousand miles away in California. The subsequent transfer of US Air Force and earlier US Army Air Forces archived film from Wright Patterson, however, proved to be a huge logistical undertaking. Given their tendency to degenerate, the older nitrate films were particularly problematic. Most of the archived film which was to be transferred to the new facility at Norton was copied onto safety film. This included McGovern's insurance print. Unstable film that was unwanted was destroyed.

6. *Iwasaki and The Occupied Screen*, Erik Barnouw, p337. In a letter to Professor Erik Barnouw dated 27th June 1968 the Historian of the Office of the Secretary of Defense, R.A. Winnacker, with reference to a full unedited copy of the *Effects* film furnished to the Columbia University states: *"....outtakes from the original production no longer exist having probably been destroyed during the conversion from acetate to safety film."* Professor Barnouw, under the auspices of *Columbia University Press,* would later produce the 16 minute *Hiroshima – Nagasaki, August 1945* from the *Effects* film itself which was provided.

7. Barnouw wrote: "At the end of the screening the audience sat in total silence for several seconds. We were at first unsure what this meant but the comments soon made clear what it meant." From Eric Barnouw, *Hiroshima-Nagasaki: The case of the A-Bomb Footage,* in *New Challenges for Documentary*, p585, University of California Press, 1988.

8. Letter of *Offer to Transfer Film Records to the National Archives*, from Department of the Air Force, Directorate of Administrative Services, William R. Boucher to Wayne C. Grover, Archivist of the United States, NARA, Sept. 15, 1961.

9. Accession Inventory, Feb. 21, 1962. Via *From the Stinko Picture Project* essay, Atsuko Shigesawa, p120, footnote #74.

10. Ward, pages 153-156. Wikipedia.

11. *Japanese Documentary Film: The Meiji Era Through Hiroshima*, Abe Mark Nornes No.43 p243.

EPILOGUE

THE RETURN TO CARRICKMACROSS

Dan McGovern never forgot the fact that he witnessed his first war in his earliest days growing up in and around the RIC barracks of his home town in Ireland. The 27th September 1999 was a typical Monday morning for me as I eased into a new working week in my capacity as a reporter in my office in the centre of Carrickmacross. The telephone rang which I promptly answered. It was our then local librarian Marita Hughes. "Joe," she said, "I have an American gentleman visiting with us down here in the library that you simply must meet."

"Who is that?" I enquired.

"His name is Dan McGovern. He's an elderly man and he tells me he's originally from Carrickmacross and he has an amazing story to tell you. Ohh…. and bring your camera," added Marita putting down the phone. A line like that is always music to a reporter's ears, so I put on my coat, grabbed by note-book and pen, audio recorder and camera and closed the front door behind me. I promptly made my way down to the library at Lower Main Street. There Marita met me inside the door and

motioned me over to a table by which an elderly but remarkably
tall man was standing examining some historical document or
other. Marita introduced me to Lieutenant Colonel Daniel A.
McGovern, United States Air Force (Retired). Dan put out his
big hand and strongly shook mine. He had one hell of a grip.

Dan had only shortly before arrived back in Carrickmacross.
This was not, however, his first return to his hometown since
leaving it was a boy in 1922. He had previously returned seventeen years before in 1982. Back then his brother, Malachy, his
sister Genevieve and he as well as some of the next generation of
the McGovern family, had visited the town and what remained
of the cottage. By then his former home was roofless, abandoned
and crumbling and being slowly reclaimed by nature. By Dan's
final visit in 1999, the cottage, which had held so many memories for him, had almost disappeared completely.

Not so the barracks. Its strong construction and constant use
as a police station have preserved it well. It still retains its
armoured window shutters and its strong but not so bulletproof
double front doors. Outside, looking up at the barracks facade,
bullet strikes and stone repairs in the limestone can still be seen –
reminders of a more troubled time which Dan McGovern
witnessed first hand as a boy. Present also at Carrickmacross
Library for my interview with Dan was our local Carrickmacross
historian, Larry McDermott[1] and our then Monaghan County
Librarian, Joe McElvaney.

As the introductions ensued we sat down around the table. I
switched on my recorder to back up my notes and the interview
was soon underway. As a keen student of military history in
general, within minutes of Dan McGovern giving me some background of his story, I was entranced. Here was a man before me
raised in my own town who not only could remember Ireland's
Easter Rising and who travelled as a boy on Crossley Tenders
with the Black and Tans, but who had also filmed President
Franklin Delano Roosevelt and then flew hazardous missions in
formations of American B-17 bombers over Nazi occupied

Europe. Then, to cap all that, he had filmed the aftermath of the Hiroshima and Nagasaki atomic bombings! It was truly remarkable. In over 25 years of journalism it was my interview with Lt. Col. McGovern that I remember most fondly.

The author with Dan McGovern in the local library back in Dan's boyhood hometown of Carrickmacross, County Monaghan, Ireland in September 1999. **Photo: ©Joseph McCabe.**

His story, as it unfolded to me during that interview and other aspects of it he imparted to me afterwards, without doubt, resulted in the most interesting interview I had ever conducted. From my interview recording and notes, as well as from the additional material he gave me that day, I ended up writing far more than I needed to fill the full broadsheet article on Dan McGovern that September. I had an embarrassment of historical literary riches so to speak but soon, even at that early stage, I started undertaking even further detailed research for something more. I knew then that it was the basis of a biography which simply had to be written.

Dan McGovern was, first and foremost, a Combat Cameraman. His greatest achievement was undoubtedly his film documentary work on the aftermath of the atomic bombs in Hiroshima and Nagasaki. However, equally it was his efforts to ensure the preservation of these films that are perhaps, his greatest monument. For these achievements alone the world owes a great debt of gratitude to a persistent and determined Irishman and his camera who, against the odds, won through in the end.

All his remarkable USAAF/USAF film documentation footage, along with thousands of his military still photographs, now resides where it belongs, in the United States National Archives, preserved for posterity for all future generations. He said once having just given an account of his remarkable career: "This was my contribution to the Air Force. It's the true story of one individual who was a cameraman doing a job that he loved to do."[2] That indeed was Mack McGovern.

Lieutenant Colonel Dan McGovern passed away from cancer[3] peacefully at his Laguna Woods home in Southern California, USA surrounded by his family on 14th December 2005. He was 96 years old. *Ar dheis Dé go raibh a anam.*[4] From his early recollections of Irish rebels right through to the historical footage he later captured for posterity on American film reels this has been his story. It is a remarkable story and it has been my great privilege to relate that story to you. Thank You for reading it.

FMPU End Frame, **Image: US National Archives.**

1. Larry points out that Dan's memories of the Irish War of Independence in South Monaghan had helped to complete an historical circle. Previously, historical narratives such as P.V. Hoey's *Farney in the Fight for Freedom* had largely only given the Republican account of events. Now, at least, accounts existed from both sides.
2. This was at the conclusion of his Air Force Oral History interview with Dr. James C. Hasdorff, Air Force Historical Research Agency in 1988.
3. Several other members of the USSBS team who worked with Dan in both Hiroshima and Nagasaki are known to have died of cancer. These were Lt. Herb Sussan and Lt. Robert H. Wildermuth.
4. *May he be seated at the right hand of God.* (Old Irish Blessing).

ACKNOWLEDGMENTS

The genesis of *Rebels To Reels* was a meeting with Lt. Colonel Daniel A. McGovern in September 1999 which involved an extensive interview conducted by the author which resulted in copious notes. Considerable information has also been gleaned from Lt. Col. McGovern's US Air Force oral history interview conducted by Dr James C. Hasdorff for the Air Force Historical Research Agency (AFHRA) in 1988, from Lt. McGovern's Library of Congress Veterans History Project interview conducted in 2003 and from his brother, Malachy's memoirs. In addition, *Rebels To Reels* has also resulted from extensive research conducted by the author over many years. To that end I wish to extend my sincere and deepest gratitude to the following people who provided me with information and indeed who assisted me in so many ways in the course of writing this biography.

First and foremost to all those members of the McGovern family who have been unwavering in their support of my efforts to enable me to finally tell Dan McGovern's remarkable story in its entirety. Without your efforts to provide me with your own personal memories of Dan, much relevant information about his life and military service, as well as your treasured family photographs, this book would be incomplete. Sincere gratitude is extended to Professor of Asian Cinema and author Abé Markus Nornes of the University of Michigan for his insight and guidance into aspects of McGovern's story in post-war Japan. Much additional information regarding Big Mack's story relating to the Nippon Eigasha cameramen used in this biography was gleaned from Professor Nornes's work *The Body at the Centre – the Effects of the Atomic Bomb in Hiroshima and Nagasaki* as well as from the historical USAAF/USSBS memos from the time held by his department at the University of Michigan. Sincere thanks also to Professor Nornes for identifying for me many USSBS photographs held by the US National Archives as well as by the Japan Peace Museum which were taken as McGovern and his USSBS crew filmed and surveyed throughout Japan in late 1945 and in the first half of 1946.

My thanks also to Rie Nakanishi of the Hiroshima Peace Memorial Museum and also to Yuki Ebisawa of the Nagasaki Atomic Bomb Museum for their assistance. ありがとう. Thanks to everyone at the US National Archives and Records Administration, College Park, Maryland and at the Japan Peace Museum for the use of those photographs.

My sincere thanks are extended to Wayne Weiss, California for his research which ultimately determined the long sought after declassification information pertaining to *Effects of the Atomic Bomb on Hiroshima and Nagasaki*. Thanks also to Wayne for relating his account of finding McGovern's partial copy of the *Effects* film at the Norton Air Force Film depository in 1994. His insight into that documentary and also of the classification, declassification and film depository storage practices of the United States Air Force with regard to McGovern's suppressed films has been invaluable. Wayne also prepared and provided many of the film still images used in this biography and also on the *Rebels to Reels* website rebelstoreels.com which were taken from the original colour *Japan in Defeat* footage as well as from the black and white *Effects of the Atomic Bomb on Hiroshima and*

Nagasaki documentary. Wayne's extensive knowledge of vintage film production processes has also greatly assisted me.

I wish to acknowledge the important input of Gary Boyd, Director, AETC History and Museums Program, Randolph Air Museum, Texas for the benefit of his recollections of Dan McGovern and also of Dan's great friend, 305th Bomb Group B-17 Flight Engineer and Top Turret Gunner, David A. Nagel. Among other things it was Gary who related to me some additional filming innovation methods which Dan McGovern employed to film much of his remarkable aerial combat footage over the war-torn skies of Europe in 1943 and which were previously unknown to me. Thanks also to Scott Bailey, Historian at Vandenberg Air Force Base and to Yancy Mailes, Director, History and Heritage Programme, Air Force Matériel Command and to all at Wright Patterson Air Force Base for their assistance.

Thanks are also extended to T/Sgt. Ashley Nicole Taylor, USAF Media Specialist, National Engagement, New York for arranging official access for me to the archives of so many individual United States Air Force bases to which my research led me. Sincere thanks to archivists Leslie Smith, Grady Simpson, Pamela Ives and Archie Difante at the US Air Force Historical Research Agency (AFHRA) at Maxwell Air Force Base, Alabama for their great efforts to retrieve archive material on my behalf. To James *JT* Tucker and all at Edwards Air Force Base Test Centre History Office in California for their valuable assistance.

My gratitude is also extended to Doug Cunningham of the First Motion Picture Unit Facebook Historical Group for providing me with relevant information as well as many original USAAF/First Motion Picture Unit photos taken of Dan McGovern in the period when Big Mack trained his USAAF cameramen at Camp Letts. My thanks also to another US Air Force man, Rick Foss, of South Carolina for his expert colourisations of Dan McGovern related photographs which have been used on the cover of this biography. In typical US Air Force style you all went *above and beyond* on my behalf.

A big Thank You is extended to Chris Coffman for providing me with Dan McGovern's long sought after B-17 mission information and for access to his fine collection of 305th Bomb Group stories which have greatly helped me to complete that sequence of Dan McGovern's story. Chris is the son of Lt. Robert Coffman who often co-piloted B-17 *Moonbeam McSwine* and who was shot down in the bomber on the Watten, mission becoming a prisoner of war. My sincere thanks are also extended to 8th Air Force veteran and B-24 Liberator crew member Frank Parkinson for his 8th Air Force mission recollections which have greatly helped me. Thanks also to Frank's daughter-in law Stephanie Minyard Parkinson for her assistance.

My gratitude is extended to John Rickard of historyofwar.org for his expertise and patience regarding my understanding of 8th Air Force bomber formations in the ETO and also to David Reichert for allowing me access to his mission thesis on the Schweinfurt missions. Thanks to Ian White and the members of the 305th Bomb Group Historical Facebook Group for information pertaining to the 305th Bomb Group and Station 105 at Chelveston. Particular thanks are also extended to Steven Quillman, Graham Meiklejohn and Shawn Favreau of the same group for their patience and efforts to retrieve mission report information and other 8th Air Force documentation on my behalf relevant to Dan McGovern's story during his deployment in England. Thanks also to Roy Tebbutt of the Carpetbagger Aviation Museum, Harrington, England and to Steve Bowman of the Birthplace of the 8th Air Force Facebook Chapter.

A huge Thank You to Brad Markell, Los Angeles, California for assisting me in finally cracking the mystery of McGovern's second crash-landing which had eluded me for so long. Thanks to Brad's recollections and notes of his discussions with Dan McGovern that mystery was solved. Brad's grandfather, 305th Bomb Group ball turret gunner S/Sgt. Charles Francis Awrajcewicz, was killed on B-17 *Eager Eagle* in an infamous mid-air collision with an RAF Bristol Beaufighter over Chelveston air base on 31st August 1943. Sincere thanks also to Larry Pederson, Maintenance Officer and to everybody at the Commemorative Air Force at AirBase Arizona for their kind assistance with B-17 bomber technical questions. I wish to extend a big Thank You to Eric Barko, Indiana who provided me with details of Dan McGovern's mission to Watten, of which I was unaware and for access to the mission diary of 305th Bomb Group waist gunner Ken Snyder, which also greatly helped piece together the story of Dan McGovern's time with the 305th Bomb Group in England. Sincere thanks also to Eric for granting me permission to reproduce in this biography many of the photographs contained in the Ken Snyder Collection and which Dan McGovern gifted to Snyder at Chelveston in 1943 as he did to so many other crew members there.

Sincere thanks are extended to Erik Nelson, the producer of *The Cold Blue* documentary (Vulcan Productions 2017) for permission to reproduce several still images from his production in this book. *The Cold Blue* was produced using the digitally restored out-takes from William Wyler's *The Memphis Belle – A Story of a Flying Fortress* much of which Dan McGovern actually filmed. Erik's restoration result is amazing. Thanks to Steve Branch, Audiovisual Archivist at the Ronald Reagan Presidential Library, California for his assistance. My gratitude is extended also to Richard Bennett and to all at cinemagear.com, Lawndale, California for providing me with many images used in this biography of historical Eyemo, GSAP and cassette camera models. Thanks also to Richard for the benefit of his historical camera expertise on so many occasions. Separately, I also wish to thank Berto Sera for the Eyemo information which he provided. Thanks to Christine Reed of *The Washington Times* Picture Desk for her assistance in helping me track down the photo of Dan with his atomic bomb test cameramen colleagues on Enewetak Atoll in 1958.

My thanks to Peter McGoldrick of the *Royal Irish Constabulary* online forum irishconstabulary.com who is the grandson and namesake of Carrickmacross RIC sergeant, Peter McGoldrick. Peter's help and guidance regarding the RIC in Carrickmacross at the time of his grandfather's service and the information on the forum he administers, has been a useful resource. Sincere thanks are extended to Neil, the curator of the PSNI Museum, Belfast who also provided me with invaluable information regarding the RIC in Carrickmacross prior to and during the Irish War of Independence and similarly to all at the Garda Síochána Museum in Dublin. My thanks also to Charles Rousseaux, Deputy Director of Public Affairs of the US National Nuclear Security Administration for permission to reproduce the logo of the Atomic Energy Commission and also to Guildings Auctioneers Ltd, Market Harborough, Leicestershire, England for their kind permission to reproduce the truncheon and handcuff image used in the chapter heads of Part 1 of this biography.

Thanks also to fellow authors Geoff Hill, Michael Wilgar, Jerry Shanahan and Ryan Robicheaux for all their publishing advice and to Mark Thomas of coverness.com for producing a great book cover and for the benefit of his extensive technical publishing expertise. Particular thanks are extended also to Pamela Cassidy, Dublin and to Peter Brown in New York for the benefit of their particular areas of expertise in relation to this biography. It is much appreciated. *Gratias tibi ago pro perito legum consilio.*

A little closer to home my sincere gratitude is extended to Marita Hughes, then a librarian at Carrickmacross Branch Library, who started it all with a telephone call to me one September morning back in 1999. A huge Thank You is extended to our local Carrickmacross historian, Larry McDermott, for his many hours of proofreading and also for his fact-checking of Part 1 of this biography. Like Marita Hughes, Larry was present for my extensive interview with Dan in 1999. My sincere thanks also to my former newspaper editor, Joe Carroll, for the benefit of his extensive expertise. A big Thank You is also extended to Theresa Loftus of Monaghan County Museum for her expertise and diligence in locating the historical photographs relevant to Dan McGovern's early life in Carrickmacross used in this biography and to Monaghan County Council for access to its Irish War of Independence files. To John Scully for some timely Carrickmacross historical Facebook posts and also to the anonymous administrator of *The Rare Old Times in Carrickmacross* Facebook page for his posting of some timely photographs also relevant to Part 1 of this biography. My thanks to the Sisters of St. Louis Carrickmacross, to the Principal of St. Louis Secondary School, Karen Patton and also to caretaker, Francie Finnegan, for arranging access for me to sites relevant to the McGovern story on the St. Louis convent property.

Grateful thanks are extended to Mary Dermody, Mary Capaldi and Denise Sewell for their words of literary encouragement to me at important times down through the years. That encouragement has always remained with me and has, in no small part, resulted in this biography. My thanks also to my friends of many years, fellow WW2 history enthusiasts, Henry and Cathal Moroney and David O'Rourke for their support. Particular thanks to Tom O'Neill for his work on the companion website for this biography and for his additional technical expertise. Sincere thanks also to my former English teachers, Breda Moroney Ward and Michael Smith, whose efforts greatly honed my writing skills during my earlier years at Inver College, Carrickmacross.

I wish to extend a huge Thank You to my family for the encouragement and support they have afforded me in the course of writing *Rebels to Reels*. To my mother Verney and to my brother Eugene for the fantastic assistance, patience and advice they have afforded me and similarly to my sisters Anne and Orla. Finally, to Sylvester the cat who provided many welcome distractions at times of intense concentration. In the unlikely event that I have inadvertently omitted anybody please know that your assistance to me has been greatly valued. Thank You to one and all. – **JMC.**

ABOUT THE AUTHOR

Joseph McCabe has worked in many different and varying aspects of the news media industry for almost thirty years. He is a native of Carrickmacross, County Monaghan, Ireland which was originally also the hometown of Lieutenant Colonel Daniel A. McGovern – the subject of *Rebels to Reels*. As a journalist he has contributed to national, international and local publications as well as to the broadcast and online media. He is a long-standing member of the National Union of Journalists (NUJ).

Joseph McCabe pictured at his work desk during an impromptu writing break with Sylvester the cat. **Photo: ©Joseph McCabe.**

Having a lifelong interest in military history and particularly that of World War 2, he has travelled to many historical battlefields across the world. He has also interviewed many veterans of World War 2 and later conflicts.

Made in the USA
Las Vegas, NV
13 February 2022

43873325R00247